Rednecks, Redeemers, and Race

Mississippi after Reconstruction, 1877–1917

BOARD OF EDITORS
HERITAGE OF MISSISSIPPI SERIES

William F. Winter, Chair
Dernoral Davis
H. T. Holmes
Peggy Jeanes
Neil McMillen
John Marszalek
Charles Reagan Wilson
Christine Wilson

HERITAGE OF MISSISSIPPI SERIES
VOLUME III

REDNECKS, REDEEMERS, AND RACE

Mississippi after Reconstruction, 1877–1917

Stephen Cresswell

University Press of Mississippi
for the Mississippi Historical Society
Jackson

Publication of this book was made possible through grants from the Mississippi Humanities Council and the Phil Hardin Foundation.

Unless otherwise noted, images contained in this volume are provided courtesy of the Mississippi Department of Archives and History.

www.upress.state.ms.us

The University Press of Mississippi is a member of the Association of American University Presses.

Copyright © 2006 by the Mississippi Historical Society
All rights reserved
Manufactured in the United States of America

First Edition 2006
∞
Library of Congress Cataloging-in-Publication Data

Cresswell, Stephen Edward.
   Rednecks, redeemers, and race : Mississippi after Reconstruction, 1877–1917 / by Stephen Cresswell.— 1st ed.
       p. cm. — (Heritage of Mississippi series ; v. 3)
   Includes bibliographical references (p.   ) and index.
   ISBN 1-57806-847-9 (cloth : alk. paper)   1. Social change—Mississippi—History—19th century. 2. Social change—Mississippi—History—20th century. 3. Mississippi—Politics and government—1865–1950. 4. Mississippi—Race relations. 5. Mississippi—Social conditions. 6. Mississippi—Economic conditions. I. Title. II. Series.
   F341.C74   2006
   976.2'061—dc22   2005024082

British Library Cataloging-in-Publication Data available

*To my parents, Ephraim and Catherine Cresswell of Durant,
with profound thanks for all of their constant and loving support*

Contents

Acknowledgments	ix
1. Civil War, Reconstruction, and 1877	3
2. Change and Continuity in Mississippi Agriculture	12
3. The Persistent Institution *Black Labor and Race Control*	37
4. The Persistent Institution *Conflict and Racial Separation*	52
5. Black Mississippians Confront the System	69
6. Politics in Late-Nineteenth-Century Mississippi	89
7. The Mississippi Constitution of 1890 and Political Dissent	110
8. Industrialization	130
9. Industrial Workers	150
10. Age of Modernization *Transportation, Cities, and Public Health*	163
11. The Era of Vardaman and Bilbo	190
12. Change and Continuity in Mississippi	228
Notes	242
Bibliography	261
Index	275

Acknowledgments

I have long felt drawn to write about Mississippi's history in the years after Reconstruction. Here was a fascinating period that saw the impressive proliferation of timbering and railroading, the rise of sharecropping, and the beginnings of Jim Crow segregation. During the years 1877 to 1917, Mississippi native Ida B. Wells was writing her hard-hitting newspaper articles, while for the first time people outside of Mississippi heard the music that came to be called the Delta blues. Spending their formative years in Mississippi during this period were artists as diverse as William Faulkner, Jimmie Rodgers, and Richard Wright. I have enjoyed immersing myself in the history of this interesting era and have learned about topics new to me, such as the impressive textile mill at Wesson and the tumultuous strikes by Illinois Central Railroad workers and by shrimp fishermen on the Gulf Coast.

Writing as I have been from West Virginia, I could not have completed this book without the help of innumerable librarians and archivists who shipped books, photocopies, and microfilm to me. They were willing to pull materials ahead of time for my frequent, but always quick, research trips. I especially want to thank the librarians and staff members at Mississippi State University, the University of Mississippi, the University of Southern Mississippi, and the Mississippi Department of Archives and History. Also helpful were staff members in the public libraries of Copiah, Forrest, Harrison, and Lauderdale counties. In hopes of finding sources untapped by earlier historians of Mississippi, I made a research trip to Louisiana State University, where I found close to one hundred important collections of papers of Mississippians of this period. The staff there was very helpful, even going so far as to help me find lodgings. I also wish to thank the staffs at the Library of Congress and at the libraries of the University of North Carolina, the University of Virginia, and West Virginia University.

On the campus of my home institution, West Virginia Wesleyan College, I found nothing but support for this project. The library staff was very patient fielding requests for interlibrary loans and helping me negotiate the intricacies of the information superhighway. President William R. Haden and Dean Larry Parsons

Acknowledgments

help foster a climate on campus where assistance for research is always available. Also supportive were my colleagues in the Department of History and International Studies, including William Mahoney, Robert Rupp, James Beeby, Katharine Lane, and Herb Costen. All of them remind me that much of the value of research for a faculty member is its ability to reinvigorate teachers in the classroom.

I salute the board of editors of the Heritage of Mississippi series. It has been a real pleasure for me to work with the expert readers they recruited—beginning at the stage of the outline. These readers made numerous suggestions for improvements, which I hope I have used to good effect. Needless to say, any remaining errors of fact or interpretation are mine.

I voice my hearty appreciation to copyeditor Robert Burchfield, who brought many improvements to the manuscript. At the University Press of Mississippi, I was happy to work a second time with director Seetha Srinivasan and editor Anne Stascavage and for the first time with editor-in-chief Craig Gill. All are consummate professionals who worked hard to make the book the best that it could be. I also thank the many staff members who work behind the scenes on book design and marketing.

I want to thank my parents, Eph and Catherine Cresswell, who first instilled in me an interest in history and specifically the history of our native state of Mississippi. The stories they told me of our forebears' lives in the state were fascinating, and while conducting the research for this book I stumbled across our kin several times. My parents' love and support over the years have been unfailing.

Finally, I thank my wife, Teresa Hamm, surely the most patient woman in the world, on matters related to this book and otherwise. I deeply appreciate the quarter century of unbroken love and support she has given me.

Rednecks, Redeemers, and Race

Mississippi after Reconstruction, 1877–1917

CHAPTER ONE

CIVIL WAR, RECONSTRUCTION, AND 1877

At the time of its secession from the Union in 1861, the state of Mississippi in many ways was a raw, frontier region. Although Europeans founded Mississippi's first white settlement in 1699, not until the 1830s did American Indian cessions allow settlement in the northern half of the state. White settlers had passed over much of southern Mississippi, moreover, because the region's sandy soil was unsuitable for growing crops. Thus, at the outbreak of the Civil War, many counties in Mississippi had been settled thirty years or less, and other parts of the state were still wilderness. The largest city in the state was Natchez, with a population of about 6,600, while Vicksburg could boast a population of only 4,600. The state capital of Jackson barely topped 3,000 residents, and Meridian was a small, unincorporated village. On the other hand, Mississippi was the key state of the great cotton kingdom. Slaves worked plantations along the Mississippi and Yazoo rivers, their tributaries, and elsewhere, and produced more than one million bales of cotton each year. A majority of the state's population was enslaved, and whites were ever vigilant for signs of slave rebellion.[1]

The young state was devastated by the Civil War. Some 78,000 men marched off to war, and an estimated one-third never returned. Economically, the Civil War shattered the state. The greatest investment in antebellum Mississippi had been the purchase of slaves, but in 1865 planters lost this "investment" as slaves won their freedom. Bonds and other notes issued by the Confederate government and by the state of Mississippi also became worthless. Land was the one remaining important form of property, but land in Mississippi had lost most of its value by war's end.

Plantation land was of questionable value because it was not clear what kind of labor force would replace the slaves or how successful such a force would be in working the land. Small farms lost value because, during the war, many acres had grown up in weeds and saplings and would require hard work to become productive once again.

In the half-century that followed the Civil War, Mississippians faced many questions about the future of their state. During the Reconstruction years, they began to shape answers, and still more answers came between 1877 and 1917. Would planters and farmers find a new system of labor to replace slave labor? Would the former slaves win a degree of true independence? Would Mississippi return to its premier status as a cotton-raising state with the highest per capita income in the nation? Or would it follow a new path, diversifying its agriculture, developing transportation links, and building factories? Would Mississippi, like the nation as a whole, see the rise of great urban centers, the flourishing of labor unions, and a sharp increase in immigrant population? Would Mississippi's leaders play an important role in national politics by, for example, helping to lead the movement called Progressivism? Would the state cling to its devotion to states' rights and small government, even as the nation itself moved toward more activist state and national governments?

Some of the earliest answers to these questions came during the period of Reconstruction. At the Civil War's end, Mississippi politics were in disarray and remained tumultuous for several years. In quick succession, various factions governed the state. A coalition of former Whig leaders gave way to military rule under Union army officers, followed by the moderate administration of Republican governor James Lusk Alcorn and then the more radical tenure of Republican governor Adelbert Ames. The state had been home to a relatively weak Whig Party prior to the Civil War, but no Mississippians became Republicans until 1865. Many former Whigs, including influential planters such as Alcorn, joined the Republican Party after the Civil War. A smaller number of former Democrats did the same. Nearly all of the Union soldiers who elected to stay in Mississippi after the war were Republicans. The largest group of Mississippi Republicans, however, were the freedmen, who soon were voting in large numbers and who were passionately devoted to the party of Lincoln. The Republicans in the state controlled a majority of county governments until 1873, when a majority of counties came back into Democratic hands.

During the period of Republican control of the legislature, lawmakers passed a number of important laws. To Democrats, however, Republican rule was most notable for a sharp increase in taxes. Republicans pointed to a number of reasons tax rates rose. First, the state lacked its most important antebellum tax, the slave tax. The tax on land now must provide the revenues formerly raised by the slave tax. Taxes also rose because the number of citizens had increased sharply with the end of slavery, and state institutions had to cater to black as well as white citizens, albeit on a segregated basis. These institutions ranged from colleges to charity hospitals. The Republicans offered costly incentives to railroads to build tracks in the state, incentives later Democratic lawmakers would continue. Most important, Republicans brought the state its first system of public schools, and building this system was a costly endeavor.

To many Democrats, however, such explanations were unacceptable. The slave tax had hit wealthy planters the hardest, but the land tax hit not only planters but small farmers as well. Public schools seemed an expensive novelty, and many farmers groused that the state had got along quite well in the 1850s without school systems. Moreover, white small farmers were uninterested in providing colleges and hospitals for black citizens. Incentives to railroads were simply special favors for investors, in the opinion of agrarian Democrats. Yet the greatest argument against the new taxes was that they were high at a time when so many farmers were still suffering from the devastation of war. While typical Mississippi farmers were not truly impoverished, they were "cash poor." Much of their income came in the form of food for their families, and many farmers saw very little cash in the course of a year. Taxes required cash, and so farmers hated taxes.[2]

Thus Mississippi's white small farmers had one strong reason for wanting to vote out Republican officials. Another reason was that the Republican Party encouraged black office-holding. Many white Mississippians had never met an articulate, educated person of color, and many doubted any existed or even could exist. Even before the middle of the 1870s, state Democrats vowed to wrest political control away from the Republicans, and they hoped the state would return to lower taxes under an exclusively white leadership.

The turning point came with the 1875 election. Democratic leaders vowed to use any tactic to end Republican control and secure white hegemony in Mississippi. Such tactics included threats, violence, and fraud. As Democrats broke up Republican meetings, threatened the lives of Republican candidates, and even killed Republican leaders, Governor Ames faced a dilemma. He could use the militia to restore peace in the state, but to do so meant sending a black militia against white opponents. In a racially tense situation like the one in Mississippi, Ames feared a full-scale race war. To fail to use the militia, however, could mean Democratic victory and a failure of democracy in the state. Ames asked President Ulysses S. Grant to send in U.S. Army troops to suppress the lawlessness. Grant, however, worried about the effect of strong-arm tactics in Mississippi. The president lectured Ames that "the whole public are tired out with these annual autumnal outbreaks in the South." Grant told the governor that if he wanted troops, he should call on the state militia.[3]

Grant's attorney general sent a negotiator to meet with Ames and with Democratic leaders L. Q. C. Lamar and James Z. George. Finally, the warring parties agreed to make peace. Democrats promised to allow a fair election, and Ames promised not to use the militia. Democratic violence and fraud continued, however, and in this 1875 election the Democrats won a clear legislative majority. The newly elected lawmakers pressured Republican state officers to resign, and by early 1876 all three branches of Mississippi's government were in Democratic hands. For nearly one hundred years thereafter, Democrats built up legends of Reconstruction-era Mississippi. They told voters this had been a period when the government was dominated by black office-holders; when soldiers ran elections at bayonet point; when state officers were ignorant, incompetent, and dishonest; and when farmers lost their land to sheriffs' auctions because of high taxes. While such legends were largely untrue, they helped keep voters voting Democratic. Party leaders warned white voters that the only way to maintain white control in black-majority Mississippi was to vote for the party that championed white domination, the Democratic Party.

Politically, however, Mississippi faced as many questions in 1876 and 1877 as it had in 1865 and 1866. Prior to the Civil War, Mississippi had featured a weak two-party system, with a dominant Democratic Party and a smaller Whig Party that occasionally won a victory in the state. After 1875, it was still not clear what kind of political system would prevail. Would there be a two-party system? If so, which party would provide the opposition to Democrats?

A number of political incidents in 1877 provided early answers to these questions. One such incident showed the dangers of Republican Party leaders attempting to continue their influence in the state. In Kemper County, there long had been "bad blood" between Democratic leader John Gully and white Republican leader W. W. Chisholm. Gully was gunned down from ambush, and a black man was arrested for the crime. Chisholm also went to jail under suspicions he was involved. Chisholm took his family with him to jail, fearing for their safety. A mob of some 200 armed men appeared at the Kemper County jail; meanwhile Chisholm and a couple of friends managed to arm themselves and "proposed to sell their lives dearly." Chisholm shot and killed the doctor who led the charge into the jail. Fearing the mob would burn the jail, Chisholm and his family attempted to leave the building but met more gunfire outside. The death toll on this bloody day included not only the Democratic doctor but also two Chisholm allies as well as Chisholm himself, his eighteen-year-old daughter, and his thirteen-year-old son.[4]

The violent incidents in Kemper County, including the assassination of a Democratic leader and the mob action against a Republican leader and his children, attracted national attention. The *New York Tribune* declared that with incidents like the "Chisholm massacre," the modern history of the South read like "the annals of a barbarous people." Southern newspapers emphasized the earlier murder of Gully and claimed that the differences between Gully and Chisholm were personal, not political. Chisholm's widow begged Governor John M. Stone to send the militia to protect what remained of her family. Stone, in the midst of a reelection campaign, declined to do anything that might give the appearance of weakening Democratic control and white solidarity. His refusal to send soldiers met great criticism in the northern states, and he was accused of not pushing hard enough for conviction of members of the mob. Prosecutors secured the indictment of fourteen men on state charges of murder, as well as federal civil rights charges, but failed to convict.

Two lessons could be learned from incidents in Kemper County in 1877. First, the tumultuous 1875 election had not determined that the Democrats would rule the state without opposition. Indeed, violent elections continued throughout the 1870s and 1880s. On the other hand, Republicans realized the high price they would pay if they sought to maintain their party. As it turned out, while opposition to the Democrats was not uncommon in late-nineteenth-century Mississippi, the most important opposition came from groups other than the Republicans. With the Republicans' ties to the Union army, to Confederate defeat, and to black officeholding, a majority of white Mississippians believed any tactic was justified to keep the Republicans from ever coming to power.[5]

Mississippi's small farmers grew restive during the depression that was widespread in 1877, and they accused Democratic leaders of doing nothing to aid yeomen farmers. In many counties, agrarian leaders set up "Farmers and Workingmen's Clubs," aiming to unite farmers and artisans in a new political movement. Cotton farmers banded together and passed resolutions declaring they would not sell their cotton unless merchants agreed to meet a specified price per pound. Many counties, lacking Republican candidates in the 1877 election, boasted slates of independent agrarian candidates instead.[6]

A typical independent ticket was the one in Clay County. At a campaign rally in Clay, W. W. Graham addressed his fellow farmers. "Gentlemen," Graham began, "we... have a class that gets their living and expects to get rich off of the farmers and I wish to ask the question, Why is it farmers should support and give riches to these idlers?" After all, in supporting the merchants and speculators, Graham argued, "we deprive ourselves of everything in life except a bare living." Graham told his own woeful story of the loss of his farm at a sheriff's sale, at which he alleged a courthouse clique had obtained his farm at an absurdly low price. The agrarians in Clay County and elsewhere vowed to bring a county government responsive to small farmers' needs. After Election Day, however, Graham reported to Governor Stone that "the election was carried by mob violence." In other counties, independents were defeated by their own lack of unity and organization. The 1877 campaign resulted in the election of only a handful of agrarian independent candidates but was a harbinger of larger and better-organized farmer revolts, including those led by the Greenback Party, the People's Party, and the "redneck" supporters of Democrat James K. Vardaman.[7]

Readers who know Mississippi well may have a difficult time visualizing the state in 1877. This was a period when neither Sunflower nor Quitman County raised much cotton and when Covington and Jones counties produced almost no timber. The state had neither paved nor gravel roads, and railroads served only a fraction of the counties. The northeastern hills had seen white settlement for less than half a century and still had many characteristics of the frontier. Biloxi had only about 1,200 residents, and neither Hattiesburg nor Laurel yet existed. The state seemed to offer boundless potential for growth but also faced troubling questions about the future, questions whose answers in 1877 seemed unknowable. Some of the most gnawing questions had to do with the future of the state's agriculture.[8]

The state had produced more than 1.2 million bales of cotton in 1860, but in 1877 Mississippi was not even close to matching this figure. The most important cotton producers had been the plantations along the Yazoo and Mississippi rivers and in the Tombigbee Prairie. These regions likely would be the chief centers in the coming years as well. Yet would plantation agriculture remain the most important method of cotton production? If so, what did plantation agriculture mean in a postslavery system? The new traits of plantation agriculture would evolve during Reconstruction and in the following decades. Also evolving was the role of white yeomen farmers in postbellum agriculture. Would Mississippi's small farmers, like farmers in northern and western states, mechanize their operations?

Would scientific farming methods be widespread in the Deep South? Would farmers, like corporate management and labor, turn to collective economic action for their own betterment?

One of the most important questions was the likelihood of the success of agricultural diversification in the state. In the 1870s and later almost every knowledgeable writer and spokesperson urged farmers to supplement cotton production with other crops and livestock. They presented their arguments with evangelistic fervor. The state's farm leaders foresaw a day when Mississippi would produce corn and oats and beef and pork as well as cotton. On the other hand, many planters suspected King Cotton would continue to dominate the state in the decades after 1877.

For the state's African Americans, as well as for white planters, the future of the state's labor system was very much in doubt in the 1870s. The freedmen felt a strong desire to operate their own family farms and were certain they did not want to toil in gangs in white landowners' fields. Planters who relied on black laborers felt just as strongly that these workers must be willing to commit themselves to harvest one crop before exercising their right to move on. By the early 1880s planters and black laborers had reached an understanding that gave both sides the things they wanted most, while each side also gave up something in these labor negotiations.

White Mississippians had come of age under a system of slavery that rested on their near-total control of the labor force. For many of the state's white residents, it was hard to imagine a large black labor force that did not rest on strict white control. During the four decades after 1877, planters, merchants, and state lawmakers developed an elaborate system for controlling the black population of the state, especially in labor matters. New laws and customs would secure white landowners and employers a ready supply of black workers who would not make great demands or leave employment at inopportune times. Job opportunities were racially segregated, with jobs low in prestige and pay set aside for black workers. In Mississippi, black unemployment became a crime serious enough to merit imprisonment at hard labor.

Given that the entire power structure was in white hands, few black Mississippians offered direct challenges to the state's system of race control. Just as slaves had found subtle ways of rebelling that had less dire consequences than an outright revolt, free black Mississippians also found subtle ways of resisting white control. Sometimes they did this by turning inward, building up the institutions of the black community and finding success in a world where whites rarely ventured. Some black writers protested the status quo by writing newspaper articles, poems, and stories that were a form of resistance. Further, these four decades did see overt protest, from streetcar boycotts to an exodus to Kansas. While these overt protests were not successful, they did demonstrate that, contrary to what whites claimed, African Americans in Mississippi were not content with second-class status.

Politically, Mississippi showed interesting divisions. The state saw some two-party political races, with Democratic hegemony challenged in turn by Republicans, Greenbackers, Populists, Bull Moose supporters, and Socialists. Yet the most important political races were wholly within the Democratic Party and might feature, for example, wets versus drys. Prohibition was an important issue in Mississippi between 1877 and 1917, and few issues excited as much voter interest. Other political divisions included the long-standing Delta-Hills split, which had been noted by political observers as early as the 1840s. This division might be more accurately described as black-majority counties versus white-majority counties. Many campaigns of the late nineteenth century featured elite reformer candidates challenged by agrarian Democrats. Another hot political division was the one that pitted states' rights advocates of small government against those Mississippians who believed in an activist government at the city, county, state, and national levels.

Mississippi agrarians organized politically several times in the late nineteenth century, seeking laws that would help small farmers. Their goals included railroad regulation and a system of government-sponsored warehouses to help farmers hold their crop off the market until prices rose. Agrarians also sought help for the indebted, as farmers fell increasingly into debt to merchants and landowners. Agrarians supported Democratic candidates such as James Z. George but occasionally turned to third-party candidates, too. The agrarians' greatest success came when they elected a new Democratic governor in 1903, James K. Vardaman. Vardaman's victory was made possible by changes in the system of elections, which agrarians had secured in the turn-of-the-century period.

Early in the twentieth century, Mississippi politicians were at the forefront of a national movement called Progressivism. Progressives pointed out problems the nation faced, studied and publicized the problems and possible solutions, and finally passed laws to solve the problems. All of Mississippi's governors between the 1903 election and the United States' entry into World War I were Progressives. During this period, the state's Progressive lawmakers passed statutes limiting child labor, ending the brutal system of convict leasing, and setting up modern consolidated schools. Not all Progressive laws "ring true" with modern-day Americans, and among Mississippi's statutes of this period were some that limited workers' right to leave their employer and seek new opportunities.

Looking to the future, Mississippians in 1877 dreamed of their state boasting factories as well as farms. Indeed, Mississippi's manufacturing output in 1917 was twenty-five times larger than its production of 1877. Yet much of Mississippi's manufacturing comprised the work of small gristmills and lumber mills, and for the most part the state lacked the kinds of large factories found in northern states. Mississippians wondered why the state seemed limited to the initial processing of raw materials and did not produce motors, steel rails, or plate glass. For those who toiled in Mississippi's factories, the labor movement initially offered great promise for improving wages and working conditions. By the early twentieth century, however, labor groups lost two major strikes in the state, and in the decades that followed Mississippi would have a far weaker labor movement than other states.

State leaders did what they could to help Mississippi modernize by aiding construction of a rail network and later a system of good roads. Cities grew, and by 1917 Mississippi was home to seventeen cities with a population of 5,000 or more. Mississippi's cities boasted all of the modern accouterments, including electric lights, natural gas service, sewer systems, ice factories, and streetcars. In the public health movement, Mississippi was at the forefront of efforts to eliminate such menaces as yellow fever, pellagra, and hookworm. Yet once again, despite some modernization, Mississippi did not keep pace with the rest of the nation. By 1917 Mississippi was still the nation's most rural state, with a wholly inadequate system of roads. Few states were as untouched by electricity, the automobile, and the telephone.

The chapters that follow will examine in detail the history of Mississippi's agriculture, its system of labor control and race control, and its political history during the years 1877 to 1917. They will analyze Mississippi's industrialization, urbanization, and improvements in transportation and public health. What will emerge is the history of a state that underwent wrenching changes in the four decades after 1877. Yet the state was clearly a place where great continuities were the rule. The citizen of 1917 lived life very much like the citizen of forty years earlier.

CHAPTER TWO

CHANGE AND CONTINUITY IN MISSISSIPPI AGRICULTURE

In 1860 Mississippi was the preeminent state in a cotton kingdom that stretched from North Carolina to Texas. The state produced 1.2 million bales of cotton that year, ranking first among all the states. By the reckoning of the U.S. Census Bureau, Mississippi had the highest per capita income in the nation. The state owed its prosperity to a number of factors. One was the presence of several regions of extremely rich, deep topsoil. Another was the vast number of slave laborers, creating great wealth for the state's planters. As might be expected in such an agricultural state, antebellum Mississippi raised most of its own food. The plantation ideal emphasized self-sufficiency, and the slaves raised corn, oats, hay, beef, pork, and poultry in great quantities.[1]

By 1880 Mississippi in some ways was a very different state. Despite fifteen years to recover from the war and rebuild its agriculture, Mississippi in 1880 produced only 960,000 bales of cotton, 20 percent below the 1860 mark. A new system of agricultural labor had appeared, based now on free workers. Further, Mississippi did not return to the antebellum practice of growing enough food to feed a farmer's family and livestock. While no other state was as rural or more agricultural than Mississippi in 1880, the state was a heavy importer of bacon, beef, corn, hay, and horses, buying from nearby states including Missouri, Tennessee, and Kentucky. Ten years before the outbreak of the Civil War, Mississippi had produced annually thirty-seven bushels of corn for every person in the state. By 1880 the comparable number was fewer than nineteen.[2]

Two other important changes after the Civil War and Reconstruction had to do with the nature of the typical Mississippi farm. After Reconstruction, the size of the average farm declined sharply. In 1880 Mississippi's average farm size was

156 acres. By 1920 it was 67 acres. Indeed, by 1910 one-quarter of the state's farmers were trying to make a living on farms smaller than 20 acres. Not only did the size of Mississippians' farms decrease, by 1920 only one-third of Mississippi farmers owned the land they worked. In 1880 fifty-six of one hundred farms were operated by their owners. By 1920 the comparable number was thirty-four. Economic success was elusive for the state's farmers. Over the years, their acreage decreased, and thousands of landowning yeomen were converted to tenants.[3]

Yet while Mississippi experienced important changes after the Civil War, in many other ways change was barely perceptible. As historian Neil McMillen has explained, "From Appomattox to the Great Depression cotton culture seemed fixed in time." The great continuity had to do with agricultural techniques and the state's labor system. Agricultural techniques were still mule-based and would be until the era of World War II. Although many farmers in the northern states used mechanized cultivators, reapers, and other implements, few Mississippi farmers mechanized any part of their operations. Part of the failure to mechanize grew out of the absence of any invention that could do the work of chopping or picking cotton. Yet the state's farmers also failed to benefit from something as basic as a tractor. As late as 1940, only 2.7 percent of Mississippi farmers owned tractors. They were vaguely aware of certain new techniques of "scientific farming," but they only rarely adopted such practices. In 1880 the amount of money Mississippi farmers spent on fertilizer was $123,000. By contrast, farmers in the adjoining state of Alabama spent ten times as much.[4]

In many ways Mississippi farmers lived a medieval existence, using the labor of animals to wrest a living from the earth. During the period 1877 to 1917, as the United States experienced rapid technological change, few Mississippians enjoyed the benefits of a telephone, electric lights, indoor plumbing, a piece of farm machinery, or an automobile. Like all farmers throughout history, Mississippi farmers lacked control over rain, hail, freezes, floods, droughts, birds, caterpillars, grubs, weevils, rodents, plant diseases, livestock maladies, and mysterious human diseases that could sweep away a human life in a matter of days. Many frustrated farmers vowed to organize to cooperate economically and politically to improve such aspects of their lives as could be controlled by human endeavor.

In addition to farmers, the state's planters formed a group of Mississippians who depended on agriculture for their living. These large-scale landowners hired wage laborers or rented plots out or both. As in antebellum times, many planters enjoyed lavish lifestyles. They lived in large homes, were attended by servants, and hosted elaborate parties. They rode in stylish buggies, wore the latest fashions, and

The Greenville cotton market in the late nineteenth century was one of the state's largest. Visible here are wagons of cotton waiting to be ginned and bales of cotton ready for shipment. Small farmer and planter alike often felt a shiver of fear as they made the trip to a cotton center like Greenville to market their crop.

sent their children away to the finest schools. Their lives were not without problems, of course, and planters did worry a great deal. Although they exercised much control over their laborers and tenants, these laborers and tenants were ultimately responsible for how much money the planter would make in a given year. Planters worried about the productivity of their workforce, and like any agriculturist, they worried about weather and other natural forces. A number of planters lost their lands over the years. A letter of Mississippi planter George Collins to his wife, written as they were on the verge of losing their plantation in 1880, was typical. Collins lamented that the nearly two decades of work operating the plantation were little else than "lost labor and mistaken effort."[5]

A variety of factors determined the success of a farm or plantation in a given year: whether the farm was large or small, whether owned or rented, and how many laborers (if any) the farmer would have to hire. The matter of which crop or crops to grow was critical. Natural forces such as rainfall, soil quality, and insect plagues influenced production. Expenses not related directly to the growing of the crop also affected income. Taxes, railroad rates, and the cost of ginning and marketing rose and fell with time. The most important determinants of income, however, were the worldwide demand for cotton and the size of the world cotton crop. Despite their isolated existence, Mississippi farmers were deeply affected by actions of cotton growers in India and Egypt and by the needs of textile manufacturers in England.

To discuss the factors that influenced a farmer's income may suggest the intelligent farmer could monitor such trends and engage in enlightened economic planning. In reality, farmers could do very little successful economic planning. For example, a farmer in June 1903 could pick up a copy of a Vicksburg newspaper and see that the price of cotton was 13½ cents per pound. The farmer might then use this information to gauge the wisdom of seeking a loan for purchasing land. Since 13½ cents was promising for a high income, the farmer might very well decide to contract the loan. Yet by late October 1903 that farmer would be dismayed to find the price of cotton had fallen to only 9¼ cents per pound and that it would be difficult to pay off the loan. The price fluctuations from month to month and from year to year made planning difficult. The reasons for these rapid swings in cotton prices were numerous. Mississippi farmers, though, believed the obvious culprit was "the middleman" and cotton futures speculators. A farmer named D. Street, in a letter to U.S. senator James Z. George, argued that growing cotton was suicidal, since the cotton farmer "is left at the mercy of the howling crowd about the so-called cotton exchanges." In fact, many of the state's farmers lobbied Congress to make commodities futures speculation a crime.[6]

While tariff policies, land taxes, corporate monopolies, and high railroad rates all angered farmers and helped lower their incomes, some of the farmers' problems very clearly began at home. One of their chief problems, according to experts of the late 1800s, was that farmers insisted on growing cotton and neglected other crops. Most Mississippi farmers raised cotton exclusively, with perhaps the addition of a garden and a small chicken-yard. On many farms, cotton grew up to the front door of the home. This monoculture, or one-crop farming, had very serious risks, which were clearly noted by Clarence H. Poe, editor of the *Progressive Farmer* (a regional publication that was the most popular agricultural newspaper in Mississippi). "When southern cotton prices drop every southern man feels the blow," Poe noted. On the other hand, "when cotton prices advance, every industry throbs with vigor." Mississippi's economy had a boom-bust cycle, depending both on the size of the cotton crop each year and on current cotton prices. Older Mississippians looking back on this period recalled the boom-bust cycle vividly. "Sometimes my father drove shouting down the hill with new suits, pretty dress goods, picture books, apples and oranges and candy," recalled Arthur Hudson of Attala County. Yet other years Hudson's father met the family carrying only the bare necessities: coffee, sugar, and utilitarian clothing. In 1877 L. N. Treadway, a Mississippi farmwife, had to tell her daughter, "Lucy, take good care of your blue dress & your Pa says he will not get you any new dresses this winter." The year had been bad for cotton farmers, and "so you will have to make up your mind to do without."[7]

Why was there such dependence on cotton, when in the antebellum years Mississippi had raised an abundance of food crops? One reason was that cotton prices at Civil War's end soared to $1.90 a pound. Farmers thus began the practice of growing little else than cotton, not suspecting that by century's end the $1.90 price would fall to just $0.0475 per pound. After the increase in taxes after the Civil War, farmers needed cash crops to pay not only the expenses of farming but also taxes. The antebellum agricultural system had been one of "safety first"—first make sure your family and your laborers would be fed and only then contemplate raising a crop to earn cash. After the Civil War, the "safety first" system became outmoded for two reasons. First, the United States was an increasingly commercial nation, and farmers decided their families needed more than beans and corn. Each visit to town reminded farmers of the existence of treadle sewing machines, pianos and parlor lamps, and apple peelers and factory-made shoes. Rather than ask their families to do without, farmers grew a crop that would provide the cash needed to buy these products. Another reason "safety first" became outmoded is that local merchants began offering credit to their customers. In a bad year, a merchant would carry over debt and help farmers feed their families the following year by advancing more credit. Thus farmers no longer faced starvation if the cotton crop failed and food crops were not grown.[8]

Cotton almost became a unit of currency. The real question was not the dollar cost of that new plow, but how many pounds of cotton would it cost? The distinction became crucial with the major expenses in a farmer's life, including taxes and land payments. A farmer who contracted a loan calling for payments of $96 per year might be in dire straits when cotton prices fell. The farmer might find that while the yearly loan payment originally had been the equivalent of 700 pounds of cotton, the payment increased to 1,182 pounds as cotton prices fell. What was originally a manageable loan became a terrible burden as the size of the cotton supply increased and prices fell. There was little use in telling the farmer that the loan payment had remained steady at $96 per year. In a very real sense, the payment had increased markedly. Unfortunately, the only way out was to raise more cotton, thus increasing the family's cash income. When farmers raised more cotton, however, cotton prices fell as the world supply increased. On a large scale across the South, low cotton prices led to distress, and distressed farmers tried to recover their cash income by raising more cotton, compounding the problem. Cotton prices fell to 4¾ cents per pound in 1898, as the size of the crop across the South rose to a staggering 11.5 million bales.[9]

The deflation of cotton prices devastated Mississippi farmers. Between 1872 and 1915 the prices of all kinds of goods fell less than 20 percent, but cotton prices fell 60 percent. Farmers found that their basic unit of currency, a pound of cotton, bought less and less as the decades passed. Inflationary times, however, were very good for farmers. Cotton prices would rise with inflation, while loan payments and taxes would remain the same. A farmer with a loan payment of $96 per year might see the loan payment fall from 700 pounds of cotton per year to 540 per year as cotton prices rose with inflation. Inflation became a cherished ideal of Mississippi farmers, and much of their political effort sought an inflation of the money supply by new issues of government greenbacks or by expanding the money supply to include dollars based on silver as well as gold.

Other problems Mississippi's agricultural community faced were the declining degree of farm ownership and the rising level of indebtedness. When cotton prices soared as the Civil War ended, farmers rushed to devote all their acreage to cotton. With no acreage devoted to grains or livestock, they would have to buy food for the coming year, yet for many of them this was an expense for which they lacked ready cash. Thus local merchants agreed to advance them credit for their "furnish"—the food and supplies needed for a year's farming. Such loans were paid back with the proceeds of the cotton crop, but if a crop was small or the price of cotton low, the farmer would begin to fall behind in repaying the debt. Eventually, merchants might foreclose on the farmer's home and land. The merchant could then choose to rent the land to the same farmer, rent it to someone else, or hire an overseer and pay day laborers to work the land. While in 1880 more than 56 percent of Mississippi's farms were worked by their owners, by 1890 only a minority of farms were owner-run. Farmers all over the country were trying to cope with serious problems in this era. However, by comparing Mississippi with the state of Indiana, for example, one can see an important difference. Both states had about the same number of farms, about 220,000 in each. Yet in 1900 tenants farmed 138,000 of the farms in Mississippi but only 63,000 of the Indiana farms.[10]

Helpless farmers could do little or nothing about floods and insects, monopolies, high tariffs, escalating railroad rates, low cotton prices, and a deflationary national economy. They also fell ever deeper into debt and lost their lands. Perhaps the ultimate insult was that farmers did not even own or control their crop. As a condition of credit, a farmer signed a lien giving the lender the right to sell the crop to satisfy the debt. Farmers complained bitterly about state laws that supported this crop lien system, arguing that farmers should be permitted to sell their own crops and settle their own debts. Little real change grew out of their complaints, however. As a number of writers have noted, the state could not abolish the crop lien system, since credit was so necessary in Mississippi's new system of cash crop farming.

Lenders would insist on some form of collateral. For many Mississippi farmers, the crop in the field was the only thing of value they had.[11]

Indebtedness was a central feature of farmers' lives in the half-century after Reconstruction. Farmers did have potential avenues for coping with indebtedness. One was to grow more of the cash crop to be able to pare down the debt or even erase it. Yet soil depletion in most areas of Mississippi meant each farmer's output per acre trended downward over time. Additional land purchases offered another way to increase output, but Mississippi's farmers were losing land more often than they were adding acreage. While growing more cotton might help the individual farmer, it was detrimental to cotton farmers as a whole.

The declining size of farms also hurt Mississippi's farmers but seemed inevitable. A rising population was farming the same number of square miles. These population figures help explain the shrinking farm size: in 1870 Mississippi had 17.9 persons per square mile; in 1890, 27.8 persons per square mile; and in 1910, 38.8 persons per square mile.[12] Mississippians tried a number of ways of coping with the increased crowding. One way was to open new areas of the state to farming. Another was to ensure that more of the land on existing farms was cultivated. Thus, where only one-third of a typical farmer's land was considered "improved" land in 1880, more than half of the typical farm's acreage was "improved" in 1920. Converting more acres into "improved" land generally meant bringing the farm's poorer land into production, and the improvement in farm output was not as much as farmers had hoped it would be. Individual farmers could, of course, cope with declining farm size by buying more land. Nationwide, farmers bought more land by not spending all their income and putting the money they saved into additional land purchases. Yet southern farmers tended to be so impoverished that declining to spend all one's income in a given year could mean death by starvation. In short, Mississippi farmers did not have capital to invest in expanding their acreage and did not have a series of rural banks willing to make loans. Further, what banker would want to loan money to a struggling Mississippi farmer who did not even own the crop that was growing in the field but, on the contrary, had signed it over to the local merchant for collateral on food purchases? Small farmers did not seem a good risk to the relatively small number of bankers in the state.[13]

On many occasions in U.S. history, farm communities have faced severe land shortages. The nation's most famous land shortage occurred in and around Salem Village in colonial Massachusetts. Social tensions there led to paranoia, mass hysteria, and accusations of witchcraft. While Mississippi's land crunch may have been less severe, serious social repercussions were inevitable. The third-party political turmoil Mississippi experienced, the waves of extremely popular though fleeting farm organizations, the rise of almost messianic demagogues, epidemics of mob violence—all were fed by social tensions growing out of farms so small farmers could barely feed their families. Such small farms offered incomes so low that expansion of the farm proved impossible. An almost perpetual cycle was continued, of low incomes that reinforced small farm size, which reinforced low incomes. Other areas of the country dealt with the decline of land available per person by turning to industrialization, which offered alternative ways for citizens to make a living. Mississippi's industrial base was so minuscule, however, that for most workers, agriculture was the only real option.

Mississippi farmers faced a tremendous number of difficulties in trying to eke out a living from the soil. Of all the difficulties they faced, perhaps the most demoralizing was that farmers lived an isolated existence. Many farms were located an hour or more from even a very small town. Many farmers never set foot outside their native county. The churches were the only social institutions in most farmers' lives, yet many congregations met irregularly, since they shared preachers with other churches. Many of the men and women who lived on Mississippi farms seldom saw neighbors. As a result, when farmers brooded about trusts and tariffs and taxes, they brooded alone.[14]

Because of the scattered population, teachers were scarce and likely to be teaching in ungraded schools. Better teachers gravitated to towns, where they were better paid. Rural schools were sparsely attended and badly funded. Parents could not pass much book learning along to their children, since a very large percentage of both black and white adult Mississippians were illiterate. In 1880, 42 percent of Mississippians aged ten and older were unable to read. The lack of education meant that when farmers took an interest in politics and attended the local, county, or state Democratic conventions, they were easily outmaneuvered by what one farmer called the "soft-hand, kid-glove, . . . clever fellows" who knew how to control meetings even if their crowd was in the minority. The lack of education also meant that many farmers could not read the agricultural newspapers or the pamphlets published by government agencies. Outside experts expressed dismay at Mississippi farmers' ignorance of modern agricultural methods.[15]

Farmers needed a way to cope with the isolation, lack of education, political weakness, and domination by business combinations such as railroads. A national organization called the Patrons of Husbandry (or Grange) appeared in the state in 1871. It came into Mississippi when its founder wrote to farm leaders urging them to start Granges in their communities. These efforts were successful, and W. L. Williams of Rienzi called together the first Grange meeting in May 1871. The Rienzi Grange was only the second to be organized south of the Mason-Dixon Line, so Mississippi played an important role in the early history of the organization. In 1872 the Patrons organized at the state level, with General A. J. Vaughan elected the first master of the Mississippi Grange. The organization spread like wildfire. There were 4 local Granges in the state at the end of 1871, 55 at the end of the following year, and 647 by the last day of 1874. Newspapers often devoted nearly half their local column space to Grange news, responding to reader demand. The organization held picnics attended by more than 1,000 persons in isolated communities. The only areas of the state that featured a tepid response to the new organization were the Piney Woods, where growing crops was not widespread, and the Delta. Growth of the Grange in the Delta was slowed by the whites-only membership policy of the state Grange and by planters' lack of interest in an organization that was led statewide by small farmers.

Mississippi's small farmers were starved for an organization such as the Grange. They joined by the thousands, motivated in part by the group's potential to alleviate loneliness with regular social functions. Farmers undoubtedly found Grange educational programs useful, as they learned both about new farming techniques and about proposals pending before the legislature. Many joined because organizers promised the Grange would sponsor cooperative economic action that could help farmers avoid going into debt at the crossroads stores. The growth of the Patrons of Husbandry in the state of Mississippi was remarkable, and Mississippi evangelists of the Grange spread out into neighboring states, helping the organization to take root in Tennessee, Arkansas, and Alabama.

Statewide cooperative economic action seemed a very promising avenue for the state's Granges. There were two extremes to which the Granges could go. At the extreme of passivity, the Granges could emphasize songfests and picnics and contests for the largest melon, while treading no path that might lead to controversy. At the other extreme, the Granges could seek to take over county and state government by aggressive political organization and action. There was, however, a middle course—to use economic cooperation to secure lower prices in farmers' purchases and higher prices in their crop sales. In looking at the larger American economy, farmers saw every day the advantages of cooperation and combination. Large corporations joined together to lobby for high tariffs and won them. Firms merged and secured greater efficiency. Workers unionized and won higher wages. There was no reason why farmers could not derive great benefit by collective action.

Grange cooperative merchandising existed at three basic levels. The first was the pooling of orders. By ordering items in bulk and distributing them at meetings, farmers could get better prices for goods that could not be produced on the farm, including coffee, pepper, baking soda, and the latest varieties of seeds. The Grange also invited bids from all the local merchants who wished to become the official Grange supplier. The winning merchant would agree to reduce prices for Grangers and in return would receive all of the Grangers' business. This plan had the potential for working very well, although some idealistic Grangers objected to it on principle. They argued that farmers had simply "changed masters," from one local merchant to another. Instead, they urged, farmers should become their own masters.

The third and most daring form of Grange cooperative economic activity was to open stores. The Lafayette County Grange, for example, operated a particularly successful store. The biggest impediment for Grange stores was a lack of cash. One solution was for Granges from several counties to come together. Members often marketed their crop through the Grange stores, too, collectively bargaining to get higher prices. The problem with this third type of collective merchandising was that the typical local Grange did not attract enough business to justify a full-time store, while if a number of Granges came together to open a store, the store would be unworkably distant from most of the Grangers who invested in it.

Cooperative stores were not the only type of collective economic action the Mississippi Granges took. Farmers found corporate monopolies galling, and they were especially irritated by a financial group that dominated the manufacture of cotton ties, the metal straps used to secure the bales. To counter the evils of the cotton tie trust, the Granges of a number of states met together in New Orleans in 1874 and founded the Planters' Cotton Tie Association (PCTA). The PCTA was a cooperative firm that planned to have ties made by a Chattanooga iron foundry and then distribute them to Granges. Local Granges were urged to buy stock in the PCTA and to give it their business. The PCTA was not a long-lived firm, but it succeeded in forcing down the costs of ties. Other Grange activities included wholesale cotton marketing efforts. W. L. Williams, secretary of the Mississippi Grange, gathered together eighty-three bales of cotton from his neighbors and shipped the bales directly to Liverpool, England. Williams's efforts resulted in a price of almost $72 per bale, even after expenses had been deducted—a much better price than other Mississippi farmers received. Yet such deals were uncommon, both because the state's farmers lacked the time and the expertise to engage in international marketing and because most Mississippi farmers were in debt to local merchants and did not fully own their crops.[16]

The biggest problem with the Grange-owned establishments was that they failed at a high rate. While not all failed, there was no section of the state that lacked a high-profile failure. This made farmers jumpy about such stores, and thus the store organizers had trouble securing investors. Lack of capital was one problem leading to the failures. The Bowling Green Central Co-operative in Holmes County had only $500 in capital when it began yet had to compete with long-established businesses. Local merchants slashed prices and accepted short-term losses until the Grange stores went under. A lack of class solidarity meant many farmers returned to the local merchants when they cut prices. Another problem faced by Grange-owned businesses was inexperienced management. Many store managers were fresh from the plow and had no experience running a store. Also, many customers were unable to patronize Grange stores because of the cash-only rule. The Granges adopted the cash-only policy not only to protect the financial health of their stores but also to encourage farmers to get out of debt. Yet the cash-only rule was a major impediment to many Grangers who wanted to patronize the stores. From Terry in Hinds County, one farmer reported glowingly of prices at the Grange store. "Flour is $8 [per barrel] instead of $12 at this point, and all other goods in proportion." The problem was that most farmers still had to pay $12 because they lacked cash.[17]

The Grange's cooperative efforts had both a strongly positive and deeply negative impact on the health of the Patrons of Husbandry. On the positive side, almost nothing could attract new members faster than plans to open a store owned and run by farmers. Successful stores, tanyards, and cooperative insurance plans encouraged growth of membership. On the other hand, those failures that did occur typically led to a rapid falling off of Grange membership. Some members quit because the promised cooperative store never materialized. Others quit because the store was too far away or because it failed. The Grange won some dramatic successes by its cooperative action, as when it forced down the prices of cotton ties. Nonetheless, Grange stores could lead to ill feeling, especially when farmers without cash were turned away.

The growth of the Mississippi Grange peaked in 1873. After a year or two of consolidation, membership began to decline. There were 31,000 members in the state in 1875, only 21,000 a year later, and 10,000 in 1877. For many farm families, participation was expensive in a cash-poor occupation. A committee of the Bowling Green Grange in Holmes County reported in 1881 that many members who could not afford the dues of ten cents per month had to quit the Patrons and "have gone out in the cold selfishness of the world to fall as a victim to the snares of the merchant, and drink down this terribly bitter dose, the mortgage, or as some term it, the death grip." Members of the Bowling Green Grange voted to waive the dues for members who could not afford to pay, and in Bowling Green, at least, membership did not decline sharply. In other areas the Grange declined because dues were expensive, because the cooperative utopia was slow to materialize, or because the organization had grown too quickly and had developed no strong roots of leadership.[18]

Efforts of the new state master, Putnam Darden, to revitalize the Granges in the early 1880s enjoyed modest success, but the Grange never again rose to the heady triumphs of the early 1870s. The Grange had an important impact on Mississippi farmers, opening their eyes to the strength that was possible through collective action. Weaknesses of the Grange included its failure to mobilize the strength of African American farmers as well as whites and its failure to organize in the Delta (an important agricultural region).

By the 1880s farmers in many areas of Mississippi were turning to organizations other than the Grange. Two of these were the Agricultural Wheel and the Great Agricultural Relief. The most important, however, was the Farmers' Alliance, which first appeared in Texas in the 1870s. Texas leader C. W. Macune encouraged the spread of the Farmers' Alliance across the South, and the first Farmers' Alliance organizers came into Mississippi in 1887, headed by S. O. Dawes. (Macune's group is sometimes called the Southern Alliance, to distinguish it from the movement's northern branch and from the all-black Colored Alliance.) Farmers founded the first Mississippi chapter at Oak Hall in Carroll County, and other local alliances quickly followed. In less than six months more than 20,000 members were enrolled in thirty-three counties, and a state organization was created. Dr. R. T. Love was elected the first president of the state alliance, and he took over the organizing work from the team sent by Macune. In these early days, Mississippi was second only to Texas among southern states in its support of the Farmers' Alliance.[19]

The Southern Alliance prospered for many of the same reasons the Grange had prospered. Here was a social club to alleviate loneliness, an educational group to spread the latest farming methods, a political organization to oversee lobbying efforts, and an economic group with bold plans for cooperative action. By merging with the existing groups and by recruiting tens of thousands of new members, the Farmers' Alliance "swept the state like a cyclone," in the words of the state president.[20]

One strength—and weakness—of the state's Farmers' Alliance was that its leadership was an elite group drawn chiefly from successful farmers, some planters, and agricultural editors. The Farmers' Alliance proved especially strong in the 1888 state legislature. Speaker of the House Charles B. Mitchell of Pontotoc County was elected with Farmers' Alliance support. Mitchell, an attorney, had close ties with powerful conservative politicians, including Senator Edward Cary Walthall. Newspaper editor E. J. Martin won election as House clerk with Farmers' Alliance backing. President pro tem of the new Senate was another Alliance-backed lawyer, Joel P. Walker of Meridian. Frank Burkitt, successful editor and another Farmers' Alliance leader, was chair of a key House committee. By tapping successful lawyers, editors, large farmers, and planters as their leaders, the Farmers' Alliance ensured the organization would have powerful and influential voices in the state capital. At the same time, this type of leadership also meant that the needs of dirt farmers and tenants often went unvoiced.[21]

By 1888 the Mississippi Farmers' Alliance had chapters in every county, with a total of 1,346 of these "suballiances." The total state membership in 1888 was about 60,000 and rising. The Farmers' Alliances became an important part of farmers' lives, providing family picnics, solemn burial services, gifts of money to those who were sick or had a disability, and educational programs. Once the groups had developed their fraternal bonds, many members wanted to turn to some of the same cooperative economic activities engaged in by the earlier Grange. Many local newspapers, perhaps serving as the mouthpieces of their advertisers, warned the Farmers' Alliance not to open stores since so many of the Grange stores had failed. But as one farmer wrote in a letter to a newspaper editor, the Farmers' Alliance members had "the lamp of past experience to guide their feet, and are proceeding with a caution born of a knowledge of past failure." Word of the coming economic ventures led more farmers to join the group, and by 1890 Mississippi had nearly 80,000 Alliance members. Eventually, more than half of all adult rural males in the state joined, forming a power to be reckoned with.[22]

When the Farmers' Alliance was first organized in the state in August 1887, no topic was deemed of greater importance than economic cooperation. After months of discussion, the plan that emerged called for creation of a centralized Farmers' Alliance Exchange, a corporation owned by the suballiances and by individual members. Farmers' Alliance members in each congressional district would pledge to buy nearly $17,000 worth of stock in the firm and would elect two members of a board of directors. The state exchange would purchase goods in bulk, then sell them to the suballiances and arrange for shipping. Because all business would be conducted on a cash basis, farmers believed the state exchange would be at no financial risk. Salaries of the employees would be paid by charging modest commissions on goods sold. This plan was more elaborate than anything implemented by the Grange and had a greater emphasis on cooperative selling (of cotton) and not just buying.

Meridian, Jackson, Winona, Kosciusko, and Durant all vied to be the site of the new state exchange, certain that the exchange offered an infallible route to future growth. Winona made the most generous bid, offering a valuable plot of land and a house as well as free use of a fireproof warehouse. Winona leaders also pledged that the suballiances of Montgomery and surrounding counties would purchase $2,000 in stock in the new exchange. When state Alliance leaders announced that Winona had indeed won the prize, local editors wrote screaming headlines: "WINONA GETS IT! A FUTURE METROPOLIS—MERIDIAN'S LOSS IS WINONA'S GAIN. THE EXCHANGE MEANS IMMENSE SHIPMENTS OF COTTON. NOW FOR THE STATE CAPITOL!" The Winona exchange opened in October 1888 and conducted a flourishing trade in plows, wagons, and other needed farm implements. The directors spoke of starting an Alliance wagon factory to meet the demand and secure even lower prices.[23]

Unfortunately, gloomy news was not long in coming. One problem was that the suballiances were slow to purchase stock. Another was that farmers were giving the exchange only a small percentage of their business. Early in 1890 Alliance leaders relocated the exchange to Memphis, where it could work more closely with the Arkansas and Tennessee exchanges. As the Methodists laid plans to build Millsaps College, a disgruntled member of the Farmers' Alliance warned church leaders not to build the college at Winona, as the state exchange had died "of the dry rot" there.

One reason for the exchange's downfall was a shift in the priorities of the state Farmers' Alliance. Only months after the group laid plans for the exchange, the state and national leadership of the Farmers' Alliance vowed to take action against the "jute trust." Southern farmers used jute bagging to wrap their bales. Farm newspapers reported that a "trust" had gained control of the jute market and doubled prices for bagging. The regional leadership of the Southern Alliance urged farmers to replace the jute with coarse cotton cloth and even to consider launching factories to produce cotton bagging, which was cleaner, more fire-resistant, and made of a product Mississippi farmers should support. Southern Alliance leaders estimated that if southern farmers switched to cotton bagging for their bales, the result would be an additional 125,000 bales purchased each year for the making of bagging. The jute boycott began in 1888 and was all but complete in Mississippi in 1889, 1890, and 1891. Finally, the jute sellers capitulated, reducing the prices of bagging sharply. One elderly Mississippi woman, interviewed in 1949 about the Farmers' Alliance, recalled first and foremost the movement to switch to cotton bagging. Though not remembered today, the triumph over the jute trust was what historian James S. Ferguson called "the most tangible accomplishment of the Alliance."[24]

Unfortunately, success was mingled with failure, as the Farmers' Alliance once again overreached. Following up on the successful boycott, the state Alliance laid plans to build a factory that would make bagging. The failure of farmers and town boosters to buy shares in the firm led to its downfall after several years of efforts by the state leadership. The editor of the *Raymond Gazette* observed wryly that if the Farmers' Alliance had instead put the cotton bagging factory money into prizes for the largest hog, Mississippi would be overrun with 425-pounders. Lack of capital was a recurring problem that hurt not only Mississippi's business owners but also its farmers.[25]

Mississippi's Farmers' Alliance could boast some economic successes. In addition to the jute boycott, local suballiances founded successful cooperative tanneries as well as cotton sheds along the railroad tracks, where farmers could store their crop and await the best price. Pooling orders at the county level helped Mississippi farmers save money and put merchants on notice that they must lower their prices to keep their Farmers' Alliance customers. Yet the major failures of the state exchange and the proposed bagging factory led farmers to believe the deck was stacked against them. Their economic salvation seemed to require new lawmakers who would be as solicitous of farmers as the current lawmakers were of business owners.

Leaders of the Southern Alliance had long been feuding about what role, if any, the group should play in politics. In Mississippi, Farmers' Alliance leaders tended to agree that members should remain loyal to the Democratic Party. Still, even within the Democratic Party, the Farmers' Alliance could take steps to be more politically active. One step the Mississippi leadership took in 1890 was to add a new level of organization. Now there would be not only state, county, and local alliances but also district alliances, with boundaries corresponding to congressional district lines. The purpose was clear—to help elect more farmer candidates to Congress. More subtly, the state Farmers' Alliance's "educational work" now concentrated less on such topics as erosion and chicken mites and more upon political education, even class education.

The Farmers' Alliance candidates for office ran as Democrats, usually seeking to wrest the nominations from incumbents. Some counties had Farmers' Alliance tickets as early as 1889, but the 1890 elections saw the real beginnings of serious

Alliance politics. The Alliance managed to elect some fifty-five delegates to the 1890 constitutional convention and at the convention came within one vote of electing the state Alliance president to chair the convention. In the fall elections of 1890, voters elected two Farmers' Alliance candidates to Congress—Clarke Lewis of Noxubee County and Joseph H. Beeman of Scott County. Both were Confederate veterans, former schoolteachers, and farmers. Beeman was chair of the state Farmers' Alliance executive committee.[26]

In December 1890 the Southern Alliance met at Ocala, Florida, and framed a document that came to be known as the Ocala Demands. The demands included: national regulation or ownership of railroads, telegraphs, and telephones; abolition of national banks; and direct election of U.S. senators. Delegates to the Ocala meeting also demanded that Congress erect a warehouse in every important agricultural county in the nation, allowing farmers to store their crops and hold the crops for the best possible price. Under this so-called subtreasury plan, the federal government would also make loans to farmers for up to 80 percent of the crop's value. If a farmer defaulted on a loan, the government could sell the crop to recoup its investment. The subtreasury idea was appealing to Mississippi farmers because it would give them leverage over the hated cotton speculators. Farmers could hold their crop until the price rose.

Farmers were beginning to favor a strong and active federal government. Even former Confederate leaders now believed that a strong central government in Washington might be necessary. Former Confederate general Stephen D. Lee, president of the Mississippi Agricultural and Mechanical College, explained that half of the nation's population "engaged in occupations other than farming" and "have accumulated wealth to an abnormal extent." Some people did grow rich from agriculture, but those who did so were merchants, railroad executives, cotton factors, wholesalers, and middlemen. Three of the dirtiest words in the farmers' vocabulary were "trusts," "speculators," and "middlemen." Only by strong federal action, such as tough railroad regulation and the building of subtreasury warehouses, could farmers hope to earn a fair living.[27]

The great political showdown within the Democratic Party came in the 1891 election for the state legislature. The newly selected legislators would have the opportunity to elect both of the state's U.S. senators. Prior to the 1891 campaign, a suballiance in Carroll County wrote Senators James Z. George and Edward Cary Walthall, asking their views on the subtreasury. Both men responded that the plan was impractical and probably unconstitutional. The state's more hotheaded Alliance members decided that both senators must go. Alliance editor Frank Burkitt

Ethelbert Barksdale was a member of Congress from 1883 to 1887. Together with Frank Burkitt, he led agrarian efforts to oust Mississippi's two U.S. Senators in 1891. Many farmers hoped the new legislature would send Barksdale to the Senate to replace Senator George.

unleashed the attack on the two men with an editorial headlined "Good-bye Senators."[28] The 1891 election was, in the words of a writer in the *Grenada Sentinel*, "one of the most exciting and serious we have ever witnessed in the state." In Chickasaw County, Burkitt was running for the legislature. His newspaper office burned to the ground one night under mysterious circumstances. Burkitt's opponent shot the crusading editor, though the wound was not a serious one. Elsewhere in the state, agrarian politician Ethelbert Barksdale debated Democratic member of Congress Hernando D. Money. Barksdale accused Money of accepting bribes from the railroads, Money called Barksdale a liar, and Barksdale threw a law book at Money and hit him in the head. Farmers' Alliance chapters were heavily involved in the county campaigns, working hard for the candidates pledged to oust the incumbent senators. Yet when the bitter campaign was over, the agrarians had to face a disappointing loss. The new legislature sent both George and Walthall back to the Senate. There was now no chance Mississippi's senators would push Congress to enact the farmers' subtreasury plan.[29]

By 1892 many Mississippi farmers had had enough of the Democratic Party. The repeated failure to elect agrarians to seats of power led to a belief that only the action of a farmers' political party could ensure victory of farmer candidates.

While some farmers remained loyal Democrats, others helped lead the Farmers' Alliances to support the new People's Party. For those who remained active in the Alliance, the Alliance itself became the poor stepchild, as all funds and all energy went into building up the People's Party. Thus the Alliance itself began to wither and die in the early 1890s.[30]

The Farmers' Alliance was a state organization that, like the earlier Grange, experienced a rapid rise and fall. Like the Grange, it saw some successes in cooperative economic action and some conspicuous failures. Like the Grange, it furnished an important social and educational agency in isolated farm communities. Both groups had some success in lobbying lawmakers and electing farmer candidates. Yet the Farmers' Alliance never realized its full potential because of serious internal divisions. The failure of Farmers' Alliances in northern and southern states to work closely together limited the two groups' influence. The failure to include women as fully participating members of the Alliances (in contrast to the Grange) also made the organization weaker than it might have been. The almost complete separation of the white organization and the Colored Alliance prevented the two groups from realizing their full potential power. Finally, the division of the Southern Alliance into those who favored creation of a new farmers' political party and those who favored loyalty to the Democrats ensured that farmers' enemies could divide and conquer. An upturn in cotton prices in the late 1890s helped farmers feel more comfortable and more prosperous, and no new farmers' organization immediately arose to take the place of the Farmers' Alliance.

Early in the twentieth century, as cotton prices neared new lows, Mississippi's agriculturalists organized again, but the new organizations never approached the size of the old Grange or Farmers' Alliance. One group, the Mississippi Cotton Association, was made up primarily of planters. Small farmers organized a second group, the Farmers' Educational and Cooperative Union. Both groups encouraged members to reduce cotton acreage. The two groups had some success in reducing the size of the cotton crop during the first seven years of the twentieth century. Yet the 1908 crop was large once again, and prices fell by two or three cents per pound from 1907 levels. Prices were also especially low during the large crop years of 1914 and 1915.[31]

The Farmers' Union was in steep decline by 1910, and on the eve of World War I, Mississippi really had no strong farmers' organization—remarkable in the most agricultural state in the nation. In fact, in 1917 it was as if no farmers' organization ever had existed in the state. Farmers were going deeper in debt, were increasingly renters rather than landowners, and still had virtually no mechanization on their farms. There was almost no state in the Union lower in number of cooperative enterprises than Mississippi. The Grange, the Farmers' Alliance, and the Farmers' Union failed to bring lasting change to the state because Mississippi farmers were at once too independent and too dependent. Mississippi farmers took pride in their independence and resented being told by their organizations' leaders to change their mix of crops, change their farming methods, vote for different candidates, boycott certain merchants, and sell their crops at a different time of year. The state's farmers were also too dependent upon merchants and creditors and thus were not always free to change their crop mix, change merchants, or hold their crop off the market. The farmers' lack of capital helped lead to the downfall of the Farmers' Alliance state mercantile house and its cotton bagging factory. It is not surprising these agricultural organizations failed to bring lasting change to the state. Indeed, it may be remarkable they were able to enjoy their many short-term successes.[32]

The farm organizations could not shrink the size of the state's cotton crop because thousands of new acres were brought into production each year in the Yazoo-Mississippi Delta. The Delta originally had been settled along rivers and large streams. Locating plantations along the rivers facilitated marketing the timber that originally covered the land and later allowed cotton to be shipped easily to market. U.S. Census Bureau reports in 1879 indicated that Sunflower and Quitman counties were among the Mississippi counties with the least cotton acreage. Yet by the early twentieth century Sunflower and Quitman counties had been cleared, cultivated, and were among the nation's top cotton-producing counties.[33]

The increasing crowding of farmers on the land in the state led to more and more Delta land being cleared and brought under cultivation. The potential of the new land was tremendous. First, there were acres of hardwoods of enormous size to be cut and sold. Sale of this lumber often nearly paid the new owner for the purchase of the land. Also, the rich Delta soil in some places was sixty feet deep. A geologist working in the state in 1906 reported, "Taken as a whole . . . the plant food percentages in this soil are probably unexcelled by any soil in the world thus far examined." Yet in 1877 vast expanses of the Delta were still largely junglelike, forming an area one Mississippi writer called "a seething lush hell." Clearing the land was extraordinarily difficult work, given the impediments of snakes, mosquitoes, poison ivy, and briars. Most of this work was done by African American day laborers who had come to the region after hearing reports of new, rich land being brought under cultivation.[34]

Clearing the Delta land was facilitated by the arrival of timber companies that set up mills and built small-gauge railroads into remote sections. Those landowners who could not wait for sawmills and railroads made a "deadening." Using an ax, the landowner or hired laborers ringed the bark of the trees and then burned the tract. The trees soon died, and the farmer or planter began growing cotton among the charred giants. The dead trees did not cast much of a shadow, and the cotton raising could proceed, even if not under ideal circumstances. For farmers in these deadenings, life could be truly isolated. Mary Hamilton's family moved to a remote location several miles from the Sunflower River. She recalled that for more than one year, she saw no other woman. Hamilton later described her frontier life: "We soon found that the country was full of all kinds of wild animals. We could hear wolves howling, see bear tracks, and hear raccoons fighting." From her frontier home, "The bears didn't bother me like the panthers and wolves did. I never could get used to hearing a panther scream nor wolves howl, though it was an every-night occurrence."[35]

Whether on new lands in the Delta or on older farms in the northeast hills, Mississippi farmers faced a frightening new menace early in the new century. On September 30, 1907, in a cotton field six miles south of Natchez, a U.S. government scientist named W. D. Hunter pulled a small beetle from a cotton plant and dropped it into a glass vial. State entomologists collected many other specimens of the boll weevil in the coming months throughout Adams and Wilkinson counties. By 1911 the boll weevil infestation was statewide. The agricultural experiment stations worked furiously to provide information. At first they helped farmers recognize this particular insect and told them what counties were most affected. Later the stations tried to give farmers advice on how to grow cotton successfully despite the weevil's presence. Many farmers, however, watched in despair as their hard work came to naught. The boll weevils caused squares, blooms, and bolls to drop off the cotton plants.[36]

Agricultural experts urged the state's farmers to cope with the boll weevil by growing less cotton. The Delta agricultural experiment station at Stoneville, for example, included a large demonstration herd of hogs. Yet many Delta farmers proved resistant to the idea of erecting hog pens on top of the Delta's legendary soil. Many farmers began experiments of their own. One Columbus man in 1915 invented a machine he claimed could move through the cotton fields picking off the boll weevils. Finally, the state's agricultural scientists developed a multifaceted plan for coping with the boll weevil infestation. One part of the plan was to grow other crops in addition to cotton. Farmers should plant early-blooming varieties of cotton to thwart the weevil's life cycle. Also, farmers should plant the cotton plants very close together, using fertilizer to make up for the smaller amounts of nutrients available to each plant. Some of the advice provided by the experts proved too onerous to be useful. One 1911 bulletin from the entomologist at the Mississippi Agricultural and Mechanical College urged farmers to move through the fields hand-picking the weevils off the crop. "We advise doing this work once each week," explained the bulletin. Yet cotton had always been a labor-intensive crop, and more so with the new method of close planting. Hand-picking weevils in an effective way was impossible.[37]

Still, Mississippi weathered the boll weevil crisis, and in fact the state was among the least hard hit by the infestation. The boll weevil may have actually improved the state's agricultural situation in some ways. The supply of cotton worldwide was already too high, even as vast new lands in the Delta were being opened up to cotton farming. The appearance of the boll weevil encouraged the farmers of Mississippi and other states to grow some crops other than cotton. This reduced the cotton supply (as did the damage of the weevil itself), and cotton prices rose.

The appearance of the boll weevil demonstrated the importance of science to Mississippi farmers. Since its founding in 1878, the Agricultural and Mechanical College at Starkville had provided scientific information to farmers. Many farmers resisted this information, however, believing that the college's professors knew only "book farming." The agricultural experiment stations, supported by state and federal funds, helped prove the practicality of the suggestions. The experimental farm in Marshall County, for example, did seemingly miraculous work converting exhausted, eroded land into a bountiful series of terraced fields. By 1910 the state had more than half a dozen experimental field stations, with farmers in many areas clamoring for more. Fearing the cost, the 1910 legislature appointed a committee to assess how necessary these stations were. The committee first visited the Delta Branch Station at Stoneville. There the legislators saw a phenomenally rich field of oats. A grain binder traversed the field, as neat bundles of oats dropped off the back of the machine. The legislators were astounded both by the lush crop and the mechanical marvel. One legislator insisted on trotting alongside the binder in a vain attempt to see how it worked. The oat fields there yielded 135 bushels per acre, an incredible achievement. Thus, contrary to expectations, the legislators wrote a glowing report, and the appropriations for experiment stations increased.[38]

The departments of the Agricultural and Mechanical College as well as the field stations printed regular reports of their findings. These discussed fertilizer use, corn smut, parasites on chickens, erosion control, and other topics. Still, there were serious shortcomings with trying to expand knowledge of scientific farming in the state by issuing these printed bulletins. First, many farmers preferred to adhere to tradition rather than try expensive new methods. Second, many farmers were illiterate or at least not prepared to wade through difficult scientific writing. Third, the farmer had to buy a stamp and an envelope and then write to the station to get a copy of the bulletins. Wise observers of the situation realized that printed bulletins did not meet the needs of Mississippi's farmers. As an alternative, in the 1880s the Agricultural and Mechanical College pioneered the Farmers' Institutes. By the early twentieth century these institutes flourished. In 1906 alone there were 142 of these educational meetings, with a total attendance of 17,645 Mississippi farmers. The Cooperative Extension Service hired agricultural experts who visited individual farms and offered advice on employing the latest methods. Agricultural training for young Mississippians improved with the advent of the Corn Clubs, forerunners of today's 4-H Clubs. The Corn Clubs originated in Holmes County, Mississippi, and soon spread to every part of the nation. By 1910 Mississippi had more than 6,000 young members, who by their projects and contests learned modern methods of agriculture.[39]

Of all the messages carried by experiment station bulletins, Grange and Farmers' Alliance speakers, and Corn Club leaders, none was more important than diversification. With the exception of an occasional Delta planter or merchant, nearly every knowledgeable person in the state urged Mississippi farmers to grow less cotton. The movement for diversification took on aspects of a religious crusade, with new converts to the cause offering testimony of their economic salvation. As farmer George J. Finley of Marshall County put it, Mississippi's croplands "have been 'cottoned' to death nearly," with soils exhausted and yields falling. Finley pointed out that pork, beef, corn, and sorghum could all be raised with great success in Mississippi, and he was of the opinion that "the man who neglects these things sins willfully."[40]

Almost no one suggested that the state's farmers should abandon cotton altogether. The point was that it made little economic sense to decline to raise food crops, then contract large debts at ruinous rates of interest to feed one's family. While in the best years for cotton it might make sense to grow only cotton, one never could know ahead of time which years would be good for cotton. Besides, going into debt often meant that farmers lost their independence, becoming increasingly reliant on merchants, moneylenders, and landlords.

A typical diversified farmer in Mississippi decided to raise cotton but also corn, hay, garden vegetables, cattle, and chickens. The advantages of this diversified approach were many. By feeding their families, farmers were saved the cost of their "furnish" and the exorbitant interest on it. By staying out of debt, farmers maintained their independence. By having a field of cowpeas or vetch to feed the cattle, some soil rebuilding occurred. Manure from the livestock allowed some additional soil improvement. If the cotton crop failed or if the price was very low for the year, at least the family was fed, and it was helpful that the farmer's problems were not compounded by indebtedness that had to be carried over to the next year. Further, there might be some corn and beef to sell, and their prices might be high. Additionally, if other farmers were also following this diversification plan, cotton acreage was reduced, and the price of cotton would go up for everyone.[41]

If the year was a good one for cotton, however, farmers would have far less cash income than they would have had if raising only cotton. They might find it hard to pay their dues to the Farmers' Alliance or to subscribe to the *Progressive Farmer*. There would be less money for shoes for the children, for land purchase, or for buying a manure spreader. But the disadvantages of diversification did not outweigh the advantages. With barely a dissenting voice, state farm leaders evangelized for diversification.

"Cotton is a tyrannical king," warned the editor of the agrarian *Batesville Blade* in 1881, and "those who pay him the greatest tribute suffer the most." The editor, Henry W. Thaten, urged Panola County farmers to "pay a little more attention to hog and hominy, and they will soon bring his majesty to terms." Even in the cotton mill town of Wesson, the local editor agreed that King Cotton "has become a tyrant, with low prices as his prime minister." Again in Vicksburg, where cotton merchants reigned supreme, a newspaper editor in 1905 urged that farmers should raise food for their families first and "then, if you will, raise cotton as a surplus or money crop." If Mississippi farmers would do this, urged this editor, they "would become the richest in the world."[42]

The best way for farm groups and journalists to boost diversification was to present success stories to the public, and this they regularly did. Readers of the *Summit Sentinel* in 1908 learned about the success of M. G. Felder, who lived near Summit. Felder, on his family farm, produced 600 bushels of corn, 200 bushels of potatoes, 100 gallons of molasses, and 13 bales of cotton. In addition, his family produced oats, hay, peas, and pumpkins and tended a variety of animals. Felder also did a little preaching on the side. "It is folly for others to assert that farming can't be made to pay," charged the local editor. It was just that it could not pay "with the all-cotton system in practice." The *Gloster Record* reported that Charles Lindenmeyer made $24 off one pecan tree, also in 1908, a tidy sum for any farmer.

With pecans at fifteen cents per pound, Lindenmeyer's pecan grove paid him handsomely. The *Wesson Herald* in 1882 trumpeted the success of W. V. Sirley, who farmed near Raymond. Sirley supplemented his cotton with hay production and grew more than fifteen tons on four acres. His four acres paid him $232 after expenses were deducted; this was far more cash than most Mississippi farmers saw that year.[43]

One of the greatest efforts to encourage Mississippi farmers to diversify involved the growing of truck crops (vegetables for commercial markets). Truck farming had its earliest beginnings in the state in Copiah County in 1874, when the Reverend J. W. McNeil and another farmer named Stackhouse began growing these crops for markets in the cities. Meeting together in 1877, local growers and railroad officials were able to plan together for their mutual benefit. Truck farming required close cooperation with the railroads because the highly perishable crops had to be rushed to market and protected from bruises and from extreme temperatures. Crystal Springs in Copiah County became the major shipping point for truck crops in the state, but residents of Harrison, Lincoln, Hinds, Rankin, Simpson, and other counties also engaged in truck farming. By 1905 truck farmers organized in Jones County, made arrangements with the railroads, and soon shipped eight boxcars of potatoes to market in one day.[44]

The most important diversification made by Mississippi farmers in the half-century after Reconstruction was the raising of increasing numbers of cattle. It is true that even as late as 1890 Mississippi had not returned to the 1860 level of the total value of cattle in the state. W. B. Montgomery of Oktibbeha County did a great deal to encourage the raising of beef and dairy cattle in Mississippi. He was a cofounder of one of the first creameries in a southern state and helped found the influential Mississippi Livestock Association. The *Southern Livestock Journal* published at Starkville helped encourage scientific stock raising across the South. One of the greatest difficulties would-be stock raisers encountered was the poor quality of breeding stock in the state. The Agricultural and Mechanical College was home to a fine herd of cattle and in cooperation with the Mississippi Livestock Association helped get superior bloodlines into hundreds of Mississippi herds.[45]

Proponents of diversification made some headway in Mississippi between the 1880 and 1920 censuses. The number of dairy cattle in the state increased from 268,000 to 789,000. The number of acres in corn increased from 1,571,000 to 2,657,000. The value of livestock being raised in the state increased from $24 million to $135 million. The value of fruit and vegetable crops, of hay, and of chickens increased sharply. Yet because cotton acreage also increased (by about 40 percent),

Mississippi still relied on cotton for a huge percentage of the state's agricultural income.[46]

Despite the problems of relying on one crop, most Mississippi farmers recognized that no crop was more suitable for the state's soil and climate than cotton. Even in the late 1800s most of the state's farmers knew what an economist put down on paper in 1926: "Nothing has been found to take the place of cotton on an extensive scale that would make the farmers as much money one year with another." While other crops such as corn could help soften the blow when cotton prices were low, "they could not bring in money and they offered little hope as a source of progress." While most farmers were deeply impressed by arguments for diversification, most also recognized that the U.S. economy was firmly based on cash. Those who wanted to buy manufactured goods and those who dreamed of buying more land must have cash. Cotton was the surest route to earning money in the state of Mississippi.[47]

On the eve of the United States' entry into World War I, Mississippi farmers were using the same agricultural methods as had their great-great-grandparents. Moreover, the daily life of the typical Mississippi farmer was nearly the same in 1877 and 1917. The new labor-saving inventions that swept the nation were rarely used by Mississippi farmers. In 1917 as in 1877, Mississippi farm homes were heated by wood and lit by tallow or kerosene. In 1917 as in earlier decades, Mississippi farmers tended to have no machinery to lighten their work, and in fact a plow and wagon were often the only implements Mississippi farmers used other than hand tools. Even more in 1917 than in 1877, the state was covered in the early fall with the white of newly open cotton bolls. While cotton had been by far the major crop in 1877, by 1917 new acreage had been opened in the Delta and in the cutover lands of Piney Woods, and cotton was the crop of choice on these new farms. To see striking changes and convincing agricultural progress, the Mississippian of 1917 would have to wait at least three decades.

CHAPTER THREE

THE PERSISTENT INSTITUTION

Black Labor and Race Control

Throughout the years 1877 to 1917, Mississippi was home to a very sizable minority group living within its borders. This minority group was the state's white citizens. At the time of the 1910 census, fifty-six of every one hundred Mississippians were of African descent. No other state in the nation had such a proportionally large black population. In fact, in 1910 one of every ten African Americans in the nation lived in the state of Mississippi. In certain counties, the percentages were even more lopsided. Issaquena County had a smaller proportion of whites than any other county in the nation. In Issaquena, black residents outnumbered whites by a ratio of sixteen to one. In Tunica County, 91 percent of residents were African American; Tunica ranked third in the nation in its proportion of black residents.[1]

The vast majority of African Americans in Mississippi in this period had been held as slaves or were the children of former slaves. A number of them had helped the Union army as laborers, and many more had served as Union soldiers. Changes came quickly after the Union victory, and a number of these were formalized in amendments to the U.S. Constitution. The Thirteenth Amendment proclaimed that slavery and involuntary servitude no longer would exist in the United States. Few white Mississippians were surprised at the Thirteenth Amendment, but most hoped the U.S. government would go no further. Instead, Congress wrote and the states ratified the Fourteenth Amendment, declaring all persons born in the United States, regardless of race, citizens of the United States with equal rights before the law. Congress then passed one additional amendment, proclaiming that no state could deny the right to vote on account of race. The states ratified the Fifteenth Amendment in 1870.

These constitutional amendments promised sweeping changes. The freedmen could expect a bold new beginning in their lives. Presumably, they would no longer toil in gangs for white landowners or feel the overseer's lash. They would be able to buy land, choose a landlord from whom to rent land, or choose an occupation other than farming. They would have the right to learn to read, denied them in slavery times, and in fact would be legally entitled to an education equal to that given to whites. The rights to vote, hold office, and serve on juries were also granted by the new amendments.

By 1917 the Fourteenth and Fifteenth amendments were dead letters in the state of Mississippi, as in other southern states. The promise of the Thirteenth Amendment would be but partly realized. An examination of Mississippi's system of agriculture and agricultural labor will demonstrate the limited progress that was made toward fulfilling the promise of the Thirteenth Amendment. This examination of sharecropping and other labor systems will occasionally include white farmers as well, and by 1917 there was an increasing number of white tenant farmers in the state. The focus of this chapter, however, is on race relations and race control, and certainly the percentage of white farmers who were sharecroppers never approached the comparable percentage for black farmers. Moreover, many of the methods of control used with black laborers were not used with white laborers.

Among the most important changes faced by black and white Mississippians after the Civil War were changes in the labor system. Heretofore slave labor had worked the plantations and many small farms, too. Now Mississippians would have to devise a new system that would provide African Americans with a way to earn a living and furnish landowners the labor force they needed. The freedmen felt strongly that they would participate in no new labor system that was similar to the slave labor system. They did not want to work large tracts of land in large gangs supervised by a white overseer. For their part, landowners wanted assurances that their land would be worked diligently and that laborers would not depart suddenly, leaving the crop untended.[2]

Thus evolved Mississippi's basic agricultural labor system, in which landowners rented out small plots of land, each of which would be worked by a family. To secure a farm to rent, the renter had to sign a one-year contract, thus reassuring the planter that sudden departures would not be the norm. In this compromise, each side gave up something while also gaining something. The freedmen were victorious in their insistence they would no longer work under a gang labor system. They would be working a small family farm, which was, after all, the American ideal. On the other hand, their absolute freedom was limited by the one-year contracts.

More seriously, the freedmen did not get what they wanted most, namely, land ownership. If they worked hard, however, in theory they would eventually be able to buy a farm of their own.

The one great flaw in the new labor system was that the freedmen were extraordinarily poor. At the time of emancipation they literally did not own the shirts on their backs, much less land or mules or plows. The only way they could rent land was to sign over a share of the future crop to the landlord. Typically this share would be half, although the landlord's share would be smaller if the tenant could furnish a mule and plow. Farmers who paid their rent with a share of the crop were called sharecroppers. Smaller numbers of black farmers worked under different systems. Some became cash renters, paying the landowner a fixed dollar amount instead of a share of the crop. Also, some black workers toiled as day laborers on the land of a white farmer or planter. Since day laborers literally were hired by the day, they had more freedom to move on but less employment security.

Descriptions of sharecropping and cash renting may imply that black farmers became independent operators, running their own farms and seeing the landlord once a year to settle. Such was not the case. In the case of the sharecroppers, it is not really true that at picking time the tenant gave the landlord a share of the crop. The landlord controlled the crop at all times, and increasingly as the years went by, the landlord supervised the black farmer's work closely. It was the landlord who actually sold the crop and distributed the share to the tenant, after certain deductions were made. The cash tenant, too, was less independent than the term might suggest. Cash tenants rarely paid in cash. The term "cash tenant" simply referred to the contract specifying the amount of rent due as a dollar amount rather than as a share of the crop. For most cash tenants, the landlord still marketed the crop and gave the tenant what was left after rent and other expenses were paid.[3]

Mississippi's planters had experienced wrenching changes in the years since the Civil War. Prior to passage of the Thirteenth Amendment, planters' wealth had been based on slaves. Now their wealth was based on land. In cold economic terms, slaves had been "liquid investments," easily converted to cash by sale. Further, slave property had been moveable property, giving the planter the option of moving to new and more fertile lands. After the Civil War, the planter's source of wealth, the land, was not always easily converted into cash, and, of course, land was not moveable property. Large tracts of land became worthless without laborers to work the land, and thus although the tenants were dependent upon the planter, the planter was no less dependent on the tenants. In the words of one recent historian, the planter became, above all, a "labor lord," and management of labor affairs was

The Persistent Institution: Black Labor and Race Control

"HOW MUCH DOES IT WEIGH?"

One key question in a sharecropper's life was how much the crop weighed. Also important was the world demand for cotton at the time of the sale.

extremely important. Landlords had numerous methods of controlling their workforce, including extending credit for a tenant's "furnish" and controlling the crop at settling time. Landlords could reward good workers with generous credit and better land, tools, and animals. They could punish other tenants with tight credit and with uncharitable treatment at settling time.[4]

Some writers have suggested that sharecropping was an ideal situation economically, since the landlord and the tenant both wanted the same thing—a large cotton crop sold at the highest possible price. Unfortunately for the tenants, however, the landlord's interests often failed to coincide with their own. For example, one technique planters used to maximize their income was to rent only very small plots to the tenants. Assuming the planter could find enough tenant families to farm the many plots, this system would maximize the planter's profit while minimizing the tenant's. Members of a large family, for instance, might work a twenty-acre plot very intensively to ensure the largest possible crop. As all the tenant families farmed intensively, the landlord's profits were maximized, while the tenant families were kept in poverty by the small size of the farm.[5]

Black sharecroppers objected to the use of overseers (representatives of the landlord) who turned them out into the fields at sunrise as a relic of slavery. Another relic of slavery was the lash. Even the most enlightened planters used it on occasion.

Plantation manager LeRoy Allen had the reputation of being a just man, but he recalled in his autobiography that "I found it advisable to apply the lash as a deterrent or corrective measure at times," though he added that "I can truthfully say that never did I do so with the feeling of pride." One planter recounted the case of a tenant whom he punished for trying to leave the plantation. The planter told how he "caught up with the man and whipped him till he couldn't stand up." The punishment was of little use, however, since "the next morning he was gone. Not a trace of him. I'd sure like to know how he got off. He couldn't stand up when I was through with him." Many black tenants wondered how much their lives had improved since the end of slavery, when they still worked under close white supervision, earned little, and were subject to physical "punishments" administered by whites.[6]

Fortunately for the tenants, there were reasons for planters to limit their use of the lash. Just as slaveholders had wanted to limit the use of physical brutality because an injured slave would not be as profitable as a sound one, so the landlords recognized that whipping tenants could make it hard to find tenants the following year. Duncan Townes was a plantation owner who, by most accounts, had little knack for agriculture or for labor management. He weighed close to 300 pounds and rarely ventured into the fields. He did, however, require the plantation managers he hired to use the lash extensively. His reputation as a sadistic landlord extended throughout the Delta, so that he was often forced to send labor recruiters into the more distant hill counties to find black tenants who had not heard of him.[7]

Cheating tenants at settling time was another way planters could maximize their short-term profits. Fortunately for the tenants, though, planters knew that landowners who had a reputation for cheating their tenants often lost their labor supply. LeRoy Allen recalled arriving in a county where he wasn't known and going to work as a plantation manager. "Riding among [the sharecroppers] as I found them picking cotton, I used the best approach and the most engaging manner of which I was capable, while attempting to interest them in talking with me about remaining on to farm the next year." Try as he might, however, "I could not crack the cold reserve that I found almost without exception among almost all with whom I talked." After several weeks of trying unsuccessfully to convince the farmers to work under his supervision the following year, Allen finally discovered the problem. The sharecroppers had misunderstood Allen's name and thought he was Allen Neely, not LeRoy Allen. Allen Neely had the reputation of being a planter "under whom few tenants cleared money." Thus planters like Townes who had an apparent sadistic streak and planters like Neely whose tenants rarely saw cash could find themselves labor lords without laborers. Even planters who treated their tenants in a fair manner could find themselves land rich and labor poor. Planter George Collins wrote his wife in the early 1880s that he had cotton and corn in the fields but not nearly enough hands to pick it. It was a situation, confessed Collins, that was so bad as "to make me tremble."[8]

Some planters went out of their way to be generous to their tenants, hoping to encourage them to stay. Planter Alfred H. Stone tried an experiment, attempting to foster an environment where his tenants would stay on the land year after year. He offered cash renting and a program to allow the tenants to purchase their own mules and implements. Tenants did agree to close supervision. Stone was disappointed in the experiment, however. From 22 to 45 percent of the tenants left each year. Stone noted that the tenants left to avoid his close style of supervision. They also knew that with their own tools and animals, they would be able to win generous contracts from almost any planter. Stone abandoned his experiment in the opening years of the twentieth century. Many other planters agreed that allowing tenants to earn their own tools and draft animals only increased the likelihood they would move on. Planters instead sought to maintain a dependent tenantry.[9]

The crop year usually began by the planter giving a "Christmas advance" to a tenant who agreed to sign a contract to farm the following year. For the planter, the trick was to advance enough credit to induce the tenant to sign and be reasonably satisfied but not so much that the tenant began to lose interest in working hard on the crop. The planter sometimes performed what seemed to be small acts of kindness, such as paying a doctor's bill for the tenant or even erasing part of a debt. Yet such actions had a clear economic purpose as well—to keep a happy and healthy tenantry, one that was able to work and was not demoralized.[10]

The tenants' lack of collateral for loans was met by a number of state laws, passed beginning in 1867, that decreed the lender had the right to sell the borrower's crop to satisfy the loan. Proponents of these crop lien laws argued that, without them, Mississippians would be unable to secure credit. Critics of the laws warned that farmers were losing all independence, as many not only lost their land to the merchant but also were denied the right to own and control their crops. The merchant kept the records of items the farm families had purchased on credit, and the merchant actually sold the crop. Often at settling time, an Anguilla sharecropper later recalled, the tenant would hear those chilling words: "You done fine Jim, . . . you come out just even." All too often, as in slavery times, the toil resulted in no cash income. It was of little use to tell the sharecropper family they had earned the food and clothing they had been charging at the store. Even slaveholders had provided food and clothing to their slaves.[11]

William H. Holtzclaw, a noted black educator in Mississippi, recalled that growing up in the late nineteenth century, he was confused because his father was a sharecropper but did not get a share of the crop. When he asked about this seeming anomaly, his parents told him that the family had eaten its share of the crop during the year. Young Holtzclaw could not understand "how it was possible for people to eat a crop—especially cotton out of which cloth is made—before it was produced." As the young man grew older he wrote that "I have seen whole crops eaten two or three years before they were planted."[12]

Planters cherished their role as creditor for two reasons. One was that it increased their control over the labor force. Planters feared an independent tenantry, but as long as the tenants were dependent upon them for food purchased on credit, landowners would have the upper hand in negotiations. When an overseer told LeRoy Percy that one of the tenants wanted permission to buy supplies at a store other than the Tralake Plantation Commissary, Percy told the overseer he must deny the request. To give in to the tenant's request, Percy lectured, "will lessen your control over him, and then it puts notions in the heads of the other negroes." Plantation stores and their extensions of credit were a method of control. They also were a very important source of income for the planters, often more profitable than the actual renting of land.[13] Interest rates at the plantation stores could, in the words of one writer, range "from 25 percent to grand larceny."[14]

Thus the credit system kept tenant farmers largely dependent and poor. The small number of black landowners and the larger but shrinking number of white land-owning farmers shared many of the problems of the tenants. They tended to be cash poor and therefore needed credit at the stores. While they owned their land, the merchant controlled their crop, and, as with the tenants, the merchant often would have conditions for the loan, such as which crops should be planted and how they should be grown. Yet if credit was the problem that led to poverty and dependence for tenants and small landowners alike, there clearly was a way out: diversification. If farmers would grow food crops, they could feed their families and avoid the problems indebtedness brought. Why in an agricultural state like Mississippi should farmers be buying cornmeal, molasses, and pork? The diversification gospel offered a way for owners and renters alike to escape indebtedness and establish economic independence.

There was an obstacle, however, that kept most small farm operators in Mississippi from diversifying, from feeding their families with home produce, and ultimately from reaching or maintaining landowner status. Take the case of a man, modestly in debt, who raised only cotton on a small farm. If the farmer worked hard, if the forces of nature and the whims of the cotton exchange were favorable in a given year, if he paid his debt at the store and had a little money left, it made little difference. The farmer could not begin to grow food crops to supplement his cotton, because the food crops would not be ready for consumption for many months. Unless the farmer's cash income that year had been several hundred dollars (a rare occurrence), he lacked the money needed to feed his family immediately. Thus, despite having had a good year, the farmer was forced to use credit to feed his family for the coming year. One condition of being granted credit was his agreement to grow cotton exclusively. The only way small farmers could really break free of the all-cotton cycle and begin to grow food crops as well would be if they could accumulate enough money not only to pay off their debt at settling time but also to feed their families during the coming year.[15]

Students of the southern states' labor system have written that landlords insisted their tenants grow only cotton. Actually, the tenants themselves recognized that growing cotton was the only logical option. Growing cotton was by far the surest way to make money by farming in Mississippi. Food crops had many advantages, but increasing one's cash income was not one of them. Farmers who were in debt recognized that they must earn cash, and cotton was the way to do that. Cotton was far more profitable than corn or other foodstuffs in most years. Tenants who dreamed of owning their own land also knew they would need cash, and they, too, tended to grow only cotton. Raising substantial amounts of food was possible only for landowners who resigned themselves to a lower cash income in an average year, in effect exchanging the lower income for increased independence and freedom from debt.[16]

A number of aspects of the tenant-farming system as practiced in Mississippi shared similarities with the system of slavery. Some black Mississippians, however, met fates worse than being a sharecropper. Some found themselves entrapped by a system of peonage, while others became prisoners of the state.

Congress defined peonage as a crime in 1867, instituting punishments for persons who used other persons' indebtedness as a reason for holding them in involuntary servitude. Although originally enacted to meet conditions among Hispanic workers in New Mexico, it soon became clear that the crime of peonage was also common in the southern states. Planters and farmers who employed black workers often felt justified in forcing them to remain and work until the debt was paid. Yet under the nation's laws a worker has freedom of movement, and workers are free to settle their own debts as they see fit. If the debts are not satisfied, the lender has the right to sue, seize collateral, secure garnishment on wages, and the like.

Certain laws of Mississippi were at odds with the federal Peonage Act of 1867. One state statute made it a crime for a worker to leave his or her employer during the year if he or she had accepted even a small advance. Under this Mississippi law, accepting the advance was held to be taking money under false pretenses if the worker later left the employer.[17]

Statistics of peonage are almost nonexistent. While records of peonage prosecutions have survived, all observers believed that only a small proportion of cases of peonage ever went to trial. In 1907 the Department of Justice sent an investigator named A. J. Hoyt into Georgia, Alabama, and Mississippi. Hoyt had previously made investigations for the department and had the reputation of being a careful, conservative employee. He concluded that in these three states, "investigations will prove that 33 per cent of planters operating from five to one-hundred plows, are holding their negro employees to a position of peonage, and arresting and returning those that leave before alleged indebtedness is paid." The U.S. attorney general therefore prodded federal prosecutors to combat peonage in their districts, and he asked for regular reports.[18]

In response to the attorney general's 1910 request for information, the federal prosecutor in southern Mississippi sent a chilling report. This attorney reported in detail one peonage case he had brought. In this case, a black farmer and his family had run away from their farm after mistreatment by the landlord. Family members were captured, stripped, tied up, and brutally whipped. The grand jury, however, refused to return an indictment. The prosecutor explained that it was all but impossible to get jurors concerned about involuntary servitude. "The Grand Jury is generally composed almost entirely of white farmers," the attorney reported, men "who have negroes in their employ, and who ... seem to be prejudiced against finding indictments for peonage." The federal attorney made it clear that this case was typical of cases he had handled, not an isolated incident.[19]

For many of the former slaves and children of former slaves who now found themselves living in a state of peonage, the Thirteenth Amendment was small comfort. Being tracked down as a runaway and beaten or held in chains clearly were reminiscent of slavery. One black farmer named Don January who lived in Rankin County found himself sold four times in the early twentieth century. Technically, it was his labor and his indebtedness that were transferred from one white buyer to another, but January's story was disturbing. After going to work for a new employer in 1907, January was bound, beaten, then captured while trying to escape and threatened with hanging before a new "buyer" was found. January, like any slave of the antebellum period, had to fear not only bloodhounds and beatings but also the uncertainty of being "sold."[20]

If peonage resulted in slavelike conditions for some black farmworkers, the convict lease system seemed to many like a true reincarnation of slave labor. Mississippi lawmakers were under intense pressure from their constituents to cut taxes, and one way to cut the expenses of the penitentiary system was to lease convicts to private individuals. These individuals would have to pay the costs of feeding and clothing the prisoners but would also have the benefit of the convicts' labor. Many counties, too, leased out their prisoners, thus reducing the costs of county government. While under lease, most prisoners worked on plantations, though some labored on railroads, roads, and levees and in timbering. As under the earlier slave system, convicts had to contend with brutal white overseers, snarling dogs, coarse clothing, and a cheap and unvarying diet.

While it is not to be expected that prisoners should be invariably comfortable and happy, several aspects of Mississippi's convict system made it especially vulnerable to criticism. For one thing, even the smallest offenses could lead to this brutal life. Under the state's so-called Pig Law of 1876, grand larceny was defined as the theft of any pig or other livestock or of any item worth $10 or more. The number of state prisoners quadrupled after passage of this law. Many citizens of the state believed one purpose of the convict lease system was to provide certain powerful individuals an inexpensive source of ready labor. The system was also useful for sending a message to black farm laborers who declined to work hard that a place had been prepared for them and that hard labor could be taken by force. The most severe indictment of Mississippi's convict lease system was its death toll. The hard work, inadequate diet, and exposure led to a death rate that even state officials admitted was unconscionably high. Official reports indicated that the death rate for white convicts was around 5 percent, while for black prisoners it averaged 11 percent. Comparable rates for prisoners of both races in six midwestern states ranged from 0.5 to 1.0 percent.[21]

Defenders of Mississippi's system might urge that, after all, prisoners must be punished and that hard labor would help repay the state for its costs and might rehabilitate the prisoner. Statistics make it clear, however, that Mississippi's system was not just a system for punishing wrongdoers. It was also a system of race control. No other state in the Union had a larger number of black prisoners per capita than did Mississippi, and no other state had a smaller number of white prisoners per capita. Mississippi had 218 white prisoners per million inhabitants and 1,425 black prisoners per million inhabitants. As for white prisoners, in many cases they were kept in the penitentiary building and were not worked at hard labor. In other cases, their labor was leased but at a lower price than that secured for black labor. In the 1890s black convicts were leased for $9 per month, while white prisoners went for $8. The lessees apparently believed black prisoners could be driven harder and if mistreated would not attract the public outrage that mistreatment of whites would excite.[22]

Even state officials could be surprisingly candid about convict leasing. Soon after the abolition of convict leasing in the first years of the twentieth century, J. H. Jones wrote an article for the *Publications of the Mississippi Historical Society* on the system and all its brutality. Jones was a former legislator from Wilkinson County and a former lieutenant governor. He believed some of the worst abuses occurred among prisoners used to build railroads, and he pointed to citizens' great desire for new railroads as one reason the state had allowed the leasing to continue. He also blamed the lessees' desire to maximize profits. Convict leasing, Jones wrote, "was evidently the product of human rapacity grafted upon the conditions that a defunct slavery had left behind it. It could only have flourished in an ex-slave state where ex-slaves made up the great majority of convicts." Jones concluded, "It is difficult to understand how a system so barbarous could have been tolerated in any Christian community."[23]

Criticisms of the convict lease system led to the founding of several state prison farms, most notably the 20,000-acre Parchman farm. Yet even under direct state custody, prisoners' conditions continued to be brutal, and just to hear the word "Parchman" was enough to send a shiver down the spine of any black Mississippian. As under the convict leasing system, a chiefly black group of convicts was driven hard for profit—only now the profit was for the state and not for individuals. By 1919, ten years after Parchman was founded, the state of Mississippi was reporting a profit of $800 per year per prisoner. An American Prison Association report noted approvingly that "the most profitable prison farming on record thus far is in the State of Mississippi." The founding of the state prison farms led to little improvement in the lives of prisoners. Overwork, exposure, lack of sanitation, and beatings took their toll, and the death rate remained high. Summing up the life of the typical Mississippi convict in the decades after the Civil War, a writer in the 1930s reported that their living conditions were "much worse than slavery." This was because "the life of the slave was valuable to the master," but if the convict died the state simply found a new one.[24]

The Persistent Institution: Black Labor and Race Control

Mississippi's heritage of slavery meant white persons accepted the usurious credit, debt peonage, and a penal system that seemed more tied to race control, labor control, and profit than to rehabilitation and reform. Did conditions of slavery really disappear in Mississippi in 1865? The best way to answer this question is to examine African Americans' mobility in Mississippi. One of the most obvious features of slavery had been the slave's inability to move to a new location without risking dire consequences. In the years from 1877 to 1917, while whites were often successful in preventing black farmworkers from moving at midyear, they seldom managed to prevent a large percentage of workers and tenants from leaving at the end of the crop year. Black tenants moved from neighboring plantation to neighboring plantation, or across the state, or to another southern state. They might move for a time into towns and cities, then back to the agricultural areas. One anecdote described the sharecropper who moved on so often "his oldest chickens just lay down and cross their legs to be tied." When asked why they moved, some of the sharecroppers said they had been cheated at the plantation store, while others resented too much supervision by white overseers. Some simply felt that surely there must be better opportunities elsewhere.[25]

Evidence suggests that in many areas, up to a third of the sharecropper families moved on each year. Thus while peonage was a tragic system where it did occur, mobility at the end of the crop year was more common than peonage. The high degree of mobility was important, because it was one of the few significant negotiating tools black tenant farmers possessed. Powerful white landowners recognized that black farmers' mobility was a source of the tenants' strength, and planters secured passage of a number of laws intended to limit black mobility.

The Mississippi legislature passed one such law in 1900, forbidding a tenant or worker to contract with a new employer without securing the permission of the old employer. The law was enforced for a dozen years until declared unconstitutional in 1913. Other laws limiting tenants' mobility included the 1906 false pretenses law (punishing those who left their employer or landlord after accepting an advance) and the 1912 Labor Agent Licensing Act, which required an expensive license for those who recruited laborers for new employment. One of the most important laws was the Vagrancy Act of 1904, allowing imprisonment of persons who could not prove they were employed. This law was vague enough that it gave law enforcement officers a great deal of discretion. In times of labor shortages, officers could round up seemingly idle workers and lease these new county prisoners out for their labor. The Vagrancy Act also sent a warning to all black workers: sign an annual contract with a landowner or risk being convicted and forced to work under armed guard.[26]

Despite these laws, and similar laws in other southern states, mobility of black farmworkers continued. During most of this period, Mississippi benefited from regional migration, as planters recruited black tenant farmers in South Carolina and Georgia to work new farmland in the Delta. An estimated 4,000 black workers came to Mississippi around 1890 from Georgia alone. Intrastate migration was also important, as black farmworkers in the northeast hills were recruited for work in the Delta, and as workers in the counties first hit by the boll weevil fled to uninfested counties. Being a labor recruiter was risky business, because there were few things white landowners feared more than someone "stealing" their labor supply.[27]

Faced with labor recruiters trying to entice their workers, the affected Mississippians acted to protect their labor supply. In 1908 Adams County planters were hard hit by the boll weevil and became alarmed as labor recruiters from the Yazoo-Mississippi Delta came to entice their workers away. Labor agents assembled a large number of workers and prepared to load them onto a steamboat. A hastily organized "Bankers and Merchants Labor Agency" met the recruiters on the wharf and ordered them to leave town on the next train. The recruiters left. Meanwhile, spokesmen for the bankers' and merchants' group addressed the black families assembled on the wharf, and a newspaper account reported their speeches were "so emphatic that the negroes concluded to abandon their idea of leaving."[28]

Thus on a number of occasions white southerners worked assiduously to prevent migration of black workers. Yet we come back to the fact that statistics show the population of black tenant farmers was highly mobile. Maintaining this mobility was the greatest success of black tenants, since the threat of leaving gave them leverage with employers and landlords. It is also the best example of how in fact the Thirteenth Amendment did have some meaning in that, unlike slaves, tenants usually were free to move on at the end of the crop year. Black tenants won their right to mobility in a number of ways. Sheer determination undoubtedly played a role. Given tenants' insistence on the right to move, planters risked complete labor demoralization or congressional interference if they did not agree to allow some mobility. The greatest reason black sharecroppers were able to win the right to free movement, however, is that whites were not unified. In fact, one part of the white population greatly desired black mobility—the group of white planters and farmers who lacked a sufficient number of black laborers. Any time white Mississippians were divided on labor issues, black Mississippians benefited. In 1884, for example, white farmers in the eastern part of the state became angry at Delta planters hiring their workers away. The legislators from the eastern counties managed to secure passage of a law punishing those who enticed away another's workers, but Delta planters convinced the governor to veto the law. A similar law finally was approved in 1890, but with many powerful whites needing laborers, movement of black agricultural workers continued.[29]

It rankled white planters and farmers to know how dependent they were upon black labor. From time to time they considered plans to lessen this dependence by importing other kinds of workers. The building of the first transcontinental railroad, in part with Chinese labor, made planters want to experiment with Chinese workers. Prevailing racial ideas of the time made many planters believe the Chinese would make excellent plantation hands. While some white landowners defended the quality of work done by black laborers, others accused blacks of being careless or "improvident and thoughtless." Planters believed the Chinese were docile and unassertive. Chinese immigration, planters mused, was a way to cope with "the costly nomadism of the negro population." The first Chinese workers came into Mississippi shortly after the completion of the first transcontinental railroad in 1869. The number of Chinese Mississippians grew modestly over the years, while the gender ratio changed markedly as single Chinese men went temporarily back to China and married, then came back to Mississippi to raise their families. In 1900 there were 183 state residents of Chinese ancestry, with a seventeen-to-one ratio of males to females. Twenty years later the total number of Chinese residents in Mississippi was 322, while the male-to-female ratio was now four to one. Planters were not satisfied with their experiments with Chinese labor, however, and the Chinese farmworkers were not satisfied with agriculture Mississippi-style. Paying the transportation costs of Chinese farmworkers proved prohibitive, and the farmworkers themselves quickly left the fields. Many opened grocery stores, backed financially by relatives elsewhere in the state and nation.[30]

Planters also dreamed of tapping into the vast flood of European immigrants coming into the United States. "Think of it!" urged the editor of the *Greenville Times* in 1881. "During the month of August 33,840 immigrants arrived in this country. . . . Now out of that great army of immigrants how many do you think Mississippi received? A few families scattered here and there in the State were all that fell to her lot." The state set up the Board of Immigration and Agriculture, which published a multilingual guide to the state that was widely distributed in northern cities and in Europe. Yet only when individual planters directly recruited European workers did any appreciable number actually arrive in the state.

LeRoy Percy arranged with a labor contractor for a large shipment of Italian laborers around 1905; he sent many of these laborers to work on Sunnyside plantation across the Mississippi River in Arkansas, while others went to work on

Marathon plantation in Washington County, Mississippi. Many writers and speakers offered their unsolicited advice. Again drawing on prevailing racial ideas, the editor of the *Vicksburg Herald* warned that if planters wanted the Italian workers to remain, they must provide "good quarters, good water, and good treatment," which planters were not providing for black workers. The Vicksburg editor explained that black sharecroppers, with their "happy-go-lucky temperament," would willingly "live in any sort of a shack, drink any sort of water, and put up with a great deal of ill treatment." The Italians, he asserted, would not.[31]

Indeed, as with the Chinese, the Italians had been primed to expect more from their American experience than a sharecropper's existence. Italian diplomats heard of peonage and mistreatment and of the cheating of Italian sharecroppers by merchants, and the U.S. government ordered an investigation. Planters by the time of World War I had given up on Italian workers, preferring to work with African American laborers who had no diplomats to look out for their interests. Publicly, Percy refused to admit his experiments had been a failure. He reported the Italians were clean and healthy, were hard working and thrifty, and were earning substantial sums of money. To a New York reporter, Percy asserted that the Italian workers were "virtuous, there never having been a bastard born on the property." Speaking privately to his fellow Mississippians, Percy's opinion of Italian workers was less laudatory. They expected too much in the way of living quarters, Percy explained, and, like black farmworkers, they required a great deal of supervision. He believed they could not be trusted to sell their own crop, although they wanted control of the crop. Percy stated that if a planter allowed Italian sharecroppers to sell their own crop, "it would require a regiment of Pinkerton Detectives to prevent them from stealing it." Percy, too, continued to rely on black labor.[32]

Thus Mississippi's labor system rested overwhelmingly on black workers, both wage laborers and sharecroppers. The system resulted in a black population that with few exceptions lived in poverty and lacked real educational opportunities and political rights. By the 1890s many white residents believed the poverty, ignorance, and disease of the black population were such that black Mississippians should be kept more nearly separate from the white race. State laws as well as customs would help ensure blacks and whites did not mingle in parks and theaters, trains and boats, restaurants and hotels. The increasingly rigid "Jim Crow" segregation would also work to the continued economic degradation of black workers, as certain occupations, for example, were deemed to be for whites only.

CHAPTER FOUR

THE PERSISTENT INSTITUTION

Conflict and Racial Separation

Mississippi had never been separated into fully distinct racial zones. Even in slavery times, the white family in the big house often lived in surprising intimacy with their black house slaves. White children suckled at the breast of black slave women is the most often cited example of this intimacy. House slaves were often companions as well as servants of the slave-holding family. On smaller farms, slaveholders toiled in the fields alongside their one or two slaves. On riverboats, black and white boatmen often worked together before, during, and just after the Civil War. Many Mississippi-born whites entered into political alignments with black politicians, not only in the Republican Party but in later Independent and Greenback Party campaigns. Yet by the 1890s whites began to embrace a rigorous separation of the races. Changing customs and an increasing number of Jim Crow laws caused the two races to draw increasingly far apart. In many ways, the change was generational. A Mississippi planter on the eve of World War I told an interviewer, "In a way I'm fond of the Negro," but he noted that his bond with black Mississippians was "not as close as it was between my father and his slaves." He added, "On the other hand, my children have grown up without black playmates and without a 'black mammy,' and their attitude is far less sympathetic toward the Negroes than my own."[1]

Changes in white attitudes reflected national currents of thought. As the nation began to collect colonies and to embrace imperialism, many whites in the North and South began to believe more strongly than before that darker-skinned people were innately inferior. There was a national backlash against "swarthy" immigrants from southern Europe. Even the young Mississippians who went off to universities in the northern states or in Europe had their racial ideas confirmed.

The latest theories advanced in the universities were the same basic ideas bruited about by Mississippi politicians and editors. Darker races were inferior, these theories held, and the superior race must be kept separate from inferior races.

Some of the changes in the 1890s and afterward were easily noticed. Certain public places in Jackson, for example, had long been open to persons of both races on a segregated basis. Black groups as well as white held meetings in Angelo's Hall and hosted picnics in Hamilton Park. By the 1890s policy dictated that these two locations were for whites only. In the 1870s and 1880s many white families provided places in their family burial plots for favored black servants. By the 1890s such burial practices were uncommon and by 1920 unthinkable. In one well-publicized event of 1900, the remains of James D. Lynch (a black citizen who had once been Mississippi's secretary of state) were disinterred from a white cemetery and moved to an all-black burial ground. The separation of blacks and whites into what were seen as appropriately separate spheres is clearly demonstrated by the case of J. C. Crittenden, a black member of the board of supervisors of Bolivar County who helped establish a new courthouse for the county in 1872. By 1915 Crittenden was employed as a porter in that same courthouse.[2]

Not surprisingly, Mississippi's first major Jim Crow law dealt with passengers on the railroads. Earlier, every city and rural community had devised its own informal system of segregating public places, but railroads were something that knit communities together. One could not have dozens of local segregation systems in effect on a given railroad line. There needed to be one uniform system of which all passengers were aware. The Mississippi legislature passed the Railroad Segregation Act on March 2, 1888, requiring railroads to provide "equal but separate accommodations" for the two races. A few days later lawmakers passed a second law calling for separate sleeping cars and separate depot waiting rooms, "where practicable." These two laws are the first examples in the nation of what became a great wave of segregation laws. The railroads resisted the new requirements because of the cost. Railroad executives argued the adequacy of the previous system, under which the first-class passenger cars were for whites only and the other cars were integrated. In 1890, however, the U.S. Supreme Court upheld the validity of Mississippi's railroad segregation law, in the case of the *Louisville, New Orleans, and Texas Railway Company v. Mississippi.* This case served notice on other southern states that the Supreme Court would permit racial segregation laws. Other laws followed in Mississippi and throughout the South.[3]

Supplementing the new laws was an evolving set of informal rules and customs of separation. Parents of both races taught their children these rules to prevent unpleasant or dangerous clashes. The rules could be complicated. A black man must tip his hat to white women, but a white man must not tip his hat to black women. African Americans driving wagons or buggies must not overtake slower vehicles being driven by whites. In any queue blacks must constantly fall back until all whites had been served. This rule applied everywhere except the cotton gin, where black farmers were served first if they arrived first. A bewildering array of rules evolved about how persons should be addressed, with special variations for children and the elderly. Generally, blacks addressed whites as "mister," "miz," "sir," or "ma'am," and generally whites addressed blacks by their first names. To make the system more complex, the rules varied from place to place. The Gulf Coast, with its French Catholic and Creole heritage and proximity to New Orleans, observed rules of race etiquette more relaxed than those elsewhere in the state. Rules in the predominantly white northeast hills seemed strict by comparison with the more relaxed rules in Greenwood. Thus when African Americans traveled to a new county, they first had to seek out a trusted local black resident and learn the prevailing rules. To fail to do so could lead to dangerous confrontations.

Yet the rules allowed blacks and whites to carry on their daily work. To prevent interaction between the races would have brought the state's economy to a standstill. The rules were designed to ensure that the two races were kept on separate planes socially and that anything suggesting equality was strenuously avoided. This was the reason for all the rules about tipping hats and saying "ma'am." For a black resident to insist on any badge of equality was risky behavior. Bishop Edward W. Lampton of the African Methodist Episcopal (AME) Church had to flee Mississippi in 1909 after his daughter tried to insist the telephone operator call her "Miss." In the tense atmosphere of white control, it was important that black residents never do anything that appeared to show resistance. A white newspaper editor writing in Mississippi in 1910 explained to outsiders that without Jim Crow laws, Mississippi would see "more race clashes and more dead niggers than have been heard of since reconstruction."[4]

The customs of segregation served the same function that good manners serve in any society. They were rituals that helped ensure someone was not accidentally insulted, since insults could lead to conflict. By acquiescing to the Jim Crow regulations, black residents avoided violence, signifying that they offered no resistance to Mississippi's racial system. Unfortunately for black residents of the state, it was not enough simply to follow the rules. It was important that they seem to enjoy the rules, to support them enthusiastically. Otherwise, whites would have to wonder what resentment and desire for change were simmering beneath the surface. One observer of Sunflower County society explained, "Whites are not satisfied if Negroes are cool, reserved, and self-possessed though polite." Instead, "They must be actively obliging and submissive."[5]

As might be expected, such an important issue as Mississippi's segregation system excited some dissent by persons of both races. Some maintained the system did not go far enough and that separation of the races should be more complete. Several white Mississippi writers suggested that blacks should be sent away from the South altogether. In his 1887 booklet, *The Negro: As He Was, As He Is, and As He Will Be*, Horace S. Fulkerson argued that land values in Mississippi were low because northerners would never come south to farm "in a country filled with a free people with whom there can be no social intercourse." Fulkerson asserted white southerners were "fixed in their determination to preserve their supremacy *be the cost what it may to the Negroes or themselves*" and that this would include farming the best land. Fulkerson believed the way to prevent race conflict was for the U.S. government to purchase new lands for black southerners to occupy, perhaps in Central America or on a Caribbean island, and he believed the government should spend "the last surplus dollar in the treasury for the purpose." A similar plan was drafted by attorney Greene C. Chandler, who suggested blacks in Mississippi and other southern states be allowed to form their own states in the West.[6] The plans set forth by Fulkerson and Chandler illustrate the belief of many Mississippians that blacks and whites would never live peacefully as long as they lived together.[7]

Other Mississippians offered direct challenges to the laws and customs of segregation. A number of white residents refused to accept streetcar segregation. The streetcar companies themselves found the segregation laws burdensome. One law called on the firms to furnish separate streetcars for the two races, which would have increased the companies' costs considerably. As an alternative, the law allowed use of a "moveable screen" to separate the two races on a given streetcar. This was the method the streetcar companies used, but most companies paid only lip service to the law. In Natchez, for example, companies provided only a small moveable sign (eight by twelve inches) that designated the division between white and black seating. Even under this relaxed method of segregation, some white citizens resisted the new system, finding it inconvenient. On August 26, 1904, Charlie Compton and three of her friends rode the Natchez streetcar out to a city park. On the return trip the black section of the streetcar filled up rapidly, while Compton and her friends were the only ones in the white section. Finally, the conductor asked Compton and her friends to move forward to give their seats to black passengers who were standing, but they refused. The conductor ejected them. Forced to walk back downtown through the mud, an angry Compton brought suit against the street railway. She won modest damages, because the Mississippi Supreme Court ruled the streetcar company's use of a small sign instead of a real screen constituted a failure to comply with Mississippi's segregation law. Railroads and streetcar companies continued to complain that the Jim Crow laws were burdensome, while citizens like Charlie Compton steadfastly objected to laws that might insist whites make way to provide an equal place for black Mississippians.[8]

Months after Charlie Compton's run-in with the Jim Crow system in Natchez, Dr. Joseph Waldauer found himself ejected from a streetcar in Vicksburg. Waldauer deliberately sat in the section assigned to black passengers, and when the conductor asked him to move, he refused. A policeman then removed the doctor from the car. Waldauer brought suit against the company, but the Warren County Circuit Court judge was so unimpressed with the doctor's case that he instructed the jury to find a verdict for the streetcar company. Unlike Compton, Waldauer was motivated by a feeling that legally enforced separation of the races was a bad idea. Other Mississippians, too, proved willing to defy Mississippi's segregation laws and customs.[9]

The most glaring defiance of the conventions of segregation was interracial marriage or liaisons. Such unions were provocative because they showed members of the two races granting the ultimate acceptance to each other, an acceptance that implied some kind of equality. In Mississippi, as in many other states, miscegenation was illegal. Still, while few dared speak the words out loud, it was nevertheless true that a very large number of state residents were of mixed parentage. Efforts to quantify accurately the number of "mulattos" living in the state were doomed to fail, but it was clear to anyone who thought about it that the ban on interracial unions was honored in theory and often defied in practice. Of course, for society to be willing to look the other way, interracial unions must be between white men and black women, and not the other way around. Under prevailing racial theories, white women were believed to be exceptionally pure and chaste and to have a natural revulsion for black men. Thus any liaison between a black man and a white woman constituted rape and could prove deadly for black men.

While few written records remain to document particular cases of interracial liaisons, there were some sanctioned marriages between white men and black women. Willard F. Bond, a white leader in the field of education in Mississippi, reported attending a teachers' conference in the 1890s and meeting a white man named J. T. Lippincott. Lippincott, who had lived in the state since the Civil War, had married a black woman. He was now a teacher in the black public schools.

Bond recalled that Lippincott "used his influence for good and was not disturbed by the white people." Perhaps Lippincott was tolerated because of his northern birth, yet a small number of native-born white Mississippians also married and raised children with black women.[10]

One of these was Newton Knight, famed Confederate irregular soldier of Jones County. Knight was married to a white woman, Serena Knight, but had a sexual relationship with Rachel Knight, a former family slave. Two of the children of Serena and Newton married two of the children of Rachel and another man. These marriages formed the nucleus of the Knight colony, a mixed-race community in a remote corner of Jasper County. In 1880 Newton, his wife, and children were all listed as white on the census schedules. By 1900 all the members of the household were listed as black. Ten years later, Newton and his daughter and grandchildren were white once again, according to the census. Other Knight offspring were sometimes listed as mulatto, but his son Thomas J. Knight, who moved away from the Knight colony, was always listed as white. Bold cases of defiance of convention, like that presented by the Knight family, can be surprising to the modern student of history. Similarly, occasional cases existed of wealthy black professionals living in white neighborhoods, of black persons being called "mister" in print, and of black timber bosses supervising white employees. If occasional cases of the color line being broken tended to shock, it was because the system of segregation in Mississippi was thorough and seldom defied.[11]

For black Mississippians, the most tragic kind of Jim Crow segregation was the separation of jobs by race. An examination of the census returns for a city like Vicksburg shows a stark racial division by type of job. Laborers, porters, and wagon drivers were black. Cooks, babies' nurses, and laundresses were also black. On the other hand, clerks, telegraphers, and bookkeepers were white. On the railroads, a strict division of labor was observed, where brakemen and firemen were black and engineers and conductors white. The skilled positions in the railroad shops were for whites, while blacks worked in positions such as "boilermaker's helper" and on track construction crews. Some occupations were filled by persons of both races—minister, teacher, undertaker—but in those cases the person in question did not serve those of the other race.[12] Factory jobs in Mississippi went almost exclusively to whites. In 1900, 94 percent of the black workforce in the state worked either in agriculture or in personal service jobs such as servants in private homes.[13]

Over the years a number of white residents turned to extralegal, violent actions to enforce their vision of black residents' place in society. Use of force in matters of race had a number of roots. In slavery, whites employed force to keep black slaves in bondage. Even whites who were not slaveholders served on slave patrols and sometimes captured and whipped slaves who were out at night without passes. Mississippi still was not far removed from its frontier heritage, where brutal fights between persons of all races were all too common. White Mississippians' folkways had a strong emphasis on "honor," especially the necessity of upholding one's honor when it was assaulted. Under this code, black citizens' asserting equality constituted an affront to white honor and would be dealt with physically. Finally, a majority of the years between 1877 and 1917 featured a depressed agricultural economy, low cotton prices, rising indebtedness, and increased crowding on the land. While both races suffered from these conditions, whites could act out their frustrations with little fear of punishment, while black residents could not. Whites controlled most land, most jobs, all law enforcement, and the state militia. Black on white violence would not be tolerated, but white attacks on black residents often excited little official concern.

One form of white mob action, most common between 1893 and 1911, was "whitecapping." The origin of the term is obscure, since there is no evidence these night riders wore caps or any other kind of uniform or disguise. Whitecapping had its origins in a number of secret organizations formed by farmers, primarily in southwestern counties such as Pike, Amite, Franklin, Marion, Copiah, and Lincoln. A rare public glimpse into the goals of these organizations was provided in a resolution passed by a Lawrence County whitecap society and published in 1893 in the *Magnolia Gazette*. The resolution spoke of the national depression then current and blamed it on wealthy investors on Wall Street and in Europe. The resolution attacked Jewish merchants, who "use every damnable idea conceivable to obtain possession of our lands." The Lawrence County organization vowed to work to "control" black labor in the county and to exert control over Jewish and other merchants. If need be, the document warned, coercion might be used against black labor, and merchants might be "forced to abandon our country."[14]

On its face, the movement was racist, anti-Semitic, and even revolutionary, as it promised to expand the rights of white farmers and deny the rights of merchants and tenant farmers. Yet many joined these organizations because leaders promised vaguely to address farmers' problems or to offer benefits such as insurance plans. One typical young member was Will Purvis of Marion County, who joined, he said, because all the other young men of the neighborhood were joining. He approved of the leaders' promise that the secret society would "promote a better regime of law and order." Yet soon Mississippians heard dire things of the new societies. A young farm woman, Allie Stokes, reported to her brother in 1893 that "there is a good deal of excitement here about what is called the White Caps." She went on to explain how "they are running all the darkeys off from people's mills and farms at a dreadful rate." One of the whitecaps' victims was "Old Man Hiller in Summit, who owned so much land in Amite County." Hiller "had his hands run off, and his large mill and farms burned down" by the whitecaps. Stokes closed by noting the current rumor that "all the Jews in Summit are going to Jerusalem."[15]

Other victims of whitecap violence included Flowers Wilson and his son, John. The Wilsons were proud and prosperous black citizens of Pike County who rode in buggies and smoked cigars. In the white vocabulary of 1893 they were insolent. A whitecap mob seized the two Wilsons, took them into the woods, and administered a whipping with a broad strap. Members of the mob warned the Wilsons to leave the area. The mob also burned the Wilsons' home and stole their corn. Flowers Wilson went to Jackson and told his story to Governor John M. Stone. Showing remarkable courage as he risked whitecap retaliation, Wilson returned to the Pike County courthouse and swore out an affidavit, naming ten of his assailants. At the autumn 1893 trial of the ten men, however, the jury took only "a few minutes" to find the defendants innocent. Wilson was relatively fortunate. In several other cases of 1893, black witnesses who swore out complaints against whitecappers were murdered.[16]

Over time, the whitecap organizations expanded the targets of their violence. Where originally they targeted Jewish merchants and black farmworkers, now the whitecaps attacked Gentile merchants, black landowners, and even some black laborers who worked for white or black small farmers. Black tenants returned home after a brief absence to discover their fences down, their livestock wandering, their corncrib plundered. Typically they found a written notice warning them to leave the county. Black farmers were beaten, and some were killed. A writer for the *New Orleans Daily Picayune* reported that in Mississippi, "the established authorities have abdicated their functions, and left the forces of lawlessness and disorder to run things to suit themselves." In the face of this carnival of disorder, citizens who were not whitecappers held mass meetings to call for an end to the disturbances. Some of these assemblies evolved into regular organizations with elected leaders and weekly meetings. Leaders of these organizations prodded Governor Stone to do something about the lawlessness, and finally Stone issued an antiwhitecapping proclamation offering a $100 reward for each person arrested and convicted of whitecap-related crimes.[17]

In the spring of 1893 law enforcement officers began to arrest whitecaps. In May whitecaps made a massed assault on the Lincoln County jail, unsuccessfully attempting to free ten of their brethren. Incidents like the assault on the Lincoln County jail pointed out to state leaders the dangers of whitecapping. The overall business climate was damaged as northern investors declined to invest in the state. National insurance companies expressed concern, and some considered canceling insurance on gins. Most important, black laborers began seeking a more congenial locale, so that southwest Mississippi was in danger of losing its labor supply. Journalists estimated 1,000 laborers had left the region already. With Governor Stone and many private citizens willing to work to put down whitecapping, success in the courts was possible.

More than any other individual, Judge J. B. Chrisman deserves credit for suppressing whitecapping. In April 1893 he presided over the trial of two Copiah County men who brutally assaulted a black farmer. The farmer was willing to identify the men in court, and Chrisman did all he could to protect witnesses and to impanel a jury that would be willing to convict. The jury found the defendants guilty, returning the first convictions in a whitecapping case. Chrisman sentenced each man to a year in the state prison. In Lincoln County, too, Chrisman acted strongly, impaneling a grand jury largely free of whitecap influence and making a tough law-and-order speech to the jurors. The grand jury returned a number of indictments. One day as his court was in session in Brookhaven, Chrisman heard an armed mob of whitecaps gallop to the steps of the courthouse. Chrisman recessed the court and walked out to meet the mob. He asked them what they wanted, and someone replied that they had come to free the whitecap prisoners. The judge responded, "If that is your game, sir, I will arrest you on the spot." Chrisman strode forward toward the man who had spoken, and instantly dozens of revolvers were trained upon the judge's head. Members of the mob said they would shoot him if he came any farther and ordered him to release the prisoners. Chrisman glowered at the mob. Finally, the sheriff's posse rode up, and the mob galloped off in disarray. Chrisman proceeded with the trials, which resulted in a number of convictions.[18]

In all counties, prosecutions proceeded with some degree of success. Unfortunately, whenever foreclosures were on the rise and black labor seemed scarce, whitecapping appeared once again. A second flurry of whitecap activity arose in 1903, in Amite, Franklin, and Lincoln counties. Local judges, prosecutors, and jurors put down this second outbreak with aid from Governors Andrew H. Longino and James K. Vardaman.[19]

Whitecapping was a complex phenomenon. Clearly it was racist and anti-Semitic. Yet it was also a class struggle between white small farmers and their enemies, the merchants (both Jews and Gentiles). At issue was who would control that valuable commodity, black labor. Black victims responded to the threats and violence with personal bravery, but their white allies in the war on whitecapping seemed most concerned about economic questions, such as whitecapping's effects on credit, outside investors, and insurance companies. Whitecapping was not the only way that some white Mississippians aimed to control the black labor supply and enforce the state's Jim Crow system. White military or paramilitary action to put down so-called race riots also served notice on the black community that proud and independent behavior would not be tolerated.

Race riots were set off by seemingly trivial incidents, but upon investigation the riots had deep roots. The most minor of incidents touched off an 1881 riot in the village of Marion in Lauderdale County. A small crowd of young black men had assembled on Marion's main street. An elderly white man took exception to their "insolence" and hit one of the men with his cane. The black men moved to retaliate, and a gun battle erupted. Blacks outnumbered whites in the initial fight. Three white men were killed, and there were no black victims—initially. Later, the sheriff's posse had a second gun battle with the black men, with casualties on both sides. Finally, a very large group of armed white men rode in from Meridian and other areas, "fresh and eager to carry the war into Africa," as one newspaper put it. The total number of black men killed in the aftermath of the Marion riot will never be known. Local newspapers simply reported that blacks were being hunted down and killed. To whites, the aftermath of the Marion riot was a case of black murderers resisting arrest, while for the black men the riot was a protest of the rule that said whites could inflict physical punishment upon black men at will. The roots of the Marion riot lay in an election campaign just ended in which black voters and many whites had worked together to support an "Anti-Monopoly ticket" in opposition to the Democrats. The specter of blacks and whites working together politically was deeply disturbing to many whites, and Lauderdale County just prior to the riot was an extremely tense place.[20]

The community of Wahalak in Kemper County had the reputation of being home to a number of black men who were deemed insolent—who did not display the required deference to whites. Twice, white mobs attacked the village. In an 1888 incident, a young white man had been fighting with a young black man. A white mob then pursued the black man to Wahalak. A major gun battle ensued as community members attempted to protect one of their own. This race riot left two whites and "several negroes" dead. In 1906 a white mob in the area lynched a black man on Christmas eve, then invaded Wahalak to "strike terror into the negroes, who had been getting defiant of late" (as a local editor explained). This time the lines were unequally drawn, as both the National Guard and white volunteers from surrounding counties streamed into the area. The estimated death toll after forty-eight hours was one white and sixteen black victims. A similar disturbance in Wiggins that same year led to an exchange of an estimated 500 shots, though apparently none proved fatal.[21]

One particularly large race riot took place in Harperville (near Forest) in 1898. As with the Marion fray, the Harperville riot was touched off by an argument between an elderly white man and a young black man. The two apparently argued over financial dealings, and the black man (William Burke) finally attacked his opponent with a hoe. The local constable arrived with a posse of fifteen, only to find Burke fortified in a cabin surrounded by sixty of Burke's heavily armed black neighbors. When gunfire broke out, a constable was seriously wounded and a member of the posse killed. A larger posse returned the next day and killed ten black men, wounded several others, and took four prisoners. Hundreds of white men from as far away as Yazoo County converged on Harperville, and at least four additional black residents were hunted down and killed. Governor Anselm J. McLaurin arrived and made a law-and-order speech, but a local man spoke up loudly: "You come to stick your nose in our business. Go back to Brandon." As had been the case with the other race riots, white and black Mississippians viewed the Harperville riot differently. For whites, it was a case of a black man resisting arrest. For blacks, it was an instance of a black man resisting being cheated at the hands of a white man. As with all of the race riots, the casualty rate was much heavier among blacks than whites.[22]

The most important race riot in this period involved the Colored Alliance of Leflore County. The Colored Alliance had many of the same goals as the all-white Southern Alliance: support for the subtreasury plan and cooperative stores. Yet on issues of black self-determination, the two groups parted company. The Colored Alliance favored new federal laws to protect black voting rights, while the Southern Alliance did not. In 1891 the Colored Alliance considered a cotton pickers' strike, while white Southern Alliance members (who relied on black pickers' labor) denounced the plan. Leflore County was a Delta county with a population that was 85 percent African American. An organizer of the Colored Alliance named Oliver Cromwell came to Leflore County in 1889, starting new suballiances and urging black farmers to stop patronizing local merchants. He recommended instead that they support a cooperative store in Durant, run by the Southern Alliance. Although thirty miles away, the cooperative store was convenient to the Illinois Central

Railroad, and Leflore farmers could pool their orders and send them to Durant periodically.[23]

Cromwell's actions should have appealed to many white Mississippians, since economic independence was an ideal of both the Colored Alliance and the Southern Alliance. Further, the white membership of the Southern Alliance should have been glad of the additional business for one of their struggling stores. Yet for whites in Leflore, Cromwell's actions were provocative. Economic independence might be an ideal for white farmers, but whites believed this same ideal did not apply to black agrarians. White merchants were concerned about losing business to the Durant store. Planters who operated their own commissaries worried about the same thing. Above all, most whites in the county feared an independent black labor force, which would be the result of black tenants making purchases on their own without the intervention of merchants and planters. Thus whites in Leflore decided Cromwell must be stopped.

A problem with reconstructing an event like the Leflore riot is that reports were heavily biased by each side. It is clear is that the sheriff moved against Cromwell and his followers, aiming to disarm the men and drive the leaders from the area. Governor John M. Stone sent National Guard troops to reinforce the sheriff's posse for a time. Cromwell fled the county. Some black residents of Leflore reported that black supporters of the Alliance were being hunted down like beasts. Estimates of the death toll in Leflore ranged from zero to one hundred. A historian who studied the incident estimated that twenty-five men were killed, none white. After the riot, the Colored Alliance disappeared in Leflore County.[24]

Another method employed to ensure continued white dominance was lynching. Lynching is the extralegal killing of someone who allegedly committed an offense, carried out by three or more people who are not punished for their acts. Statistics of lynching present certain problems, because many lynchings were committed in isolated areas and were not reported in the press. While major organizations such as the National Association for the Advancement of Colored People (NAACP) compiled lynching records, the NAACP statistics were based on press reports from major southern cities. Lynchings that did not attract regional press attention went uncounted. Even so, thousands of lynchings were counted. Some 4,750 were enumerated from 1882 to the present, and 581 occurred in Mississippi. While most southern lynchings were instances of white mob violence against black victims, in Mississippi this was true to an especially high degree. The percentage of lynch victims nationwide who were black was 72 percent, while in the southern states the percentage rose to 84 percent. In Mississippi, fully 93 percent of lynching victims were black.

White Mississippians who condoned lynching claimed they did so because black men had a propensity to rape and that white women were the preferred victims. As for why a rapist should not be entrusted to the courts, apologists for lynching had several explanations. One was that black rapists did not deserve the dignity of a trial. Another was that white women should be spared from having to testify about the traumatic crime. Yet another was that in a trial, there is always the possibility of an acquittal (although acquittals of black defendants accused of attacking white women were almost nonexistent in Mississippi). Some lynch mobs actually made a pretense of holding a rudimentary trial, having witnesses identify the alleged criminal and perhaps permitting the man about to be lynched to speak on his own behalf. Typically, however, little care was taken to ensure that the lynch victim was really the wanted criminal. One hapless black man known only as Bear was lynched after he was interrogated about a murder and "at once manifested a degree of nervousness that was convincing of his guilt." Needless to say, anyone facing the possibility of a lynching would manifest "a degree of nervousness."[25]

Few white Mississippians stated publicly that lynching was wrong. An 1877 press report described a rape allegedly committed by two black men. The editor of the *Jackson Clarion* complained that "the strange part of this horrible affair is that swift punishment was not visited upon the fiends" and "that they were not hung to the first tree or burnt alive" but instead taken to jail. The editor warned that "if jails and penitentiaries are to be the 'be all and end all' of brutes who commit such crimes, their frequent perpetration may be expected." Former U.S. senator William V. Sullivan bragged in 1908, "I led the mob which lynched Nelse Patton and I am proud of it. I directed every movement of the mob and I did everything I could to see that he was lynched." James K. Vardaman, when running for governor, made campaign speeches praising the work of lynch mobs. As governor, he did take some action to put down lynchings, but overall there was a reported lynching every twenty-five days while Vardaman was governor. In every decade Mississippi was the number one state for lynching in the United States, and in the 1880s the state's lynching rate was twice that of any other state.[26]

Mississippi's governors did take steps to suppress lynching. They were willing to send the National Guard to isolated counties to prevent lynchings there, and governors occasionally went in person to ask mobs to disband. Even Vardaman, who as a candidate declared himself in sympathy with those who lynched, intervened some nine times to stop lynchings. The governors justified their actions chiefly by stating that the majesty of the law must be upheld, that the reputation of the state was at stake, and that a demoralized labor force was of no benefit to Mississippi.

Governor Andrew H. Longino took a courageous stand against lynching. He used his inaugural address to urge lawmakers to pass legislation that would have discouraged lynching, but the legislature failed to act.

Some clergymen and journalists also denounced lynching. Methodist bishop Charles B. Galloway wrote a stinging indictment of the practice of lynching in 1906, but he did not focus on humanitarian concerns. Like the governors, Galloway feared that when southerners stepped outside the legitimate legal system to punish crimes, "the very foundations of society become insecure." To his credit, Galloway did urge that black criminal defendants be given genuinely fair trials, arguing that "racial and social lines have no place in courts of justice."[27]

Of the governors, Andrew H. Longino took the most courageous stand against lynching, and he paid dearly for it. During his successful gubernatorial campaign of 1899, Longino did not talk about lynching, but in his inaugural address he devoted a quarter of his time to the subject and made startling proposals. Longino warned the assembled legislators that if lynching continued unchecked, investors and settlers from other states would stay away, helping to keep Mississippi economically underdeveloped. Longino denied lynching was a practice aimed primarily at punishing rape, noting that some lynch victims had been killed after the most trivial of alleged crimes. Respect for the laws would decline if lynching went unchecked, Longino reasoned, and he called the practice the "most demoralizing, brutalizing, and ruinous species of lawlessness known to any brave and free people." His first proposal was that the legislature pass a law "giving to the family of anyone who may hereafter be lynched a right to recover in the chancery court a fixed sum in damages against the county wherein the lynching occurred." The sum must be large to act as a proper deterrent to lynching. In addition, the plaintiffs should only have to prove that the lynching did occur and that it took place in the county in question. Longino also recommended a second law aimed at officers who seemed almost glad to allow lynch mobs to take their prisoners. This law would declare the office of sheriff or constable vacant if a prisoner was taken from custody by a mob.[28]

Longino hoped the two proposed laws would discourage citizens from lynching. If citizens seized and killed a black prisoner, their elected sheriff would automatically be removed from office, while the victim's family would receive a large sum of money from the taxpayers. In closing his remarks on lynching, Longino admitted that the two proposals were "stringent" but said he hoped the legislature "will prove itself equal" to the task. The legislature did not so prove itself, however. Legislators took no action, and Longino himself did not push for the measures. After his term ended, Longino tried to win other offices, but in each case his enemies stymied his ambitions by reminding voters of his proposals on lynching. Longino even went so far as to admit his proposals had been wrong, but voters gave little respect to a man who had suggested state payments to the families of alleged rapists.[29]

Lynching continued to be widespread during and after World War I. Critics of the practice urged that justice be allowed to take its course through the court system. Yet detailed studies of state courts in this period show that little real justice was meted out to black defendants. W. E. B. Du Bois once said it was common knowledge that the courts in the South "have been used largely as instruments for enforcing caste rather than securing justice." A white attorney and future judge from Sunflower County, Sidney Fant Davis, agreed that race and caste were central to Mississippi's legal system. Davis explained in 1914 that an outsider reading Mississippi's laws would be led to believe they applied equally to whites and blacks, as one might expect under the Fourteenth Amendment. Actually, Davis asserted, "Nothing could be further from the truth." In practice, law enforcement officers knew that certain laws applied to whites, certain laws to blacks, and certain laws to both. In criminal cases involving African Americans, a major question always was, "What white interests have been affected?" Thus black men fighting with each other would not likely be charged with assault or would not have their case taken seriously. Crimes like adultery and rape also would not be taken seriously if the victims were black. Yet vagrancy was severely punished because it limited the supply of labor available to whites. Similarly, courts dealt severely with black defendants accused of stealing from whites or assaulting whites to prevent further such crimes and to ensure the position of the dominant race was not compromised.[30]

Black defendants sometimes received absurdly lenient treatment from the courts. As one writer has noted, a crucial question early in the investigation of a case was, "Whose nigger are you?" Black defendants who worked for respected planters might be released early in the proceedings or be assessed a fine with no prison term. After all, why punish planters by depriving them of their laborers? Those who worked for poorer whites or those who had no white patrons at all fared not as well. Some black crime victims were incensed that black-on-black crimes received scant attention from law enforcement officers or the courts. Many black citizens accused of crimes were left out of the official justice system altogether, being punished for their alleged crimes by their white employers. As a Mississippi planter's wife explained, "They can't afford to send them to jail because they need them on the farms; so they just . . . give them a good beating, and that teaches them."[31]

Statistics demonstrated the racial biases of Mississippi's criminal justice system. As we have seen, the population of the state's prisons and prison farms was overwhelmingly black, not matching the racial proportions of the general population. Further, white prisoners were often spared hard labor. Capital punishment statistics, too, show an overwhelming bias. Of those prisoners who were executed between 1891 and 1910, 92 percent were black. What cannot be measured, of course, is whether black Mississippians were more criminal than white Mississippians—if they were, this would account for some of the lopsided statistics. Yet even conceding for the sake of argument that black Mississippians may have committed more crimes per capita, one reason would be that crimes that carried prison sentences included such things as vagrancy, leaving one's employer without permission, or stealing anything worth $10 or more. There can be little doubt that justice Mississippi-style was in part a system of race control, and attorneys such as Sidney Fant Davis recognized this.[32]

Former slaves in Mississippi in 1870 were living in pleasantly exciting times. By decree of the federal government they were living in freedom. The Thirteenth Amendment promised involuntary servitude never again would exist. The Fourteenth Amendment pledged equality before the law, and the Fifteenth Amendment promised political rights. The freedmen could reasonably have expected to spend the next few decades farming, saving their money, and getting a good education. If anyone sought to deny them their rights, the courts would protect them, as the Fourteenth Amendment promised.

As we have seen, however, the former slaves and their children discovered the federal amendments made hollow promises. It was true that the Thirteenth Amendment led to an end of slave auctions, and at the end of the growing season many black farmers did exercise their right to move on. Yet planters tended to think possessively of "their" labor supply, and legislators passed laws to discourage workers' movement. Some employers held workers in a system of peonage, and while federal prosecutions helped discourage this practice, one state law helped protect the peonage system. The nightly slave patrols were replaced by new kinds of night riders, such as whitecap bands. Blacks were still living in tremendous poverty and relying on whites for clothing and food. Many blacks were called to the fields by the same bells that had been used on the antebellum plantations. Many were still subjected to white overseers and corporal punishment.

Contrary to all promises of the Fourteenth Amendment, blacks did not receive the same legal protections as whites. Members of white lynch mobs were never punished, while the murder of a black man by a white was almost automatically deemed to be an act of self-defense. Black crimes were trivialized or ignored if they did not affect white citizens' lives, while if a black man committed a crime that harmed whites, the punishment would be severe. Rates of incarceration and capital punishment of blacks were much higher than for the white population, and the death rate for black prisoners was far greater than that for white convicts. A Jim Crow system of laws and customs barred blacks from the better schools, from many neighborhoods, and from the most-prized jobs. Black political rights were severely curtailed, and attempting to exercise those rights could prove deadly.

Mississippi's system of race control was designed to keep ever available for white benefit a ready supply of black workers, including tenant farmers, agricultural day laborers, and domestic servants. Those who refused to work at all, those who resisted white oversight, and those who insisted on a better situation would incur white wrath and some form of punishment. Peonage laws, labor agent laws, vagrancy prosecutions, and acts of violence were designed to keep the black population intimidated and subordinate. Mississippi's racial system was largely successful in its goal of keeping a large, cheap labor supply available for white employers. Yet despite the dangers, black Mississippians did offer a surprising degree of resistance to white dominance, and this resistance is the subject of the next chapter.

CHAPTER FIVE

BLACK MISSISSIPPIANS CONFRONT THE SYSTEM

Between 1877 and 1917 black Mississippians faced a system of race control that relied on force to keep them on the bottom rungs of the social and economic ladder. By formal and informal systems, including indebtedness, peonage, convict labor, whitecapping, and lynching, whites assured themselves of an available, subservient labor force. Yet persons of color in Mississippi grappled with the system, resisting in direct and indirect ways.

Moses Weston of Washington County confronted Mississippi's Jim Crow system in a direct way. In 1889 he entered a white saloon in Greenville. The proprietor ordered him out, but Weston said he could patronize any business he pleased. When a man moved forward to eject Weston, Weston shot him dead. The proprietor then shot and killed Weston.[1]

Most African Americans in Mississippi behaved in more circumspect ways than Weston, recognizing that they lived in a state where power was concentrated in white hands. Black Mississippians who wanted to keep their sanity and preserve their lives developed two distinct personae. Howard Odum, a white man who taught school in Mississippi before moving on to graduate school, reported that each black resident "has two distinct selves, the one he reveals to his own people, the other he assumes among the whites." Among whites, black Mississippians were agreeable and unassertive, avoiding controversial topics. Whites insisted on this persona, for they used it to justify the system of Jim Crow segregation.

The most quoted black spokesperson nationally was Booker T. Washington of Alabama. Washington was chief exponent of the "accommodationists," who urged publicly that black southerners not assert their civil and political rights but instead stress literacy, vocational education, and hard work. Many black Mississippians, including Isaiah T. Montgomery, agreed with Washington that as black citizens grew to be better educated, to develop useful job skills, and own their farms and homes, whites would grant them grudging respect and eventually some civil and political rights. As historian Neil McMillen points out, leaders like Montgomery made serious errors in their calculations. Montgomery and Washington believed that well-to-do whites were their potential allies and that a skilled black workforce and black home ownership would be pleasingly impressive to their white allies. Actually, while wealthy whites seldom expressed vulgar racism, they nonetheless had abundant reasons to perpetuate a tradition where black Mississippians were poor, uneducated, and skilled at little save raising cotton.

Other black Mississippians denounced both Washington and Montgomery. Yet even those who criticized Washington's ideology agreed that black citizens should build up their own communities. Indeed, one of the most successful methods of coping with the system of segregation and race control was to develop strong blacks-only churches and fraternal lodges. These social institutions fostered black leadership—a leadership that functioned only within the black community. Black efforts at self-help also included aid to education, including such private schools as Utica Institute and Piney Woods Country Life School. An old saying is that the best revenge is to live well, and some of the greatest black triumphs in this period came when black Mississippians were able, against great odds, to own and operate successfully their own businesses and farms.

Black leaders like Blanche K. Bruce, John R. Lynch, and Isaiah T. Montgomery were among the larger planters in the state. In the early twentieth century, a black citizen named E. W. Green, orphaned as a child, worked his way up from agricultural wage laborer to own 1,000 acres of choice Jefferson County farmland. His seventy black workers helped provide him with an imposing, elegant home. Most black landowners owned property on a more modest scale; nonetheless, they won some notable successes. In Tunica County, one out of three landowners was black. Yet even this small army of black landowners owned only one-tenth of the land in Tunica County. Further, some might suggest that since black residents outnumbered white residents by a ratio of nine to one in the county, black land ownership there should have been greater. Statewide, there were tragic cases of white entrepreneurs scheming to get black families to make payments on overpriced land, then repossessing the land when the inevitable missed payment came. Few black farmers could afford to hire an attorney to protect their interests in such cases. Given the handicaps of poverty, land ownership was an remarkable achievement. In the first decades of the twentieth century, 15 percent of black farmers in the state owned their own farms.[2]

African American senator Blanche K. Bruce personally opposed the back-to-Africa movement, but he did present to Congress the petition of his constituents seeking a $100,000 appropriation to aid black southerners who wished to go to Liberia.

Mack Parker of Tunica County was born into slavery. He worked hard as a tenant, and observers later remembered he was able to walk the fine line between self-confident pride and fatal assertiveness. He warned his neighbors that white Mississippians aimed to control them with the pencil, not the lash. Though not well educated, Parker made sure that his children received good educations. On one occasion he boldly insisted that his well-educated son examine the planter's book for errors. Parker's tenacity paid off, and he was able to purchase a farm that remained in his family for at least eight decades. Robert Flagg was a tenant who also lived in Tunica County. He was discharged from his plantation in 1876 for being too interested in politics. He went to work as a schoolteacher, while he also worked part of his father-in-law's land. He taught himself bookkeeping and kept books for the local cottonseed press. Along the way Flagg bought land and inherited more. By the early twentieth century he had tenant farmers working his land, while he devoted his own attention to a grocery store and a dance hall.[3]

Renters were sometimes able to gain independence and self-sufficiency, as they rented lands that had not yet been cleared. Planter George Collins recorded in one letter that many of his black tenants wanted to become "independent of me and each other" by renting land "back there among the wolves and other wild things." Collins initially resisted renting land in the backwoods, where tenants could not easily be supervised. The planter finally yielded on the condition that the tenants agreed to clear and farm some of the land. These backwoods renters did clear some land and grow some cotton. They lived a self-sufficient life as they fed on blackberries, venison, rabbit, fresh-caught fish, and greens from their large gardens. Richard Jones recalled that his father, who lived in the Delta in the early twentieth century, supplemented his farming by trapping mink and selling the pelts. "He carried $400 around in his pocket," Jones recalled, and knew that "he could get up and go any time."[4]

For African Americans, getting up and going was a bold act—one that could arouse the fear of planters who depended on black labor. In the mid-1870s a number of black Mississippians supported a back-to-Africa movement. The movement had its roots in the 1820s, in efforts of the American Colonization Society to send freed slaves to a colony in Liberia. In 1877 a number of black constituents asked U.S. senator Blanche K. Bruce to present their petition to Congress, seeking a $100,000 appropriation to aid Liberian immigration. Bruce did as they asked but noted his own personal opposition. He pointed out that Liberia could not easily absorb a large number of new black residents, especially poor ones. As a black planter himself, Bruce was unlikely to support a plan to move laborers out of the South. A black organizer known only as Dr. Collins came into the Mississippi Delta from Arkansas in 1878, advocating Liberian immigration. Collins started a number of secret Liberia clubs, which in turn were infiltrated and sabotaged by representatives of a black planter named Louis Stubblefield. Stubblefield later explained that he was concerned about his black neighbors being swindled, but he was also concerned about keeping a steady labor supply on his Bolivar County plantation.[5]

Some plans for black separation involved emigration rather than immigration. In the 1870s black entrepreneurs in the South began to establish black enclaves in Kansas. They encouraged black citizens who had accumulated some capital to move to Kansas, where (it was said) the soil was rich and rights were not suppressed. Several prominent black Mississippians moved to Kansas, including J. C. Embry of Vicksburg. In February 1876 Embry wrote to Senator Bruce that unless white Mississippians began to respect black political rights, he would encourage black Mississippians to follow him to Kansas. By his letters to northern newspapers and his publication of a booklet entitled *Thoughts for To-day upon the Past, Present, and Future of Colored Americans*, Embry helped to stir an interest in more widespread black immigration to Kansas. Soon the interest in moving to Kansas became a "Kansas fever" among black residents of the Deep South. One black

Mississippian who migrated to Kansas in 1879 told a St. Louis reporter that the movement to Kansas really began in the fall of 1877, when some black residents of the Mississippi Delta received letters from their friends and relatives who had already gone to Kansas. The letters told "of the glorious country, and how easy it was to make a living out there." As these reports spread, a mass movement was born.[6]

By the second week of March 1879, great crowds of black Mississippians were headed for the banks of the Mississippi River, carrying all their possessions. Roads leading to the river were choked with ramshackle wagons of those intending to leave. Uncharitable white observers likened the participants to sheep, who dumbly followed one another, giving no thought to where they were going or why. One white resident of the Delta recalled stopping a black farmer who was headed for the river. "We questioned him and discovered that he knew not to what particular point he was going, knew not the value or kind of land he was to occupy, knew not the conditions on which he was to take it, and in fact knew absolutely nothing." This white resident may not have stopped to consider that articulating hopes and dreams to a white stranger would have been unlikely for any black citizen of the Delta. Still, there undoubtedly was an irrational tone to the Kansas exodus of 1879. Many of the participants had little money to finance their move. A black preacher in Kansas who ministered to many of the Mississippi migrants explained that the motivation of the "exodusters" was their belief that "slavery is not dead, but sleeping in disguise, as [if] it were a wolf in sheep's clothing." As black political rights in Mississippi were vanishing, and as independent farming grew increasingly unlikely, many blacks believed that they would soon need passes from their landlord to travel the roads of their county. Tens of thousands of black Mississippians showed an interest in getting out of the state before this happened.[7]

Black Mississippians' belief that they could make it to Kansas and obtain land despite their poverty was not as illogical as it first appeared. The existence of the federal Homestead Act of 1862 gave hopes of free federal lands. Since Reconstruction, Republican politicians had occasionally spoken of helping freedmen obtain land, and Congress had passed a few modest laws encouraging this homesteading. One black Mississippian wrote to President Rutherford B. Hayes to ask for federal aid for those who wanted to leave the state for Kansas. In his letter to the president, J. T. Brewington made it clear he knew that reaching Kansas required money. Federal aid was necessary, Brewington urged Hayes, because "we are in the first place entirely unable to reach those lands [in Kansas], secondly to raise means to subsist the first year, thirdly to raise means to get implements with which to commence labor to get sheltering." Senator Bruce put former Vicksburg resident J. C. Embry in touch with Senator William Windom of Minnesota, and Windom introduced a resolution calling on the Senate to investigate aiding those black southerners who wished to migrate to "such Territory or Territories of the United States as may be provided for their use and occupation." An investigation followed. Word spread throughout black communities that federal aid for migration to Kansas was a real possibility. Windom's dream of providing aid to migrants died a lingering death in the Senate, but the rumors continued to be remarkably lively.[8]

Meanwhile, thousands of Mississippians lined the banks of the Mississippi, awaiting passage to Kansas. Those who had funds boarded the steamboats with their families. Many could afford to purchase tickets taking them only part way to Kansas. In some cases, white residents forcibly prevented black families from going to the river, using the justification of indebtedness or broken contracts. In at least one instance an exoduster on the riverbank was shot dead after a confrontation with whites who wanted him to return.[9]

On the riverbanks, white violence and intimidation diminished after local business owners convinced steamboat captains that they should not stop for black passengers. They persuaded the captains that if the region were depopulated of black laborers, the boats would have no cotton to carry. Steamboat crews were coerced as well. One boat captain complained, "They have armed every white man ... to mob the first captain that lands a boat ... with colored people on board." Finally, after thousands of black Mississippians gave up their dreams and returned home, the boats again began accepting black passengers. The captains may have feared federal prosecution for racial discrimination, or local whites may have acquiesced since the exoduster movement had lost its steam.[10]

Despite the obstacles, several thousand black Mississippians managed to reach Kansas during the height of the 1879 and 1880 migration. Thousands of others failed, unable to secure transportation. For some, Kansas became their home, and their children raised children there. Others grew disillusioned and returned to Mississippi. Those who remained in Kansas bettered their lots. Mississippi-born black Kansans had higher rates of literacy and home ownership than black Mississippians who remained in Mississippi.[11]

Historians have long been puzzled by the actions of Isaiah T. Montgomery in the period of Kansas fever. A wealthy black planter himself, Montgomery went to Kansas on an inspection trip, hoping to convince some of his own tenants to return. Montgomery reported widespread poverty among black Mississippians who had gone to Kansas and publicly pronounced the Kansas experiment a failure. Yet

Montgomery also quietly purchased Kansas lands and generally assisted in the various colonizing plans developed by other black entrepreneurs. In a letter to the governor of Kansas, Montgomery explained why he would invest in black colonies in Kansas while at the same time denouncing the exoduster movement. He admitted in his letter that he did not always speak his true feelings in public. If he had uttered even a few words in favor of black migration to Kansas, the number of black Mississippians leaving the state would have been staggering. To prevent the destruction of Mississippi's labor force, Montgomery had issued public statements describing the suffering that he had allegedly found in Kansas. He closed his letter by asking the governor not to put a return address on his reply, since in Mississippi it had long been the custom "to ransack the mails to prevent the circulation of documents breathing the spirit of freedom." While Montgomery undoubtedly believed Kansas would offer hope and freedom to some black southerners, he chose not to create turmoil and disruption of the labor supply that he and others depended on by praising the migration to Kansas.[12]

The exoduster movement had promised to be one of the greatest mass movements in American history. As a Greenville newspaper put it after the movement was over, "We all know that could the negroes have gotten off while the fever was on them, there would hardly have been a man, woman or child left in this county." The black exodus would have made Delta lands unprofitable, and thus many whites would have been forced to leave to find better opportunities. The exoduster movement saw the departure of some 3,000 migrants from Mississippi in the space of two years. For thousands of other black Mississippians interested in the movement, the Kansas exodus failed, and for two reasons. One was that powerful planters and merchants would not permit it. Through both persuasion and intimidation, they convinced steamboat captains to refuse to carry black passengers until the movement subsided. They employed intimidation against black participants, and they used their political power to suppress any congressional plans to aid those who wanted to leave the South. Second, the movement failed because of the poverty of the participants, most of whom had money neither for transportation nor for land, tools, and shelter. As it was, St. Louis became home to a large refugee camp of exodusters who had run out of money, and only the charity of the nation prevented starvation.[13]

If black Mississippians were not going to go to Liberia or to black enclaves in Kansas, there remained the possibility of separatism within Mississippi. One of the best examples of black separatism was the founding of Mound Bayou, an all-black town in Bolivar County. For those who participated in the building of Mound

Bayou, the town served a number of purposes. First, it was a source of profit for early investors. Second, it would be a haven from peonage, whitecapping, lynching, and the daily insults of Jim Crow Mississippi. Third, it would be a showcase, a focal point of race pride in a state where the power structure did not encourage black pride. Isaiah T. Montgomery conceived the idea of a model black town in 1885, when officers of the Louisville, New Orleans, and Texas Railroad spoke to him about land sales. The railroad owned large tracts of forested Delta land but had difficulty selling it because it was so wild and because of whites' fears of fevers in the region. The railroad's officers believed black Mississippians were immune from tropical fevers and more willing to work in oppressive heat and humidity. They also knew that many black farmers had experience clearing land. The railroad representatives offered Montgomery a deal whereby he would sell land on commission.[14]

Given Montgomery's background, however, the plan would go beyond selling scattered tracts of land to black farmers. Montgomery had participated in experiments to develop ideal plantation labor systems, notably at the Davis Bend plantation owned by Joseph Davis (brother of Jefferson Davis). Montgomery himself later owned and directed this plantation as well as others. As we have seen, he also traveled to Kansas and invested in lands there to encourage the building up of an enclave of black Mississippians. Now Montgomery envisioned a model town, populated exclusively by black Mississippians and serving a larger community of rural black farmers. As a first step, Montgomery and his cousin Benjamin T. Green purchased 840 acres of Bolivar County land.

The first settlers arrived early in 1887. Twelve years later the town was incorporated, with Montgomery as the first mayor. By 1904 the town had 400 residents and served 2,500 outlying farmers. Early residents lived on scant rations, as they struggled to finance their land purchase. Most worked not only their own land but also hired themselves out to work the lands of others.

A typical pioneer of Mound Bayou was Simon Gaither, a former slave. Gaither bought a forty-acre farm in the earliest days of Mound Bayou, but constant privation was his lot. His initial land payment left him almost broke. The first year he built a crude log house and planted corn, cane, rice, and garden crops—on the less than one acre he was able to clear. Gaither hired himself out to clear land for other Mound Bayou farmers at $4 an acre and cut timber for $6 a cord. Meanwhile, his wife and children traveled more than ten miles to chop cotton and to do similar work for others. After a dozen years in Mound Bayou, Gaither was able to purchase another forty acres, attributing his success to his family's willingness to endure privation.[15]

The early settlers soon were able to congratulate themselves on their success. By 1910 Mound Bayou boasted a population of about 1,000. It was home to two doctors, two lawyers, a funeral home, a photographer, a hotel, a number of boardinghouses, and a weekly newspaper, the *Mound Bayou Demonstrator*. The town also could boast a brickyard, an ice plant, a bakery, and four cotton gins. One special point of pride was the two-story brick bank, which allowed the typical resident to avoid going into debt to unsympathetic white merchants. Some of the homes in Mound Bayou were impressive by any standards. Civic leader Charles Banks owned a home worth $12,000, while Isaiah T. Montgomery lived in a twenty-seven-room brick mansion.

The town benefited from the contributions of outsiders as well. From Alabama, Booker T. Washington cast an approving eye on Mound Bayou and did what he could to encourage northern philanthropists to aid the town. Andrew Carnegie's foundation donated money for a building for a municipal library. The American Missionary Society financed the Mound Bayou Institute, a school similar to Washington's Tuskegee Institute. The General Baptist Convention operated a similar school. The most important philanthropy was Julius Rosenwald's investment of funds in a cottonseed oil mill, which was to provide an industrial alternative to agricultural work for area residents.[16]

Unfortunately, the town experienced financial woes in the years just before and after the United States' entry into World War I. Most of the problems stemmed from the cottonseed oil mill, which proved to be a more expensive undertaking than its backers had predicted. Backers of the mill had to ask Rosenwald to contribute a second time to the mill, and he reluctantly did so. Meanwhile the Mound Bayou Bank became all too involved in the risky venture. State bank examiners closed the bank in 1914, although residents soon organized a new bank to take its place. Finally, the backers of the oil mill realized that the only way to begin operations was to lease the mill to a wealthy industrialist. Accordingly, the mill was leased out, but the lessee embezzled some of the mill's funds.[17]

Just after World War I, Mound Bayou was a place of disappointment for many residents. The impressive cottonseed oil mill stood idle. The Carnegie library was devoid of books, since the Carnegie Foundation had specified the town must buy the books, but the town government had not been able to do so. The two church-sponsored vocational schools were languishing and were forced to merge to survive. Many observers reported the relatively new town was beginning to look run down. A visitor in the 1940s found a town "more dead than alive," with a predominantly older population.[18]

Still, for those who participated in the building up of Mound Bayou between 1887 and 1917, the successes greatly outweighed the failures. Montgomery confided to Booker T. Washington in 1904 that he hoped Mound Bayou would teach black Mississippians "high class farming, improvement of homes, thrift, saving, and abandonment of the mortgage systems" and would feature urban attractions sufficient to keep young residents in the area. Mound Bayou did provide a place where enterprising black Mississippians could buy land and deal on terms of dignity with black merchants, bankers, and town officers. Most important, Mound Bayou offered pride in a state where black pride was a scarce commodity. As the editor of the *Mound Bayou Demonstrator* wrote in 1910, "What chance has the negro boy or girl who lives in the 'nigger quarters' of the cities? . . . They soon learn to think they can never amount to anything and to despise their race no matter how hard they work or moral they be." Mound Bayou showed black residents of the state that members of their race could successfully run banks, gins, stores, real estate offices, and town governments.[19]

There were other attempts at founding all-black towns in Mississippi in this period. One of the more successful was Moorhead in Sunflower County. Initial leadership for Moorhead came from a white railroad executive, Chester H. Pond, an Ohio-born Mississippian. Pond believed the existing sharecropping system led to demoralization of the typical black farmer and to a feeling "that every white man is against him." Moorhead was designed to offer alternative, industrial employment for black workers and an opportunity for them to purchase homes. Pond also hoped the town would be a haven from the evils of alcohol. In 1906 Moorhead had an estimated population of 700 persons, including a sprinkling of whites. Its industries included a small cottonseed oil mill, a textile factory, a stave plant, and a lumber mill that turned persimmon wood into shuttles and shoe lasts. Two northern church groups supported a vocational institute, the Industrial School for Girls. While few details of Moorhead's utopian history have survived, it appears that black home ownership was common and that blacks participated in the running of the town. On the other hand, the white leadership and the modest number of white residents may have diluted some of the impact Moorhead had on race pride within the state.[20]

Another source of pride within the black community were private boarding schools for African American children. Laurence C. Jones founded Piney Woods School, and William H. Holtzclaw set up Utica Institute. These schools did important work in basic and vocational education but endured a precarious financial existence. Northern philanthropy helped, but without grassroots support from black residents of Mississippi the schools would not have survived. These schools did risk white antipathy. Prior to founding Utica Institute, Holtzclaw considered opening a school in the Delta but met a great deal of white resistance. One otherwise friendly planter, speaking of a possible vocational school in the Delta, said, "I really think it would do harm." He offered to contribute to a school located elsewhere in the state, as long as Holtzclaw sent the graduates "somewhere else when they are educated." In founding the Piney Woods School, Jones met white indifference or opposition. Finally, a respected white sawmill owner, who was a socialist, offered his support and helped Jones mold local public opinion.[21]

Some black professionals turned to journalism for their careers and in so doing helped build up black communities. In any one year, African Americans published twenty to thirty newspapers in Mississippi, but many lasted less than a year. Surviving issues of these publications are exceedingly rare, making generalizations about their contents difficult. One of the more important titles was the *People's Journal*, published at Jackson beginning in 1877. It survived approximately five years, publishing under several titles. The *Delta Light House* of Greenville lasted nearly three decades, although it is not clear if its publication was continuous or broken. At Mound Bayou was the *Demonstrator*, published for about fifteen years beginning in 1900. It distributed an impressive 4,000 copies of each issue in 1912, showing that its circulation extended far beyond the town limits of Mound Bayou. Statewide, these newspapers were short-lived primarily because of a lack of advertisers. To make up for a lack of black-edited Mississippi newspapers, some black residents turned to out-of-state papers, such as the *Chicago Defender*. The *Defender* was considerably bolder in race matters than Mississippi black papers, and for this reason whites were vigilant to keep the paper out of the state. Pullman porters, though, sneaked it in. Musician W. C. Handy supplemented his income by quietly distributing copies in the state.[22]

Black journalist George S. Schuyler explained that "juggling torches in a powder magazine" was child's play "compared to editing a newspaper for Negroes in Mississippi." Papers tended to be bolder in the late nineteenth century, then more circumspect during the administration of Governor James K. Vardaman and thereafter. A number of black newspapers vigorously attacked the new constitution of 1890 after it was drafted, especially its disfranchising provisions. These papers included Meridian's *Fair Play*, the *Jackson Colored Citizen*, and the *Natchez Brotherhood*. After 1900, black editors tended to be more cautious. Some observers have suggested the editors were careful because they had white financial backing and feared losing it. There is undoubtedly some truth in this, but the bigger fear was of white violence. In Brookhaven, Eugene N. Bryan edited the *People's Relief*. Bryan printed something too bold—precisely what is not recorded—and he was accused of "stirring up race hatred." Local whites drove him from Brookhaven, and a mob that included members of the police force torched his home and office. As an afterthought, several months later a mob burned his five rental houses, and local prosecutors even considered prosecuting him for criminal libel. Thus most black editors protected their lives and livelihood by avoiding discussion of race relations or mob violence.[23]

Generally, black community leaders did not confront the state's system of segregation and labor control head-on. To do so could have been suicidal, as numerous incidents demonstrated. Occasional complaints about Mississippi's evolving racial system were voiced in the 1880s, when many black citizens still voted and a few still served in the legislature. As racial ideas hardened in the state and nationwide in the 1890s, most black leaders avoided controversial topics, guided by their own instinct for self-preservation. Only rarely did a black Mississippian speak out publicly and bitterly. Among those who sometimes did so were Blanche K. Bruce, John R. Lynch, and, later, Perry Howard. These men were able to speak out because they held federal jobs in Washington, D.C., had influential friends, and did not have to live permanently in the state of Mississippi.

One of the most important black Mississippians to speak out against racial injustice was journalist Ida B. Wells. Wells grew up in Holly Springs and was a schoolteacher in Marshall County. On the invitation of her aunt, she moved to Memphis, where she taught school and began writing for several newspapers. By 1889 she was co-owner and co-editor of a Memphis paper called *Free Speech*. While on a journalistic trip through the South, Wells visited Natchez, Mississippi, on March 9, 1892. There she learned that three close friends in Memphis had been killed by a mob. Their only "crime" seemed to be that they had operated a business called the People's Grocery in competition with white-owned stores and had refused to be cowed by whites. Wells wrote and published a heartfelt denunciation of the killing of her friends and of lynching generally. In retaliation, a mob of white men in Memphis destroyed her newspaper office and vowed to kill her on sight if she ever returned to Tennessee. Wells continued her journalistic career in New York City, and the antilynching campaign she spearheaded was the most notable achievement of a remarkable career.[24]

Wells's antilynching writings were published in the *New York Age* and were reprinted in other newspapers and collected into small books. In *A Red Record*, Wells provided lynching statistics taken from news reports in the *Chicago Tribune*.

Between 1892 and 1894, she reported, there were 453 lynchings of African Americans. White apologists for lynch mobs explained that the "usual cause" was black men's rape of white women. Wells contradicted this, proving that only 143 of the lynchings had been of men accused of rape, attempted rape, or behaving improperly toward white women. Of the 453 lynchings in three years, less than 32 percent of them targeted men who allegedly assaulted or insulted white women. In *Mob Rule in New Orleans*, Wells examined one particular case of lynching and rioting, then looked at overall statistics of lynching. By 1899, she found, only one in six lynchings was for the "usual crime." The "usual crime" was not very usual. Wells rebutted the idea that black men were lustful beasts who would not be content until they raped white women. Wells pointed to the Civil War period, when white men were away and yet virtually no black rapes of white women occurred. She also pointed to the Reconstruction period, when single white women came south to live in black communities and teach school and no rapes occurred. The rape allegations, Wells concluded, were simply part of a mythology of lynching that served to prevent whites from objecting to lynching.[25]

Wells wrote at length about a lynching near Quincy, Mississippi. Members of a white family named Woodruff grew ill, and at least one family member died. The Woodruffs' neighbors suspected a black resident named Benjamin Jackson had poisoned the well, and the sheriff arrested him along with his wife and mother-in-law. During the coroner's inquest into the alleged poisoning, a mob seized Jackson and hung him. After Jackson's death, the official inquest resumed to determine if others were involved in the possible poisoning. The coroner's jury found there was no evidence whatever against the wife and mother-in-law and set them free. Still, a mob appeared and hung the two women. The following day a mob lynched a fourth black resident for involvement in the alleged well poisoning, despite the coroner's failure to find that he had been involved. Wells remarked that "the moral degradation of the people of Mississippi" was evident from the fact that there was no outcry over the lynchings; in fact, there had been very little notice of any kind of this quadruple hanging that included two women. Wells remarked that if African tribes had hung four people under similar circumstances, the Christians of the United States would have denounced such barbarism. As it was, the nation hardly noticed this crime and this assault on the legal system.[26]

In her most provocative allegation, Wells asserted that many victims of lynch mobs were not rapists but were black men involved in consensual relationships with white women. The lynchings sometimes occurred because a husband discovered his wife in bed with a black man and assumed force had been involved.

In other cases, the husband knew force was not involved but alleged that it had been in order to protect his own family's reputation and to incite the mob. Occasionally, white women manufactured the story of a rape to protect themselves, when they discovered they were pregnant with a child fathered by their black paramour. Wells told of a Mrs. Marshall, a white woman in Natchez who gave birth to a dark-colored baby whose skin color was attributed to some dark-complected but white ancestor. Later, Marshall gave birth to a second baby whose skin color was even darker, and while the mother weakly asserted the baby was dark from not getting enough oxygen, the doctor spoke the obvious: "It was a Negro child." A black servant fled, and Mr. Marshall disowned his wife. Wells also narrated the case of Ebenezer Fowler, "the wealthiest colored man in Issaquena County." In 1885 a mob of white men riddled Fowler's body with bullets on the streets of Mayersville after discovering he had written a letter to a white woman. Unfortunately for the woman's reputation, the letter made it clear she and Fowler had long been intimate. Those facts did not spare Fowler's life, however.[27]

Wells's allegations about white southern women's willing liaisons with black men were extremely controversial, and many southerners claimed Wells had made up stories like the one about Mrs. Marshall in Natchez. To buttress her case, Wells produced dozens of excerpts from white southern journalists' writings, in which they reported that some white women slept with black men. She quoted editors from North Carolina, South Carolina, and Tennessee. The editors told of young white women who produced mulatto children and refused to tell authorities the name of the father. She quoted Alabama editor J. C. Duke of the *Montgomery Herald*, who complained in 1887 about "the growing appreciation of white Juliets for colored Romeos." Wells also documented a large number of cases where white men had assaulted young black women and were punished by neither mobs nor courts.[28]

Wells was attempting nothing less than the dismantling of the racial and gender stereotypes that made lynching not only possible but inevitable. She sought to counter the reputation of black men as uncontrollably lustful. She hoped to disprove white men's claim that there was no such thing as rape of black women because (whites said) black women had no sense of honor to violate. Wells attempted to demonstrate white women sometimes had strong sexual feelings and were sometimes attracted to black men. She aimed to disprove white men's statements that lynching was designed to eliminate the rape of white women by black men. Lynching was simply an illegal and improper use of terror, Wells wrote, and the alleged criminals being killed by mobs should instead be tried in court. During

William H. Holtzclaw was a noted educator and the founder of Utica Institute. He corresponded with Governor Edmund F. Noel about the need to suppress lynchings in the state.

most of her campaign against lynching, Wells was fighting alone, although by the early twentieth century some members of women's clubs (both black and white in the North and South) added their voices in denunciation of the practice. Lynching would continue to be widespread during and after World War I, however.

Wells was not the only black Mississippian to denounce lynching. Noted black educator William H. Holtzclaw wrote privately to Governor Edmund F. Noel,[29] denouncing the epidemic of lynchings that was sweeping the state. "Here in the South white men make the laws," Holtzclaw wrote, "they interpret the laws, and they should enforce the law to the last letter, not override it." Holtzclaw warned the governor that "every time you make a law and fail to abide by it, so long as it is on the statute books you have done just that much to undermine the structure of civilized government." Noel answered the black educator cordially and said he agreed completely. The governor pointed out that he had repeatedly said in speeches "that the people are in a sad condition when they look upon laws as something to use when it suits them and to defy or evade when it does not suit them." Noel said he had worked against lynch mobs in the past and would do so in the future, and he invited Holtzclaw to send any information he could about recent lynchings. Unfortunately, Holtzclaw could not speak out publicly against lynching. If he had, his effectiveness as an educator and fund-raiser would have

Attorney Samuel Alfred Beadle was the author of several volumes of poems and stories that protested injustices toward African Americans in Mississippi and nationwide.

been destroyed, and he would also have placed himself at great personal risk. Wells could speak more freely because she no longer lived in the state, and her livelihood did not depend on the goodwill of white Mississippians.[30]

Another writer who, like Ida B. Wells, made some very direct challenges to Mississippi's racial system was Samuel Alfred Beadle, and Beadle made these challenges while living in Mississippi. Beadle was a black attorney, but it was as a writer of stories and poems that he made his bold statements. Beadle published several slender volumes in his lifetime. *Sketches from Life in Dixie*, which appeared in 1899, included his very best work. Beadle's books are currently out of print.

One allegorical tale in *Sketches from Life in Dixie* is "The Abduction and Rape of Themis," which deals with the theme of whitecaps, murder, and miscarriages of justice. The story centers on Thomas Ebon and Roderic Vulcan (whose names suggest "black" and "hell," respectively). Ebon, who represents the black everyman, finds himself in the horrible position of being "an industrious and well-to-do fellow, who had in some way incurred the displeasure of his neighbors." This situation was all the worse "because of his ignorance of the offense said to have been committed." Indeed, the offense might have been that he was black and prosperous. Ebon is murdered by a mob including Vulcan, and the townspeople determine to prosecute the killers. Vulcan then plots with some of his comrades, including Leon Caste and Ed Malice, and they plan and execute a two-part scheme. First, they start a newspaper with which they could sway public opinion, and second, they plot against Themis, who represents justice. As they approach Themis, she is in consultation with Washington, Jefferson, and Lincoln, debating whether the American experiment had failed at securing equal justice to all. As if to answer their question, a character named Prejudice drags Themis away and rapes her. The tale ends by explaining that the rape of Themis was how Judge Lynch was conceived.[31]

The more provocative writings in the volume are Beadle's poems, including one entitled "Strike for Civil Rights," which urges African American men to be brave and strike a blow against lynch law:

> *Say, Must we longer trust the law,*
> *Class-enacted to hide the flaw*
> *Of the crimson hand that strikes to awe,*
> *And terrorize us into slaves?*

A headnote explains that another poem, entitled "Lines," was composed after Beadle read about attacks made on African American soldiers passing through the South before and after the Spanish-American War.

> *As the smoke of the fight goes by,*
> *And the bugle calls to repose,*
> *By my countryman's hands I die,*
> *As well as by the hands of its foes;*
> *Yet I love you my country, I do,*
> *Here's a heart, a soul that is thine,*
> *Pregnant with devotion for you,*
> *And blind to your faults as to mine.*

Similarly, in "A Message for Janett," a dying black soldier asks his comrade-in-arms to

> *Tell them of our negro heroes,*
> *Of the valiant black brigade,*
> *And the gallant charge it made.*

Beadle's denunciations of white mob violence and appeals to race pride would undoubtedly have raised white ire in Mississippi if whites had routinely read volumes of poetry and stories by African American writers. As it was, they did not, and Beadle's work went unnoticed by white Mississippians. He undoubtedly helped ensure white ignorance of his work by using a Chicago printer for *Sketches from Life in Dixie*.[32]

The greatest mass movement opposing segregation in Mississippi in this period came in response to the 1904 law mandating racial segregation of streetcars. As we have seen, a few whites protested the new law and the way it was enforced. But at least five of Mississippi's seven cities that had streetcars saw organized protests from the African American community. The protests took the form of boycott, of walking rather than acquiescing to this new extension of Jim Crow. Black citizens of Montgomery, Alabama, would use a similar technique in protesting segregation on city buses more than half a century later.

The boycotts against municipal streetcar systems sprang up across the South as states passed laws mandating segregated public transportation in the cities. Unfortunately, it is very difficult to trace the history of these protests in Mississippi, because the state's major newspapers claimed the protests were small and unimportant. Jackson newspapers, for example, reported that hardly anyone was boycotting. But from Monroe County, the editor of the *Aberdeen Weekly* reported that only an "occasional lone negro" still rode Jackson's streetcars. The boycott seems to have been almost universal among black residents of these five cities over the summer of 1904. In August the *Natchez Daily Democrat* editor admitted the boycott was "knocking flinders out of the Mississippi streetcar business." By fall, however, the boycott began to deteriorate, and it failed by year's end. Conservative black preachers urged their congregations to shun the protests. The impoverished nature of the black community also meant that a large segment of the black populace had never ridden the streetcars to begin with. The protests were also defeated by absolute white solidarity, such that financial losses would be tolerated rather than see retreat from the ideal of total segregation.[33]

In deciding how directly they dared confront Mississippi's system of Jim Crow segregation, its system of labor control, and its tolerance of mob violence, each black Mississippian had to decide how much personal risk was acceptable. One black Mississippian who determined to preserve his dignity and his rights no matter the cost was William H. Foote. Foote was a native of the state but had managed to secure an education at Oberlin College in Ohio. During Reconstruction, he had won a Yazoo County legislative seat. After Reconstruction, the once-dominant Yazoo County Republican Party was destroyed by violence and intimidation, but Foote maintained his own links to the statewide party and served in the lucrative position of deputy federal revenue collector. Foote's fatal decision, however, was his refusal to adopt the subservient persona that might have saved his life. White men who did not know Foote looked in amazement as he walked, well dressed and with head erect, on the streets of Yazoo City. "Why look at that nigro; who is he?" they would ask. "He has the audacity of a white man." One observer wrote that a white Republican postmaster at Yazoo City was tolerable, but "How could 'our nigros' be made to 'keep their places'" with a dignified, articulate, proud man like Foote living in Yazoo County? White citizens believed he set a very bad example for black residents.[34]

The fatal encounter came when a black man came to Foote for protection as he was chased by a whip-wielding white mob. Foote protected the man, confronting members of the mob and quarreling with them. Gunfire broke out, and when the smoke cleared five white men lay on the ground, three fatally injured. Foote's friends urged him to flee the county, but he refused. Officers took him to jail, and soon the inevitable lynch mob appeared. When the mob broke down the door to Foote's cell, he struck down the first to enter and continued fighting with the white men until his own body was riddled with bullets. The coroner's inquest found Foote's death came at the hands of a "body of unknown men."[35]

For most black Mississippians, Foote's example was an uninviting one. Whites controlled the power structure of Mississippi, including the great majority of plantations, banks, stores, and newspapers. Whites controlled most of the cash and credit in the state and distributed most of the nonagricultural jobs. Whites had complete control of the sheriffs' offices, the constable and jailer positions, municipal police forces, the state militia, and the courts. For most black Mississippians in the forty years after 1877, the best way to prove their own self-worth was to turn inward, building up their own local institutions, including black churches, black-owned businesses, black fraternal lodges, even black towns such as Mound Bayou and Moorhead. The remarkable thing is not that black Mississippians did not more often confront the state's racial system directly. The remarkable thing is the large number of successes in building up prosperous black-owned businesses, flourishing community organizations, and thousands of farms run by black landowners—in spite of innumerable handicaps.

More direct protests would have to wait for a time when black Mississippians had powerful allies outside the state. These would include politicians from states outside the South and a large bloc of black voters in northern cities. Many of these voters, in cities such as St. Louis and Chicago, had once lived in Mississippi, and by the 1950s they demanded justice for their friends and families still living in their native state. With the help of outside forces, black residents of Mississippi and other southern states won notable civil rights victories beginning in the 1950s and 1960s. Such victories were not possible in the early twentieth century, when the nationwide intellectual climate was overwhelmingly racist and when black voters were relatively scarce in all regions.

CHAPTER SIX

POLITICS IN LATE-NINETEENTH-CENTURY MISSISSIPPI

The student of Mississippi's history can have trouble making sense of the state's late-nineteenth-century politics. For many voters, the most important issues were local ones: whether the county government should fence the courthouse, or select new textbooks, or impose a quarantine to control yellow fever. Voters were influenced by a variety of factors, including their religion, their place on the economic ladder, even the neighborhood clique to which they belonged. Yet white voters agreed on one cardinal tenet—that white supremacy was of paramount importance and that the Democratic Party was the vehicle to ensure this supremacy. Some Mississippians, both white and black, challenged the Democratic Party, but such challenges were viewed as seditious and almost revolutionary, whether the challengers addressed racial issues or not. Republican, Independent, and third-party movements had to be put down in much the same manner that an insurrection would be suppressed.[1]

One notable political division was a rivalry between the Delta and the Hills, or between white-majority counties and black-majority counties. Another schism that divided the Democrats into two groups was the split between elite reformers and agrarians. Yet another division was the struggle between those who believed in activist government and those who believed government should be small, inexpensive to the taxpayer, and offer no special privileges to any persons or corporations.[2]

Mississippi's most important Democratic leader in the late nineteenth century was James Z. George. Born in Georgia, George came to Mississippi with his

U.S. senator James Z. George was popular with small farmers and wealthy planters alike. He played key roles in both the overthrow of Reconstruction in 1875 and in the disfranchisement of black voters in 1890.

mother at an early age and attended informal "field schools." During the Mexican War, George served under Colonel Jefferson Davis. On his return from the war, he read law and was admitted to the bar in Carrollton in 1847. George first attracted notice as a delegate to the 1861 Secession Convention, where he coauthored a plan that would have paid for the defense of the state with a heavy slave tax. The plan went down to defeat but raised George in the esteem of the state's small farmers. During the Civil War, George served as a colonel in the Confederate cavalry, then won promotion to brigadier general.[3]

In 1875 and 1876 George managed the Democratic Party campaigns that wrested control of the state away from Republicans. Northerners rebuked George for leading political campaigns that quickly turned to bloodshed. For his part, George never publicly condoned election violence. After the 1876 election he rose quickly, winning appointment as a justice of the state supreme court, then elected chief justice by his colleagues. In 1880 the legislature elected George to the U.S. Senate, to the seat previously occupied by African American senator Blanche K. Bruce. George served in the Senate until his death in 1897. He was the most important of the state's "redeemers"—Democrats who took control of their state from Republicans and effectively ended Reconstruction. Some called George "The Commoner," referring to his humble upbringing and his friendship for the state's small farmers. As senator, George worked with agrarians to keep tariffs low and was a key supporter of the bill that established the U.S. Department of Agriculture.[4]

George again played a key role in the political history of the state when he served as chair of the Franchise Committee in Mississippi's 1890 constitutional convention. He had originally opposed the convention call, seeing no need for a convention since black voting had already been sharply reduced. At the insistence of his constituents, however, George finally backed the idea of a constitutional convention and helped guide the legal disfranchisement that followed. Many small farmers showed great devotion to George throughout his career. Yet as he sought reelection in 1891, some small farmers turned against him, arguing that a more radical agrarian should take his place. After a bitter campaign within the Democratic Party, George won reelection. Throughout his career, he was a moderate conservative supported by a surprisingly broad array of Mississippians: planters, business owners, and small farmers.[5]

Another important redeemer was L. Q. C. Lamar. Like George, Lamar was born in Georgia. In his formative years, he moved several times from Georgia to Mississippi and back. He graduated from Emory College, read law, and practiced in Georgia and then in Mississippi. Voters in northeast Mississippi elected Lamar to Congress in 1857 and reelected him two years later. Lamar resigned in December 1860 and returned to Mississippi, where he served as a member of the Secession Convention. During the war, he was colonel of a Mississippi regiment and also undertook diplomatic missions for the Confederacy. Before and after the war, Lamar served short stints as a professor at the University of Mississippi, teaching mathematics, social sciences, and law.[6]

Lamar's constituents returned him to Congress in 1872 and reelected him until his elevation to the Senate in 1877. Lamar was Mississippi's unofficial spokesman in Washington. While he did not defend the use of mob violence in elections, he did offer explanations of why the Ku Klux Klan arose and why black voters sometimes felt intimidated and failed to vote. Following the Hayes-Tilden disputed presidential election of 1876, Lamar was one of the most influential southerners arguing for the seating of the Republican candidate Rutherford B. Hayes. By acquiescing in Hayes's election, Lamar hoped to avert a potentially violent confrontation between the two parties nationally, and he sought and received assurances that, as president, Hayes would remove federal troops from the South. Lamar is also noted for his warm eulogy in praise of radical Republican Charles Sumner, delivered on Sumner's death in 1874. Many observers felt his speech helped heal the breach between North and South.[7]

More conservative than Senator George was his colleague L. Q. C. Lamar. Many credit Lamar with helping hasten reconciliation between North and South. (Photo courtesy of the Library of Congress.)

Lamar served in the Senate until 1885, when he resigned to become secretary of the interior under President Grover Cleveland. Three years later Cleveland appointed Lamar a justice of the U.S. Supreme Court, and Lamar served on the Court until his death in 1893. Unlike George, Lamar had few close ties with agrarians. In 1878 an agrarian legislature instructed Mississippi's U.S. senators to vote in favor of the inflationary Bland-Allison Silver Bill. Lamar refused. Like most conservatives, he abhorred inflation and believed the money supply should be based firmly on gold. Legislators snubbed Lamar by passing a resolution praising the black senator, Blanche K. Bruce, for following the legislature's instructions. Still, many Mississippians praised Lamar for statesmanlike leadership during his two decades of service in Washington.[8]

Another redeemer who served in the U.S. Senate for many years was Edward Cary Walthall of Grenada. Walthall was a railroad attorney, and as a politician he continued to be a spokesman for the railroads. For this reason, he seldom won the praise of small farmers, even though he sometimes voted in an agrarian way—supporting low tariffs, for example. The legislature elected Walthall to the Senate in 1885, and he served until his death in 1898.[9]

Mississippi's governors in this period were conservative, often supporting banks and railroads and opposing the agrarians' most cherished goals. In an era when the

Frank Burkitt was an agrarian editor and Democratic legislator from Chickasaw County. In 1892 he cast his lot with the Populist Party and three years later was the party's candidate for governor. This photo was taken about ten years after his run for governor, as he prepared to return to the legislature as an agrarian Democrat.

governors were relatively weak and the legislature strong, Mississippi's chief executives served their terms and retired into relative obscurity. The governors were John M. Stone, Robert Lowry, and Anselm J. McLaurin. Stone returned to the governor's office after sitting out for the eight years of Lowry's administration.

No radical agrarian won election as governor or U.S. senator in this period. Certainly agrarian candidates contended for high office. The worthy master of the state Grange, Putnam Darden, made a credible run for governor in 1885. Newspaper editor Ethelbert Barksdale ran for a U.S. Senate seat on a radical agrarian platform in 1891. But the most influential agrarian leader was Frank Burkitt.[10]

Burkitt was the state lecturer of the Farmers' Alliance and traveled the state organizing new chapters of the organization. He was also a newspaper editor, whose articles in the *Chickasaw Messenger* were widely reprinted by other newspapers across the state. Burkitt called for tough regulation of railroads. In his famous Wool Hat pamphlet of 1886, he accused lawmakers of wasting the taxpayers' money and accused the new Agricultural and Mechanical College at Starkville of failing to meet the needs of the state's small farmers. Throughout his career, Burkitt was a champion of low taxes, arguing that small farmers found it difficult to meet their tax obligations. As chair of the Appropriations Committee in the state House of Representatives, he kept his promise to slash state expenditures.[11]

In 1890 Burkitt served in the constitutional convention, fighting the poll tax and literacy test because he saw that they would disfranchise tens of thousands of white small farmers. He was one of four delegates who refused to sign the new constitution. By 1890 he was supporting free silver and the subtreasury system, two of the paramount goals of radical agrarians nationwide. In 1892 Burkitt left the Democratic Party, running as a Populist for Congress and later for governor. Early in the twentieth century he returned to the Democratic fold, returned to the legislature, and resumed his role as watchdog of the state treasury. He was an influential supporter of James K. Vardaman, the state's first important champion of the small farmer in the twentieth century.[12]

The Democratic Party first showed its postwar strength in the 1875 state election. Party leaders urged all white voters to join the Democratic Party and to topple the Reconstruction governments, which allegedly had brought ruinous taxes and gross misrule. A large majority of white voters did rally around the Democratic banner that year. There remained, however, the question of the future of political parties in the state. Those who had been Whigs before the Civil War, and some Democrats who disagreed with the state party's current leaders, suggested that Mississippi should develop a new two-party system. Politicians who made such suggestions suffered bitter attacks. In 1881 the *Yazoo Herald* asserted that "the white people of this state, with now and then an exception, are all of one mind, politically speaking, and are animated by the single purpose, to keep the State in the hands of the Democratic Party." Yet the question arose—why support a party whose "single purpose" was to maintain its own power?[13]

Senator Lamar admitted that there were problems inherent in such a large, inclusive party as the Mississippi Democrats. The state Democratic organization was made up, Lamar noted, of "incongruous and unsympathetic elements" and had a natural tendency toward divisiveness. For example, merchants and small farmers both worked in the Democratic Party, but each sought vastly different goals. The only way to keep the party from splintering beyond repair was to stress white solidarity. "The safety of Mississippi," lectured Lamar, "lies in the maintenance of the Democratic organization and in its wise direction by conservative leaders." The new system was an excellent one for elites in power. Nominations for office were made by county, district, and state conventions, which lawyers, planters, and merchants dominated. The convention delegates handed down the list of persons they wanted to hold office, and the voters were expected to ratify their decisions. Anyone who questioned the actions of the Democratic convention was deemed an enemy of the white race, a foe of the only organization working to maintain white supremacy in a state with a dangerous black majority. Thus in the great majority of cases, the nominees tapped by the Democratic convention in due time became the county and state officials, often with no opposition in the general election.[14]

For many years writers referred to the principal struggle within the state Democratic Party as one of the Delta versus the Hills. The problem with this scenario is that many Mississippi counties were neither in the Delta nor in the Hills. The terms may still be useful if we agree that "Delta" includes such southern river counties as Adams and such Black Belt counties as Noxubee. Similarly, the term "Hills" must be understood to include the Piney Woods, the coastal plain, and other flatlands. A more appropriate division may be the one that was more widely recognized in the late nineteenth century, one that was similar in makeup to the Delta-Hills split. This was the rivalry between the white-majority counties and the black-majority counties (often simply referred to as white counties and black counties). Of course, in citing this rivalry, it must be made clear that it does not refer to a contest between blacks and whites. The rivalry was between white leaders of the black counties and white leaders of the white counties.

The political power of the state lay in the hands of the black-majority counties. These counties dominated the Democratic state convention, the Democratic state executive committee, the state legislature, and the 1890 constitutional convention. Delegates from white-majority counties grew angry when the 1877 state Democratic convention named all five new members of the state executive committee from black-majority counties. Similarly, of the fourteen state at-large candidates the Democratic executive committee nominated to serve as delegates to the 1890 constitutional convention, eleven were from black-majority counties. In the legislature, black-majority counties held seventy-eight seats, while white-majority counties held only forty-two. White counties could cite numerous examples of what they deemed unfair apportionment. Jackson County had 1,673 white voters, while black-majority Lowndes County had only 1,430. Yet Lowndes was entitled to six Democratic state convention delegates and Jackson County only four. Leaders from counties such as Lowndes offered explanations. Lowndes County's overall population was considerably larger than Jackson's, and anyway the black-majority counties tended to be wealthy plantation counties and thus paid more in taxes. White-majority county leaders, however, wanted to go back to the antebellum system of apportionment, where representation in the legislature and in Democratic Party councils was based on white population. Leaders of black-majority counties remonstrated that black Mississippians were citizens and must be counted in apportionment plans. White county leaders countered that Delta leaders were unconcerned about rights of black citizens except in the apportionment schemes.

Aside from arguments over apportionment, a number of other battles in state politics were fought along regional lines. Delta leaders wanted levee construction, for example, but politicians from white-majority counties saw no reason why taxpayers from the Hills should support extensive levee building. Residents in the northeastern hills experimented with raising wool and asked the Mississippi congressional delegation to support high wool tariffs to protect American producers. Members of Congress from the Delta, however, favored uniformly low tariffs. The white-majority counties tended to have more small, independent farmers than the black-majority counties, and they sought laws to protect small farmers from merchants and bankers. Leaders in black-majority counties, on the other hand, were more likely to work to protect the prerogatives of lenders and other commercial elites. Politicians in white-majority counties favored a plan giving a larger share of school funds to white counties, but Delta leaders argued that black-majority counties paid a higher share of the taxes and were thus entitled to keep a larger share of the school funds.

Politically active Mississippians also divided on questions of the proper size of government. Mississippians had a long tradition of favoring low taxes and small government. Most white Mississippians believed that citizens should guard against expansion of power of the local, state, and national governments. Mississippi went to war in 1861 in part to counter the threat of an activist federal government. White Mississippi's overthrow of Reconstruction in 1875 was fueled partly by anger at activist county, state, and national governments. Antigovernment feelings led to toleration of lynching and whitecapping and in some areas to the widespread acceptance of moonshining and illegal liquor sales. When some Mississippi farmers advocated a federally built system of agricultural warehouses and a new subtreasury system of government-sponsored loans, they met bitter attacks from those who said Mississippians should not be asking the federal government for help. The popular southern evangelist Sam Jones laid aside ecclesiastical matters for a moment when he told a Mississippi audience that the subtreasury system was a bad idea, since "no true man or proud American citizen with the right spirit wanted government aid."[15]

Yet most white Mississippians paid only lip service to the ideal of small government. Prior to the Civil War, planters had used slave labor to develop their own system of levees. After the war, planters pressed hard for federal aid for building levees, and they sought federal aid to clear the tributaries of the Mississippi and Yazoo rivers for navigation. Planters and merchants also wanted the state government to protect the interest of creditors and to aid railroads in expanding their lines.

Agrarians, too, despite their professed love of small government, sought dramatic federal action to inflate the money supply and favored the massively expensive subtreasury system. They also sought strong federal regulation of railroads. At the state level, agrarians wanted the state government to build an agricultural college and a large number of experiment stations (with some federal aid as well). Elite reformers sought new agencies that would investigate banks to ensure safe financial practices, and they promoted expanded county, state, and national health services. Throughout the period 1877 to 1917, Mississippians overcame their aversion to big government and continually developed ideas for how government might be of service.

In campaigning for office in Mississippi in the late nineteenth century, opposing candidates often traveled together and met the voters at "joint speakings." Voters came from miles around to compare the candidates. Some candidates used thundering oratory to attract attention, while others used racist invective. A number used humor to pique the interest of the crowd. The most notable of these humorists was John Allen, a multiterm member of Congress from Lee County. One of Allen's anecdotes has justly won fame in the annals of American political humor. Allen was at a "joint speaking" with his opponent, a former Confederate general. The general told how on the night before the Battle of Shiloh, he was inspired by looking out from his tent occasionally to see a brave sentinel marching back and forth in the rain. When Allen's turn to speak came, he remarked that the general's story was perfectly true—Allen knew, because Allen was that sentinel. Allen then urged all those who had been generals in the Confederate army to vote for his worthy opponent. All those who had been privates, however, should vote for Allen. From that day forward, Allen was invariably known as "Private John Allen," as a humorous counterpoint to the many politicians who put a "colonel" or "general" before their names.[16]

Mississippi's members of Congress regularly were reminded of the importance of local issues to voters. Senator John Sharp Williams's friend and biographer recalled one campaign trip where Williams rode out by wagon to visit each "one-gallus sovereign who was plowing among the sassafras shoots." Williams visited with a farmer named Yarber and seemed to convince him that the proposed national subtreasury system was a bad idea. Williams was turning to go when the farmer remarked that Williams should not take his vote for granted. Asked why, Yarber explained that "when our folks held that election last year in Beat Three, you come out square agin the people." Yarber accused Williams of having voted in that Beat Three election for a law requiring farmers to fence their livestock. Williams admitted he had supported that stock law, and Yarber commented, "Folks is got cattle, and no land to pasture 'em on. How kin they feed a bunch o' bull yearlin's after you git the country all fenced up?" Both Williams and his biographer seemed to enjoy telling this story, believing Yarber was not educated enough to realize members of Congress dealt with issues weightier than the fence laws in Beat Three of a rural county. Yarber and his neighbors undoubtedly put a different interpretation on the story. A man who did not understand poor farmers' need for free range would probably not understand their other needs.[17]

For Yarber and thousands of other farmers, local issues often seemed most important. County and beat fence laws, plans for new dirt roads, decisions to place a county under yellow fever quarantine—these issues affected farmers directly, and citizens felt passionately about them. A new state textbook law requiring that a special commission in each county select textbooks for all the county's schools became a raging issue in the 1890s. These commissions, generally made up of elites, selected what they believed were the very best textbooks available. The citizen revolts against their decisions, however, were bitter. The opposition was based primarily on cost—the books that were available locally would no longer be used, and parents would have to buy new textbooks, even as cotton prices were low. The Farmers' Alliance of Oak Ridge in Madison County passed a resolution stating, "We repudiate the hasty and ill advised action of the Text Book Committee and declare that we will not buy nor use the books which said committee would foist upon us." In Choctaw County, the local editor reported that schools were legally required to use the newly chosen books, but "Will the people of old Choctaw buy the books adopted by the Text-book committee? Will they?" Citizen ire was so intense in Holmes County that the textbook commission came back into session, repealed its earlier recommendations, and instead urged schools to use the old books. The *Durant News* editor noted smugly that the county textbook commission might as well have rescinded its decision, because the people of Holmes County would not have changed textbooks in any event.[18]

At the state level, no issue aroused more citizen interest than the crop lien law. The 1867 statute was generous to merchants and onerous to borrowers. One part of the law curtailed farmers' rights to contest the lenders' books. Another section declared that absolutely all of the borrower's property was subject to seizure to satisfy the debt. When the state codified its laws in 1880, agrarians tried to get the crop lien provisions dropped from the new code, but to no avail. Republicans, Independents, and third-party leaders won many new converts because of the Democratic legislature's refusal to drop the lien provisions. Many agrarian

Democrats also promised to fight lien laws. The Grange, and later the Farmers' Alliance, vowed to defeat legislators who favored strong crop lien laws.[19]

The crop lien issue highlighted many of the rivalries within Mississippi politics. Legislators from black-majority counties strongly favored the crop lien law, while their colleagues from white-majority counties generally sought repeal. Planters believed the crop lien law made the state a better place for all. Without it, they argued, lenders would deem loans to farmers too risky to make. Small farmers, on the other hand, believed the crop lien law granted special privileges to bankers and merchants at the expense of tillers of the soil. Republicans, members of the Greenback Party, and Independents fought the crop lien laws, while elite lawmakers argued that fighting over the crop lien issue weakened the Democratic Party and thus put white supremacy at risk. Elites saw the crop lien law as a method of labor control, giving landlords power over their tenants. Landlords probably were correct in arguing that without the law, credit would be even tighter, to the dismay of many farmers.

The crop lien issue was not an abstraction. Statistics showed clearly the decline in numbers of farmers who owned their farms, as farmers unable to pay merchants lost their land. The *Batesville Blade*, a Greenback Party organ, asked its readers, "What do the tenant farmers of Panola County think of the legislature that has given the landlord the right to dispose of his (the tenant's) household furniture for rent?" The Greenback Party editor urged that "the landlord should not expect, nor the law allow him to exact more than the land produces." The Republican Party, too, made good use of the lien issue. A Republican handbill from 1881 reproduced a printed notice of a sale by a landlord of all a tenant's possessions, even his bedding. A Democratic editor in Greenville admitted that such sales did happen but claimed they were "rare." Agrarian Democrats pushed hard in 1885 to elect legislators committed to repealing the lien laws. They succeeded, and in 1886 the state's lawmakers rescinded the laws. Unfortunately for agrarians, repeal had little effect, as conservative judges continued to protect creditors' prerogatives under the common law. They explained that if creditors' rights were not protected, credit would be unavailable, tenants would face starvation, and Mississippi would become a wasteland.[20]

Another hotly contested issue at the state level was railroad regulation. Debates over railroad legislation showed clearly the split between elites and agrarians and between the black counties and the white counties. Greenbackers, Independents, and Populists used their support for railroad regulation to attract new converts, but agrarian Democrats also favored regulation. During the 1870s, farmers had often supported government actions friendly to the railroads, but by the 1880s their attitude had changed. As farmers grew more experienced with railroads, they developed a list of grievances. For one thing, railroad rates, like taxes, were one of the few expenses in the farmers' cash-poor lives that absolutely must be paid with cash. Farmers believed that larger shippers won excellent rates while small farmers paid full price. John M. Simmons, writing in the *Hinds County Gazette*, provided the example of a buggy shipped from San Francisco to the Hinds County town of Edwards. The shipment from San Francisco to Vicksburg cost $18, while the very short trip from Vicksburg to Edwards cost $15. Farmers sought to bring order and fairness to the setting of railroad rates.[21]

Farmers were especially bitter about high rail rates when they recalled that railroads had been built with their tax dollars. Under an 1871 law, the state of Mississippi paid each railroad $4,000 per mile for track laid after the first twenty-five miles. Under an 1882 statute, newly built lines were exempt from taxation for a ten-year period. Moreover, local governments often used taxpayer dollars to purchase stock in railroad companies, and railroads sometimes repaid the localities' confidence by changing the route to bypass the towns and counties that had invested. Agrarian editor Frank Burkitt used the pages of his *Chickasaw Messenger* to keep a number of examples of the railroads' perfidy before the public. One such example was provided by the Memphis, Birmingham, and Atlantic Railroad, which sold stock to many eastern Mississippi towns, counties, and individuals, promising a good network of service to the region. Later, the firm changed its route to better serve the newly discovered Alabama coalfields. Burkitt led the opposition to the proposed route change, but a majority of lawmakers agreed to modify the railroad's charter. He introduced legislation requiring the railroad to reimburse those along the abandoned route who had purchased stock, but the legislature defeated his proposal. Burkitt and the agrarians were sure the legislature was a tool of the railroads.[22]

Putnam Darden, leader of the Grange and, like Burkitt, a voice for agrarian Democrats, offered proof that the railroads had "bought" officers of the state government. Darden charged that railroads put state lawmakers on general retainer, paying them a generous fee for unspecified services. While state judges were not given fees, they were given free railroad passes, a valuable gift at a time when most travel was by train. When Darden made his charges in 1883, many public-spirited citizens were incredulous that he would make such wild accusations. Judges denied the charges and demanded proof. Judge J. A. P. Campbell, a widely respected jurist, published a letter in state newspapers saying he paid his own way on railroads. Several days later, however, Judge Campbell published a second letter admitting that, come to think of it, he had used passes on a number of occasions. "In accepting these unsolicited compliments to my official station," Campbell explained, "I conformed to long established and general usage, and took them when offered, as a matter of course, without a thought of any obligation for them." Judge H. H. Chalmers wrote a letter to state newspapers, proclaiming he used railroad passes "openly, without the slightest hesitation or concealment, feeling at entire liberty to follow a custom long established." Farmers had to wonder, however, whether private citizens would be likely ever to prevail against the railroads in court when judges used free passes issued by the companies and many prominent attorneys were on the companies' general retainer.[23]

Legislators created the Mississippi Railroad Commission in the 1884 session. The law required railroads to submit a list of their rates to the commission, and the commissioners would have the power to revise the rates if the charges were deemed unfair. Commissioners were required to consider the overall financial condition of the railroads in reaching their decisions and to allow the companies a fair rate of return. Railroads must post the rates at the depot and charge all customers the posted rates. Giving better rates to selected customers could result in a fine of $10 to $500 per offense. Mississippi's Railroad Commission was a strong one, when compared with those in other states, since it had the power to revise the company's rates. Governor Robert Lowry agreed to sign the bill only after lawmakers added a provision saying the governor would appoint all three members of the new commission. Many believed this provision gutted the new law, as Lowry appointed three very conservative men to the body. Railroads promptly brought suit challenging the existence of the new agency, and the state attorney general refused to represent the state in court, saying he agreed with the railroads that the Mississippi Railroad Commission was unconstitutional. Finally, a private attorney stepped in to defend the state. In 1885 the U.S. Supreme Court ruled the commission was legal.[24]

In revising railroad companies' rates, the Mississippi Railroad Commission was left open to one very serious charge: that it was regulating interstate commerce, which was the job of Congress. Indeed, the federal courts took a dim view of the commission setting railroad rates. In time, the Mississippi Railroad Commission ceased its efforts to revise railroad rates and concentrated on less controversial topics, such as whether a railroad should be required to build a new depot in a certain small town.

Few observers were impressed with the Mississippi Railroad Commission's record. Many town boosters and many lawyers and judges believed railroad regulation would discourage railroad expansion and retard municipal growth. Agrarians were disappointed in a railroad commission that seemed incapable of successfully regulating rates or even providing better schedules and more serviceable depots. State legislators were so unimpressed with the commission that, in 1887, they added penitentiary oversight to the commission's duties to give its members something to do.[25]

Why was the Railroad Commission, despite agrarians' high hopes, a failure? First, the commission could not be strong when so many other bodies had the power to overrule its decisions. These included state and federal courts, the federal Interstate Commerce Commission, and the Mississippi legislature. Under court rulings, the Railroad Commission could only act in matters that did not constitute interstate commerce—but most Mississippi railroad matters were at least partly interstate. Railroads were extremely complex corporations, and the commissioners did not have the staff to gather needed evidence and lacked expertise to study the minutiae of personnel and fuel costs, engineering, and seasonal variations in traffic. One historian who studied the Mississippi Railroad Commission concluded its accomplishments were largely nebulous.[26]

A very emotional issue was the movement for prohibition of alcoholic beverages. Black-majority counties generally opposed prohibition, while white-majority areas were more likely to favor it. Still, there were exceptions, and new political divisions appeared. Most agrarians favored prohibition, but some very important agrarian leaders—including Frank Burkitt—did not. Prohibition laws were a major objective of elite reformers, but many other members of the elites, including most planters, opposed new state liquor laws. In many cases, townspeople opposed prohibition while rural folk favored it. Religious divisions also appeared. Baptists and Methodists tended to favor prohibition, while Catholics, Episcopalians, Jews, and those who did not attend church were less likely to favor outlawing liquor sales.[27]

The start of Mississippi's prohibition movement came in 1879, when the Reverend John B. Gambrell fired the opening shot in what would be a long political fight. Writing in the *Baptist Record*, Gambrell called liquor the "matchless evil" and vowed to fight it. Within a matter of months he was advocating statutory prohibition of the sale of alcohol. Gambrell believed the forces of good were locked in deadly combat with the forces of evil, and he asked which should be prohibited, "the saloons or the church?" He asserted that if liquor sales were outlawed, crime would diminish, homes would be blissful, and the Sabbath would once again be sacred.[28]

Elite reformers continued a long-standing Mississippi tradition in pushing for statutory prohibition. Just as white citizens in antebellum Mississippi had feared an uncontrolled black population and chastised certain of their white neighbors for not being vigilant enough against the slaves, so now the elite reformers argued that widespread use of alcohol made black Mississippians brutish and criminal. In order to control the black underclass and whites who displayed weakness for alcohol, elite reformers sought to ban alcohol from the state. Some of those who favored prohibition did so after watching promising young people blight their own futures. The young man who drank heavily, according to one Mississippi reformer, "would snatch the shroud covering his dead mother's remains, and barter it for whiskey." While alcoholism was considered a man's problem, women suffered, too, from the indignity of being pointed out on the streets as "the drunkard's wife."[29]

Others were concerned that alcohol poisoned state politics. Journalists reported widespread drunkenness each election day and debauchery at the highest levels of state government. In 1882, when the sergeant-at-arms of the state Senate wrote to his hometown paper that "he had not yet seen a single member of the Mississippi Legislature drunk," the *Vicksburg Herald* responded that the officer "has our heartfelt sympathy for the severe affliction which has befallen him—the loss of his eyesight." Allegations of severe drinking problems were made against a number of prominent Mississippi officers, including Senator John Sharp Williams, Congressman Walter M. Denny, and Governor Anselm J. McLaurin. Williams and McLaurin admitted their weakness and asked voters' forgiveness. Many Mississippians envisioned a day when all public officials would be sober at all times.[30]

Reformers spread across the state organizing prohibition clubs. A farmwife noted in her diary in 1889, "Miss Belle Kearney from near Jackson organized a young women's temperance union last night." Frances Willard, national leader of the Woman's Christian Temperance Union (WCTU), came to Mississippi and helped organize chapters of her organization, and soon there were WCTU groups in sixty counties. Among African Americans, many church leaders started prohibition groups among their congregations. Statewide, a biracial Prohibition Convention met annually, and a Prohibition State Executive Committee helped provide leadership throughout the year. Several newspapers aided the temperance cause, including the WCTU's *Mississippi White Ribbon*, the *Clinton Sword and Shield*, and the *Brookhaven Leader*. Though initially led by males, the state prohibition movement was increasingly directed by women. Some men feared the prohibition movement was the beginning of a drive for woman suffrage. Many WCTU leaders spoke of women's rights, especially a woman's right to be free of the domination of a drunken, tyrannical husband.[31]

Occasionally prohibition advocates grew impatient and turned to vigilante action. Lillie Stokes wrote her brother in 1891 that "the Braininger house in Kirksville was burned down last Tuesday night, and they lost nearly everything they had. It was of course set on fire, and no one seems to be sorry for them." She added that the Brainingers "have been threatened so often for selling whiskey they might have expected it." In 1890 prohibitionists of Calhoun County marched on a local still and destroyed it. The *Batesville Blade* of February 25, 1881, reported that "some women crusaders made a raid on the liquor saloons of Grenada recently."[32]

In the early 1880s state prohibition leaders declared themselves ready to push for major new legislation. The so-called local option bill would give citizens of a county the power to vote their county dry. To support their cause, prohibitionists offered statements from the American Medical Association that alcohol was no longer considered a medicine but a poison. They produced the statement of a judge from a dry county that after the legislature had outlawed liquor there, his criminal docket had shrunk considerably. Those who opposed the law argued that it was impossible to legislate morals. They also pointed out that much of the funding for education came from taxes and fees paid by liquor dealers. The wet advocates charged the prohibitionists with bringing dangerous division to the Democratic Party. They also warned that white supremacy was at stake, since in local option elections both sides would try to recruit black voters.

Prohibitionists succeeded in electing enough legislators in 1885 to pass a strong local option law the following year. Under this law, voters could petition for a local option election, giving them the option of prohibiting the sale of alcoholic beverages in their county. To safeguard counties from constant political agitation, such elections could be held no more frequently than once every two years. To lessen dangerous divisions within the Democratic Party, local option elections could not be held within two months of any national, state, or county regular election. Some prohibitionists sought to have the law declare that once a county went dry, it could never go back to allow the sale of alcoholic beverages. Lawmakers, however, thought it fairer to give the voters complete choice in the matter. Many prohibitionists were sorely disappointed with the law, since it could make areas currently dry to go wet. For example, small towns that were currently dry (having had a state law passed to that effect) could be forced to go wet if the entire county chose to defeat prohibition.[33]

Some of the most exciting elections in late-nineteenth-century Mississippi did not involve candidates but were local option elections deciding the future of liquor in a given county. In many areas, it was the closest thing Mississippi had to a two-party system: the wets versus the drys. Each side raised large amounts of money, organized at the precinct level, held mass meetings, printed posters, and carried on debates in newspapers. Methodist bishop Charles B. Galloway urged prohibition supporters not to rush into local option elections but first to organize carefully. Galloway published the *Handbook of Prohibition*, telling local dry leaders to build up their clubs, cultivate black citizens, and avoid in the local option campaigns all political issues except prohibition.

Feelings ran high in these campaigns. Bloodshed occurred in the Hinds County local option election of 1886. Here the Gambrell family led the dry forces, while the most prominent leader of the wets was Jones S. Hamilton, a penitentiary lessee, state senator, and planter. Most newspapers in Hinds County favored the wets, while several religious papers, most notably the Gambrell family's *Sword and Shield*, championed prohibition. The wet forces encouraged black citizens to participate in the election, while the *Sword and Shield* editors charged that Hamilton and others gave gifts of liquor to black voters as bribes to win their votes. On Election Day, Jackson voted with the wets, but the larger number of rural voters put Hinds County in the dry column.[34]

The Hinds County local option election involved violent rhetoric and some outright violence. Several wets accosted Dr. G. W. Luster on his way home from a prohibition precinct rally. They stabbed him, but he managed to shoot and kill two of his assailants. Luster was not charged in the incident. Meanwhile, in the pages of *Sword and Shield*, Roderick Gambrell fanned passions that were already hot. He accused the antiprohibition leader Hamilton of having defrauded the state of $80,000 while he leased convicts and also of fraudulently padding his own vote totals when he had been elected state senator. Under the moral code of the time, Hamilton was almost sure to try to vindicate his honor.

One May evening shortly after the local option election, citizens found the body of Roderick Gambrell lying in a pool of blood on a bridge in the city of Jackson. Investigators found that Hamilton had wounds in the stomach and arm, and in fact he admitted killing Gambrell, though he claimed Gambrell was the instigator. A majority of the state's newspapers viewed the young editor as a martyr, although a few wet papers believed Hamilton's claim that Gambrell was the aggressor. One of Hamilton's employees admitted Hamilton had been shadowing Gambrell for some time. Hamilton's attorneys managed to get a change of venue to Rankin County, and the ensuing trial lasted forty-eight days. The crucial moment came when the judge ruled that Hamilton and his associates must be tried separately, and thus prosecutors had a difficult time proving a conspiracy to murder. Since Hamilton and his friends were the only eyewitnesses, the jury returned a verdict of not guilty, unable to say beyond a reasonable doubt that Gambrell had not fired the first shot.[35]

Other violence stemmed from the Gambrell killing. Two Winona editors, one a wet and the other a dry, disagreed over Hamilton's guilt and denounced each other. When they met on the street, a shoot-out ensued. One editor was shot and seriously wounded, while the other escaped unharmed. The *New Orleans Picayune* correspondent noted that, given the number of bullets that were flying, the shoot-out was "the poorest piece of marksmanship on record." In Jackson, John H. Martin used the pages of his *New Mississippian* to denounce Hamilton repeatedly as a murderer. Hamilton's friend Wirt Adams took offense. When Adams and Martin met on the street, they shot and killed each other. Thus the list of casualties related directly or indirectly to the 1886 Hinds local option election included five killed and three seriously wounded. Among these casualties were some of the state's most prominent citizens, including three newspaper editors, a state senator, and a former Confederate general and railroad executive.[36]

In many counties, black voters assumed an importance they had not had since Reconstruction. In Clay County, the antiprohibition forces recruited hundreds of black voters, and WCTU leaders noted with disgust that these black voters "surged like a swollen stream to the polls." In Grenada, the dry forces solicited and received a statement from black leader Frederick Douglass, asking Grenada's black voters to aid, "by voice, vote, and co-operation, the grand Prohibition movement now happily inaugurated in Mississippi." Church bells rang constantly on Election Day in Grenada County, but in Grenada County, as in Clay County, the wets won. Of the thirty-two counties that held local option elections in the first months under the law, exactly half voted themselves dry.[37]

After several years of local option elections, prohibition leaders began to divide on future tactics. Many Methodist leaders, like Galloway, believed the local option system was a sound one, and he urged continued efforts to win new counties for the dry cause. He also called for increasing attention to getting the prohibition laws successfully enforced, or else the wets would be proved right in their assertion that "prohibition did not prohibit." Many WCTU leaders, however, and many Baptist ministers argued that the local option system was a failure. They claimed that many areas, including populous Adams and Warren counties, would never vote themselves dry, especially because of the wets' manipulation of black voters. Events strengthened the hands of Galloway's critics. One could hardly claim the local option system was a success after Hinds, Lauderdale, and Lowndes counties returned to the wet column after having earlier voted themselves dry.[38]

For an increasing number of prohibition leaders, one or both of two actions must be taken. First, they believed, black voting in Mississippi must be eliminated, so black votes could not be used to win local option elections for the wet forces. Second, the state should simply prohibit the sale of alcoholic beverages in all counties. The calling of the state constitutional convention offered drys a chance to win both of their goals. Prohibition leaders worked hard on behalf of dry candidates for delegate. At the constitutional convention, the dry forces did help secure new voting procedures that nearly eliminated black voting, but the convention declined to approve a system of statewide prohibition. Not until early in the twentieth century would the legislature give serious consideration to such a plan.[39]

Penitentiary reform was another emotional issue in late-nineteenth-century Mississippi. The state's convict leasing system arose after the Civil War for two reasons. One was that the penitentiary had been destroyed in the war. Building an adequate penitentiary would be expensive, and the state was short of funds. Leasing the prisoners to private individuals or companies would actually raise money for the state. Other reasons included the uneasiness felt by many white Mississippians at emancipation and their fear that freedom would lead to crime, violence, and an undisciplined workforce. Black Mississippians who got into trouble with the law would be returned to a system like slavery, working in chains, if necessary, and under the watchful eye of armed guards. Moreover, many white Mississippians regularly perceived a labor shortage in the state, and the convict lease system served as a visible reminder to black Mississippians that labor could be given freely or taken by force. Most Mississippi convicts were black, and nearly all of those performing hard labor were black. Even the theft of a young pig or a crime as mild as vagrancy could lead to hard labor under the convict lease system. According to noted southern author George Washington Cable, writing in the late nineteenth century, Mississippi had the worst prison system in the nation. While most southern states leased their convicts, Mississippi went a step farther and allowed the lessees to sublease the convicts. Thus the state never knew where all its convicts were, and the lessees and sublessees had total control over the hapless prisoners.[40]

During the lease period of Jones S. Hamilton and his associates, the death rate among the prisoners was 8.8 percent per year. This compared with an antebellum prison death rate in the state of 2.5 percent. Mississippi's escape rate for prisoners during the tumultuous Civil War period was 2.5 percent, but under Hamilton and his colleagues it reached 13 percent. Governor Robert Lowry reported in 1885 that fully one-quarter of Mississippi's prisoners had died or escaped during the past year. With an almost unlimited supply of potential convicts, the lessees allowed a high rate of deaths and escapes and simply had the state send more prisoners. Northern states' prisons typically had a death rate of about 1.5 percent per year, while southern states, with their convict lease systems, had a death rate averaging 4 percent. Mississippi's convict death rate was typically 8 percent, and it sometimes reached 15 percent per year.[41]

Several news stories of the 1880s turned public opinion against convict leasing. Editors Frank Burkitt and Roderick Gambrell broke the story of how Hamilton, Hoskins, and Company (lessee of the state's prisoners) fell behind nearly $80,000 in their payments to the state. The lessees then devised a plan to sublease the convicts to the Gulf and Ship Island Railroad for construction work, and they secured a certificate from state attorney general Thomas Catchings to the effect that they owed no money to the state. Burkitt charged there was a corrupt conspiracy between the executive branch of the state government and the dishonest lessees. Many state residents began to believe the editors' allegations of corruption in high places. Another key news story broke when, on February 18, 1884, lessees sent prisoners from a Delta plantation to the state penitentiary in Jackson. The prisoners had to transfer from steamboat to train at Vicksburg, and townspeople were horrified at what they saw. The prisoners showed unmistakable signs of malnutrition, disease, frostbite, and beatings. City authorities refused to let the lessees walk the prisoners through town and provided a covered wagon to shield citizens from the terrible sight.[42]

A legislative investigation followed the 1884 Vicksburg incident. In 1886 a committee of the legislature reported that the sublease system had led to "a state of servitude worse than slavery." Even slaveholders had a motive to keep their workers strong and healthy. Convict lessees' goal was to reduce expenses—for food, shelter, and medical care. The committee noted the system had produced "an epidemic death rate without the epidemic."[43]

Reforms followed. In 1886 the legislature repealed the Pig Law, which had allowed imprisonment at hard labor for minor instances of theft. The number of convicts had quickly quadrupled after passage of the Pig Law in 1876 and was cut in half after its repeal. To prevent the worst abuse of prisoners, state lawmakers prohibited lessees from subleasing state prisoners. The legislature created a board of control to oversee penitentiary affairs beginning in 1887. From time to time, board members visited convict camps, and if conditions were especially bad, they would order the return of the prisoners to direct state custody. With the cancellation of subleases and creation of a board of control, the death rate declined sharply, from 15 percent per year in 1887 to 3 percent in 1890.[44]

Further reform came with the state's constitutional convention of 1890, where delegates enacted a section declaring the state would lease no prisoners after 1894. Prisoners would work instead on state-owned prison farms or on other state projects. Mississippi was the first southern state to abolish convict leasing. Alabama's system flourished until 1927, while North Carolina's system was not completely dismantled until 1933. Unfortunately, the legislature was slow to enable the changes it had mandated. Land was not purchased for the new prison farms until 1894, and land for the large Parchman farm was not purchased until 1901. It would be a number of years before the prison farms were ready to hold all the state's prisoners.[45]

As the state began to operate its prison farms, the escape rate dropped drastically, but the death rate fell less impressively. One problem was that the state began to depend on the profits of convict labor, and these profits could be perpetuated only by keeping costs low. As the *Jackson Weekly Clarion* editor pointed out in 1898, "Convicts can be made a source of revenue, instead of a constantly increasing financial weight for the taxpayer to carry." Governor Stone reported the cost of raising crops at the state's prison farms in 1896 was $95,000, while the crops produced $155,000 in revenue. Thus, by the beginning of the twentieth century, Mississippi had stopped the barbaric practice of granting private individuals complete dominion over state convicts, yet convicts were still seen as a source of income. The death rate no longer would reach occasional highs of 15 percent per year, but it was still above that of other southern states and far above that of northern states.[46]

Reform of the convict lease system was one issue on which agrarians and elite reformers could unite, though they favored reform for different reasons. Elite reformers opposed the convict lease system because it was barbaric—they believed government functions like reform of prisoners should be conducted in a more rational way. Reformers saw that the convict lease system was very profitable for the lessees, and they mused that these profits more properly belonged to the state. Agrarians favored an end to convict leasing for two reasons. First, a convict lease was a special privilege granted to a small group of men. Also, agrarians tended to have a working-class ideology and believed an end to the convict lease system would make more working-class jobs available in the private sector, as private citizens began doing the labor convicts had been performing but under improved conditions. The clamor for penitentiary reform was one of several factors leading to the 1890 constitutional convention, the subject of the following chapter.[47]

CHAPTER SEVEN

THE MISSISSIPPI CONSTITUTION OF 1890 AND POLITICAL DISSENT

One issue on which agrarians and elite reformers could agree was black disfranchisement. White agrarians sought it because each time they raised a tough issue—such as crop lien law reform—their opponents said the issue endangered white supremacy and urged Democrats to unite behind the status quo. If black voting could be eliminated, whites could tackle difficult issues without any claims being made that white political supremacy was threatened. Elite reformers favored disfranchisement because they favored a rational and scientific government chosen by an educated and tax-paying electorate. Elite reformers believed a great many black citizens—and some whites—were drunken, criminal, depraved, and ignorant. By limiting voting to intelligent taxpayers, elite reformers believed government would be in better hands. Both elite reformers and agrarians generally favored prohibition and recognized that in local option elections, the wet forces had used black voters to defeat prohibition. Agrarians and elite reformers favored the calling of a convention to write a new state constitution that would effectively disfranchise black citizens.[1]

Agrarians had another reason for seeking a constitutional convention. The farmers' fondest political goals were blocked by conservative legislators from black-majority counties. Agrarians hoped the constitutional convention would award a number of new seats to white-majority counties, thus increasing the agrarians' power. If legislative seats were to be apportioned based on the number of active voters in each county, then it was true that the black counties held more seats than they should have. If legislative seats were to be apportioned based on the number of citizens in each county, whether they were voters or not, then the state of Mississippi would undoubtedly be dominated by the black-majority counties for many years to come. Agrarians believed in the justice of their cause, and some Delta lawmakers hinted they would support increased power for the white counties as an added insurance of white supremacy.[2]

The drive for a constitutional convention was not, of course, a drive to secure white political supremacy in the state. Whites already enjoyed political supremacy and had since at least 1875. In the 1888 presidential election, nearly every black voter who participated voted for Benjamin Harrison, but Grover Cleveland defeated Harrison in Mississippi by a vote of 85,000 to 30,000. Of the 160 members in the 1890 legislature, only 6 were black, and even these black members had been elected with the support of white voters. Yet every time a close political battle threatened in any Mississippi county, both sides were tempted to recruit black voters to tip the balance. Once black voters had been recruited for one side, the other side would turn to violence or fraud to negate the black vote.[3]

In the 1881 elections, for example, Democrats triumphed over a biracial Independent movement. The triumph came in large part because of Democrats' willingness to threaten or assault black voters and to stuff ballot boxes with Democratic ballots. Few Democratic newspapers were jubilant over their party's victory. The *Greenville Times* published a letter by a Democratic participant in this election who stated, "We have won, but I am disgusted, and never again will I make another such fight." Another letter came from a local attorney, a Democrat who wrote that "for the first time I have lost the faith, and feel like leaving the State of my boyhood's home." With Democrats feeling remorse after winning a major victory and with whites soon perpetrating frauds on each other in elections that did not involve black voters, many politically minded Mississippians believed the time had come for change.[4]

Solomon S. Calhoon, who chaired the constitutional convention of 1890, wrote an article in 1902 explaining the reasons for calling the convention. Calhoon stressed his colleagues' desire to replace the constitution of 1868, framed during Reconstruction by a "nondescript body composed of negroes, mulattos, and brazen adventurers of the white race from the States recently in arms against us, who came here for plunder." Calhoon argued that under this document, the state was governed for a time by "recently emancipated slaves, led by a set of vultures whom it would be flattery to denominate as disgusting, men without manhood enough to appreciate their own shame." Calhoon acknowledged that "there was revolution" in 1875 and that in 1890, the state's white citizens wanted to complete the revolution by discarding the old Reconstruction-era constitution. Calhoon admitted that the 1868 document itself "strangely enough, was not, as a whole, a bad constitution." Given its history, however, the 1868 constitution was doomed. Calhoon's explanation is not satisfying, however, because it does not explain why in 1890 the state's political leadership decided to produce a new constitution. Why had the movement not come in 1878, as Democrats consolidated their control? Why did it not come later, in 1903, as a new generation of leaders took control of the state?[5]

Several events of the late 1880s led whites to believe white supremacy in the state was not quite complete. In 1886 ten black residents of Carroll County had the temerity to accuse a white citizen of attempted murder and were willing to identify the man in court. This assault on white supremacy was countered by a white mob that opened fire on the ten in the Carroll County courtroom. Many citizens believed white supremacy could be made secure without such violent outbursts. The Leflore County massacre came in 1889. It was sparked by black residents demonstrating economic independence and allegedly stockpiling arms. In 1889 a black convention in Jackson asked the Democrats for a fusion slate for state offices, one that would include some black Republican candidates. When the Democrats refused, the state's Republicans brought out a Republican slate of officers for the first time in twenty-two years. This slate was headed by white Republican James R. Chalmers, former Confederate general and former member of Congress. Although the Republicans abandoned their campaign after Democrats threatened violence, once again many white residents believed the state should be protected from the threat of Republican revivals and widespread black voting. In 1890 Congress moved to consider the Lodge Election Bill, which called for federal supervision of federal elections. Democrats feared U.S. soldiers soon would be on duty in Mississippi elections, protecting black Republican voters. The Lodge Bill passed the U.S. House of Representatives, increasing the feeling that the state of Mississippi should take action to guarantee perpetual Democratic hegemony and white political supremacy.[6]

Agrarians pushed hard to call a constitutional convention. In 1886 Frank Burkitt introduced a bill calling for a referendum on a constitutional convention; his bill passed only in the House of Representatives. In 1888 a call for a convention passed both houses, but Governor Robert Lowry vetoed it. "Quiet reigns throughout our borders," Lowry argued, so "why agitate and convulse the country?" The Farmers' Alliance continued to push for a convention, and in the fall of 1889 the cause won an unexpected convert when U.S. senator James Z. George also began calling for a new state constitution. The fairly conservative senator may have jumped on the bandwagon to prevent agrarian radicals from dominating the proposed convention. As it was, few people would have as great a role in shaping the convention's actions as George, who served as a delegate and Franchise Committee chair. George cited as his chief motivation the pending Lodge Bill. The 1890 legislature passed the convention bill, and newly inaugurated governor John M. Stone signed it.[7]

The convention bill called for delegate elections in July 1890, with the same number and apportionment of delegates as in the state House of Representatives. State voters would also elect fourteen at-large delegates. Apparently, white county delegates believed the at-large delegates would be mostly from white-majority counties, to prevent unfair domination of the convention by the black-majority counties. The state executive committee of the Democratic Party had other ideas, however, and nominated a slate with eleven of the fourteen hailing from black-majority counties.[8]

Each Democratic county executive committee decided on its own how party nominations for delegate should be handled, and thus some Democratic nominees for delegate were selected by county conventions, while others were chosen in county primaries. As might be expected under a one-party system, the delegate elections strained the "big tent" Democratic Party. In a number of areas, the Farmers' Alliance was very active in the selection of Democratic nominees for delegates and met the sharp opposition of more conservative Democrats. In Yalobusha and Lauderdale counties, these divisions proved especially hard to heal. In Yalobusha County, the voters on general Election Day could choose between a regular Democratic slate and a Farmers' Alliance slate. In Lauderdale County, the Farmers' Alliance and labor groups nominated one ticket while conservative Democrats nominated another. At a "peace meeting" in Lauderdale, however, each side agreed to drop one of their two nominees, and the county would thus be represented by radical agrarian John A. Bailey and the extremely conservative insurance executive H. M. Street.[9]

Black and white Republicans were as active as they dared to be in these 1890 delegate elections. Black Republicans in the summer of 1890 held a mass convention in Jackson, declaring their wish to be included in the drafting of the new constitution. They expressed confidence that if the two races worked together, the constitution would prove acceptable to both. The editor of the *Jackson New Mississippian*, however, urged black Mississippians to abandon their interest in the coming convention and warned that to fail to do so would lead to bloodshed. Similarly, black citizens of Rankin County held a mass meeting to consider nominating candidates for delegates, but they first asked the Democratic nominees for delegates to address them. The two Democrats refused to do this, instead advising black Mississippians to put their trust in the Democratic Party. The *Brandon Republican*, with its Republican editor, attacked the county's Democratic nominees, but the Rankin Republicans made no nominations themselves.[10]

In Adams County, with its large black majority, black Republicans prepared to nominate one of their local leaders, George F. Bowles, to serve as a delegate. Democrats asked the Republicans to withdraw Bowles's name, and Bowles made a speech to the effect that Republicans could trust Democrats to frame a just constitution. Thus on election day, Adams County voters could vote for only the Democratic nominees. In Jasper County, longtime white Republican F. M. B. "Marsh" Cook offered his candidacy for delegate. Democrats warned Cook, a leader of the Farmers' Alliance, to abandon his campaign, but he refused and was assassinated on a lonely road before the election. Democratic newspapers claimed Cook was an obnoxious Republican who was odious even to his own family and who had stirred up racial strife in the county. Yet the local Farmers' Alliance chapter declared their fallen brother was well known for "speaking words of prudence, wisdom, and calmness."[11]

The delegate elections resulted in an overwhelming victory for the Democratic Party. Although the convention would have three members who considered themselves Republicans and one delegate who had moved freely between the Democratic and Republican parties over the years, in fact the Republicans had nothing to celebrate. Republican delegates included former governor James Lusk Alcorn, noted Reconstruction-era politician Horatio F. Simrall, and Mound Bayou founder Isaiah T. Montgomery. Montgomery's fellow delegate from Bolivar County was George P. Melchoir, who had regularly supported state and county Republicans in the 1880s but who called himself a Democrat on the convention roster. Coahoma Democrats nominated Alcorn because they respected him as a lawyer and planter and Confederate veteran and because he did not favor mass black voting. Simrall was included among the Democratic nominees of Warren County primarily because he was a respected leader of the Farmers' Alliance. The Montgomery-Melchoir ticket's credentials were briefly challenged at the convention, not because of its Republican roots but because the powerful Walter Sillers faction of Delta politicians opposed the slate, while the rival Charles Scott faction of Democrats supported it.[12]

Thus the convention would have three or four Republican members who were completely acceptable to their Democratic neighbors. The convention would also include two Farmers' Alliance Independents from Yalobusha County who defeated their Democratic rivals, although one of these called himself a Democrat on the convention's roster. The closest thing to a real anti-Democrat in the convention was John E. Gore, Webster County's delegate who called himself a Greenbacker and who defeated a Democrat in the delegate elections. Yet the Greenback Party was defunct in every corner of the nation save Webster County. Agrarian Independents went down to defeat in delegate elections in Alcorn, Jones, Marion, and Warren counties, among others. If there was a single Republican running on a Republican ticket and opposing the Democrats in this 1890 election, he has escaped detection after a diligent search. Marsh Cook's death sent a message to other Republicans that actively opposing the Democratic nominees could prove fatal.

All of the 134 delegates, except for Isaiah T. Montgomery, were white, and a change of two votes on election day would have denied him his election. Ninety-two of the 134 delegates were Confederate veterans. According to the convention roster, the delegates included fifty-two lawyers, forty-two farmers, and seven planters. This breakdown by occupation boded ill for agrarians, as did the breakdown by county. Eighty-nine of the delegates hailed from black-majority counties and only forty-five from white-majority counties. These numbers would make it exceedingly difficult for the white county delegates to demand a reapportionment in their favor.[13]

Among the delegates were former congressmen W. S. Featherston and Wiley P. Harris and future members of Congress Walter M. Denny, William F. Love, and Frank A. McLain. Also serving were incumbent U.S. senator James Z. George and future governor and U.S. senator Anselm J. McLaurin. Only about forty-four of the 134 delegates were reliably agrarian on the convention's roll-call votes. Among these were agrarian editor Frank Burkitt; John E. Gore, the Greenbacker; and the two Independents from Yalobusha County. At least fourteen members of the constitutional convention would, in two years' time, abandon the Democratic Party and build up the agrarian People's Party.[14]

The first order of business for the convention was selection of a presiding officer. Agrarians nominated Farmers' Alliance president Robert C. Patty. Patty did not attract widespread criticism since he was not a radical but was a substantial planter of Noxubee County. He came within one vote of being elected, losing to Hinds County lawyer Solomon S. Calhoon. In a show of goodwill, Patty moved that Calhoon's election be made unanimous, and for his part Calhoon said he would have been glad to see Patty serve. Calhoon delivered an opening address, reminding the delegates why they were there and setting the tone for the convention. He began by pointing out the "unfortunate fact" that in Mississippi, "two distinct and opposite types of mankind" lived together. It was only natural each of the two races should seek to have the strongest political voice, Calhoon acknowledged. Delegates must recognize, however, that in the history of the world, the rule of dark-skinned races had always meant "economic and moral ruin," while rule of whites had meant "prosperity and happiness." Thus, Calhoon said, delegates must ensure that the dominant race continued to dominate and bring good government and economic success to the state. Calhoon addressed no other topic in his lengthy address.[15]

In organizing the convention into committees, it was clear the Committee on Elective Franchise, Apportionment, and Elections was to be the premier committee. It was instructed to meet in the Senate chamber of the state capitol (while the convention itself met each day in the House of Representatives chamber). Alone among the committees it was given its own staff (a clerk, page, and porter) and priority in all print jobs so its important work would not be delayed. More than half of the committee's membership came from the black-majority counties, but overall its membership was varied, including conservatives, agrarians, and Republicans.

Virtually none of the 134 delegates favored mass voting or a continuance of the status quo. Isaiah T. Montgomery believed voters should meet a county residency requirement of one year, pay a poll tax, and be sufficiently literate to make out their ballot. Another Republican delegate, Horatio F. Simrall, believed a strict residency requirement of one year in the precinct would be the most important tool of black disfranchisement. He believed this rule would disfranchise many black voters because of "the disposition of young Negroes ... to change their homes and precincts every year." Agrarian spokesman Frank Burkitt was willing to consider a number of forms of disfranchisement but felt strongly there must be no property requirement for voting or holding office. Delegate A. J. Paxton, a Washington County planter, would couple disfranchisement with a provision that "no negro, or person having as much as one-eighth negro blood, shall hold office in the state." Delegate R. H. Taylor of Panola County would add to the number of white voters by giving the right to vote to those males aged eighteen to twenty-one who were literate and who owned (or whose parents owned) $500 worth of property. Taylor believed a large majority of the young persons who could meet this requirement would be white.[16]

Thinking along the same lines as Taylor was delegate John W. Fewell, an attorney who proposed to enfranchise any woman who owned (or whose husband owned) $300 in real estate. He intended this as a way of increasing the white vote and not so much an advancement of women's rights. Since he and others believed women must be protected from the tumult of Mississippi elections, Fewell proposed that a woman's ballot would be cast by a male voter who had her written authority to cast her vote.[17]

With Fewell's proposal, Mississippi became the first state in the South to consider woman suffrage. Public opinion, as reflected in the state's newspaper columns, was not in step with the proposal. Some editors chided Fewell for seeking to use women to protect white men from the danger of black domination. Others worried that, under these proposals, "propertied black women would be permitted to vote while the wives of the state's poor white men would not." For many newspapers, the proposal was simply a source of levity. The *Choctaw Plaindealer* reported that "John W. Fewell is trying to fix up a plan for the women to wear the breeches." The Franchise Committee, however, warmly received the proposal. Writing a report for his hometown paper, delegate T. L. Hannah noted the woman suffrage proposal "has a strong support and I fear will pass." Hannah reported the committee had approved a plan granting women the right to vote if they owned $400 worth of property in their own right and could read and write. There had been only one dissenting vote.[18]

Ultimately, the Franchise Committee moved away from the woman suffrage proposal and focused on alternative plans instead. At the urging of conservative delegates from black-majority counties, the committee called for a poll tax to be paid by would-be voters and the administering of a literacy test. To agrarians who pointed out that many intelligent white farmers could not read and write, the committee responded with the "understanding test" proposed by Senator George and others. The understanding test was a loophole designed to let illiterate white citizens vote. Under the understanding test, illiterate voters who could explain a section of the state constitution—to the satisfaction of the voting registrar—when it was read to them could be placed on the voter rolls. All these proposed voter qualifications were designed to disfranchise black voters. There was one nagging question in delegates' minds, however. Would the proposed suffrage requirements pass federal muster? The Fifteenth Amendment said no state could deny the right to vote on the basis of race. The Fourteenth Amendment declared that if any state denied the right to vote to any group of adult males (except insurrectionists or criminals), the state's congressional representation would be proportionally reduced. Moreover, the Mississippi Readmission Act of 1870 stated Mississippi must not limit the suffrage of adult males, except perhaps by a residency requirement.[19]

Convention president Solomon S. Calhoon appointed committees to examine such federal questions. In due time a committee chaired by Wiley P. Harris reported that the proposed suffrage rules were not in danger of invalidation by the

Isaiah T. Montgomery believed the Constitution of 1890 embodied a compromise between the black and white races. He urged white Mississippians to accept compromise, or else the state's black citizens would have to "press forward to the impending conflict."

U.S. Supreme Court. They did not conflict with the Fifteenth Amendment because the new rules applied to blacks and whites alike. As for the Mississippi Readmission Act, it was unconstitutional, since northern and western states were not subjected to such limitations. Harris's committee concluded that "there can hardly be a conception of unequal States in the Union," and therefore Mississippi could not be subjected to suffrage requirements not placed on the other states. While the committee admitted that Congress at one time had possessed extraordinary power over the defeated southern states, it concluded that such powers had ended when the southern states were readmitted to full membership in the Union. Another ad hoc committee also addressed federal questions. By a vote of eight to one this committee declared Congress should repeal the Fifteenth Amendment, sending the question to the states for ratification. Members argued that only white persons could ensure honest and competent government. The committee even proclaimed that Mississippi stood ready to accept a reduction in its congressional representation, since it would be reducing the number of voters.[20]

Black delegate Isaiah T. Montgomery addressed the delegates and explained that the new constitution offered a chance for compromise between Mississippi's two races. More than 100,000 black voters would give up the franchise in exchange for whites' promises of fair treatment. He said that black Mississippians would rejoice if whites accepted this compromise, while if whites rejected it then black citizens would "gather their armor closer about them and press forward to the impending conflict." Addressing his black constituency directly, Montgomery assured them that delegates "have not taken away your high privilege," the right to vote, "but only lifted it to a higher plane." Montgomery's hope was that after many black voters were disfranchised, "the two great races shall peaceably travel side by side, each mutually assisting the other mount higher and higher on the scale of human progress."[21]

In supporting the plan presented by the Franchise Committee, including the poll tax and understanding test, Montgomery predicted the plan would disfranchise about 123,000 black voters. He turned to his fellow delegates and said dramatically, "[I] press the fated question home to your conscience and to your hearts—'What answer?'" Montgomery asked his fellow delegates, "Is our sacrifice accepted? Shall the great question be settled?"[22]

For many authors writing since 1890, Montgomery has been a traitor to his race, enjoying a certain amount of wealth and power himself and neglecting the great mass of black Mississippians. Yet he was in step with the prevailing "accommodationist" ideas espoused by many black leaders of the time. He thought that to press for full political rights at this time would be suicidal. Montgomery believed that in the near future, black southerners should devote themselves to education and hard work, aiming to acquire job skills or a farm of their own. After blacks elevated themselves, the accommodationists believed, the better class of whites would come to their aid, agreeing that educated and tax-paying citizens should vote regardless of their race. Such accommodationists were overly optimistic about the goodwill of white elites, but they were quite correct in recognizing that to confront the prevailing tide in a direct fashion would be to no avail and might lead to renewed racial violence.[23]

In its final form, the suffrage proposal before the convention would limit suffrage in seven new ways. (1) Voters must pay a poll tax of at least $2 for at least two years prior to the election and must prove they had paid this tax. (2) Voters must demonstrate literacy or else pass an understanding test administered by a local official. (3) Voters must be literate enough to cope with the new Australian ballot (which listed the candidates of all parties) and to mark the names for whom they wished to vote. (4) Voters must have resided in Mississippi for two years and in their town or rural precinct for one year. (5) Voters must never have been convicted of any of nine named crimes, including theft, arson, and bigamy. (6) No voter could vote in a given election unless he had been registered at least four months prior to the election. (7) Prior to the 1892 election, all voters in the state would be dropped from the rolls, and a completely new voter registration would be held. Thus the new rules applied to all voters, not just those who wished to register after 1892.

According to the suffrage plan's backers, black citizens were more likely to fail to pay the poll tax, more likely to fail the literacy test or be unable to mark their ballots properly, more likely to move from precinct to precinct, and more likely to have been convicted of theft or bigamy. Voting registrars could give white illiterates an easy understanding test, while refusing to pass intelligent black applicants who took the test. Still, conservative leaders like Calhoon were undoubtedly aware that many poorer white men would also decline to pay the poll tax, also moved regularly, and were so uneducated they either would fail to mark the ballot properly or else would decline to undergo the humiliation of an understanding test. The plan favored the "courthouse cliques," since voters must pay the poll tax for two years prior to the election and must register four months before the election. In other words, voters must take steps to register well before the excitement of the campaign began. Those who had traditionally been politically active might be willing to register early, but new converts won in the excitement of an agrarian campaign might discover it was too late to register.

The Franchise Committee's report also included two unusual proposals that were meant to be the final bulwarks of white supremacy. First, the committee provided an electoral college system for choosing the governor and other state officers. The committee intended that the white counties would dominate this electoral college, and if no gubernatorial candidate received an electoral college majority, the legislature would elect the governor. Also, the committee's plan declared that the legislature could give the governor the power to appoint the officers of any county. Thus if black voters somehow gained a majority in a given county, the legislature could authorize the governor to choose that county's officers—and presumably the governor would choose white Democrats. The Franchise Committee's report generally satisfied the membership of the convention. Some conservatives attacked the plan because too many ignorant and propertyless whites were still permitted to vote, and some agrarians protested that too many whites were disfranchised, but in the end the committee's plan won acceptance.[24]

The other potentially divisive plan before the convention was the proposal to reapportion the legislature. A chief motivation of white-majority counties in supporting the idea of a constitutional convention had been their desire to reduce the dominance of the black-majority counties in the legislature. On the surface, such plans were doomed from the start. The apportionment of the constitutional convention was based on that of the state House of Representatives, with fourteen additional members chosen from the state at-large. The state House of Representatives was very strongly dominated by the black counties, and, as we have seen, eleven of the fourteen at-large delegates were from black counties. Thus, unless the black-majority counties voluntarily gave up some of their power, white-majority counties could not expect to make progress toward reapportionment. Yet there was a chance the delegates from the black-majority counties would voluntarily give up power. Some delegates from the black counties admitted that the white counties deserved a larger representation given their large numbers of active voters. The Franchise Committee announced plans to add thirteen new seats to the state House of Representatives, many of them to be given to the white counties. Delegate William G. Yerger from Washington County argued that the new seats from the white counties would be an "added bulwark of safety" for white supremacy. Senator George made the same case, pointing out that while Congress might pass the Lodge Election Bill and the Supreme Court might overturn the understanding test, everyone agreed Mississippi had unlimited power to apportion itself. The new seats could ensure that the white voters always selected a majority of the legislators.[25]

If we compare the state House of Representatives elected in 1885 to the one elected in 1895, we can see some of the effects of reapportionment: in 1885 forty-two members were from white majority counties, and seventy-eight were from black-majority counties; in 1895 fifty-one members were from white-majority counties, and eighty-two were from black-majority counties. Thus white-majority counties held 35 percent of the seats in the 1886 legislature and 38 percent of the seats in the 1896 legislature. This was hardly the gain white county delegates had hoped for.[26]

One of the most important actions of the convention was putting the details of apportionment into the constitution itself. While the new constitution said that the legislature could take its own decennial census and reapportion after each, the legislature declined to take advantage of this power. Even if the legislature had chosen to reapportion, another provision of the new constitution divided the state's counties into three districts (northeast, southeast, and west) and said no section would ever have more than forty-four members of the House of Representatives. While this may have been intended as another "bulwark of safety" for white supremacy (so that the heavily black western counties would not dominate the legislature), as it turned out, this provision hurt the white-majority counties a great deal. By the early twentieth century, the fastest-growing section of the state by far was the southeast, but short of a constitutional amendment, there was no way to give these predominantly white counties their fair share of legislators.[27]

If agrarians were disappointed with the reapportionment provisions of the constitution, they were even more displeased by the defeat of their elective judiciary proposal. Farmers believed that judges sided with railroads, bankers, and merchants, and they wanted to return to the antebellum system where Mississippi voters had elected judges. On a number of close votes, however, delegates voted down the elective judiciary. As a sop to the agrarians, the convention agreed that the clerk of the state supreme court should be elected. Also, agrarian delegate Frank Burkitt of Chickasaw County managed to secure passage of a section requiring new judges to take this oath: "I will administer justice without respect to person and do equal right to the poor and to the rich." [28]

The new constitution declared Mississippi would never again attempt to secede from the Union and outlawed both slavery and dueling. The governor was given a line-item veto, and all tax bills had to pass the legislature by a two-thirds vote. This provision allowed the Delta to protect itself from "soak the rich" taxes that might be framed by agrarians. In turn, agrarians won a provision forbidding railroads from giving free passes to most public officials and a section protecting workers from employers' interference in their political or civil rights. Workers who were injured on the job could sue their employer even if a fellow employee had caused the accident. Convict leasing after 1894 was prohibited. The constitution instructed the legislature to provide pensions for indigent Confederate veterans and their widows.[29]

A number of delegates urged that the document be submitted to the voters for ratification, but the Judiciary Committee ruled these proposals were "unnecessary and inexpedient." Delegates tabled one such proposal by Frank Burkitt by a vote of 80 to 26, with 27 delegates not voting. On final passage, delegates approved the document 104 to 8, with 21 delegates absent. The eight dissenters included agrarians like Burkitt and Gore and conservative Deltans who were irritated at the understanding test loophole in the literacy test. Four delegates declined to sign the document. In his farewell address, Calhoon returned to the themes of his opening speech, saying Mississippi whites refused to be governed by blacks, since he claimed that the black race "has shown no science, no literature, no art, no enterprise, no progress, no invention." He predicted northerners would come to agree with this assessment and added that he hoped African Americans would make a better record for their race in future years.[30]

Public reaction to the new constitution as recorded in the state press was overwhelmingly negative. The *Choctaw Plaindealer* had opposed the constitutional convention from the first session, referring to it derisively as the "Con. Con." The *Plaindealer* favored prohibition but commented with disgust that few delegates did. The *Ellisville Alliance Eagle* wanted an elective judiciary but noted that delegates to "the $4 a day convention believe in a centralization of power." The *Eagle* editor scoffed at the delegates' apparent belief that under the elective judiciary system, there was the danger of black judges being elected. The *Natchez Democrat* disliked giving new legislative seats to the white counties and believed Senator George had pushed the apportionment plan to win votes, "due to the fact that [his] Senatorial term expires in 1893." As there was no provision for popular ratification, however, the newspapers soon moved on to other topics.[31]

The framing of the constitution of 1890 was the most important political event in Mississippi in the late nineteenth century. Almost immediately after its passage, writers began debating the effects of the constitution, and they have been debating these effects ever since. When the new voter registration numbers became available in 1892 and 1896, some surprising patterns emerged. The understanding test was less important than the delegates had thought it would be. Designed to provide a loophole allowing tens of thousands of illiterate whites to register to vote, actually only about three out of one hundred registrants (white or black) used the understanding test. Surprisingly, far more black applicants than white registered under the understanding test—the opposite trend from what the constitutional convention delegates had expected. Nearly 12 percent of successful black applicants used the understanding test, while less than 2 percent of white registrants used it. Quitman County actually had a small black majority of voters after the new registration. After the new registration, 49 percent of Bolivar County's voters and 48 percent of Coahoma's were black. On the other hand, white leaders were so entrenched in Quitman, Bolivar, and Coahoma counties that white domination was never in danger. Interestingly, in the 1892 presidential election, despite the large number of black voters in these counties, Republican Benjamin Harrison won only 8 to 15 percent of the vote in the three counties. It is not clear whether the weak Republican showing was caused by black voters being urged to vote Democratic, whether black voters did not vote on election day, or whether fraudulent counting of votes occurred. Clearly, though, Republican voting and black office-holding were not to be part of the near future of any of these counties, despite the presence of a large number of black registrants.[32]

Statewide, the racial patterns of voter registration varied widely by county. In several black-majority eastern counties, black voting became very uncommon. In Noxubee County (in the Black Belt), Republicans and Independents had earlier been forced to disband by Democratic threats of violence. Now less than 1 percent of Noxubee's adult black males registered, while 92 percent of the county's adult white males did so. The same pattern prevailed in nearby Lowndes County. Despite the very large black population there, only nineteen black citizens succeeded in registering. Racially balanced Jasper County registered only 6 percent of adult black males but 87 percent of adult white males. Yet in counties with large white majorities, black voting often was tolerated. In Marion County, 77 percent of black men were registered in 1896. In Covington County, black registration reached 74 percent. In these counties, it appears that both conservative Democrats and agrarian insurgents encouraged black voters to register and join their side.[33]

In terms of raw numbers, it is safe to say the constitutional convention formalized the disfranchisement of some 100,000 black voters. The new constitution also led to the disfranchisement of some 50,000 white voters. Mississippi was left with an overwhelmingly white electorate and one that had been purged of many white voters of more modest means.[34]

In 1898 the U.S. Supreme Court considered the validity of Mississippi's new suffrage rules under the Fourteenth and Fifteenth amendments. In the case of *Williams v. Mississippi*, justices ruled the poll tax, literacy test, and understanding test were constitutional because they applied to both races equally. Yet the justices did show that they were not naive about Mississippi's new constitution. They observed that the state supreme court justices had acknowledged that the convention delegates "swept the horizon of expediency to find a way around the Negro amendments to the Federal Constitution." While the federal justices recognized the purpose of Mississippi's new constitution, they declined to interfere. Having received a constitutional green light, other southern states followed Mississippi's lead and enacted new disfranchising constitutions.[35]

In the 1940s some writers suggested that southern states' disfranchisement provisions were not as important as they first appeared, because they reflected a fait accompli. Since black voting and Republican politics had already declined in the southern states, disfranchisement became possible. Yet while the number of black voters in Mississippi fell sharply after Reconstruction, the number was not negligible even in 1890. In 1888, for example, the Republican presidential candidate Benjamin Harrison actually carried seven Mississippi counties, largely with black votes. In 1890 the legislature had six black members, but after passage of the new constitution not a single black legislator would win election for some eight decades.[36]

By the final decade of the nineteenth century, Mississippi voters were showing a new interest in national issues. In 1891 Mississippi had an exciting political campaign (described in Chapter 2) centering on the Farmers' Alliance proposal that the U.S. government build a series of subtreasury warehouses to aid farmers. Interest in proposals to inflate the nation's money supply by silver coinage reached a fever pitch in Mississippi in 1896. Residents of the Delta pushed with increasing vehemence (and increasing success) for federal aid to levee building. Mississippi's congressional delegation won points with voters as they helped secure new rural free delivery mail routes for their constituents.

The Spanish-American War of 1898 led Mississippians to debate issues of imperialism. A majority of politically active Mississippians opposed the concept of the United States forcibly governing colonies. Typical in this respect was rising young star James K. Vardaman, who served in the U.S. Army in Cuba. Vardaman opposed the colonizing of Cuba or Puerto Rico, in part because it was unjust to govern people without their consent. (Vardaman conveniently ignored Mississippi's disfranchisement of black citizens.) Vardaman was also motivated in his anti-imperialistic stands by his low opinion of the residents of the Caribbean islands. "The American nigger is a gentleman and a scholar," Vardaman wrote, compared with the average Cuban. The reluctance of white Mississippians to support U.S. colonizing efforts was in step with the national Democratic Party, which was similarly averse.[37]

In the nation's political battles, Mississippi often found itself ignored by the rest of the country because it was seen as a state that had a one-party system. Mississippians invariably voted Democratic, so there was no reason for national political leaders to visit the state or to reward the state with patronage or party honors. Yet Mississippi never was, strictly speaking, a one-party state. The agrarian Greenback Party arose in the late 1870s, offering a number of programs to help indebted farmers. The Greenbackers took over several Mississippi counties in the 1879 election and sent seventeen Greenback legislators to Jackson. Independent legislators were a common phenomenon in the 1870s, 1880s, and 1890s. Without fraud and violence, the state would likely have seen the election of 1881 gubernatorial candidate Benjamin King, the nominee of the Greenback and Republican parties. The People's Party elected more than one hundred county and local officers as it argued for strong national and state governments that would act to solve farmers' problems. In 1894 twenty-two incumbent Democratic legislators went over to the new party, forming a Populist caucus.

The Mississippi Republican Party was toppled by what Solomon S. Calhoon called the "revolution" of 1875. By threats and violence against Republican activists, Democrats ensured Republicans would no longer offer a credible challenge in state elections. Yet the Republicans won some surprising successes after 1875. In 1882 they elected two congressmen (one in cooperation with the Greenbackers). The Mississippi Republicans were a major power in municipal elections in Jackson, Natchez, and Vicksburg. The Republican mayor of Jackson was reelected until 1887. The prohibition issue sometimes helped the Republicans win local elections. Dry Democratic voters helped elect a Republican legislator from white-majority Attala County in 1885 and helped elect a Republican mayor of Summit as late as 1895.[38]

In a number of counties along the Mississippi and Yazoo rivers, Democrats agreed to divide the offices with local Republicans. Typically, Democrats took the sheriff's office, the circuit and chancery clerks' offices, and three of the five seats on the board of supervisors. Republicans took the remaining offices and took about half of the county's legislative seats. Under such plans, there was only one county ticket on election day, and violent campaigns became a thing of the past. Planters and merchants were happy because their tenants were not constantly agitated by office-seeking politicians, and black leaders were pleased because they were not shut out of the political process. Some Deltans, however, attacked the plan. White politicians who were passed over took offense at continued black office-holding, and some white citizens did not like having to deal with black officials such as county tax collectors. If the white majority on the board of supervisors was divided, a black member might cast the deciding vote. Black politicians and their white Republican allies sometimes reasoned that in counties that were more than 75 percent black, Republicans should not have to divide the offices. Thus occasional "straight Republican" tickets appeared and were at times victorious.[39]

Despite the stray successes of Republicans, Independents, Populists, and Greenbackers, the fact remains that Mississippi displayed an astonishing devotion to the Democratic Party. In one and a half centuries of gubernatorial elections between 1833 and 1987, Mississippi elected a non-Democrat only four times. In only two presidential elections between 1836 and 1960 did the state give its electoral votes to the Whig or Republican nominee. There are a number of reasons for Mississippi's steadfast devotion to the Democratic Party. One is that the roots of Mississippi's Democratic devotion went decades into the past. Antebellum Whigs were always a decided minority in the state, and only a set of unusual circumstances ever led the Whigs to win a statewide race. In the post-Reconstruction years, the various opposition parties had difficulty in starting from scratch in their battle against the powerful Democratic machine.[40]

Time after time, candidates were warned their life was in danger if they did not drop their opposition to the Democratic Party. From Jefferson County, respected white leader R. H. Truly dropped out of his race for state senator as an Independent.

"I *thought* I had a *legal* and *constitutional* right to run for office, but subsequent events in this county have *convinced* me that *possibly* I have no such ... rights," Truly explained in a letter to the local newspaper. "I therefore withdraw." Repeatedly, candidates who refused to give in to threats were gunned down. The slain dissidents included Marsh Cook in Jasper County, Print Matthews in Copiah County, and a number of others. Republican gubernatorial candidate James R. Chalmers dropped out of the race in 1889 after threats were made and meeting places denied him. Black Republican leader John R. Lynch said it was clear that "so far as this state is concerned we do not live under a republican form of government." Henry M. Dixon refused to abandon his independent bid to be sheriff of Yazoo County in 1879 and was gunned down on the streets of Yazoo City. Typical of a large number of incidents was one in which a group of black citizens was fired upon from ambush as they walked to a political meeting in Sharkey County in 1881. Three of them were killed and two seriously injured. A number of state newspapers tried to start the rumor that Democrats had not been involved and that in fact the killing was not political, but the editor of the *Greenville Times* urged his fellow editors to play fair. "From our information," he wrote, "it is certain that this wanton, wicked murder, was committed by white men; and that the contest over a local office was its cause."[41]

Violence was so common in Mississippi politics that Democrats soon turned to violence against other Democrats. Newspaper editors were particularly at risk, since they often were the ones responsible for "heating up" political campaigns. As we have seen, editor Roderick Gambrell was shot and killed for his role in the 1886 local option election, including his attacks on a noted wet leader. On the day of his election as constitutional convention delegate, Democrat J. W. Cutrer shot and killed a fellow Democrat who had charged that Cutrer's ancestry was not entirely white. The two men's enmity grew out of a political battle over where the county seat should be located. Newspaper editor James K. Vardaman denounced local residents who had posted a cartoon critical of Greenwood's municipal government. He was then accosted by those he had criticized, and he shot and killed one of them on the streets of the city. In Attala County, two legislators, one a Populist and the other a Democrat, attacked each other so bitterly in the local press that their friends suspected a gunfight was inevitable. Though Democrat S. A. Jackson initiated the gun battle, Populist W. P. Ratliff proved the better marksman and shot and killed his legislative colleague on the courthouse grounds in Kosciusko.[42]

While there were some cases where Democrats attacked Democrats and a few where non-Democrats prevailed over Democrats, in most cases of intimidation and violence Democrats suppressed non-Democrats. Democrats could afford to be more aggressive, since juries were unlikely to convict Democrats for assault or murder if their attorney could show they were only working to ensure white control of the state. Violence did diminish as the years went by. Most observers believed the political assaults and murders became less common as Democrats replaced violent tactics with fraud. Fraud incited less criticism and was harder to prove in court than assault.[43]

The political parties opposing the Democrats were deeply hurt by provisions of the constitution of 1890. The new suffrage rules made it clear the great majority of black citizens in the state would not be voting in the future; thus a revival of the Republican Party after 1890 seemed highly unlikely. The Populist Party arose just as the new suffrage rules were going into effect. In one sense, the Populists benefited from the new rules, as the Democrats were now less likely to say white supremacy was in danger—after all, Democrats had framed the new constitution with its guarantees of white control. On the other hand, Populists were deeply hurt by the poll tax provisions of the new constitution. Populists had great potential appeal with poorer white farmers, but such farmers were unlikely to pay a $2 poll tax for two years in succession simply to win the right to vote. Many farmers in many years earned less than $40 a year—if they made any money at all—and $4 proved a steep price to pay. With fewer white farmers of modest means voting, the Populists did not come close to carrying the state.[44]

The years 1877 to 1900 were exceptionally important in the state's political history. The Democratic Party consolidated its control, so that in 1902 all eight Democratic congressional candidates won 100 percent of the vote. Black disfranchisement, championed by most white citizens, was finalized by the constitution of 1890. Most state residents still paid lip service to the ideal of small government. Increasingly, though, citizens did call for government actions to aid the people. Town boosters supported state and local government aid to railroads and new factories. Deltans supported local, state, and national aid for levee construction. Farmers dreamed of a federally constructed system of warehouses, which would make farmers more independent of merchants and bankers and which would inflate the money supply. A large majority of Mississippians favored federal government spending to bring rural free mail delivery to the nation's farmers.

Agrarians managed to meet some of their state-level objectives, such as cutting state expenses and taxes, but failed to achieve most of their cherished goals. By 1900 farmers' crops were still liable to seizure by creditors, convict leasing had not been eradicated, the state Railroad Commission was exceptionally weak, state judges still were not elected by the people, and black-majority plantation counties continued to hold a large majority in the state legislature. While many counties had voted themselves dry by local option voting, future progress at the county level seemed unlikely, and in fact some of the dry counties had reentered the wet column. Early in the next century, agrarians would succeed in taking firm control of the state government, would make black disfranchisement even more complete, and would take bolder steps to make Mississippi the driest state in the nation.

CHAPTER EIGHT

Industrialization

Looking back on his boyhood in Attala County in the late nineteenth century, Arthur Hudson well remembered what industrialization had meant to him. It meant a trip to the gristmill, where water raced through chutes and kept the giant mill wheel turning. The place was so loud Hudson had to shout to get the proprietor to come out. Soon the miller emerged, "hat, eyebrows, beard, and shirt dusty as a corn weevil." Invariably the miller handed young Hudson a fishing pole so he could try his luck on the millpond while the grain was ground. Finally, the deal would be made, and Hudson would be on his way with a sack of fresh meal. The transaction was cashless, as the miller claimed a portion of the product for his pay. For Hudson, visits to this small industrial establishment provided some of the most vivid memories of his boyhood.[1]

In 1880 Mississippians were proud of their state's industrial progress. The state boasted 1,479 manufacturing establishments that year, up 69 percent from 1850. Yet most of these establishments were small gristmills like the one Hudson visited or one-person blacksmith shops or neighborhood sawmills. Moreover, while the number of manufacturing establishments in Mississippi had risen 69 percent since 1850, the number of such establishments nationwide increased more than 105 percent during the same period. Thus, in the three decades leading up to 1880, Mississippi had impressive actual industrial growth, but growth that was significantly behind that of the nation as a whole.[2]

U.S. census figures showed industrialization increasing quickly in Mississippi during the years after 1880. By 1910 more than 50,000 persons were employed in manufacturing in the state, and in 1920 the number reached 57,500. The 1920 figure was nearly ten times as large as the number for 1880. Moreover, the jobs were not in gristmills and blacksmith shops alone but in sawmills, some of which were huge. Smaller numbers of workers were employed in textile mills and in railroad shops that could produce a locomotive from scratch.

The move toward industrialization was a wrenching one. By 1915 state residents often observed industrial workers roaming from town to town. Robert Powell's memories of industrialization in Mississippi were not as positive as Arthur Hudson's. A laid-off textile worker, Powell walked more than 200 miles with his wife and small children looking for work. The family finally gave up and collapsed in a deserted cabin near Natchez, where locals found them "starving to death and desperately ill from fatigue and exposure." They explained they intended to stay in the cabin "until death came to their relief."[3]

In Mississippi agriculture, local landowners were always ready to provide credit at the local store in exchange for a promise to work. Rural churches and the local Granges helped members who experienced hard times. Industrial workers, however, had few safety nets. In 1914 the *Meridian Star* reported that every night dozens of men descended on the local police station, where they asked for (and were given) a place to sleep. The paper added that these men were not ne'er-do-wells, as a look at their callused hands instantly showed. They were simply workers from sawmills and railroads who were unable to find work.

Mississippi's lumber industry in the years between 1877 and 1917 grew rapidly, enriching investors, creating jobs, and generating a host of problems. The lumber boom involved the development of three separate types of economic activity, each of which was mutually dependent upon the other two. Timbering operations consisted of cutting the trees and delivering the logs to the sawmills. Milling the logs into boards or molding comprised another industry. Finally, the development of railroads encouraged rapid expansion of timbering, allowing sawmills to ship their products quickly and cheaply.

Mississippi's Piney Woods section in the southern part of the state offered an especially rich harvest of timber. Trees were huge, and many areas had seen little timbering prior to 1880. As area resident H. J. Smith put it, "I remember the great pines which covered the land as the most imposing, the most magnificent and the most glorious sight of my whole life." The enormous trees were in uncrowded stands, with all branches located far above the ground. Thus the forests were dark, quiet places of remarkable beauty. Smith recalled he could see for great distances because of the height of the branches and the absence of underbrush. He remembered that no matter where he traveled in Pearl River County, he never left the shade of the great forests. The *Biloxi Herald*'s editor agreed that most parts of the Piney Woods were "a howling wilderness" and that in a week's ride on horseback, "a man would see [only] at long intervals a human habitation."⁴

The "howling wilderness" was not to last. The *Southern Lumberman* in 1911 applauded the cutting of an "ancient landmark" near Osyka, an enormous poplar tree well known to local residents. Timber operator V. J. Wroten "happened by" and noticed the tree, and he ordered his crew to cut it down. With their hand tools, they shaped it into a beam seven feet square at the wide end, and with twenty oxen they pulled the "stick" to Osyka. Few Mississippians stopped to mourn the passing of ancient landmarks or cathedral-like forests. Piney Woods soil supported only an impoverished agriculture, so with the coming of railroads and sawmills, area residents looked forward to a bright future.⁵

The Delta was another region of wild, forested land. LeRoy Allen recalled in his autobiography that when his family moved into the Delta, cotton was the main crop. Yet timber was a close second. Mary Hamilton's recollections were similar. When she moved to the Delta, many of the logs being carried out were so large that only one could fit on each massive, eight-wheeled wagon. When she crossed the Sunflower River to join her husband in their new home, the roads were so indistinct through the dark forest that her husband tore up and dropped pieces of paper to prevent her from losing her way. A subsidiary of the Schlitz Brewing Company and several other firms began harvesting oak trees to make barrel staves, and Hamilton recalled that the companies imported 500 Slovenian woodsmen to do the cutting. As they marched into the woods, Hamilton was impressed by the haunting folk songs they sang and by the wagonload of whiskey kegs that accompanied them. Hamilton had a difficult time keeping her husband out of the Slovenians' camp.⁶

While the barrel makers sought the huge hardwood trees of the Mississippi Delta, the larger part of Mississippi's timber boom was based on the yellow pine trees growing in the Piney Woods. Yellow pine in many ways was a superior wood. Harder than the white pine produced in northern states, it had a marked resistance to decay. It also had a great tensile strength. At first, however, carpenters in northern states rejected Mississippi yellow pine because it was not as easy to work with—heavy resin content made yellow pine difficult to saw. Northern white pine merchants spread false information about yellow pine, saying it decayed quickly and that it could not be painted. By the 1880s and 1890s, however, the supply of white pine in northern states was dwindling.⁷

The new source of the nation's timber could either be the heavily forested states of the Pacific coast or southern states such as Mississippi. The South had the advantage of being closer to the eastern population centers than were the Pacific states.

Timber could be shipped more cheaply to New York and Baltimore and other eastern markets from Mississippi than from Oregon. The Piney Woods also seemed preferable to the Pacific states as a source of timber because loggers would not have to cope with snow and freezing temperatures or hilly and mountainous terrain. Moreover, northern industrialists began to discover the superior qualities of yellow pine. Railroad companies, for example, found it was an excellent product from which to produce railroad cars, especially the sills, which were prone to decay. Many Michigan lumbermen came to Mississippi after their northern holdings were cut over, and they invested heavily in Mississippi lands.

In the late nineteenth century, the timbering industry and the sawmill industry were essentially separate. Individuals hired crews and supervised them in the cutting and delivery of timber to the mills. The mills took possession of the logs at the mill itself and then sawed the logs into boards. The loggers might cut timber on their own lands or might pay other landowners for the right to cut timber. They also might purchase logs that had been cut and stacked by landowners and simply undertake to get the logs to mill and to sell them there at a profit. On the timber crews, one most highly valued worker was the axman. The typical axman cut about ten trees per day. The most adept could produce a timber as square as that produced by a mechanized planer. A disadvantage of using axes to fell trees was that the stumps were three to four feet tall, thus subtracting several feet from the length of each log. Saws, however, were useless because they became coated with rosin and would not slide through the kerf (slot) being cut, and also the kerf became clogged with sawdust.

By the late 1880s southern timber operators had made improvements in the crosscut saw and methods for its use. The improvements consisted of teeth called "cutters" that cleaned the kerf of sawdust with each pass. The gumming of the blade was solved by generous use of kerosene to keep it clean. When the first crosscut saw arrived, people assembled from miles around to see what it could do. Contests were sometimes improvised, pitting the saw against the ax. The saws proved much faster, and even though they required two men to use, they were more than twice as fast as the ax. Not only was the new method faster, but trees could now be cut near ground level, resulting in less waste.

At streamside, the logs were branded with the mark of the logger and left to wait for the first appearance of steady rains. When the rains came, loggers rushed to streamside to dump the logs into the water. Quick work was essential, since a fall of the water level could strand the logs temporarily or even until the next year. For weeks, if the rains held, the sound of logs knocking against each other could be heard for miles. Logjams were an ever-present danger. Such jams began when one log failed to make a turn in the creek and ended up perpendicular to the banks. One of the greatest logjams in the state's history occurred in 1900, near the mouth of the Pascagoula River. The jam was twenty-five feet high at its tallest and more than seven miles long. It took six weeks to clear. On larger streams, the creek runners fashioned logs into rafts. This was a more efficient way of handling the logs, but rapid currents could lead to excessive speed and lack of control, endangering the workers. Rafting was a grand adventure. Young men looked forward to it as a great coming of age. Old men recalled their rafting adventures with a detail that showed how vivid their memories still were.[8]

One of the most noted timber operators and creek runners was Wes Fairley, a black man who legend says was fully seven feet tall. He could not find shoes to fit and went everywhere barefooted—even to the federal land office, where he made repeated purchases of pinelands. Fairley was the main operator along Black Creek, floating his logs to the mills at Moss Point. He also purchased logs from area landowners. Fairley was popular with all. His skill was so great that whites thought nothing of sending thousands of dollars worth of business to this black entrepreneur, and white workers competed for positions on Fairley's crews.[9]

There were several other black loggers working in south Mississippi, including Sandy Williams in Harrison County and Israel Breland in Perry County. While such entrepreneurs were the exception and not the rule, virulent racism seemed less common in the timber camps than in the Cotton Belt. Skilled labor was at a premium in this rapidly expanding industry, and an expert axman, saw filer, ox driver, or creek runner was valued no matter the color of his skin. Interviewed in the 1960s, former timber workers recalled that on the great timber drives, race seemed almost forgotten—all of the men "ate out of the same pots, slept in close proximity around campfires, and joined in singing at night."[10]

Timbering shared a number of similarities with Mississippi agriculture. Timber operators pledged to supply a certain quantity of timber, and the sawmills made an advance to help with expenses. The operator then hired crews of skilled workers, in turn giving them an advance. Timber operators were often as dissatisfied at settling time as were Delta sharecroppers. Mill managers rejected certain logs for being a fraction of an inch undersize, then would cut them up for lumber anyway. The manager often rejected logs for containing too much sappy wood. Some creek runners became expert at hiding the flaws of the logs they were selling.[11]

In the early twentieth century, small timber operators began to disappear. The mills sent their own agents into the backcountry to purchase timber rights, supervise cutting, and deliver logs to the mill. Most of the timber along rivers and creeks

INDUSTRIALIZATION

Engine number 202 of the Gilchrist-Fordney Lumber Company headquartered in Laurel. The building of railroads like the one shown here was of critical importance to expansion of Mississippi timbering. By the same token, railroads could not have expanded without enormous numbers of cross-ties made from Mississippi trees. (Photo courtesy of Lauren Rogers Museum of Art.)

had already been cut. A sizable investment would be required to cut logs and transport them overland. At first, mills built plank roads that allowed logs to be carried to the mills by log wagon. Later the companies laid primitive rails made of logs, over which special wagons could roll. These wagons might originally be powered by draft animals and later by small steam locomotives designed to hug the log rails. Finally, steel rails were laid, at first with a less expensive narrow gauge and later with the standard distance between the tracks. Sometimes these company rail lines incorporated and became common carriers. The railroads and the timbering industry in Mississippi aided each other's rise. The timbering industry could not expand much beyond the rivers until the railroads were built. Railroads could not be built without millions of wooden cross-ties. Railroads flourished as they carried logs to mills and lumber to northern states. Timber companies' cutover lands were worth more if they were near a railroad line.[12]

Industrialization

Early in the twentieth century, mechanical marvels took over some of the tasks previously performed by humans and draft animals. Shown here is a steam loader owned by the Gilchrist-Fordney Lumber Company. The steam loader quickly and efficiently raised logs and placed them on waiting railroad cars. (Photo courtesy of Lauren Rogers Museum of Art.)

The steam skidder made its appearance early in the twentieth century. This machine had a huge reel of steel cable and could drag logs up to 1,000 feet to waiting railcars. Although skidders could move more than 500 trees per day, the land was almost totally devastated. The skidders pulled topsoil along with the logs, and rains soon eroded the loose topsoil. Reforestation was impossible on lands that had seen use of a skidder. Many lumber companies argued that the use of oxen in the twentieth century was archaic. Other industry observers pointed out that future costs of unproductive land should be factored into the equation. By World War I, Mississippi timber companies were only beginning to think of replanting cutover lands instead of selling them to farmers. To do so, of course, required a mental shift toward long-term investment.

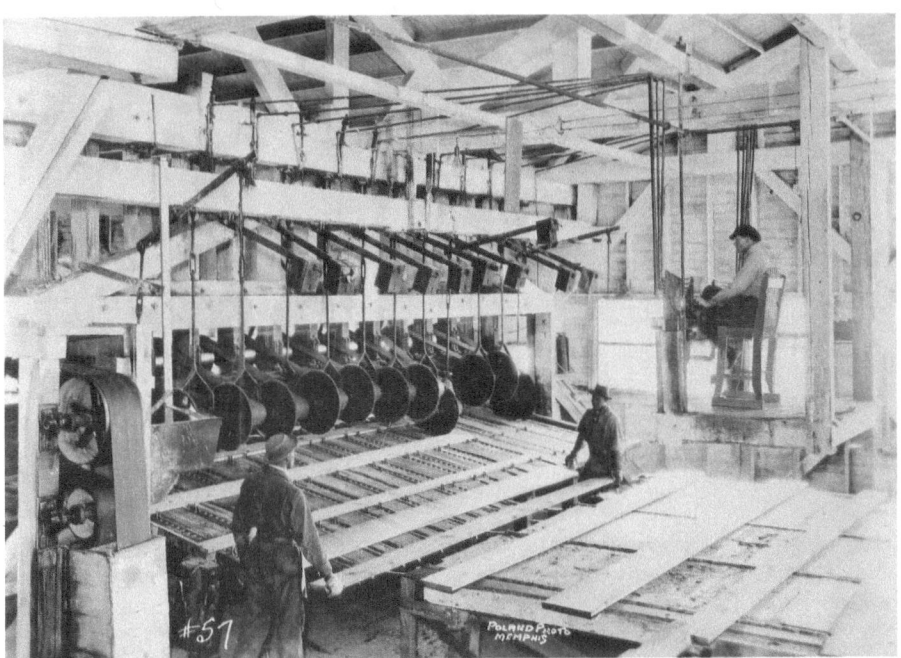

Part of the machinery at the Lamb-Fish Lumber Company sawmill in Tallahatchie County. The firm claimed to have the world's largest hardwood sawmill. Shown here is the trimmer saw, which cut boards into pre-set lengths. (Photo courtesy of Memphis Public Library.)

A number of technical developments led to a phenomenal growth in annual lumber production in Mississippi. In the late nineteenth century, sawmills began to use gang saws. These saws had a whole set of blades set in a single frame and could cut an entire log into boards in a single pass. The increasing use of drying kilns reduced the weight of lumber and slashed shipping costs. Yet even with all the technical developments, sawmills were still dependent for their success on their skilled workers. The sawyer was the prince of the mill. He was expected to cut up a log within seconds, making quick mental calculations to determine the most profitable kinds of boards to produce. The edger trimmed each board and was responsible for determining the final length and width. He, too, had to make rapid mental calculations—would it be more profitable to cut off this knot and have a shorter board or leave the knot and have a longer board of a lower grade?[13]

The benefits of the timber and lumber industries to the economy of Mississippi were great. The number of employees working in the state's lumber mills increased from 1,200 in 1880 to more than 37,000 in 1920. The value of lumber products grew

INDUSTRIALIZATION

Part of the Enochs Brothers sawmill operations at Fernwood are shown in this photo circa 1907. The mill pond is visible at rear. Fernwood was also home to a hotel, ice cream parlor, the Enochs Brothers corporate headquarters, and the company commissary.

in the same period from $2 million to more than $94 million. Increasingly, the economic importance of the state of Mississippi to the nation was based on both cotton and lumber. In 1915 Mississippi ranked third among the states in lumber production and fifth in cotton. Cotton was still king in the state. The value of the state's cotton crop in 1910 was $83 million, while the value of the state's lumber products was $38 million. Cotton was of paramount importance, but the tragic effects on the state's economy of a bad year for cotton now would be blunted since cotton was no longer the sole important commodity.[14]

The timber boom developed south Mississippi in a short period of time. Laurel was a mere crossroads in 1890, but it boasted a population of 8,465 in 1910 and reached 13,037 ten years later. The effect of lumbering on people's lives was dramatic. In south Mississippi, Richard S. Davis had fallen on hard times and faced the bank's foreclosure of his farm. He told his sons they must forget their dreams of attending college. Five days before the foreclosure, agents of the Great Southern Lumber Company offered Davis a large sum of money for the right to build a railroad across his land. The farm was saved, his sons' futures again looked bright, and local people enjoyed the prosperity brought by the building of a new timber camp to house 700 persons.[15]

Fernwood, in Pike County, was in many ways a typical sawmill town. Home to a large sawmill and planing mill owned by Enochs Brothers Lumber, it also featured

In 1915 the town of Wisner was physically picked up and moved to a new location. As Mississippi began to modernize and industrialize, residents sometimes found it hard to put down the kind of deep roots enjoyed by their forebears. (Photo courtesy of Lauren Rogers Museum of Art.)

the firm's corporate headquarters, a post office, a brickyard, an ice-cream parlor, a small barbershop, the company commissary, and a company-owned hotel, where as a little girl Maggie Carruth was kept busy polishing lamp chimneys. Little Fernwood was simply a sawmill town, however, and when the nearby trees were all cut, the mill was dismantled and moved elsewhere. When Margaret Carruth Moore returned to the Fernwood area decades later, hoping to find the site of her girlhood labors, not one building remained at the old site. Similarly, Annie Louise D'Olive enjoyed growing up in the sawmill town of Ten Mile. Later in life she wrote a reminiscence of the town for the *Journal of Mississippi History*. But when she tried to go back to Ten Mile, she found not even a highway sign. Local residents directed her to the old town site, but not a building remained—all had been dismantled when Dantzler Lumber ended its operations there. Lumberman Isaac Enochs enjoyed the role of town founder, and he started a number of new communities, the names of which all ended in "o": Barto, Kioto, Davo, Carto, Knoxo, and Kokomo. When the timber was all cut and the sawmills closed, however, these towns disappeared.[16]

Remarkable in many ways was the history of Wisner, a logging town of 800 people located in Smith County. Residents cut timber for the Eastman-Gardiner Company's mill. Wisner boasted one of Mississippi's most active Young Men's Christian Associations (YMCAs), a drugstore, a grocery, a butcher shop, a barber, and even an electric generating plant. It was an incorporated town with a mayor and board of aldermen. In 1915, however, the timber played out. The company made plans to move the town twelve miles to a site in the midst of standing timber. To prevent confusion, residents chose a new name for the town—Cohay. Town officers were forced to probe some interesting legal questions. Could the officers of Wisner continue in office in Cohay? Would the ordinances of Wisner automatically become the ordinances of Cohay? Would the funds of the old town belong to the new town, even though some residents decided not to make the move? Cohay flourished and was visited by a *New York Evening Journal* reporter in 1922. He found a prosperous village of 1,000 souls. The reporter noted, however, that Cohay had an uncertain future. Its houses were ready to be loaded onto railroad cars at a moment's notice.[17]

Timbering exhibited the same boom-bust cycle that was common in cotton farming. While timber production did not fall significantly statewide, the localities that were enjoying the prosperity did change. As timber was cut, both mills and houses were moved to new locations. Workers and their families were not able to put down the same deep roots enjoyed by their Mississippi forebears. The portability of mills, people, and towns had unfortunate aspects for investors. The Enochs Brothers founded and invested heavily in a railroad, originally named the Fernwood and Gulf. Railroads are most profitable carrying goods both in and out of a given area. The brothers sought to build up towns along the railroad line, including Fernwood, Mesa, Barto, and Tylertown. Only Tylertown really survived the departure of the sawmills, and the deaths of the other towns meant that the brothers' railroad lost money in more years than it showed a profit. The rapid decline of these towns devastated the people who had purchased town lots or opened stores.[18]

Timbering and lumber production offered a great boost to Mississippi's economy. They also produced unfortunate side effects. The naval store industry, too, was an economic blessing with associated ill effects. Prior to the Civil War, this industry produced gummy substances such as pitch that could be used to caulk ships and to waterproof rope and sailors' clothing. The antebellum naval stores industry operated with slave labor, chiefly in South Carolina and Georgia. After the war, many naval stores operators moved to Mississippi as their eastern "orchards" were exhausted. The operators brought with them a skilled black labor force. Once in Mississippi, they gradually recruited new laborers, continuing to rely almost exclusively on African Americans. The chief product was no longer pitch but turpentine.[19]

Mississippi's turpentine orchards were located in remote corners of the Piney Woods. "Chippers" were employees who lived in the forest and cut gashes in the sides of pine trees. Sap dripped down the gashes into a box. Every three weeks a "dipper" collected the sap. The sap was then taken by boat or wagon to a distillery, where workers heated it to boiling. Vapor from the heated sap entered a tube that ran through cold water, and the vapors condensed to form water and turpentine. The water and turpentine were collected in a barrel. The turpentine rose to the top and was skimmed off. Needless to say, the constant scarifying was bad for the pine trees, and in the early years of the industry landowners were reluctant to allow the destruction of their trees in this way. By the early twentieth century, chippers worked the trees for three seasons, and then the landowner harvested the trees for lumber.[20]

Black workers who had the skills and did not mind an isolated existence in the forests were highly valued by their employers and hence were often well treated. The supply of such workers was limited, however, leading some employers to do almost anything to prevent their workers from leaving. Armed guards patrolled roads leading away from the turpentine camps. One former chipper recalled that one of his co-workers was tracked by bloodhounds when he tried to leave while owing his employer fifty cents. Holding workers in this kind of peonage was a violation of federal law, but prosecutions were few. In some areas, management posted "runaway notices," reminiscent of similar handbills printed during slavery times. White supervisors ran the isolated turpentine camps and did not hesitate to mete out corporal punishments to black workers. Interviewed years later, a black naval stores worker estimated that about one out of four of his employers treated him well. One of the better managers was J. A. Simpson of the Finkbine Lumber Company. The camp Simpson set up near D'Lo featured a YMCA, baseball teams, a church, and chapters of black fraternal organizations. In most camps, however, shooting craps and playing cards were the only entertainment. Legal marriages were uncommon because of the lack of ministers in most camps. Children could not receive even a rudimentary education. The lack of education meant a ready labor supply for the operators, and sons of naval stores workers also became naval stores workers, despite the low pay.[21]

The peak year for the naval stores industry in the state came in 1914, when Mississippi produced 2.4 million gallons of turpentine and 77 million pounds of rosin. The value of naval stores products in 1914 was about $2 million. Prices for turpentine and rosin shot up during the World War I era because of inflation and increased demand. The supply of virgin trees was down sharply by 1919, however, and the industry entered a steep decline in the postwar period.

Similarly, Mississippi lumber producers had to cope with the decline in the number of available trees. Until 1910 or so, nearly all timber producers immediately sold the lands after clear-cutting. Most of them believed that it would be foolish to pay land taxes for thirty or forty years while waiting on a new stand of mature trees. Timber companies operated demonstration farms, enticing young farmers to buy the inexpensive, cutover land. With its low humus content, the land was disappointing to the new owners. In the years before and after World War I, expert foresters preached the gospel of replanting timberlands. Increasingly this was done, ensuring that the timber industry would not vanish the way the towns of Wisner and Ten Mile had.[22]

Production of turpentine, lumber, doors, and moldings provided Mississippi some industrialization. Still, the great dream of Mississippians had always been to see the rise of a textile industry in the state. The state produced about one million bales of cotton each year, yet the product was sent off to prosperous cities such as Lowell, Massachusetts, and Manchester, England, to be spun and woven. Lowell and Manchester seemed to flourish, while the areas that produced the key raw material—cotton—remained mired in poverty. The first steps at building up a textile industry in Mississippi came prior to 1850, and on the eve of the Civil War Mississippi boasted four cotton mills employing 152 workers.

After the Civil War, investors rushed to build new cotton mills in the southern states. They sought to take advantage of the proximity to cotton and the region's untapped waterpower (especially in the Piedmont of Virginia and North Carolina). Mississippi's sluggish streams could not provide the waterpower of the eastern states, but the state offered a greater proximity to the most important cotton supply in the world. By 1880 Mississippi had flourishing textile mills in Wesson, Natchez, Enterprise, Corinth, Bay Springs, and other localities. The census enumerator counted eight cotton mills in Mississippi in 1880, and most of these mills also spun and wove wool.

Some Mississippians expressed disappointment with the textile mills. One farmer reported that even though he and his neighbors lived only fifty miles away from a cotton mill, they did not sell their crop there because the prices mills offered for cotton were the same as anywhere else. Still, Mississippi's textile mills consumed millions of pounds of cotton each year, thus helping to support cotton prices. A journalist from Wesson who attended an 1883 press convention at Columbus in Lowndes County reported that Columbus was a nice city but that its leaders were not progressive since they had not opened a textile mill. "What a grand thing it would be for Columbus," he wrote, "to hear the rush, rattle, and roar of the spindle and the loom, to witness the joyous faces of the hundreds of young people given congenial employment." Various cities exerted great effort in organizing textile companies. By 1910 there were fourteen cotton mills in the state producing yarn and cloth valued at more than $3 million.[23]

The most impressive industrial establishment in the state was Mississippi Mills, located in Wesson in Copiah County. Hundreds of men, women, and children worked at the factory manufacturing cotton and wool cloth of all grades. (Illustration courtesy of Wesson Public Library.)

The most impressive industrial installation in the state was Mississippi Mills in Copiah County. The mill's founder, Colonel J. M. Wesson, had operated a textile mill in Choctaw County in the 1850s but saw the plant destroyed during the Civil War. As the war ended, Wesson relocated to Copiah County and built a modest mill. Grateful locals named the town in his honor, but in 1871 Colonel Wesson sold the mill to New Orleans businessmen John T. Hardy and William Oliver. Oliver moved to Wesson and became the manager of Mississippi Mills. He built several new buildings during his tenure. For added effect he fronted his mills with tall but shallow buildings, up to five stories, some with mansard roofs and gables. Three clock towers, ranging from six to eight stories tall, made the facility even more impressive. Behind the front buildings were lower buildings more conveniently laid out for milling. Even without the front facade, Mississippi Mills was impressive. The carding room alone occupied five acres. Fire was Oliver's constant fear, since the boilers consumed fifty cords of wood per day and the air was filled with flammable cotton fibers. After a fire in 1873, Oliver used only brick in his construction, and he even isolated the wooden structural supports with liberal use of asbestos.[24]

Oliver's partner, John T. Hardy, eventually sold out to cotton merchant Edmund Richardson, but Oliver continued to manage the mill. Under Oliver's direction, the mills turned out cotton cloth that won major awards at the 1876 Centennial Exposition at Philadelphia and wool cloth that won the gold medal at the 1881 Atlanta Exposition. The mills produced everything from mattress ticking and prisoner stripes to high-quality tweed and a cotton cloth so fine it was called "Mississippi silk." Oliver became something of a hero to leaders of Copiah County. The editor of the *Wesson Herald* praised Oliver for saying to the young men of the state "that there is a future for them besides the drudgery of clerk-life" or "the eternal planting of cotton." Without Oliver, Wesson would have been only a sleepy town, but because of him the town enjoyed "the deep loud whistle of the mighty Corliss Engine, as it floats out at early morn, echoing and re-echoing amid the hills and valleys of Copiah County." [25]

Oliver brought electric lights to Wesson only one year after Edison had demonstrated his incandescent bulb. Thus Wesson residents were ahead of most New Yorkers in enjoying the novelty and utility of electric lights. People came from all over the South to see the "light in a bottle," and locals still talk about how the trains nearly tipped over as passengers rushed to one side of the cars to see the lights of Wesson. Yet most locals believed that Oliver's real contribution was providing employment for hundreds of Mississippians. Some came to Wesson to escape the drudgery of farm life or to earn the cash Mississippi farmers so rarely saw. Some had tired of the isolation of farm life and looked forward to being a part of a small but growing city. Some families made up mostly of women and their children came to Wesson because Oliver made a practice of hiring women and children.[26]

The 1880 census revealed some interesting employment patterns in Mississippi Mills. The demographic breakdown of the mill employees was 64 percent white female; 35 percent white male; and 1 percent black male. No black females were employed. The census showed that almost all of the female employees were unmarried. The few married female operatives generally were newlyweds who had not yet had children. The male workforce, on the other hand, was overwhelmingly made up of married men. These patterns reflected the prevailing social ideals of the time. Married women should not hold jobs, it was believed, but should be supported by their husbands. Factory jobs were for whites, but a tiny number of custodial and messenger jobs in the mills went to black men. Unmarried women might properly enter the workplace, but the propriety of their working was clarified by the fact that their male co-workers were respectable, married men.[27]

Demographically, Wesson was an unusual Mississippi town. Not only were six out of ten residents female, but 93 percent of residents were white. Copiah County had a black majority. More than 40 percent of mill workers were aged ten to sixteen. Adult males were in a distinct minority in Mississippi Mills, comprising less than 22 percent of the workforce. About a third of the mill employees could not read, and illiteracy was more common among the youths than among those aged twenty or over. Those who came to the Mississippi Mills as young adults were often literate, but those who grew up in the mills typically received only a year or two of education. Like mill owners everywhere, Oliver tried to compensate for the tragedies of child labor by giving generously to the local schools. His generosity aided those children who did not work at the mill but left the young mill workers uneducated.[28]

Mississippi Mills was the pride of Copiah County and indeed the pride of the entire state. Yet the factory's demise came with surprising swiftness. The mills were hurt by the national depression of the 1890s, then by another national depression beginning in 1907. In 1909 and 1910 several economic factors combined to spell devastation for the mill. First, cotton prices advanced sharply, but the price of manufactured cotton goods did not. Thus in October 1908 the mills were paying nine cents per pound of cotton, but by the following fall the mills were forced to pay nearly fifteen cents. Since the prices of yarn and cloth did not go up, Mississippi Mills had to curtail its production sharply. The firm was soon $50,000 in debt, and in 1910 the General Electric Corporation (one of its creditors) petitioned a federal court to appoint a receiver. Mississippi Mills had no sources of new investment, and credit costs at the time were high. Plans to allow the mills to continue to operate and raise funds were rejected by the court, and finally the once-proud and prosperous Mississippi Mills was closed and sold to satisfy the debt.[29]

The closing of the mills was a tragedy for the people of Wesson. The managers of Mississippi Mills tried to secure places for mill hands at other mills at Natchez and Enterprise. They even paid the train fare for these former employees. As Wesson's town leaders stared at the empty mills, they tried to be optimistic. The editor of the *Enterprise* was hopeful "that the mills will soon awake from their long winter's nap, and that Wesson will echo with the voices of all the happy operatives again." Yet the mills remained eerily silent, and finally the land and machinery were sold to satisfy the firm's creditors. In 1919 the buildings themselves were torn down to salvage the materials. Today only one building from the once-impressive complex remains.[30]

Adding to the variety of industrial work were the state's cottonseed oil mills. These mills pressed the cottonseed to recover the oil, an inexpensive alternative to butter and lard. The crushed seeds themselves were sold for cattle feed or fertilizer for exhausted soils. As early as 1880 Mississippi was home to eight cottonseed mills, with Jackson and Meridian the most important production centers. A Coahoma County farmer reported in 1894 there were no textile mills nearby but said the presence of cottonseed mills helped local farmers enormously. The sale of cottonseed repaid farmers for their ginning costs—leaving larger profits for them to enjoy. By 1914 the cottonseed oil mills provided employment that surpassed the employment of textile mills. Mississippi in 1914 was home to sixty-seven cottonseed mills employing 2,300 persons.[31]

The fruit and vegetable packing business was another industry that utilized Mississippi's agricultural products. Strawberries, tomatoes, and other fruits and vegetables were packed into wooden boxes—made in state from Mississippi wood—and shipped to northern cities such as Chicago and St. Louis. By June 1895 Crystal Springs was shipping twenty boxcars of tomatoes daily. Speed was of the essence, and the Illinois Central Railroad aimed to get Copiah County vegetables to Chicago in fifty-four hours. Early in the twentieth century, use of refrigerated cars reduced the necessity of great speed. Railroads like the Illinois Central and the Mobile and Ohio operated their own agricultural extension services, urging Mississippi farmers to raise fruits and vegetables as well as dairy products. The railroads assisted local residents in organizing cooperative canneries where tomatoes, cabbages, figs, peaches, and other products could be preserved prior to shipment. While Copiah County remained the center of the fruit and vegetable canning business, canneries also operated in Biloxi, McComb, Jackson, and other cities.[32]

On the Gulf Coast, a number of canneries packaged Mississippi seafood. Mississippi was the third largest shrimp producer in the United States in 1908 (behind Louisiana and Florida), and it was the nation's largest shrimp canning center. In fact, New Orleans was the only other locale that canned shrimp. The Mississippi Gulf Coast was the nation's second-largest oyster canning center, after Baltimore. In many cases, Bohemian laborers staffed the canneries of Baltimore, then relocated to the Mississippi Gulf Coast with the change of season. Like the textile factories, the canneries provided employment for women and children as well as men. Most canneries hired white workers only. Mississippi had eighteen canneries of all types in 1914, employing approximately 1,000 persons.[33]

Mississippi saw impressive growth in manufacturing and in the size of its industrial workforce. The timber and lumber industries expanded rapidly, leading the state to be one of the top three lumber producers in the nation in the years before World War I. Other industries, including the naval stores and the textile and cottonseed oil industries, provided the state with increasing numbers of wage earners and an expanding tax base. While only three in one hundred Mississippi workers were engaged in manufacturing in 1880, thirteen in one hundred were so engaged in 1920. Yet while Mississippi's growth in manufacturing was impressive, the state never came close to meeting the national percentage of workers engaged in manufacturing. Mississippi's percentage of the workforce in manufacturing rose from 3 to 13 percent, but the national rate rose from 18 to 26 percent. Thus Mississippi's growth of manufacturing employment was steeper than the growth for the nation as a whole, but only because Mississippi was starting with such a low number. When we compare Mississippi's percentage of the workforce that was engaged in manufacturing with the comparable number for the United States as a whole, the national percentage was higher in 1880, higher in 1920, and higher in every year in between. In 1920 the nation's percentage of the workforce engaged in manufacturing was twice as large as Mississippi's.[34]

There are a number of reasons Mississippi did not industrialize to the extent other states did. One was a shortage of investors. Mississippi was an impoverished state with little history of manufacturing and was distant from large consumer markets. It was not the first place northern industrialists thought of when they contemplated building a factory. While it was true the state's poverty might mean a labor force eager to work for low wages, this advantage was not great enough to lead northern investors to risk their money in an unfamiliar and unproved area. In the late nineteenth century, northern investors also expressed concern about yellow fever and other diseases found in the South, fearing epidemics that could paralyze economic life for months at a time.

It is true that Mississippians invested in Mississippi. The wealthier individuals in various towns invested heavily in railroads and factories that promised to come and bring greater prosperity. Mississippi railroad, lumber, and insurance companies invested in various types of factories. Planters invested in railroads, cotton gins, cottonseed oil mills, and sometimes textile mills. Yet when profits of up to 60 percent per year were possible by providing credit to impoverished sharecroppers, it made little sense to undertake a risky investment in a factory. Some writers have suggested Mississippi's legislature was anticorporate in its policies, frightening away outside investment. Yet the legislature did pass a number of laws enticing corporations, and no writer has demonstrated that other states were friendlier to corporations.[35]

Experts at the time had their own scapegoats for Mississippi's unimpressive record of industrialization. Writing in 1909, University of Mississippi chemistry professor Anthony M. Muckenfuss claimed southern states like Mississippi were held back by lack of the kind of "inventive genius" demonstrated in northern states. He supported his assertion by showing that fewer patents were issued to southerners than to northerners. Turning to prevailing racial theories of the time, the professor asserted that Mississippi suffered under a terrible disadvantage by having a larger African American percentage of the population than any other state. He also claimed Mississippi was held back by having fewer of its black residents "mulatto" than any other state save Alabama. Muckenfuss concluded that "the presence of the negro is perhaps after all the greatest deterrent to progress" in Mississippi. Reports such as Muckenfuss's led to defeatism. It would be difficult to achieve a sudden rise in "inventive genius," and there was no way to change the state's racial demographics.[36]

Muckenfuss was correct in saying ignorance held the state back. What he did not say was that not only black illiteracy but also white illiteracy was high in Mississippi. Mississippi's children attended fewer days of school than children in other states, and the state's schools were poorly funded when compared with those of other regions. Many Mississippians suspected that good education only led young people to leave the state, and so for many, education was not a high priority. Residents who received six years of education at inadequate schools found it difficult to become machinists or millwrights.

Mississippi's relative lack of urbanization also kept industrial growth low. Few industrial plants would be likely to locate in very rural areas, but Mississippi had few large cities to attract factories. In fact, the greatest cities serving Mississippi residents were the four large metropolises outside the state's borders: New Orleans, Memphis, Birmingham, and Mobile. Manufacturers who did locate in the region tended to build in these four cities, and Mississippi's newly improved system of railroads carried a number of the state's would-be industrial workers out of Mississippi altogether. The industrial installations that did locate in Mississippi did so only to be close to certain raw materials. Thus lumber mills located in the Piney Woods because it was cheaper to establish the mills where the timber was than to ship the timber out of state to be sawed. Cotton gins and cottonseed oil mills were located in Mississippi to process the cotton before it was shipped elsewhere. To a large extent, Mississippi's industrialization was nothing more than the initial processing of raw materials near the point of production. Mississippi produced turpentine, lumber, and cottonseed oil. It did not produce furniture, steel rails, or motors. The state produced some cotton cloth. It did not produce clothing.[37]

Given its agricultural traditions, scarcity of capital, relative lack of skilled and well-educated workers, and lack of major cities, Mississippi was likely to see major industrialization only if there was some special reason why factories would flourish there. Birmingham, Alabama, for example, became a major steel center because iron ore was found nearby. The Piedmont region of Virginia and North Carolina became a major textile center because of abundant waterpower. Pittsburgh, Chattanooga, and Wheeling flourished as industrial centers because local sources of coal led to low energy costs. Mississippi had none of these advantages. In this period of its history, it had almost no mineral resources that were being exploited. No iron deposits meant no steel mills. No coal deposits meant few mills would locate in the state, unless waterpower was available.

Waterpower was tragically lacking in the state of Mississippi. In an era when waterwheels were the favored source of power for spinning and weaving, sawing, and grinding, Mississippi's sources of waterpower were few and inadequate. A federal survey of waterpower noted that the great Yazoo-Mississippi valley was characterized by "scarcely moving streams." Most of the state's large rivers had such a low rate of fall, and such unsuitable banks, that it was the small streams arising in the hills that were most successfully tapped for waterpower. Indeed, the federal survey noted a number of cases where mills "are run by streams almost within a stone's throw of the fountain head from which they spring." Such streams offered a great degree of fall, a never-failing source of water, and secure banks on which to build a waterwheel. Unfortunately, such streams were so small they could power only a gristmill or a very modest sawmill. In 1887 Mississippi had 301 waterwheels creating power to run mills. By contrast, Tennessee had 1,882, Georgia had 1,917, Massachusetts had 3,046, and Ohio had 6,684.[38]

Lacking waterpower, coal reserves, ores, a well-educated workforce, and adequate investment capital, Mississippi remained an area where manufacturing trailed far behind agriculture as a source of wealth. Mississippi in 1890 accounted for 2 percent of the nation's population but only 0.2 percent of the nation's industrial output. The state did make efforts to improve its climate for manufacturing. Chapter 10 examines Mississippi's efforts to develop its transportation system, modernize its cities, and cope with the prevailing diseases that made northerners reluctant even to travel in the region, much less invest there.[39]

CHAPTER NINE

Industrial Workers

Mills producing lumber, cloth, cottonseed oil, and fertilizer provided new employment opportunities for Mississippians. Yet industrial workers found such employment had advantages and disadvantages. In exchanging the life of the farmer for the life of a mill hand, one gained the regularity of a cash paycheck and a workplace protected from extremes of cold and storms. The work was less exhausting than plowing, chopping, and picking. On the other hand, the factory worker no longer had the freedom to decide what to do next, or how to do it, but was subservient to the time clock and supervisor. The workplace was loud, the air was filled with fine sawdust or cotton fibers, and factory workers had less opportunity for fresh air and sunshine than did farmers. Factory workers also saw much less of their families.

Workers were paid on the fifteenth of each month for the previous month's work. New workers had to wait up to forty-five days to receive their first paycheck. The mills therefore agreed to make advances to any employee in the form of scrip good at the company commissary. Prices at the commissary were high, and the firm made a tidy profit on sales at these establishments. To any who complained about being forced to trade at the company store, companies agreed to exchange the scrip for cash—for a 10 percent fee. Since the value of the scrip was deducted from the next paycheck, some workers never caught up and had to go on requesting scrip advances every month. Like sharecroppers, these workers seldom saw cash. Like planters, mill executives sought profits through the commissary system.[1]

An unfortunate part of life in a factory was the danger of injury. Recalling her childhood in the sawmill town of Ten Mile, Annie Louise D'Olive remembered the mill accidents that punctuated the town's history. A steam boiler exploded and killed one man. The bursting of a steam pipe scalded a number of workers. One man's arm was caught in a planing mill roller that left him paralyzed. Similarly,

The photograph album of young Maggie Carruth of Fernwood documents a pleasant array of social activities in the Pike County logging town. Several times, however, her entries note the untimely death of a friend—here, by an accident in the Enochs Brothers sawmill.

an 1885 issue of the *Wesson Times* detailed two recent accidents at Mississippi Mills. In one, Emma Mann lost part of a finger while she was cleaning off looms one Saturday. "A few days before," the newspaper added, "Mr. Ike Smith's little girl lost part of her thumb, the tendon attached to the thumb extending to the elbow was torn out." The lesson, according to the *Times* writer, was clear: "These accidents should teach our Mill friends to be careful." Corporate efforts to provide a safer workplace were tragically slow in coming.[2]

Many of Mississippi's industrial workers had to cope with seasonal work. Cottonseed oil mills laid off workers in the spring and summer, then resumed hiring in September and worked at capacity through May. In 1919 the number of employees in this industry ranged from 3,319 in December to only 1,496 in August. Workers could not count on steady work, and employers undoubtedly won only partial loyalty from their workers. The canning industry showed the most acute variation in employment each year. Oyster canneries employed no workers for two months of the year. In the other months, the number of workers ranged from 313 to 514. The vegetable canning industry had fewer than 100 employees statewide during several months of the year but then peaked at 624 workers in November. The seasonal work was a hardship on employees. Even as they developed skill and experience, they moved on to other work as soon as they could. On the Gulf Coast,

INDUSTRIAL WORKERS

Photographer Lewis Hine took this photograph in 1911. Eva Streety was a widow's daughter and earned twenty-eight cents a day at the textile mill at West Point, Mississippi. Eva told the photographer she was twelve years old—"Which is doubtful," Hine noted—but admitted she had been spinning in the mill even before she was twelve. (Photo courtesy of the Library of Congress.)

workers sometimes cobbled together reasonably full employment by moving from oyster canning to fruit canning to fishing to shipbuilding, as one opportunity opened and others closed.³

Most manufacturing jobs were closed to African Americans, who found their chief employment options to be sharecropping or domestic labor. A small number worked in turpentine camps, where conditions were no better than those experienced by sharecroppers. A few obtained employment in railroad shops as boilermakers' helpers or in similar positions. Some found work in the sawmills, but whitecaps took a dim view of black mill workers. In Jackson County logging camps, whitecaps posted notices warning operators to cease using black or foreign-born workers. Whitecaps warned black workers at a Dantzler sawmill in Van Cleave to leave their jobs or be killed. At the Norwood and Butterfield Lumber Company in Lincoln County, whitecaps burned the engine house after company managers refused to fire black workers. The northern owners of the firm sent a sarcastic telegram to Governor John M. Stone: "Your state offers great inducement for investment of money and protection of property."[4]

Industries in Mississippi employed children at grueling, dangerous tasks. In 1880, 47 children aged ten to fifteen worked around dangerous machinery in sawmills, and 261 worked in textile mills where they inhaled fibers for sixty hours each week. The total number of children working in manufacturing in Mississippi in 1880 was 527. By 1910 the number had risen to 6,538. Some observers believed that those who complained about child labor were being hypocritical, since children in Mississippi had always worked. In fact, the federal government estimated that in 1919, more than 88,000 children in the state were working on home farms. Yet these 88,000 children were under the supervision of their parents; were getting plenty of sunshine, fresh air, and exercise; and were rarely around hazardous machinery. Most worked hard at peak seasons of agricultural work, but they had time for play much of the rest of the year, and they did attend school.[5]

The *Wesson Herald* pointed out that although the town had 650 school-aged children in 1883, only 100 actually attended. Wesson was one of the few towns in the state with a ten-month school year, but financing the long school year was made possible by the small number of children who actually went to the town's schools. The *Herald* promised its readers an article that would call formally for securing an education for more of Wesson's children, but the promised article never appeared. Several weeks later the paper was running an ad that had become all too familiar: "WEAVERS WANTED. Also families that have girls aged 14 to 30 years, and boys from 12 to 16 years. Apply at once to Mississippi Mills."[6]

The Greenback Party led the earliest fight against child labor. In 1881 its Jackson newspaper, the *Crisis*, attacked Democrats for permitting child labor and pointed out the tragedy of children at Wesson who in the winter months never saw the sun except through the factory windows. The Populist Party also called for an end to child labor, and later so did the state's Socialist Party. Some Democrats attacked the system, but for the state's industrialists, child labor had one compelling advantage: children worked cheap. In 1896 the prevailing wage for southern textile workers was 67 cents per day for a man doing unskilled work, 47½ cents for a woman, and 31 cents for a child. This explains why 88 percent of the employees at the Wesson mills were women and children. In 1900 there were 411 children (aged ten to fifteen) working in the state's textile mills, and ten years later 836 children were working in sawmills.[7]

In 1908 the state legislature did pass a law to reduce the evils of child labor. Despite vocal opposition from the textile industry, the new law declared that no child under twelve could be employed in factories. Children aged twelve to fifteen could be employed no more than fifty-eight hours per week and could not work at night. Age was to be determined by parental affidavit, and sheriffs were to inspect local factories monthly. Public health officers were to make factory inspections twice yearly. Judges were instructed to require grand juries to investigate allegations of child labor law violations.

Mississippi's Child Labor Act of 1908 was one of the stronger such statutes in the nation. The limit on hours was exemplary for that day, and while many argued the enforcement mechanisms were weak, some states (such as Georgia and South Carolina) barely had enforcement mechanisms at all. The National Child Labor Committee (NCLC) organized a chapter in Mississippi, and national and state groups lobbied for even stronger child labor laws. The NCLC also won the support of a variety of women's groups in the state, including the United Daughters of the Confederacy, the Federation of Women's Clubs, and the WCTU. Over time, the legislature modified the state's child labor laws, usually tightening them but occasionally lowering the age at which children could work. Several NCLC inspection trips into Mississippi, however, showed little actual progress against the evils of child labor.[8]

The number of child laborers in Mississippi declined, according to U.S. government figures. The 1910 census showed 6,538 children doing nonagricultural work in the state, while only 4,491 were documented in the 1920 census. Still, it is not clear whether the statistics improved because child labor was actually declining or because it was increasingly hidden. NCLC investigators found cases of textile factory owners who said they had no child laborers at all. When the inspectors pointed out numerous children who were present, the owners explained that these were simply children who enjoyed coming in and helping their mothers or older siblings. These children were not on the payroll but were able to increase the amount of work done by another family member and thus increased the family's pay. In this case, the child was an employee in everything but name.[9]

While some modern writers have suggested that Mississippi Mills closed because of disputes over wages, the pages of Wesson's newspapers at the time of the mills' demise do not mention wage disputes. Rather, editors blamed the legislature for passing the Child Labor Act of 1908. "When the children were shut out of the mills," argued the *Wesson Enterprise* editor, "grown men and women had to be secured to take their places" at higher wages. Thus, as Mississippi Mills was coping with a national depression coupled with higher cotton prices, it also had to increase its wage scale. The *Enterprise* argued that the mill children "were rarely

In May 1911 photographer Lewis Hine captured this image of two mill operatives, Elsie and Sadie, at their machines. The two girls were employed at the Yazoo City Yarn Mills. Each claimed she was thirteen, but Hine noted that they looked younger. (Photo courtesy of the Library of Congress.)

ever sick," and "there has never been a dwarf seen in the mills during its history." Yet while the Child Labor Act may have played a role in the downfall of Mississippi Mills, it is clear that the company was already in trouble from other factors, chiefly the high cost of cotton and low prices of cloth. Other textile factories survived the new laws, in many cases by firing the ten-year-olds and replacing them with youths aged fourteen to seventeen. While Wesson residents felt justified in their bitterness toward the new laws, many Mississippians argued that what was needed was not employment of grade school children but jobs for adults.[10]

For Mississippians of modest means, industrialization offered new employment opportunities. While a very large percentage of Mississippians still farmed, many state residents found employment sawing lumber, tending the machinery in textile mills, and repairing steam locomotives. These new opportunities, however, had hidden costs—the loss of contact with the land, the lack of sunshine, the need to follow the dictates of an ever-present supervisor. In antebellum Mississippi, industrial workers were employed in gristmills, saddleries, and blacksmith shops.

They had a close relationship with their employer and could suggest changes to improve working conditions. Employees of Mississippi Mills or Enochs Brothers Lumber, on the other hand, would likely never meet their employers. Industrial employment in Mississippi thus took on an impersonal aspect.[11]

To address problems in the workplace, workers in Mississippi organized themselves into unions. The earliest were the railroad "operating brotherhoods," made up of the employees who staffed the trains. The Engineers' Brotherhood organized at Water Valley in 1869. The brotherhoods of firemen, trainmen, and conductors all organized by the 1890s. Railroad shop employees—such as the machinists—also organized by the 1890s. By the early twentieth century, unions of bricklayers, painters, plasterers, printers, and electrical workers were flourishing. Several early organizations attempted to unite farmers and laborers in the same group. Among these were the Farmers and Workingmen's Association that flourished in Hinds and Lincoln counties around 1877. The Greenback and People's parties similarly attempted to unite the state's farmers and laborers.

One of the most important labor groups, nationally and within Mississippi, was the Knights of Labor. The Knights sought to be a union for all workers, and in Mississippi both black and white workers joined. In some cases, Knights of Labor locals were open to both blacks and whites, while in other cases the Knights of a given city organized segregated locals. The group reached a peak of influence around 1890, when there were an estimated forty locals in the state, each with about fifty members. The Knights enjoyed some success in organizing the state's sawmills and led some successful sawmill strikes in the late nineteenth century. Efforts to organize Mississippi Mills, however, led to firings of union backers and ended in failure.

Unions offered a rare opportunity in Mississippi for blacks and whites to work together in the same organization. In the case of sawmill workers, both blacks and whites joined the Knights of Labor but participated in segregated locals that were loosely allied. Longshoremen's and laborers' union locals were usually integrated, with a largely black membership and a largely white leadership. The Jackson bricklayers' union was predominantly black, and its leaders were black, except for the secretary, who was white. The interracial aspects of unionism in the state undoubtedly led many Mississippians to fear the labor movement. At the same time, deeply ingrained racial rivalries made it difficult for union members to work harmoniously together.[12]

The worst nightmares of conservative leaders seemed to come true in Vicksburg, where a labor movement made up of the railroad brotherhoods and the Knights of

Labor grew powerful in the late 1880s and early 1890s. The labor groups dominated the mayoral and city council elections of 1888. They then asked the new city council to cut the workday for all city projects to nine hours, and the city council agreed. As work began on the new Pacific Hotel, labor union members were riled when the contractor brought in eight non-union plasterers from New Orleans. Union members brought work on the hotel to a standstill, and finally the plasterers agreed to join the union. Reporting on these events, the Vicksburg correspondent of the *New Orleans Daily Picayune* commented, "Labor is so well organized here at present that it is difficult to see how its position could be made stronger."[13]

Many merchants and planters undoubtedly felt a shiver of fear and revulsion as they watched the Vicksburg Fourth of July parade in 1890. Marching in the parade were predominantly white unions such as the carpenters, predominantly black groups including the bricklayers, the interracial Knights of Labor, veterans of the Grand Army of the Republic, and the local Farmers' Alliance. From the speakers' platform, the interracial crowd heard speakers from the Knights of Labor, the Farmers' Alliance, and the Republican Party. Representing the city's conservative leadership, the editor of the *Vicksburg Commercial Herald* complained, "We never could see . . . how [these labor groups] can prove beneficial to either race." Criticizing black participants in the parade, the editor asserted that most had no idea what the Fourth of July was or why it was celebrated. The editor closed by warning that white labor leaders aimed to use the mass of black voters and union members for their own selfish advantage.[14]

The Vicksburg editor was angered more by the appearance of the parade than by anything said from the speakers' platform. Knights of Labor leader W. B. Eldridge did ask that basic rights of black citizens be upheld, but he added that socially the two races would always remain separate. Eldridge also said it was clear Mississippi's political system was characterized by white supremacy and that the upcoming constitutional convention was therefore unnecessary. Even the Republican Party speaker declared, "I maintain before the white and colored people, that intelligence alone must and can rule supreme over the boundaries of the South." In other words, mass black political participation was a thing of the past. Thus, while Vicksburg's labor groups won some notable victories, they did not seek to topple Mississippi's racial or social system but only sought concessions on wages, hours, and union recognition.

The largest and most acrimonious strike in Mississippi was that of the shop employees of the Illinois Central Railroad, beginning in 1911. The strike grew out of efforts of the various railroad unions to unite into the Railway Employees

Department, a loose federation allied with the American Federation of Labor (AFL). Several major railroads recognized the federation, but the Illinois Central and other lines controlled by the Harriman financial group refused to do so. The Harriman group feared the federation was the first step in the formation of one large union of all railroad employees. When the Harriman lines refused to negotiate, members went out on strike in early October. In Mississippi, the strike was centered in McComb and Water Valley, two towns where Illinois Central Railroad shops were located. The chief issue of the strike was recognition of the union federation, although the unions also sought minor concessions in wages and working conditions.[15]

The Illinois Central responded to the strike by sending a train carrying 450 strikebreakers into McComb. Most of the strikebreakers were destined for the railroad shops in New Orleans, although some were to be put to work in McComb. All stopped at McComb to secure their dinner. According to the *McComb City Enterprise*, the strikebreakers were "a gang of hoodlums, probably picked up in the slums of northern cities." They had plundered stores in Durant and Winona and had made insulting gestures to the women of those towns. The *Enterprise* narrated how the McComb strikers went home and got their guns when they saw "the class of human rubbish the railroad had brought into the town." Most accounts say the strikebreakers fired the first shot in McComb, but soon the air was filled with hundreds of rounds of ammunition fired by strikers. When the strikebreakers saw the danger, they fell to the floor of their railroad car. Thereafter, the fate of the train and the strikebreakers inside remained something of a mystery. Observers at nearby Magnolia said the train rushed through their town at full speed, with every window broken out and not a soul in sight as the strikebreakers lay down to avoid further gunfire. The railroad claimed no strikebreaker was hurt, but the *McComb City Enterprise* reported seven strikebreakers were dead and fifteen wounded. Observers at New Orleans, the train's final destination, confirmed that some of the strikebreakers had been killed. At least three strikers were shot, one fatally, and McComb was also rocked by a mysterious dynamite blast near the railroad shops.[16]

After the riot at McComb, Governor Edmund F. Noel sent the National Guard to McComb and Water Valley. The strikebreakers who remained in McComb begged to be given safe passage out of the town, and Colonel E. B. Baker of the National Guard arranged this after making certain that was what the strikebreakers wanted. Baker secured the promise of union federation president Claude Bailey that the strikebreakers would not be molested as they were evacuated. The Illinois Central reluctantly supplied a train to evacuate the men, and the National

Guard escorted the train as far as the Louisiana line. After the removal of the last of the strikebreakers, the situation in McComb calmed, but the National Guard remained in town for some months.[17]

The situation was tense at Water Valley as well, although the lack of surviving newspapers from the town means fewer details have survived. There were at least two major gun battles in the Yalobusha County town. One was between the sheriff and his deputies, on the one hand, and the Illinois Central guards, on the other. The second disturbance occurred about two weeks into the strike, when a lawyer (a former railroad fireman) gave a rousing speech to strikers, and the strikers went home and got their guns. Union members went to the paint shops and opened fire on the strikebreakers through the windows. The casualty rate among the strikebreakers was undoubtedly high. Reports stated that no strikebreakers returned the fire of the strikers. Once again, a mysterious train left the city the next day. Residents reported it contained the bodies of twenty-six strikebreakers. As in the earlier incident at McComb, Illinois Central officials denied any of their replacement workers had been injured. Still, many of the strikebreakers who remained fled town the following day.[18]

Meanwhile, the company again sent strikebreakers into McComb, after having built a huge stockade around the town's railroad shops. The strikers referred to it as "Fort McComb," with its ten-foot-tall fence topped by two feet of barbed wire, a searchlight, and a machine-gun tower. Strikebreakers were horrified by the warlike conditions, and many quit and asked to be given transportation out of town. The company at first refused, but at the urging of the National Guard it finally did provide passage for departing strikebreakers.[19]

The strike met a bewildering array of responses from the city, county, state, and national governments. The local mayors, city councils, and sheriffs supported the strikers, reporting that the disorders in McComb and Water Valley were sparked by provocative actions of the strikebreakers. The circuit judge serving Pike County, on the other hand, claimed the union men who fired into the train were "assassins and murderers." Governor Noel attempted to remain impartial, hoping to broker a negotiated settlement. Still, he felt strongly that railroad property must be protected, and he sent the National Guard to the strike scene and kept the troops there even as local officials argued they were not needed. Governor Earl Brewer, who took office during the second part of the strike, told a newspaper correspondent the strike was dragging on because the reasonable Mississippi unionists were being led by "dangerous agitators." Senator-elect James K. Vardaman stated, "I sincerely hope from the depths of my heart that the laborers will win in this contest." He added that unions offered the only hope for workers "to force capital and predatory wealth to yield to them a fair share of the products of their own toil."[20]

About a month after the strike began, Governor Noel called a special session of the legislature to appropriate funds to pay National Guard expenses. The session became something of an embarrassment for him. Several legislators, including Murray G. Felder of Pike County, questioned Noel's use of the National Guard to protect the rowdy strikebreakers. Noel responded that the McComb riot allegedly involved 2,000 shots fired at the strikebreakers' railroad car and that an estimated 400 to 500 shots were fired at the Water Valley railroad shops. A number of legislators focused on the claim by the sheriffs of both Pike and Yalobusha counties that National Guard troops were not needed. Noel responded that the officers in question had wanted the troops at first and later attempted to change their minds. He also justified the troops by saying the district attorneys (elected from multicounty districts) had favored sending in the National Guard. Some legislators continued to be unimpressed. Moze Hunt Jones of Franklin County expressed his belief that the sending of troops was part of the railroad's scheme to enlist the state government in defeating unionism. Senator Frank Burkitt was incredulous the Illinois Central actually sought reimbursement for transporting troops to defend its property, and he worked to have the reimbursement for Illinois Central deleted from the appropriation.[21]

The governor's proposal to appropriate $46,000 to pay National Guard expenses failed to receive a majority of members' votes and thus went down to defeat. Finally, after Noel carefully itemized and justified the expenses, the legislature made the appropriation. The strike, meanwhile, wore on.[22]

By November union members were trying desperately to be heard, issuing two open letters to the people of Mississippi. One complained that the Illinois Central was scouring rural Mississippi to find men to "SCAB on the shopmen," and it urged Mississippians to refuse to be hired for this purpose. A second open letter tried to counter reports common in the press that the strike was over and railroad functions were getting back to normal. The letter asserted that 97 percent of Illinois Central workers had gone out on strike and that almost that number were still striking. Unfortunately for the strikers, however, the open letters got little publicity outside McComb. Wider circulation was given to the Illinois Central president's statement (in mid-October) that the strike was all but over, and there was "nothing to arbitrate."[23]

Throughout the strike, a chief goal of both sides was to win the battle of public opinion. McComb's newspaper, the *City Enterprise*, clearly favored the strikers. Just after the riot, for example, the paper's headline read, "Scabs Insult Citizens and Start Fight." More typical of the state press at large was the *Hattiesburg News*, which took an antistriker tone, warning that the strike had been caused by labor leaders being "drunk with power" and that union members were "arrogant" and "greedy." Nonetheless, the *News* was fair enough to add that management's own "mean and selfish and short-sighted" policies had forced labor to organize in the first place.[24]

During the strike, the operations of the Illinois Central were severely curtailed, with passenger trains running hours late, if at all, and freight service drastically cut. Value of the company's stock fell sharply, and the firm's overall business losses were about $3 million. As the railroad's rolling stock deteriorated, some of the company's competitors actually loaned locomotives and boxcars in order to help prevent a labor victory. With this outside help, the Illinois Central persevered. The corporation's officers believed the enormous cost was justified to prevent creation of one railroad union group representing all employees.[25]

Costs for the company were fearful, but the costs for employees were even higher. Union investigators reported that 90 percent of strikers had been forced to move to smaller quarters during the strike. Some 68 percent had seen their families scattered among relatives or even permanently broken up. Many of the workers showed incredible staying power, but after three years the funds of the Railroad Employees Department were exhausted, and strikers received their last strike payments. Early in 1915 the AFL formally abandoned the strike. Most state residents had seen nothing in their newspapers about the strike for more than two years. Workers who had stuck to the union to the bitter end were not rehired by the Illinois Central and indeed had trouble finding railroad work at all. An elderly former employee of the Gulf, Mobile, and Ohio Railroad, interviewed in 1964, said part of his job had been to screen job applicants to ensure they had not been union members at the time of the Harriman lines strike.[26]

Mississippi's early labor unions have a mixed record of success. The unions won some early sawmill strikes because the lumber industry in Mississippi was booming and because it would be very difficult to replace skilled sawmill employees. Some of the successes in the sawmill strikes must be attributed to the leadership of the Knights of Labor, which was strong enough to launch one strike after another in various Mississippi sawmills. A 1915 shrimp fishermen's strike on the Gulf Coast failed because the fishermen were relatively poor and easily replaced.

In theory, the workers should have been able to win the strike that paralyzed the Illinois Central beginning in 1911. The highly skilled strikers would prove hard to replace, and the Illinois Central took a real financial battering during the strike. The firm was, however, a very powerful company backed by a major national financial group, and with the aid of the courts and even help from competing lines, the Illinois Central survived the strike. Management was willing to accept fearful losses to secure the long-term goal of preventing the rise of one big railroad union.

By 1917 there were few strong labor unions remaining in Mississippi. The Knights of Labor had fallen apart in the state, as it had nationally. The railroad unions were reeling after the battering they took in the Harriman lines strike that ended in 1915. The state press gave unions largely negative coverage, and the public attitude toward unions was increasingly hostile. Nationwide, legislation during the New Deal and during World War II would aid the rise of unionism, but in Mississippi public opinion would hinder union organizing.

CHAPTER TEN

AGE OF MODERNIZATION
Transportation, Cities, and Public Health

Few eras of history have seen as much technological growth as the period from 1877 to 1917. Mississippians of this era witnessed the development of the telephone, phonograph, electric lights and appliances, moving pictures, automobiles, and airplanes. Yet these inventions changed the lives of relatively few Mississippians. Certainly air travel was nothing but a novelty to be observed—and discussed—by state residents. Electric lights and labor-saving appliances were something that improved the lives of prosperous residents of the state's cities but failed to reach rural areas of the state until the 1930s and 1940s. Three agents of modernization did touch the lives of a great many Mississippians—transportation, increasing urbanization, and advances in public health.

Transportation was closely linked with industrialization in Mississippi. There were thirty wagon-making establishments by 1900, producing in that year 910 wagons and 235 carriages. Railroad shops in the state built and repaired locomotives and freight cars. The *Water Valley Central* reported proudly in 1881 on the first run of Engine 13, pulling fifty-four cars. Number 13 "is as good on the pull as can be found in any locomotive on any road," the *Central* editor boasted. In May 1881 six more locomotives were under construction at Water Valley. Mississippi had nine railroad shops in 1900 employing more than 1,500 machinists, boilermakers, carpenters, and other workers. Value of the repair work they did was estimated at $870,000 yearly. Shipbuilding was a small industry on the Gulf Coast offering irregular and seasonal work. Mississippi in 1900 produced twenty-five steam-powered wooden boats, fourteen large sailboats, eight barges, and four small sailboats. The number of persons employed in the shipyards in 1900 ranged from a high of 162 to a low of 40.[1]

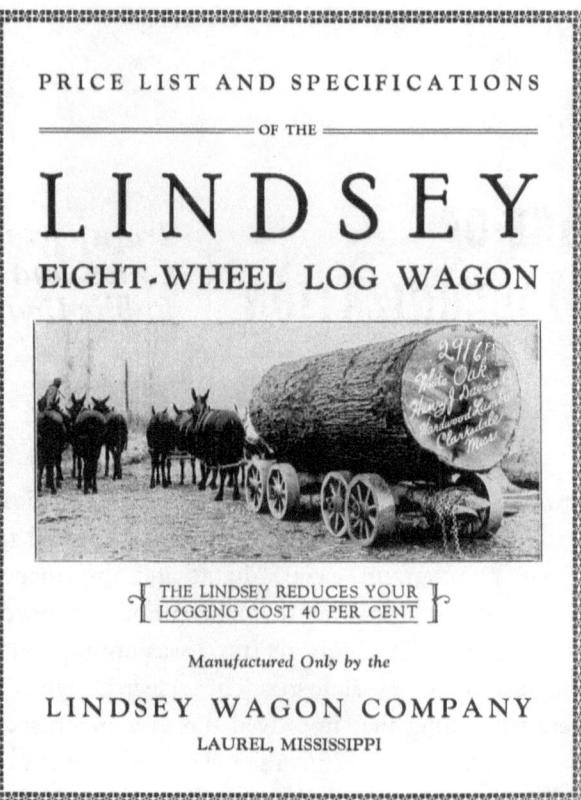

The Lindsay Wagon Company provided employment to a large workforce in Laurel. The firm developed one particularly successful product, the eight-wheeled log wagon that became a standard fixture in logging operations across the nation. (Photo courtesy of Lauren Rogers Museum of Art.)

For Mississippians, the railroads symbolized a new era of progress and development of their state. Ocean Springs resident Thomas Park remembered, "In my childhood the steam engine was perhaps the most admired mechanical object that man had created and I quite enthusiastically joined in this adoration." Similarly, another Gulf Coast resident, Laura Taylor, recorded in her diary the 1896 opening of the Gulf and Ship Island Railroad. "The boys seem never to tire of the R.R.," Taylor wrote; they "go to see it every day, I believe." Grown men, too, were infatuated with railroads. The most common postwar activity of Confederate generals was railroad building. General James Lusk Alcorn was a driving force behind the development of the Memphis and Vicksburg Railroad. General Absalom M. West was an early president of the Mississippi Central, while General Rufus Polk Neely was another Mississippi Central leader. General P. G. T. Beauregard of Louisiana was president of the New Orleans, Jackson, and Great Northern Railroad. General William T. Martin of Adams County was the primary booster of the "Little J" railroad between Natchez and Jackson.²

Yet railroad boosters in Mississippi faced a number of obstacles. One of the most serious was that the population was widely scattered throughout the state. The state in 1870 had only five towns with a population greater than 2,500. Railroads lacked passengers. The Delta shipped massive amounts of cotton, and the Piney Woods transported vast quantities of lumber, but other parts of the state had considerably less to ship. Even the Delta and Piney Woods railroads suffered from the one-sidedness of shipments—a great deal of material left the state but relatively little came in. The Illinois Central benefited from having two great cities as its termini (Chicago and New Orleans), but Mississippi towns along the Illinois Central tracks found that they received inadequate service. The company's chief goal seemed to be to give rapid service between the two great metropolitan areas. Natural barriers also interfered with railroad building. Crews that constructed the Yazoo and Mississippi Valley Railroad encountered mosquitoes, poison ivy, briars, quicksand, and poisonous snakes. The Yazoo River at the crossing near Vicksburg was thirty-one feet deep under normal conditions but eighty-one feet at flood stage. Engineers could find no bedrock upon which to build a bridge. This Yazoo River bridge ended up costing three times the amount that had been estimated.³

The giant of Mississippi railroading was the Illinois Central, a north-south line that absorbed several antebellum Mississippi railroads. A major problem that the Illinois Central encountered was consolidating its new holdings. Northern railroads used a gauge of 4 feet 8½ inches, while Mississippi's railroads used the traditional southern gauge of 5 feet. Through passengers had to change trains at the midpoint of their trip, or the cars had to undergo a tedious modification before proceeding. On July 29, 1881, the Illinois Central made railroading history when it converted all its southern track (from Kentucky to New Orleans) to the new gauge in a matter of hours. The process required some 3,000 workers scattered along the 550-mile section of track. At sunup, the crews began drawing the spikes on the western rails, then moved the rails 3½ inches eastward and spiked them back into place.⁴

The Illinois Central gave reasonably good service to Jackson and to several dozen smaller towns such as Grenada and Durant. Yet railroad magnate Collis P. Huntington of New York noted that the Mississippi Delta was badly underserved by railroads. A new Delta railroad, he perceived, would spark new development of the region. He began construction of a railroad that would constitute a rival north-south line to the Illinois Central. The dream of Huntington and his collaborators became a reality in 1884, with the opening of the Louisville, New Orleans, and Texas Railroad, offering service to Memphis, Vicksburg, and New Orleans. Huntington acquired 774,000 acres of prime Delta land, and with his land sales and the operation of his railroad, he did a great deal to develop the Delta. Nationally, however, Huntington overextended himself, and he was forced to begin liquidating assets. One of these assets was his Delta railroad, which he sold to the Illinois Central in 1892. The Illinois Central merged Huntington's road with its own smaller line that ran from Jackson to Yazoo City. The new Delta enterprise operated under the name Yazoo and Mississippi Valley Railroad.[5]

One of the largest railroad-building projects in Mississippi was the Gulf and Ship Island Railroad, chartered by Congress in 1855. Congress promised the railroad promoters a federal grant of 500,000 acres if the road were completed by 1865, but the disruption of the Civil War meant that the line would have to be built largely with private funds. In 1886 the state put the bulk of its convict population at the disposal of the railroad promoters, and under conditions of great brutality prisoners graded the roadbed from Gulfport to Hattiesburg. The railroad's cost for this work was $50 per prisoner per year. In 1892, during a nationwide depression, the Gulf and Ship Island went into receivership, and a new group of investors took over led by Joseph T. Jones, an oil investor from West Virginia and Pennsylvania. Although the road hauled prodigious amounts of lumber in the 1890s, not until July 4, 1900, did the Gulf and Ship Island reach the state's capital city. Under Jones's leadership, contractors dredged a deep channel from Gulfport to the harbor on Ship Island and built a pier there that was nearly one mile long. Jones thus facilitated the shipping of Mississippi lumber to world markets.[6]

Several railroads besides the Illinois Central and the Gulf and Ship Island were responsible for fueling the Piney Woods timber boom. The Mobile, Jackson, and Kansas City Railroad was built from Mobile, heading northwest through the Mississippi Pine Belt and on to Hattiesburg. There was barely a village along the line when the railroad was first built, but the area developed quickly with the railroad's aid. Another great line through the Piney Woods was the Mobile and Ohio, one of Mississippi's oldest railroads. It entered Mississippi northwest of Mobile and then extended almost directly north and served a number of cities along the eastern edge of the state. The state was, in fact, much better served by north-south lines than by east-west routes. One of the most important east-west lines was the Alabama and Vicksburg, which served Vicksburg, Jackson, and Meridian. Another was the Columbus and Greenville, serving those two cities and a host of cotton towns along the way. A line of the Louisville and Nashville linked New Orleans and Mobile as early as 1881, making tourist hotels in towns like Biloxi accessible to wealthy urbanites.[7]

William C. Falkner, grandfather of the novelist William Faulkner, was one of the most interesting characters in the story of Mississippi railroad building. The elder Falkner was also an author, and his novel, *The White Rose of Memphis*, brought him a good income, which he invested in his dream of connecting his home of Ripley, Mississippi, to Middleton, Tennessee, by rail. Before the building of the railroad, Ripley farmers had no choice but to take their goods to market over nearly forty miles of rough roads that were impassable in winter. As Falkner constructed his railroad, he earned the state's standard incentive of $4,000 per mile. Never one to think small, Falkner called his road the Ship Island, Ripley, and Kentucky Railroad—and later the Gulf and Chicago. Falkner boasted that his railroad was the cheapest ever built, but later engineers came to regret the railroad's meandering course, which followed ridgetops to avoid the cost of building bridges.[8]

Railroads employed thousands of Mississippians, offering good pay and benefits. The tragic downside was the dangerous nature of the work. The death or maiming of a railroad employee was almost a daily occurrence in Mississippi. Fortunately, a number of mechanical improvements brought increased safety to employees. The most important was the invention of an automatic coupling device. Previously, workers had to get the couplers of two cars into the right position by hand, then drive an iron pin into the couplings to hold them together. Loss of fingers and hands was all too common. With the automatic coupler, the cars joined themselves when they rolled into each other at low speed. Another important safety improvement was the air brake, replacing the ineffective hand brakes beginning in the 1870s. Danger of collision was lessened by the construction of double sets of tracks with automatic signaling devices. Passengers and employees alike benefited from the elimination of unsafe iron stoves for heating and their replacement with more advanced heating systems. The "vestibule" system of covered walkways between passenger cars prevented many deaths and injuries.[9]

While Mississippi's railroads were of central economic importance, the place of steamboats in the state's history is also substantial. Steamboats began service in the state well before the Civil War and increased in number and in carrying capacity throughout the late nineteenth century. Photographs from the period show steamboats so covered with cotton bales that the boats themselves are all but invisible. These boats were active on the Mississippi River, the Yazoo, and various small tributaries. U.S. government records from 1904 indicate the Mississippi River between Memphis and Vicksburg carried 88 million tons of cotton that year, and the river between Vicksburg and New Orleans carried 47 million tons. Moreover, the river between Memphis and New Orleans typically carried three-quarters of a billion tons of logs annually. The *Belle of the Bends* and the *City of Wheeling* served Vicksburg and other cities and as early as 1905 were "brilliantly lighted" with electric lamps in every stateroom. The *Betsey Ann*, which operated out of Natchez, had a post office aboard, served meals, and boasted a saloon specializing in mint juleps. On a smaller scale, many small towns were served by packets, bringing goods and the U.S. mail. As late as 1917 packets served such towns as Carthage, Gainesville, and Pearlington, along rivers including the Pearl and Tombigbee.[10]

Railroads and boats were important links of transportation in Mississippi, the more so because the state's roads were so bad. At the turn of the century, there were no paved roads in Mississippi, and only 0.5 percent of the roads had gravel on them. No other southern state had a smaller percentage of its roads improved. The poor roads kept farmers isolated. Senator John Sharp Williams estimated that Mississippians were able to get their mail only about once every six days, as they went to the nearest crossroads post office. Although Congress inaugurated a rural free delivery system in 1893, the new mail routes were slow in coming to Mississippi. Because the routes had to be approved by the postmaster general, and because the postmasters general were Republican between 1897 and 1913, few routes were approved in the Democratic state of Mississippi. In 1900 Ohio boasted 225 rural mail routes, while Mississippi had none. When pressed for explanations, the postmasters general pointed to widespread illiteracy among southerners and the poor quality of roads in the region—two explanations that only angered Mississippians and other citizens south of the Mason-Dixon Line.[11]

It is difficult to appreciate how isolated were the lives of many state residents in the days before good roads. Samuel G. Thigpen recalled growing up in rural south Mississippi. "There were communities that I heard people talk about," Thigpen mused, "from 10 to 25 miles away from us that I never did go to because they were so far away." From his family's Lake Como home, the closest rail point was Heidelberg, eighteen miles away. The roads in that direction were so bad, however, that Thigpen's father generally took goods to Laurel to ship. Laurel was twenty-five miles distant. In 1898, at the age of eight, Samuel made his first trip to town with his father. The eighteen-mile trip to Heidelberg was a long one, over bad roads. The boy and his father camped out overnight. Seeing a town like Heidelberg (population 228) was a momentous occasion for the boy.[12]

The poor quality of Mississippi's roads could be traced to state road laws, which dated to 1822. Under these laws, every male aged eighteen to fifty had to work on the roads for up to ten days per year. Alternatively, he could pay a $5 fee to the local road supervisor. Each of the five members of the county board of supervisors was responsible for the roads in his beat, and each was required to appoint a road supervisor for the beat. Anyone who refused to serve as road supervisor would be fined $50 for contempt. The road supervisors occasionally called the men out for a workday, and residents showed up with plows, saws, picks, and shovels. The system was utterly free for the taxpayers. Materials were purchased using the $5 fees of those who chose not to work. The negatives of the system, however, were overwhelming. No beats actually saw ten days of work put in, as citizens exerted pressure on the supervisor to minimize the work draft. The quality of the roadwork was very often bad. Observers frequently said the roads were better before the work was done than afterward.[13]

One of the most serious problems with Mississippi's road building and maintenance was that no planning was done at the county or state level. Roads were built and maintained at the beat level, meaning Mississippi did not really have a system of roads but only a collection of locally useful routes. That the quality of roads and bridges was bad may be seen by a state law levying a stiff fine for anyone who crossed a bridge on horseback at a speed faster than a walk. In particularly marshy areas, road crews laid "cross-ways"—logs laid across the roadway. Not only did these cross-ways make for a very bumpy ride for wagons, they were also treacherous for horses, mules, and oxen, which routinely injured their legs. Bridges were so costly and so prone to loss by flooding that in many areas farmers doubled as ferrymen—on call twenty-four hours a day. Mississippi's dirt roads were barely adequate for horses and wagons, and they proved almost completely unusable by that new mode of transportation, the horseless carriage.[14]

Ocean Springs resident Thomas Park felt pride when his father traveled to St. Louis and purchased a car called the Locomobile. "How he got it to Ocean Springs," Park commented, "I'll never know." The Locomobile spent a lot of time at the mechanic's being fixed. While young Park won new popularity with his friends, his father made enemies among farmers. After hitting a pig "with a glancing blow" on a country road, Park's father had to defend himself with a tire iron when a farmer strode up with a bullwhip. The Park family concluded that Mississippi was not ready for automobiles. An excursion from Ocean Springs to Biloxi was cause for both pleasant anticipation and dread. At least two blowouts were to be expected. Typically, the car would bog down in the mud, leading a sheepish Park to ask a farmer to come to his rescue—with a horse.[15]

Other pioneering auto owners complained loudly about the condition of Mississippi's roads. An Alabaman who traveled through east Mississippi reported that Greene County's sandy roads and Wayne County's roads of red clay were especially treacherous. In all of east Mississippi, this traveler reported, only George County had bothered to erect road signs. In other counties, it was necessary to inquire of local farmers which roads went where—often turning out of bed the early-retiring agrarians. Gulfport's postmaster N. D. Goodwin was one automotive pioneer. He reported a six-mile stretch of road in Forrest County that took three hours to traverse because of the poor quality of the roadbed. After a trip from Gulfport to Hattiesburg that took seven hours, Goodwin concluded that "the roads were worst where they had been worked" by inexperienced road crews.[16]

With the coming of the automobile, many Mississippians organized to press government at all levels for better roads. Citizens founded a number of "Good Roads Clubs," supplementing the ones organized in other states. By 1915 there was the Mississippi Highway Association. Local clubs of auto owners, such as the Jackson Automobile Association, took weekend excursions, making inspections and lobbying local governments along the way. Politicians at the very highest level joined the good roads movement. The list of Mississippi delegates to the Pan American Good Roads Congress, held in California in 1915, reads like a who's who of prominent Mississippians of the time. The list included Governor Earl Brewer, U.S. senators John Sharp Williams and James K. Vardaman, member of the U.S. House of Representatives J. W. Collier, and Jackson editors Fred Sullens and R. H. Henry.[17]

Surprisingly, the railroads were among the greatest boosters of good roads in the state. The first statewide good roads conference was held in 1901, under the sponsorship of the Illinois Central Railroad. Both the Illinois Central and the Southern Railroad sponsored "good roads trains" that traversed their territories showing off the latest in road-building equipment and offering exhibits demonstrating the benefits of well-made roads. By the 1940s and 1950s trucking would challenge railroads for primacy in hauling freight in Mississippi, and the automobile would cut drastically the demand for rail passenger service. In the early twentieth century, however, it seemed clear that better roads would aid the railroads. For one thing, better roads could lead to population growth and to increased industrialization, and such growth would benefit railroads. Also, most freight and passengers came to the railroads by roads. Rail traffic might increase if it were easier for shippers and passengers to get to the depots.[18]

Proponents of good roads had to persuade a majority of Mississippi's citizens that good roads were needed. Many rural residents believed that good roads primarily benefited urban car owners; therefore, car owners should bear the burden of building good roads. Indeed, expense was the great obstacle to road improvement. Good roads enthusiasts stressed how better roadways would aid farmers. If a farmer took two full days to haul 2,000 pounds to the depot over rough roads in two trips, good roads enthusiasts pointed out how much more efficient it was for the same farmer to spend five hours carrying 2,000 pounds in a single load over a graded gravel road. The good roads boosters pointed out that it could be taxing for a mule to pull a load downhill on Mississippi's muddy roads. Draft animals would live longer, and be in better condition generally, if they did not have to haul up steep hills or through boggy bottoms. Literature of the good roads associations pointed out the inefficiency of days of enforced inactivity, when farmers needed to do hauling but could not. Farmers who raised perishable crops never knew if the roads would be passable while the crop was still fresh. Some good roads writers argued that young Mississippians would be more likely to stay on the farm if they could occasionally slip away to the city and enjoy bright lights and moving pictures.[19]

Some early good roads literature admitted that a system of gravel roads for Mississippi might be prohibitively expensive. A field station at the Agricultural and Mechanical College at Starkville published a pamphlet in 1901 called "Good Dirt Roads for Mississippi." The publication called upon the state to abandon the citizen labor draft and have the boards of supervisors hire experienced contractors to maintain an excellent system of dirt roads. A 1910 report by a national expert stated that Mississippi had so little good road material (few gravel quarries, for example) that macadam roads could cost up to $9,000 per mile. This expert reported experiments with the firing of lumps of clay to use in place of gravel—the resulting material could make an adequate though not excellent road. Still, like the field station publication, this 1910 report argued that dirt roads would be adequate if they were improved. Dirt roads must be graded and ditched, the author explained. Even such a simple practice as building roads in sunny areas wherever possible could help enormously with the problem of mud.[20]

One of the most active counties in improving its roads around 1915 was Lauderdale, site of the state's then-largest city, Meridian. Lauderdale County planned and built a series of five major roads radiating out from Meridian. Residents reported that farm values nearly doubled along the routes. Farmer Joe Clark told an interviewer he would rather have a small farm on a good road than a large farm on a bad road. Most residents along the road declared themselves willing to pay new road taxes, given the improvement in their daily lives. Charley Odum was a

Lauderdale County farmer not fortunate enough to live along one of the five main roads. He reported great difficulty in marketing his crop. In fact, he reported, "The people in my community have actually had to go without oil for their lamps for a week at a time because they couldn't get it" over impassable roads. Odum concluded that the costs of not having good roads were greater than the cost of building them.[21]

For farmers, the aim of the good roads movement was to reduce the costs of marketing their crops and reduce the isolation and loneliness of farm life. Town boosters, on the other hand, dreamed of a major system of highways that would link Mississippi's towns and cities with New Orleans, Memphis, Birmingham, and Atlanta. Such highways would facilitate commerce, attract industries, and promote hotels, restaurants, and gasoline stations. Since most of these larger highways would be regional or national, Mississippi's leaders had to cooperate with the leaders of other states. Meanwhile, Mississippi towns often competed fiercely with each other. To be left off the proposed highway route could mean a town would languish as an economic backwater.[22]

Improvement of the state's roads was made possible by a reworking of the road laws, slowly inaugurating a system to replace the one set up eight decades earlier. In 1900 the legislature authorized boards of supervisors to hire contractors to work the roads, rather than rely on a labor draft. By 1910 counties were regularly issuing road bonds to allow the hiring of contractors, and roads were more professionally surfaced and graded. The emphasis was still on dirt and gravel roads, however. In 1909 there were nearly 40,000 miles of road in the state; of these, 219 miles were of gravel or stone, and no road was paved. For a community to build a new gravel road could be a signal achievement. Arthur Hudson recalled that when Attala County built a single mile of gravel road just south of Kosciusko in 1913, "I used to drive out there sometimes just to hear the buggy's wheels click and scrunch." The Washington County Board of Supervisors authorized the state's first paved highway in 1918, a section of road connecting Glen Allen and Lake Washington with Greenville. The more tight-fisted members of the board wanted to pave only two tracks, to accommodate vehicles' two pairs of wheels, but the progressives won out, and the entire road (one lane) was paved. Paved roads were a godsend to the Delta, where an especially sticky mud called "gumbo" could pull the wheel off a wagon.[23]

In 1916 Congress passed the Federal Roads Act, providing money to the states for highway construction if the states set up state highway departments to plan and maintain roads. Mississippi nearly lost its chance to obtain these highway funds, being one of the last states in the nation to organize a highway department. The legislature created the Mississippi Highway Commission in 1916, but federal officials complained that the state's weak support for the commission raised doubts about whether Mississippi should receive highway funds. Certainly the appropriations for the Highway Commission were tiny—$13,000 in 1916, for example. Federal complaints about Mississippi's inadequate highway funding led the state legislature to enact a one-cent-per-gallon gasoline tax. The new tax was wholly necessary for highway construction, since the existing property taxes could not even maintain roads, much less build or upgrade them. By 1925 the state was maintaining 2,600 miles of highway, while the counties continued to maintain smaller roads.[24]

The history of the good roads movement in Mississippi illuminates some important trends in the state in the early twentieth century. Certainly the movement was a part of the Progressivism that swept the state—a movement to use scientific and technological advances to solve the problems people faced. Yet the good roads movement also showed the division between agrarian reformers and urban progressives. The former believed good roads should be used to improve the lives of farmers of modest means. The latter were more interested in roads that would bring prosperity for cities in general and merchants in particular, roads that would encourage commerce and lead to industrialization. As in so many other cases, Mississippi made great strides in absolute terms, as thousands of miles of nearly impassable muddy roads gave way to graded and ditched roads, some dirt, some gravel, and even some paved. Yet in relative terms, Mississippi remained at the bottom of the list of states in terms of the quality of its roads. In 1900 no state had a smaller percentage of its roads improved; by the time of World War I this was still true. While Mississippi founded a highway commission, no state gave less support to its highway commission than did Mississippi. It would take decades for Mississippi to develop a highway system comparable to those enjoyed by other states.

In efforts to modernize the state's cities, the building of roads and streets was a key goal. City governments were sometimes willing to press their populations hard in order to achieve an excellent system of streets. For example, Biloxi's city government in 1910 passed an extremely tough city street ordinance. Ordinance 417 stipulated that Biloxi's male citizens must labor six days per year upon the city streets. Those who refused would be fined $2 per day for each day of refusal and would be sent to jail if the fine were not immediately paid. The only way to win release from jail was to post a $100 bond and go to work on the city streets. The most controversial feature of the new city law was that by paying a fee of $3, in advance, men could win release from the work requirement. To many Biloxians, this was "class legislation," whereby the more prosperous could avoid onerous labor, but the average citizen (who earned perhaps a dollar a day) could be forced to work. Several Democrats announced their candidacy for city council on a platform of opposition to the new ordinance, and the Socialist Party brought out a full slate that was similarly opposed to the new system.[25]

In the face of citizen protests, the board of aldermen relented slightly. Ordinance 419 provided that those who refused to work on the streets would be fined $6 but not forced to work. Still, several of the anti–street law candidates won election to the board of aldermen, including Socialist candidate Sumner W. Rose. At Rose's urging, forty Biloxians refused to labor on the streets or pay the $3 fee. Rose criticized the law because it forced poorer citizens to work, an involuntary servitude in violation of the Thirteenth Amendment. He also pointed out that poorer citizens had to labor six days since they could not pay the $3; thus the city in effect was paying fifty cents per day for grueling roadwork. In February 1911 Rose went to jail when he refused to pay a fine or fee or to labor on the streets. With him went another Biloxi Socialist, the noted art potter George Ohr. The men attempted to have the city, state, and federal courts overturn Biloxi's street ordinance, but while they gained national publicity, they failed in their quest. By the time of World War I, however, cities (like counties) were beginning to abandon the citizen labor draft system. Residents of the state's cities came to enjoy paved streets long before farmers had paved roads in their neighborhoods.[26]

Almost every modern convenience of the period 1877 to 1917 came first to city residents. These conveniences were available to country folk later or not at all. Citizens living in Jackson and Vicksburg enjoyed local telephone service, and long-distance service connecting the two cities, by 1881. Yet the new invention came so slowly to rural areas that in 1900 a traveling circus displayed a telephone as a novelty that attracted more interest than the elephants. At Lake Como, for example, circus operators set up a telephone at the circus tent and put another at a general store a quarter mile away. For a dime, circus patrons could call and speak to the storekeeper. Many older farmers insisted the whole thing was a trick devised by dishonest circus managers, even though the voice on the other end was clearly the familiar voice of the storekeeper. In 1902 Mississippi had more than 15,000 telephones and 297, mostly female, operators. The phone service was centered, however, in some thirty cities and towns. Few farm families would enjoy phone service for years to come.[27]

City residents enjoyed other convenient utility services that were unavailable to rural residents. In 1902 Mississippi had eighteen city-owned power stations and twenty-five private electric companies. Several of the electric plants were outgrowths of city streetcar lines, which required large amounts of electricity to operate and whose surplus power could be sold to city residents. Jackson, Meridian, and Columbus had city-owned natural gas plants, offering piped gas for heating, lighting, and cooking. Cities set up municipal water systems to replace dependence upon wells. Hazlehurst got its impetus for clean water in 1883 when a routine cleaning of the well near the courthouse revealed "the carcasses of some dead cats, almost decayed."[28]

Urban population growth was rapid in this period. Meridian, for example, saw a quadrupling of its population between 1870 and 1890, then another doubling by 1910. The state's largest city in this period, it benefited from sawmills, railroad shops, and a variety of industries. Meridian also served the large agricultural population of east-central Mississippi. In 1890 the highly successful Rothenberg Brothers mercantile firm used some of its profits to boost the city of Meridian and erected a beautiful new opera house. Nine years later the firm opened a gigantic department store that occupied an entire city block.[29]

For all the state's cities, rapid growth caused problems. Poverty, prostitution, drunkenness, assault, and theft became increasingly common as cities grew. Carpenter J. T. Cochran came into Hattiesburg looking for work. When he failed to find it, he was arrested and charged with vagrancy. In the mayor's court, however, Cochran won release as the mayor pointed out that Cochran's vagrancy was "through no fault of his own." The mayor served notice that he would not enforce vagrancy laws against "white men who are searching for employment." At the time of Cochran's hearing in the mayor's court, the *Hattiesburg News* reported the case of a woman and her sixteen-year-old daughter who had come to town looking for work and now had no food and no possessions. Local citizens helped the two unfortunate women. A few months later, however, another young woman attempted suicide by jumping out of the window of her Hattiesburg boardinghouse because she was "penniless and without employment."[30]

Mississippi's cities grew and modernized at a rapid pace during the forty years beginning in 1877. The cities of 1917 were all but unrecognizable when compared with their earlier forms. Automobiles, bright lights, movie theaters, opera houses, ice-cream parlors, soda fountains, and the conveniences of electricity and the telephone led many Mississippians to enjoy fully the inventions and other improvements of this period. As with so many measures, however, while Mississippi's actual growth was impressive, its relative growth was not. Mississippi in 1870 was the least urban state in the Union, and in 1920 this was still true.[31]

Modernization of Mississippi's transportation system and of its cities helped lead to economic growth and diversification. Yet Mississippi would never reach its economic potential while disease killed many workers and left others tragically enervated. With depressing regularity, epidemic diseases swept through Mississippi, bringing anguish and mourning to thousands of families. The epidemics also brought business to a standstill for months at a time. In addition to epidemics, Mississippi suffered from diseases that were present at all times, including pellagra, hookworm, and tuberculosis. Sometimes these diseases proved fatal, while in other cases they deprived a person of energy and ambition. Northerners were reluctant to invest in the Deep South because epidemics regularly paralyzed business. Prevailing endemic diseases hurt the quality of work in the state. Before Mississippi could participate fully in the national economy, it would have to conquer several diseases—none more terrifying than yellow fever.

Although doctors at the time believed that yellow fever was indigenously American, modern evidence suggests that yellow fever was West African in origin and was thus a scourge brought to this country along with the scourge of slavery. We now know that yellow fever is a viral disease, carried from human to human by the mosquito *Aedes aegypti*. Once in the human body, the virus enters the lymphatic system, attacking and destroying the tissues of internal organs. Every doctor practicing in the state knew the symptoms. These began with headaches, chills, a lack of energy, and aching joints. Patients with milder cases might begin to improve after these symptoms ran their course. The less fortunate, however, saw a worsening of symptoms within three days. Nausea, headaches, suppressed urine flow, and constipation were among the symptoms of moderately severe cases. In the most severe cases, the patient would bleed from any or all of the body's orifices. One horrific symptom was the dreaded "black vomit," the body's expulsion of matter the color and consistency of coffee grounds. This was actually blood from hemorrhages in the stomach lining, darkened by the gastric fluids. Sleeplessness and nervous agitation were common symptoms, and the patient might finally experience real mental unbalance caused by cerebral hemorrhages. One symptom that came on late in the disease, and even after death, was jaundicing of the skin, ranging from a bright canary yellow to a bronzy color. The bodies of yellow fever victims often seemed to decompose quickly and gave off odors believed to help spread the disease. Many families found themselves with no one willing to help bury their dead.[32]

In the late nineteenth century, medical experts disagreed sharply about how yellow fever spread. Many knew it was caused by some sort of "germ" or microbe, but it was unclear how the microbe spread from patient to patient. Some believed the disease could be spread by objects touched by sick persons. Such clothing, papers, and personal effects were called "fomites" and were to be avoided at all costs. Many believed the disease was more easily spread in the presence of poor sanitation—stagnant pools of water, neglected privies, and dirty streets. Others believed the disease floated through the "miasma," carried by polluted air from privies or rotting carcasses.[33]

The worst outbreak of yellow fever in recorded human history struck the region between Memphis and New Orleans in 1878. Mississippi was the state hit hardest during this horrendous epidemic. The tragedy of this epidemic can be seen by looking at the experiences of one man, Samuel Agnew, a minister who kept a diary. Agnew recorded with sorrow in 1878 that his very young daughter had contracted the dreaded fever. Agnew tells the story:

> *October 12, 1878.* She looks better in the face. She eats as much as she ought to eat.... We feel cheerful and think she with Gods blessing will now be spared to us. *Later.* At 2 o'clock I was called down stairs.... They had tried to give her Brandy and she could not swallow it. There was phlegm in her throat and I thought she was dying. The poor dear Babe struggled for breath. I was filled with sorrow and my eyes came dimmed by tears. By 3 o'clock she had got over the trouble and breathed without trouble. *October 13, 1878.* Mary at this time lies quietly, noticing persons pass by. The preceding sentence was written about 10 o'clock and in 2½ hours thereafter my little Mary had breathed her last. [I saw her] looking at me earnestly as if she wanted me. I took her from the cradle and walked with her. She smiled most pleasantly and noticed different objects as she passed them. Before a great while I noticed a change in her countenance which excited my fear.... She was so weak she could not struggle. Every once in a while she would raise her little feet sometimes one and sometimes the other. She commenced dying 15 minutes before twelve and her last breath was drawn 30 minutes after twelve. I sat and watched with eyes dimmed with tears her spirit departing from the body.... So my little darling has "become a lump of cold clay."[34]

Agnew sent a friend to Baldwyn to purchase a coffin, and the family put Mary's body on a table in the parlor. Friends and family sat up all night. The next day Agnew recorded how "she lay in her coffin with a white flower in her hand. Her face was natural except that it was pale and icy.... The coffin was a fine one. The finest I have ever seen. I do not know what it cost. I kissed her on her left cheek.... With tears we took our last look. The coffin was closed at 10 o'clock."[35] The frosts that ended the epidemic came four days after the death of Agnew's daughter.

One of many communities hit by yellow fever in 1878 was Dry Grove in Hinds County. Newspapers warned their readers that the news from Dry Grove "appalls the stoutest heart." The local correspondent noted that residents had lost all hope. One nurse, reported a newspaper correspondent, "has placed in rough boxes with his own hands seven of one family, the Castors. Other families are entirely swept away." Six doctors were at work ministering to the sick at Dry Grove, but three of the six practitioners were dreadfully ill themselves.[36]

The Episcopal rector's wife, Emily Douglas, wrote a reminiscence describing the fearful events at Dry Grove. Douglas sent her children to a friend's isolated farm where she believed they would be safe, and the children considered the trip something of a lark until they learned that their father had contracted the fever back at Dry Grove. Then came the news that the cases were becoming fatal. Even in their rural retreat, three of the children were "struggling between life and death in the embrace of the heartless invader." Douglas recorded how she prayed for the restoration to health of her family members but added that "God did not think best to grant [my] prayer but in part," since two of her sisters died. The Douglas children as well as their father did recover, however. In this little community, forty adults died, leaving many orphans. Local clergy worked to find homes for the bereft children. Douglas reported the children found good homes, "but Oh there was a longing for the 'touch of a vanished hand and the sound of a voice that was still.'"[37]

One factor that added to the terror of the 1878 epidemic was that all the traditional rules were broken. Physicians had long noted that children seldom died of the yellow fever. Yet in 1878 a great many children died. Mississippians knew that African Americans were less likely to contract yellow fever and less likely to succumb if they did contract it. Yet in the 1878 epidemic, thousands of persons of color died. Epidemiologists had noticed that yellow fever never struck areas with an elevation higher than 500 feet above sea level. In 1878, however, many such towns were hit, including Holly Springs at 625 feet elevation. In 1878 many towns that had seldom been touched by yellow fever were hit by the prevailing epidemic. These included several that initially had been refuges for those fleeing the fever—Holly Springs, Grenada, Greenville, Jackson, and Meridian.[38]

Why was the 1878 epidemic so lethal? First, the viral strain of that year was more deadly than usual. This would explain, for example, why African Americans succumbed in such large numbers. Also, it is clear that weather conditions previous to the epidemic were ideal for mosquitoes. There had been an exceptionally mild winter, and many towns in south Mississippi had seen only one frost all winter.

Thus mosquitoes flourished in 1878 in towns like Holly Springs and Grenada, where they had had only a tenuous foothold before.[39]

Coupled with the disease was a wave of economic devastation. The state came to a standstill. Railroads did not operate, newspapers ceased publishing, banks closed, mail delivery stopped. One Delta correspondent noted, "The fields are white, and the cotton is being blown off into the mud and ruined." He added that "the negroes on most of the plantations have suffered fearfully, and in many places they have died in the fields, being stricken with the fever while at work." Those who wanted to carry on business during the tragedy were prevented from doing so by quarantines forbidding communication between towns. Meanwhile, news of the economic standstill confirmed to northern investors that the Deep South was no place to locate factories or to invest in banks or railroads.[40]

Yellow fever had traditionally been an urban disease, its spread hastened by large numbers of people for the mosquitoes to infect. In 1878, however, the disease hit rural areas as well as towns. The little farming community of Lake (straddling the line between Scott and Newton counties) had about 350 residents. Of these, 330 contracted the fever and 78 died. Larger towns like Greenville were also devastated. Greenville, with a population of 2,500, had never before experienced yellow fever. All but 450 people fled in the face of the epidemic. Of the 450 who remained, 435 contracted the fever and 296 died. Greenville's epidemic ended before the frosts arrived. "The fever is dying out," explained one resident, "because the supply of live material is exhausted." Except for the 15 people who had very strong resistance, there was no healthy person left in Greenville for mosquitoes to infect.[41]

Most doctors repeatedly told the public that yellow fever was not contagious by contact. Those who worked around the sick had no higher incidence of the disease than those who had no contact with them. Doctors urged a cleaning up of the poisonous environment that they said was causing the disease. This included cleaning out (or treating with lime) privies and draining old wells, cisterns, and standing pools. Town officers of Magnolia issued pine firewood to citizens, requiring them to light bonfires to purify the "miasma" that carried the disease. Some towns sprinkled carbolic acid on the streets and yards. The use of this acid was so extensive that tree branches drooped and fish in nearby creeks died. Did all this emphasis on sanitation do any good? Perhaps a little—at least the cleaning out of old wells and cisterns. *Aedes aegypti* mosquitoes prefer breeding in containers of water with vertical or near-vertical sides. They do not typically breed in pools of water and are finicky enough to avoid breeding in muddy ditches or in privies. Much of the energy invested in the sanitation campaigns therefore had little effect on the mosquito vector of the disease.[42]

Citizens demanded quarantines. By excluding all outsiders, residents hoped to keep their uninfected communities free of yellow fever. Many doctors argued that quarantines were a wasted effort, but city officers came under considerable pressure from locals to enact strict quarantines. Some residents established informal shotgun quarantines. Citizens near Water Valley burned bridges to keep outsiders away. The "Maritime Report" for the lower Mississippi Valley warned boat captains to avoid the upper Yazoo River because of the danger from bands of armed farmers. A Louisiana doctor traveling to help the citizens of Winona described the strange sights he saw from his train window as he passed through various Mississippi towns. The depot platforms looked like scenes from Currier and Ives prints of snowy New England, having been liberally covered with lime. Repeatedly the doctor saw rope barriers, with grim-faced men carrying shotguns prepared to exclude newcomers. At night the doctor observed dozens of bonfires, lit in hopes of somehow inhibiting whatever manner of germ was causing the fever. The quarantines did little good. While it was easy to exclude the obviously sick, those who were only recently infected were sometimes admitted if they were known to the quarantine guards. People who fled pestilential communities would do almost anything to find safe haven in another community. All it took to infect an entire community was one infected person successfully getting around the quarantine guards.[43]

With all the many theories about yellow fever that were circulating, it was inevitable that people would occasionally stumble on the right answer. One newspaper account during this 1878 epidemic reported that old-timers in Mississippi knew that the appearance of a certain gray-backed mosquito was "a certain forerunner of the yellow fever." The *Aedes aegypti* mosquito was indeed notable for its gray back. In 1881 an eccentric Cuban doctor published a paper implicating *Aedes aegypti* in the transmission of yellow fever. Unfortunately, Dr. Carlos Finlay's writings were ignored, and it is true that his experimental efforts to indict *Aedes aegypti* were inconclusive. Scientific breakthroughs allowing victory over yellow fever were still years in the future.[44]

The yellow fever epidemic of 1878 left 15,000 to 20,000 people dead in the lower Mississippi Valley. The highest death tolls were in Mississippi and Louisiana. In Vicksburg, 10 percent of the city's populace died, and other Mississippi towns were hit just as hard. The financial and business costs of the regional epidemic were estimated at some $200 million. In order to meet future crises, Mississippi's U.S. senator L. Q. C. Lamar late in 1878 introduced a bill to establish a national bureau of public health, an agency whose director general would have cabinet rank. The new bureau would oversee quarantine and sanitary matters. Southern members of

Congress jettisoned their devotion to states' rights and supported this strong new federal agency, while the American Public Health Association (dominated by northerners) preferred to leave public health matters to the states. Fearing the power concentrated in a director general, northern members of Congress substituted a weaker bill for Lamar's proposed law, and this weaker version passed. Persistent southerners in 1879 finally secured passage of a law giving the National Board of Health quarantine powers.[45]

While the yellow fever epidemics of 1888, 1897, 1898, and 1899 were less deadly than the 1878 epidemic, business losses were nevertheless severe. It was never clear until the frost came whether the state was going to be spared massive loss of life. Thus, during each of these epidemics, Mississippi communities enforced quarantines that effectively brought commerce to a standstill. Citizens turned to vigilante action if the quarantines were not enforced. Outside Jackson, for example, angry citizens tore up the tracks of the Alabama and Vicksburg Railroad when they believed the railroad was disobeying the spirit and letter of the quarantine.[46]

Local, state, and national public health authorities took some experimental steps to combat the yellow fever in the epidemics of the 1890s. In 1898 the U.S. Marine Hospital Service conducted an especially vigorous disinfecting program at fever-ridden McHenry, Mississippi. Objects that had been touched by yellow fever patients (fomites) were subjected to sulfur smoke or formaldehyde gas. Five homes of yellow fever patients were put to the torch under U.S. government supervision. The ashes of the homes were soaked with bichloride of mercury. All passengers on the Illinois Central Railroad were required to get off the train at both Kenner, Louisiana, and at McComb, Mississippi (one hundred miles apart), and each time they were examined by federal medical officers, had their luggage exposed to formaldehyde gas, and changed to a fresh, newly sanitized coach. In 1898 Jackson experimented with a policy of "depopulation." The city government urged citizens to live elsewhere temporarily, especially in areas north of Mississippi where the fever was not present. Carbondale, Illinois, became a favorite destination, and "when one stepped off the train there he could almost imagine himself in Jackson when he saw the many familiar faces around him." Those who did not have the funds to relocate were sent to live in tent camps north of Jackson. Meanwhile, public health officers visited the homes that had once been occupied by fever patients and subjected the houses to a thorough disinfecting.[47]

Efforts to combat yellow fever were better organized in the 1890s than they had been in 1878. Unfortunately, the lack of sound medical knowledge meant that these public health efforts were generally wasted. Since the fomite theory of yellow fever was wrong, the burning of houses and disinfecting of luggage did no good at all. Use of dangerous chemicals including formaldehyde, carbolic acid, and bichloride of mercury undoubtedly caused health problems rather than solved them. Tent camps near the center of fever did no good. Relocation to Carbondale was useful, since *Aedes aegypti* was not present there. On the other hand, Mississippians had known for decades that relocation was a useful practice, but only those with ready cash could make the trip. Perhaps recognizing the futility of state and local efforts, in 1898 the Mississippi legislature petitioned Congress for the creation of a powerful national public health agency with a mandate for quarantine work and research. Once again Mississippi lawmakers laid aside their states' rights scruples. With the coming of war with Spain, the petition from Mississippi was forgotten, but since the war involved tropical locales the U.S. government did put renewed effort into studying yellow fever.[48]

Mississippi played an important role in the research that led to the eradication of yellow fever. The U.S. Marine Hospital Service sent Dr. Henry R. Carter to investigate an 1898 outbreak of yellow fever in Taylor, Mississippi. Local residents blamed the appearance of the disease on a bunch of bananas sent to a local general store. After all, bananas were tropical, and the yellow fever was considered tropical. Carter rejected the banana theory, noting that the fruit had arrived in Taylor fifty-one days prior to the onset of the first case of fever. Fifty-one days struck the doctor as an improbably long incubation period. Carter successfully traced the fever to a railroad construction gang that had been quartered along the tracks near Taylor—members of the crew had recently been in Jackson, where the fever was widespread. As he studied the cases at Taylor, Dr. Carter was especially interested in the progress of the disease over time.[49]

Carter soon moved on to Orwood, a Mississippi farming community near Taylor but much more isolated. Orwood was not on any railroad. Outside visitors were few and were quickly noticed by residents. Orwood provided an ideal locale to study how the fever came into a community from outside. Carter discovered it took twelve to fifteen days after the arrival of an infected outsider for the first case of fever to appear. He called this period the "period of extrinsic incubation." Once fever cases were present in a locality, however, any nonimmune newcomer might come down with the illness as quickly as three days after arriving in the community. Taylor's findings pointed intriguingly to some kind of host that carried the disease, one that required a minimum of twelve to fifteen days before it could pass the disease on. Since Walter Reed had recently linked malaria with the *Anopheles* mosquito, a mosquito vector seemed a distinct possibility.[50]

Walter Reed read Carter's article in the *New Orleans Medical and Surgical Journal* with great interest. Reed was conducting his own studies attempting to prove the *Aedes aegypti* mosquito was the carrier of yellow fever. Reed undertook his most important yellow fever studies the year following Carter's work in Mississippi. In Cuba, Reed had medical corps personnel subject themselves to the bites of *Aedes aegypti* mosquitoes from neighborhoods infected with yellow fever. These subjects contracted yellow fever, while a control group living behind mesh and protected from mosquitoes did not. Reed's studies showed how accurate Carter's work in Mississippi had been. Once inside a mosquito's body, the virus took twelve to fifteen days to replicate and reach the insect's salivary glands. After one of these "primed and ready" mosquitoes bit a person, the symptoms of yellow fever could appear in three days. Carter, Reed, and the other researchers at last had found the answer. To control yellow fever, you must control *Aedes aegypti*.[51]

The strain of yellow fever that appeared in Mississippi in 1905 was particularly deadly. The Mississippi legislature was not in session, but Governor James K. Vardaman wrote to every legislator at home, asking each lawmaker's written authorization to finance a strong campaign against the fever. While the state's efforts did not entirely neglect quarantines, the new emphasis was upon mosquito control. The state board of health took control of several towns hit by the fever and organized oiling and screening gangs. Whenever a new case appeared, crews rushed to the infected household and screened the premises. This kept infected mosquitoes from leaving the house and protected the occupants from the entrance of additional infected mosquitoes. The crews also put oil on the surfaces of wells and cisterns to hinder the growth of mosquito larvae and screened the wells and cisterns to prevent escape of any of the mosquitoes that managed to reach the adult stage. Citizens drained water barrels, emptied buckets and cans of rainwater, cleaned gutters, and participated in the oiling and screening. Guided by the new scientific discoveries, the hard work paid off. The number of deaths in the 1905 epidemic was only sixty-three, and that year marked the last yellow fever epidemic in U.S. history.[52]

The work of the U.S. Marine Hospital Service in eradicating yellow fever was so impressive that the Mississippi legislature moved to slash the appropriation of the state board of health. The state board's most important function had been control of yellow fever, and with the national government now playing the leading role in fever eradication, the state board had little to do. The state board of health officers had to prove to the legislature that Mississippi still had pressing public health problems. One of these was the mysterious disease called pellagra.[53]

Dr. Joseph Goldberger's studies and experiments in Mississippi provided the answer to the riddle of what caused pellagra.

Pellagra in the United States had a murky early history. Since the disease was not recognized in this country, cases of pellagra were misdiagnosed as other ailments, depending upon the dominant symptom. Pellagra caused severe peeling of the skin wherever the skin was exposed to light, and it also caused digestive failures. In advanced cases, patients experienced complete loss of energy, wasting, and sometimes delirium and death. Thus in the eighteenth and nineteenth centuries, cases of pellagra were diagnosed as sunburn, psoriasis, intestinal flu, or mental illness. Pellagra was well known in other nations of the world, including Italy, and some researchers linked it to a diet rich in corn. Perhaps corn was an inferior grain, or perhaps the patients had eaten tainted batches of corn.[54]

Medical researchers began to realize pellagra was widespread in the South. Earlier misdiagnoses had hidden the prevalence of the disease, but by 1910 it was clear there were tens of thousands of cases in the South. Despite the claims of some European doctors that pellagra was caused by inadequate diet, American doctors refused to admit malnutrition was common in America. Besides, pellagra seemed to sweep through certain neighborhoods and through prisons and asylums. Surely this was an infectious disease, doctors reasoned. Some physicians believed the malady was carried by rats or mosquitoes. Others treated patients with strychnine or arsenic to kill the microbes that were allegedly causing the ailment. Patent medicine entrepreneurs offered an array of pellagra "cures" that were useless against the disease and gave patients false hope.[55]

The state of Mississippi was at the center of discoveries about pellagra and its cure. The U.S. Public Health Service assigned Dr. Joseph Goldberger of New York to study pellagra, and he came to Mississippi where the disease was widespread. Goldberger began to study two Jackson orphanages, one Baptist and one Methodist. About half the children at the orphanages had clear symptoms of pellagra, and doctors suspected the children had been catching the disease from each other. Goldberger noticed several interesting things. First, none of the staff members showed any sign of pellagra—odd, if this were an infectious disease. Also, at the Methodist orphanage Goldberger discovered that neither the youngest nor the oldest children had pellagra, but only the children in the middle age group of six to twelve years old. Goldberger suspected the pellagra cases were caused by poor diet. The staff did not develop pellagra because they ate some meals at home. The youngest children did not contract the disease because they were given milk regularly, and the older children were given meat because they worked hard in the orphanage gardens and elsewhere.[56]

To prove his contention about the nature of pellagra, Goldberger made sure each child received milk, buttermilk, eggs, and beans regularly. He saw to it that each child's allotment of meat was increased from one to four servings per week. After twelve months, the number of pellagra cases in the two orphanages had fallen from 209 to 1. Many Mississippi doctors suspected Goldberger's study was flawed and remained convinced the disease was infectious. Many had long been perfecting their own treatment for pellagra and refused to believe that milk and eggs could cure this crippling illness. Goldberger therefore turned to another experiment.[57]

This time Goldberger conducted his study at a state prison farm in Rankin County. Governor Earl Brewer made the politically risky decision to offer twelve inmates pardons if they would participate in a six-month dietary study. Twelve men quickly volunteered. Goldberger proposed to produce pellagra in healthy subjects simply by modifying their diet. Goldberger's assistant explained to the men that they would be fed a diet of cornbread, biscuits, grits, mush, rice, molasses, sweet potatoes, cabbage, and collard greens. Many of the prisoners thought it "a huge joke" to win their freedom by eating a diet not unlike that they had eaten on the outside. Goldberger secured newly constructed, carefully screened quarters for the men, wanting there to be no doubt that mosquitoes had not caused pellagra in the men.[58]

The men grew dissatisfied with their diet. One man escaped, while two others wrote the governor asking to be excused from the experiment. On one occasion,

Goldberger's assistant took pity on the men and fed them a serving of meat. As the six-month period drew to a close, a worried Goldberger even removed the buttermilk from the biscuit recipe, thus giving the men a diet based exclusively on plant products. Finally, on October 30, 1915, Goldberger sent the news to his wife. Seven doctors had independently examined the eleven men who were still participating in the project, and all agreed that five of the eleven had developed pellagra, including its characteristic rashes. "This is way beyond anything I had anticipated," the doctor told his wife. "The most I had hoped for, the most I prayed for was two cases. We have five!" The convicts finally got some meat and won their release, while Goldberger had again proven his point. Still, a professor at Columbia University publicly accused Goldberger of faking his study. Many Mississippi doctors believed Goldberger was ignoring the fact that pellagra repeatedly swept through whole neighborhoods, and these doctors argued that pellagra was clearly an infectious disease not unlike yellow fever or smallpox. Goldberger therefore prepared to embark upon a truly horrendous experiment.[59]

In his last major pellagra study, Goldberger aimed to disprove once and for all the notion that pellagra was an infectious disease. In this 1916 experiment, Goldberger, his wife, and eighteen others ingested "diabolical concoctions," including capsules containing the blood, urine, and feces of pellagra patients. Goldberger and his coresearcher put the nasal secretions of pellagra patients into their own noses. Goldberger's wife and several others received blood transfusions from patients dying of pellagra. Physicians finally came to admire Goldberger's determination and accepted the results of his research. Pellagra could be easily cured by providing meat, eggs, and dairy products to patients. Goldberger encountered resistance for a number of reasons. The *Jackson Daily News* editor suspected many Mississippi doctors were resistant to findings that would allow patients to cure themselves.[60]

Goldberger's work in Mississippi also challenged the whole direction of the national public health movement. In the late nineteenth century, the public health movement had emphasized sanitation—cleaning up cisterns, privies, and filthy city streets. In the early twentieth century, public health officers emphasized the role of microbes in spreading disease, and fighting disease required microscopes, laboratories, and syringes. Now Goldberger told the medical community that a major public health menace could be met with a little beef and cheese. Moreover, medical science had always believed disease was caused by something. With his Mississippi experiments, Goldberger proposed that disease might be caused by a lack of something. It was an idea doctors in Mississippi and elsewhere were slow to accept.[61]

Over time, Goldberger came to be a hero in Mississippi, winning praise from editors and invitations to address state medical groups. Yet the promise that this terrible disease could be easily conquered was not easily delivered. Pellagra was caused by poverty, and Mississippi could not easily eradicate poverty. Many poor people the world over were able to avoid pellagra by raising a few chickens or keeping a goat. Yet in Mississippi, the prevailing sharecropping system called for farmers to grow only cotton. Their food needs were met by "furnish" from the plantation commissary, an issue of food that included mostly cornmeal, molasses, and coffee and perhaps a small amount of salt pork. Raising livestock was not possible for most sharecroppers because the planter expected them to grow cotton right up to the front door of their cabins. Undoubtedly, pellagra had existed in Mississippi from the earliest territorial days. There was a dramatic upturn in cases during 1905–7, as the state experienced bad crop years, low cotton prices, and hard times generally. While patients with advanced cases of pellagra could now be saved from death, the appearance of new cases continued at an alarming rate.[62]

Members of the Mississippi state board of health conferred regularly with Goldberger and mapped out a plan of action. They printed flyers about pellagra and how to prevent it and delivered these to country stores across the state. The board encouraged schoolteachers to teach about pellagra and its prevention. The incidence of pellagra in Mississippi declined sharply after 1916. Its decline can be traced both to the state board of heath's educational efforts and to an economic upturn before and during World War I. Unfortunately, pellagra returned in bad crop years and in years when cotton prices were low.[63]

After yellow fever and pellagra, hookworm was Mississippi's most severe health menace. As had been the case with pellagra, hookworm was widespread in the state from its earliest days but went unrecognized. Finally, medical writers postulated that hookworm must be present in the American South, and researchers with microscopes fanned out across the region, discovering widespread infestation. The first Mississippi case was discovered in 1904 in Wilkinson County.

Hookworms are minute worms that enter the body through the skin, often through the feet. They enter the bloodstream and eventually attach themselves to the intestinal walls. Thousands of eggs are expelled with human feces, and the eggs hatch in the soil and the cycle begins again. Hookworm went undetected for many years because the symptoms were vague and difficult to pinpoint. Hookworm sufferers showed a loss of energy, and afflicted children might fail to reach their full potential height. Even after discovery of the first case, few Mississippi doctors suspected how widespread the infestation was. In 1910, when doctors examined the twenty students at a school for white children in Marion County, they discovered that every one was a victim of the parasites. Hookworms affected black and white, young and old. Only those few Mississippians who invariably wore shoes and had indoor plumbing were safe from being infested.[64]

Aided with funds from the Rockefeller Sanitary Commission, Mississippi was the first state to organize a campaign against the hookworm. The campaign had several phases. First, the public was educated about the parasite and encouraged to be tested for the presence of hookworms. Second, those who had the illness were treated. Fortunately, the treatment was cheap and effective. Thymol killed the parasites, and Epsom salts purged them from one's system. Finally, state residents must wear shoes, especially in farmyards and near privies. Privies must be reconstructed so that they were deep, were screened, and had no noticeable runoff.[65]

Some Mississippians suspected that since the money of a northern philanthropist was financing the campaign, the antihookworm crusade must be a Yankee plot to get southerners to wear shoes made in northern factories. Yet in reality the crusade was a homegrown affair, led by Mississippi doctors, editors, teachers, and county officers. Newspapers like the *Hattiesburg Tribune* printed an honor roll each week of those families who had added a sanitary privy to their home or farm. In Pearl River County, officials displayed at the courthouse a huge county map with homes with sanitary privies circled. As the map filled up with circles, farmers worked to ensure their home would not be the only nonprogressive one on the map. Local editors warned that factories would never come to Mississippi as long as so many workers were lethargic and stunted in their growth.[66]

The hookworm eradication project was a massive undertaking. Doctors and nurses treated 44,000 Mississippians for the disease in 1912. Health officers in Jones and Harrison counties found a 70 percent infestation rate, while 35 percent was more typical statewide. In the space of a few years, 167,000 state residents were tested for hookworm, and about a third of those underwent the thymol treatment. Stunted children and lethargic workers became increasingly uncommon in Mississippi, although as in the case of pellagra, public health officers had to guard against revivals of this menace.[67]

The campaigns against yellow fever, pellagra, and hookworm (as well as efforts against tuberculosis, diphtheria, and other diseases) helped integrate Mississippi and the other states of the Deep South into the national economy. In the 1870s most national life insurance companies would not write policies in Mississippi or excluded certain regions of the state where disease was prevalent. Northern policyholders who wished to travel in the Deep South were required to receive written permission from their insurers before they could do so. These irritating restrictions helped lead to the founding of Mississippi's Lamar Life Insurance Company in 1906. The national press portrayed black and white southerners as lazy. Few northern investors would be interested in bringing a factory to Mississippi if the workers there were lethargic or if quarantines regularly paralyzed commerce. Progress over pellagra and hookworm helped end the era in which hundreds of thousands of southerners were medically deprived of their energy and ambition. The eradication of yellow fever meant the Mississippi economy would no longer shut down completely every few years.[68]

Mississippi made great progress in improving transportation, modernizing its cities, and eradicating public health menaces early in the twentieth century. Economic growth was strong, thanks in part to this modernization. Yet when compared with the progress experienced by the nation as a whole, Mississippi lagged well behind. Mississippi's roads were far inferior to those of other states. A smaller percentage of Mississippians enjoyed electric lights and telephones when compared with Americans as a whole. While the state's cities grew rapidly, Mississippi remained the most rural state in the nation, one that was unlikely to industrialize to any extent. Progress over disease was impressive, but good health was scarcer in Mississippi than in other states and would be for many decades to come. Poverty prevented greater progress in Mississippi. While a number of Mississippians boasted impressive wealth, the state's per capita income was the lowest in the nation. With a relatively small consumer market, underfunded schools and widespread illiteracy, and only a modest tax base, Mississippi found itself unable to attract new settlers, investments, and industries.

CHAPTER ELEVEN

The Era of Vardaman and Bilbo

At the dawn of the twentieth century, a new group of state political leaders came into office. The domination by Confederate colonels and generals ended. Anselm J. McLaurin, whose term of office ended in 1900, was the last Civil War veteran to serve as governor. Senator James Z. George, a Confederate general, architect of the overthrow of Reconstruction, and guiding force of the 1890 disfranchisement of black voters, died in August 1897. Mississippi's other U.S. senator and former Confederate general, Edward Cary Walthall, died eight months later. Taking the place of the aged Confederate veterans was a new generation of eager politicians. Yet despite the change in personnel, many of the key issues facing the state remained the same. Prohibition was still a lively issue. Race and race control were of central importance in a majority of canvasses. Education funding was still a controversial topic, as it had been since the 1870s. Woman suffrage, first considered in Mississippi in 1890, excited further debate early in the twentieth century.

Political observers continued to point to the important political split between the Delta and the Hills. This key political division resembled a two-party system. The Delta-Hills divide did not reflect an invariable geographic reality. In the eastern part of the state, Lowndes County was a plantation county with a large black majority, and its politicians cooperated with Delta planters. Franklin County in the southwestern part of the state was neither in the Delta nor the Hills; its leaders tended to vote with the agrarian, "hill" faction of Democrats.[1] Some issues and some geographical political trends remained the same. State politics in the early twentieth century also saw some new players and new geographical trends. One increasingly important group was town boosters, who sought to develop their own localities. Both planters and small farmers often opposed the town boosters because of the costs of encouraging development. The geographic split between the Delta and the Hills began to give way to a three-way division between the Delta, the Northeast, and the South. The southern region of the state included the rapidly growing Piney Woods and Gulf Coast areas. It contained some of the fastest-growing cities, including Hattiesburg, Laurel, Biloxi, and Gulfport. The southern counties demanded a larger share of the seats in the legislature. Delta and Hills politicians, however, cooperated to ensure that their counties did not lose power to this upstart area of the state.[2]

Increasingly, Mississippians abandoned devotion to small government and sought governmental activism at all levels. Prior to the Civil War, roads were built by neighbors working together. Quarantines were unofficial and enforced by local citizens arming themselves and blockading the roads. Levees were built by slave labor, as slave-holding neighbors cooperated together. By the early twentieth century, these communal ideals and practices were giving way to citizens' calls for activist government. Citizens demanded that government at various levels conquer disease, build highways, encourage but regulate railroads, ensure a safe food supply, eradicate drunkenness, regulate professions, dredge rivers and harbors, deliver parcels, and provide scientific information to farmers. Many of the new calls for government activism came from Progressives—people who documented the problems society faced, rallied public support, and secured new laws to cure society's ills.

Two events of 1903 marked the coming of a new era in state politics. On Jefferson Davis's birthday, the state dedicated a new capitol. Thus "The Old Capitol"—site of Mississippi's Secession Convention, its interracial Reconstruction legislatures, and its constitutional convention of 1890—fell into disuse. The new legislative halls would see important actions, too, as lawmakers responded to the urgings of Governors James K. Vardaman, Edmund F. Noel, Earl Brewer, and Theodore G. Bilbo.[3]

The other key event of 1903 was passage of the direct primary election law. The advent of the statewide primary system in Mississippi grew out of popular dissatisfaction with the existing system. After the framing of the 1890 constitution, not only did black voting drop precipitously, but white voting also fell. The constitution required a poll tax and a literacy test for would-be voters, and as William Alexander Percy noted snidely, poor white farmers "were not blest with worldly goods or mental attainments," and many were disfranchised. Thus political power was more restricted than before, and under the convention system for making nominations, the real power lay in the hands of small cliques of politically active men. Planters, merchants, and bankers dominated party conventions and chose the candidates who would run in Mississippi's one-party elections.[4]

Agrarians, by any measure a majority in Mississippi, had been keenly disappointed by the recurring demonstrations of their political weakness. The agrarian Greenback and Populist parties had failed to gain power. Agrarian Democrats like Ethelbert Barksdale and Putnam Darden failed in seeking election as governor or senator. Agrarians' failures could be traced to the concentration of power in the hands of entrenched leaders of the Democratic Party. A statewide primary system for making party nominations could take power away from the old party leaders and increase agrarian power sharply. The primary election system would also add a new level of racial disfranchisement. If a black voter braved community disapproval by registering to vote, if he paid the poll tax and passed the literacy test, it still would make little difference, because the state Democratic Party chose to open its primary to white voters only. Black voters could still legally participate in the general elections, but in most general elections there would be only one name on the ballot for each office, that of the Democratic nominee.[5]

The state Senate passed Noel's direct primary bill in 1900, but the House did not. In 1902 Governor Andrew H. Longino used his annual message to urge lawmakers to pass the bill, and this time both houses did so. Many Mississippi counties had held primaries for years, but the Noel Primary Election Act made primaries mandatory for all state and county elections. In the event no candidate received a majority of the vote, election officers would hold a run-off primary three weeks after the first primary. Mississippi was the first state to pass such a mandatory primary election law for state and local offices. The law had the immediate effect of revolutionizing state politics.

One of the law's effects was to shift some political power from the black-majority counties to white-majority counties. A Delta county like Bolivar, for example, lost much of its influence in gubernatorial elections. Heretofore, candidates for governor had considered Bolivar County important, since it controlled a considerable number of delegates to the state nominating convention—its allocation of delegates based in large measure on the county's sizable black population. After the system of primary elections was initiated, however, few candidates would spend much time in Bolivar, where there were only about 1,200 white voters. Planters would have a smaller voice in choosing the governor than they had enjoyed formerly, while agrarians' voices would grow louder.[6]

Indeed, after the new primary law went into effect, many conservative politicians did not have the heart to continue. James McCool, for example, was a railroad attorney who had enjoyed a successful political career. In 1906, however, he had to decide whether to run for reelection to the legislature under the new primary system or simply retire and avoid the indignities he was sure to experience at the hands of agrarians. His son encouraged him to retire, since to run "will take so much money and an iron constitution to go through with it." McCool's son had put his finger on one of the ironies of the new system. Running for governor or other high office began to cost a great deal of money, and few who were not wealthy could undertake such a statewide campaign. Under the old system, the candidates need only lay their credentials before the Democratic convention. The politically active delegates at the convention would already know something of the candidates' qualifications. Under the new primary system, there would be the expense of extensive travel, of holding barbecues, of printing posters and handbills. The irony, then, was that agrarians sought the new system to give themselves a greater voice, but few tillers of the soil would be able to run for statewide office because of the expense. Under the old convention system, a candidate needed to be skilled at diplomacy and negotiation. Under the primary system, the candidate must be skilled at moving and motivating great crowds of people. Thus the new system could encourage the rise of demagogues and the use of dangerous techniques such as fanning the flames of race hatred to arouse and motivate voters.[7]

One of the masters of motivating voters under the new primary system was James K. Vardaman. Vardaman had little formal education but had read poets and historians and was a self-educated man. He had read law with a relative but was never a successful attorney. As a young man, he secured an interest in a Montgomery County newspaper, the *Winona Advance*. In 1890 he took his editorial skills to a larger town and purchased the *Greenwood Enterprise*. Vardaman became a town booster, launching successful newspaper campaigns to help Greenwood secure a city-owned water system, a volunteer fire company, electric and telephone service, streetcars, a new high school, and even an opera house.[8]

In his early newspaper work, Vardaman was not a venomous racist. He did not use the word "nigger" in his early editorial writing, though many other Mississippi editors did. In one incident, Vardaman the editor sided with a black county prisoner who had been unable to pay his $14 fine. The prisoner had been subjected to fearful overwork and abuse by the farmer who leased his labor—when the prisoner's fingers were frostbitten, the lessee cut them off with an ax. The crusading editor scolded county residents, writing that Leflore County was a land of Bibles and preachers and charity, yet it permitted incidents such as this one, a crime sufficient "to make crimson the souls of the whole community." When Isaiah T. Montgomery in 1891 sought funds to build a high school to educate black youths in the Delta, Vardaman urged his readers to contribute and praised Montgomery's work "for the improvement and elevation of the negro" through education.[9]

In 1889 Vardaman won a seat in the legislature representing Leflore County. He was a typical Delta lawmaker, conservative in his voting. He opposed the elective judiciary and a progressive income tax that would have hit wealthy planters severely. He even voted against a proposal for a statewide primary, although later no politician would benefit more from the primary system than Vardaman. He approved of the idea of a poll tax to limit voting in the state, even though it would disfranchise some whites, and he fought bitterly with Frank Burkitt's agrarian band of legislators. In 1894, when Vardaman was only thirty-three, lawmakers rewarded his reliable conservatism by electing him Speaker of the state House of Representatives.[10]

In 1895 Vardaman ran for governor, dropping out of the race when it became clear he was hampered by not being a Confederate veteran. He soon served as an officer in the Spanish-American War and announced his second bid for governor in a letter from Cuba written late in 1898. The state Democratic convention, however, passed over Vardaman in favor of Longino. In the elections of both 1895 and 1899, Vardaman chafed at the knowledge that he seemed to enjoy great popular support but that the small core of party leaders handpicked the nominee for governor. Meanwhile, Vardaman went back to newspapering, now editing another Leflore County newspaper, the *Greenwood Commonwealth*. In his editorial work of the late 1890s and early 1900s, Vardaman aimed to position himself for a successful gubernatorial bid. He also sought to win a statewide readership, offering annual subscriptions for one dollar, delivered anywhere in the state. To attract a statewide readership, his writing became spicier. When Vardaman attacked Governor Anselm J. McLaurin in print, *Vicksburg Dispatch* editor Charles E. Wright accused Vardaman of inaccuracy. Vardaman responded that Wright was a "moral pervert and cowardly liar" and a "scurvy biped without courage, conscience, or conviction—an irresponsible and unscrupulous cur fit only for things filthy." Reaching out for a statewide readership, Vardaman also became more willing to race-bait. When a mob at Corinth in 1902 seized a black man accused of rape and burned him alive, Vardaman commented editorially that "when one of these devils commits such deeds as this nigger did, somebody must kill him." When white educators prepared to teach a summer institute for black teachers, editor Vardaman expressed his horror, arguing that the whole theory of separation of the races was endangered. "Let niggers teach niggers," he concluded.[11]

Passage of the Noel Primary Election Act in time for the 1903 election was a godsend for Vardaman, who was sure he could do better with the mass of the voters than with cliques of party leaders. To win a statewide primary, however,

James K. Vardaman twice failed to win the Democratic nomination for governor under the convention system, then became the Democrats' first nominee chosen in a statewide primary election.

Vardaman the conservative state legislator of 1889 would have to become Vardaman the friend of white laborers and small farmers. This transformation was a thorough one, made over the period of about a decade. By 1900 Vardaman supported primary elections, favored heavier taxes for the wealthy, attacked black education, and assailed large corporations. His most important political idea was that lawmakers should devise a new way of distributing school taxes in order to benefit white education at the expense of black education and to benefit school systems in the white-majority counties. Many observers were surprised that a Delta politician would advocate funneling more tax dollars to the white-majority counties, but Vardaman was playing on a new stage now. It little mattered if he irritated the Delta aristocracy as long as he pleased the large masses of voters in the white-majority counties.[12]

Edmund F. Noel was one of Vardaman's opponents in the 1903 primary election. A resident of Holmes County, he stole much of Vardaman's support in the Delta, especially as Vardaman began to adopt some stances that seemed anti-Delta. Noel had won high praise for his authorship of the primary law, and his credentials as a proponent of prohibition were impeccable. Even stronger than Noel, however, was Frank A. Critz. Unlike Noel and Vardaman, Critz had strong support from the state's Civil War veterans, since he had served in the Confederate army. Critz had been the strong second-place finisher in the 1899 race for the Democratic nomination for governor, and many argued the nomination was rightfully his, while Vardaman and Noel could try again another time. Critz championed many of the same Progressive issues as Vardaman, while adopting a more statesmanlike stance on racial issues. Critz promised to seek industrial development, while Vardaman countered that Critz would give special favors to corporations. Both Critz and Vardaman favored prohibition, though not as strongly as did Noel.[13]

Vardaman was a memorable campaigner. He was an excellent stump speaker and attracted attention with his white pants, shirt, coat, tie, and shoes, topped with a black Stetson hat covering his shoulder-length black hair. Supporters called him the "White Chief," referring to both his attire and his statements on racial issues. Vardaman attracted almost idolatrous support from the mass of Mississippi voters by hitting three key issues that struck a collective nerve with the electorate. These were taxes, class, and race. Vardaman charged that policies of a Noel or Critz administration would favor wealthy Mississippians, giving tax breaks to investors and corporations while forcing farmers and laborers to bear a heavy burden. He pointed out that alone of the three candidates, he was a self-made man, rising from humble rural roots to become a lawyer, editor, and Speaker of the House. Vardaman attracted attention by his statements on matters of race. He argued that black rapists were a perpetual danger to the white women of Mississippi and added that he would willingly help lynch a black "brute," stating, "I haven't much respect for a white man who wouldn't." Vardaman favored finding a new way to fund education, spending less on black education and more on schooling for whites. To accomplish this, the Fourteenth Amendment with its promise of racial equality must be modified. Vardaman also advocated repealing the Fifteenth Amendment's voting rights guarantee.[14]

The *Jackson Clarion-Ledger* found it amazing Vardaman could claim that black Mississippians endangered "in the remotest degree the social, industrial, or political supremacy" of whites. Many argued that Vardaman was recklessly fanning the fires of race hatred, when in fact a majority of the state's black residents were law-abiding and were of tremendous economic importance to the state since they raised most of the cotton. Critz and Noel both argued that white schools were already far superior to black schools, that black voting was a thing of the past, and that it was pointless and in fact dangerous to invite national attention to issues of black voting and black legal equality. If race hatred grew to ominous levels under Vardaman's agitation, Critz pointed out, the state could see an exodus of its black labor force or new interference by Congress in the state's affairs. Noel brought out Vardaman's record as a state legislator, arguing with some justification that everything that Vardaman now advocated he had opposed as a legislator. Primary elections? Vardaman had voted against those. The elective judiciary? Vardaman had fought that, too. Cutting funding for black education? Actually, Vardaman had favored generous appropriations for black education.[15]

Vardaman came in first in the initial primary with 39,679 votes, followed by Critz with 34,813 and Noel with 24,233. Since Critz's vote was close to Vardaman's, and since Noel threw his considerable support to Critz in the runoff, Critz was in the strongest position entering the second primary. Ironically, the turning point came when Senator Anselm J. McLaurin endorsed Critz, leading McLaurin's many enemies to campaign hard for Vardaman. In the final days of the campaign, Vardaman benefited from the aggressive support of John Sharp Williams, "Private" John Allen, LeRoy Percy, and Charles Scott. Vardaman won the second primary with 54 percent of the vote.[16]

Anyone who hoped Vardaman would discard race-baiting and deliver a statesmanlike inaugural address was disappointed. The new governor proclaimed that the Fourteenth and Fifteenth amendments comprised a mistake that "stands out naked to all the world in all of its stupid ugliness." The South should take the lead in correcting the mistake by working to modify or repeal the amendments. Turning to education, the governor declared that the state had squandered millions of dollars on educating black Mississippians. Despite this, he alleged, black residents were "deteriorating morally every day." There was no point trying to educate black citizens morally, the governor continued, because the black citizen "has never felt the guilt of sin, the restraining influence of moral scruples, or the goading of an outraged conscience." In fact, "slavery is the only process by which he has ever been even partially civilized." In a very brief moment of charity, Vardaman admitted that history provided some examples of intelligent black persons, but he hastened to add that these were "mixed breeds and freaks of the race." Black men sought to rape white women because they sought social equality, Vardaman charged, and he promised to ensure social equality never arrived in the state of Mississippi.[17]

In the 1904 legislative session, Vardaman asked lawmakers to take a number of decisive actions. He urged expansion of Jim Crow segregation, tougher vagrancy laws, and penitentiary reform. Lawmakers passed a statute bringing Jim Crow segregation to the state's streetcars and a draconian vagrancy law that could lead to a term of hard labor for loafing. Lawmakers put the penitentiary under a board of control and brought a final end to convict leasing by the state. The legislature created a textbook commission, with the goal of adopting a uniform system of textbooks resulting in lower costs for parents. Many lawmakers were surprised when Vardaman vetoed the state's usual tiny appropriation for a black teachers' college, Holly Springs Normal Institute. Though the appropriation was only $2,000, Vardaman explained that the kind of book learning stressed at the school had done the typical black Mississippian no good "but serves rather to sharpen his cunning, breeds hopes that cannot be fulfilled, inspires inspirations that cannot be gratified, creates an inclination to avoid honest labor, promotes indolence and in turn leads to crime." Holly Springs Normal Institute, already experiencing precarious financial health, soon closed from the lack of funds.[18]

In 1906 Governor Vardaman urged the legislature to enable the state government to take bold actions to improve the lives of citizens. He asked lawmakers to fund generously public health programs. To aid impoverished sharecroppers, he urged a new state usury law. In 1906 and until the end of his term, Vardaman urged legislators to outlaw child labor. When corporate lobbyists argued that a strong child labor law would keep new textile mills from locating in the state, Vardaman disputed the point but said that "I would not give the soul of one of these little ragged boys or girls for all the cotton factories in Massachusetts." The legislature did do the progressive things Vardaman asked, though in the case of child labor laws the action did not come until just after he left office. The creation of the Mississippi Department of Agriculture in 1906 was especially important, given the recent appearance of the boll weevil in the state. State and federal scientists working together would help the state's cotton farmers cope with this new crisis.[19]

Given the nature of Vardaman's race-baiting campaign for governor in 1903, political observers paid more attention to racial issues than to any others during the governor's four-year term. Delta merchants, planters, and editors told the region's black residents to ignore Vardaman's invective, saying it was simply empty rhetoric designed to capture votes. Isaiah T. Montgomery wrote Booker T. Washington, suggesting that Washington should try to get northern newspapers to reprint "the inflammatory mess" Vardaman was serving up in Mississippi. If northern papers would do this, the Vardamanites might feel pressure to tone it down. Yet Harris Dickson, a noted white author, wrote two apologia for Vardaman and published them in the *Saturday Evening Post*. A 1905 article entitled "The Vardaman Idea" told the national audience that the Fifteenth Amendment had been a terrible mistake, because "the Negro . . . is congenitally unqualified to exercise the most responsible duty of citizenship." Dickson argued that the black citizen must be kept away from the political process because "he is physically, mentally, morally, racially, and eternally the white man's inferior."[20]

While Vardaman's use of racist rhetoric was politically useful for him, there is no evidence he said things he did not believe. On the other hand, as governor, he understood it was his duty to enforce the law. This meant, for example, that he must protect black prisoners from mobs and ensure that the only punishments given to black citizens were the punishments meted out by courts. By his repeated statements as governor and by his actions, Vardaman made it clear his administration would not tolerate lynching. Whenever the governor learned of a threatened lynching, he contacted the local sheriff and urged him to be vigilant and offered to send the National Guard. To prevent the lynching of a black man from Batesville accused of murdering a white man, Vardaman rushed by railroad to his hometown of Greenwood, assembled the National Guard, and proceeded to Panola County. The governor sent the prisoner to Jackson for safekeeping. In 1905, when a white woman in Jackson accused a black man of raping her, Vardaman repeatedly urged calm, and prisoner Stewart Johnson was not lynched despite feelings that ran high. In fact, a Hinds County jury acquitted Johnson, and the *Daily Clarion-Ledger* reported that Johnson must be the first black Mississippian ever to be acquitted of the charge of raping a white woman.[21]

Whitecapping reappeared in Mississippi in 1902 after a period of dormancy. Governor Longino had worked hard to see the whitecappers brought to trial, while in 1903 gubernatorial candidate Vardaman expressed his view that Longino was overreacting and should let the local sheriffs handle whitecappers. Many whitecappers and their supporters were sure that, given his racist campaign rhetoric, Governor Vardaman would pardon those already convicted of whitecapping and discourage new prosecutions. They were mistaken, however. Vardaman continued Longino's policy of strong actions against the whitecappers. After local merchants and landowners warned that economic life in southwest Mississippi was coming to a standstill, Vardaman made it clear he disapproved of whitecapping, and he urged prosecutors to take strong actions. Vardaman hired a Pinkerton detective to infiltrate the whitecap groups, and by 1905 whitecapping in Mississippi was again at an end.[22]

Given his actions to prevent lynchings and punish whitecapping, some have suggested Vardaman does not deserve his reputation as a hateful racist. Moreover, while he eliminated the appropriations for Holly Springs Normal Institute, he supported vocational education at another black school, Alcorn Agricultural and Mechanical College. With his hands-on approach to penitentiary management,

Vardaman helped eliminate some of the brutalities in black prisoners' lives. If indeed his worst offenses were uttering hateful things he did not act on, perhaps Vardaman's reputation may deserve some rehabilitation. Yet so much of Mississippi's troubled history in the twentieth century grew out of grandstanding politicians' provocative racist statements. If Vardaman the candidate said he would gladly help lynch a black rapist or murderer, the message was sent to hundreds of thousands of white Mississippians that white brutality toward African Americans would be tolerated. Some politicians and editors spoke out against him, arguing that most black citizens were hardworking and law-abiding and deserved at least basic rights and a basic education. Given Vardaman's great success and his opponents' many defeats, politically active citizens soon learned that Vardaman's course was the one more likely to lead to success.[23]

In 1907 the state prepared to choose a governor and U.S. senator. Although legally the legislature was called upon to elect the senator, by general agreement legislators would elect the victor in the Democratic preference primary. The two contenders for the Senate seat were Vardaman and John Sharp Williams. Vardaman was the outgoing governor (prevented by the 1890 constitution from succeeding himself), while Williams was the minority leader of the U.S. House of Representatives. Superficially, the two men had a great deal in common. Both were from the Delta, both were trained as lawyers, both were financially comfortable, both were avid readers, and both were able speakers. Yet Williams had been born into a prominent and wealthy family and had attended the finest schools in the South, the North, and Europe. He loved the law and loved to debate. Vardaman came from a middling farm family and received little formal education. Though he had done a creditable job of educating himself by reading, he had displayed only lukewarm interest in his law practice. He enjoyed writing editorials and making stump speeches, but he was not a debater and did not like being contradicted. Williams, like most Delta politicians, had a fairly conservative outlook and favored calm race relations. He favored moderate Progressive reforms such as tariff reduction and railroad regulation. For his part, Vardaman adopted most of the old Populist Party platform. He favored direct election of U.S. senators, election of judges, and government ownership of railroads.[24]

Williams believed his greatest opportunity for victory was to challenge Vardaman to a series of debates. Vardaman, however, persistently refused to debate Williams. Finally, Williams's supporters at Meridian simply announced a major senatorial debate to be held July 4 at Meridian and implied that both candidates would be there. Vardaman realized he would look like a coward if he refused to appear, and reluctantly he prepared for the debate. As expected, Williams was at his best in the debate venue. He criticized Vardaman severely for his promise to modify the Fourteenth Amendment and argued that a race-baiter like Vardaman would never convince Congress to go along. Dramatically, Williams offered Vardaman a pencil and a copy of the U.S. Constitution and invited him to come forward and indicate what changes he would make. Warming to his subject, Williams asked why Vardaman had exerted no leadership as governor to secure repeal or modification of the Fourteenth and Fifteenth amendments. Was it not true that the issue was simply a vote-getting scheme, Williams asked. Williams closed by noting that every intelligent Mississippian knew white supremacy had been settled by the constitution of 1890.[25]

Vardaman responded with his standard stump speech, ignoring the conventions of a debate. He praised Confederate veterans and lauded the virtues of the state's farmers. He praised the black mammies who had raised so many white Mississippians so well, but he soon began to describe alleged incidents of black men's rape of white women. Vardaman ended his Meridian speech by telling of one young white woman, forced to come into court to testify against the black man who had raped her. She testified "with her eyes red and weeping," while the black defendant coolly whispered suggestions to his lawyer, aware of the seriousness of his situation but "unable quite to hide a grin of delight." While Williams's supporters were certain their champion had won, Vardaman's supporters rushed forward and carried their candidate away on their shoulders. Thus ended the first and only debate of the campaign.[26]

The early news on election night was favorable to Williams, as the towns and cities tended to favor the congressman. As results from rural precincts began to come in, however, they were overwhelmingly for Vardaman, and at last the governor delivered his victory speech to well-wishers gathered in front of the governor's mansion. Yet when all the votes had been counted, one week after the election, Williams had won by 648 votes out of 118,344 cast. In his 1903 race for governor, Vardaman had carried a number of Delta counties. This time he carried none. In fact, he carried only counties in the northeastern hills and in south-central Mississippi. Vardaman did best in many of the same areas in which the Populists had done well. The 1907 Senate race was an aberration. Former governor McLaurin's political machine was still strong in the state, but in this 1907 race both candidates were anti-McLaurinites. In future elections, Vardaman would likely find himself opposing a McLaurin machine candidate, and chances were good that he would win, as he had in 1903.[27]

Vardaman decided not to retire to Greenwood but to remain in Jackson and start a newspaper called the *Issue*. He hoped his newspaper would enjoy national circulation and be read by tens of thousands of progressives nationwide—as were the newspapers of Robert La Follette and William Jennings Bryan. The newspaper's virulent racism doomed its circulation outside the South, however. The newspaper was not much of a moneymaker, and Vardaman turned to the lecture circuit to supplement his income. He toured nationally, repeatedly delivering a speech called "The Impending Crisis." Vardaman began by informing his audience of two supposed scientific facts about black people. Black and white children developed in the same way, he explained, but the intellectual growth of black children stopped at puberty. According to Vardaman, African Americans had no innate sense of right and wrong. He argued that the United States faced a great crisis because black Americans were demanding social and political equality. The lecture circuit allowed Vardaman to hone his already considerable platform skills. He planned to challenge incumbent U.S. senator Anselm J. McLaurin in the 1911 primary.[28]

In late 1909 McLaurin suddenly died, throwing state politics into turmoil. Governor Edmund F. Noel, elected in 1907, appointed James Gordon, an elderly Confederate veteran, to serve as senator until the legislature could elect someone to finish out McLaurin's term. The legislature met in January 1910 and recognized that Vardaman wanted very much to be a U.S. senator. Anti-Vardaman forces vowed to defeat the former governor at all costs. The reasons for their opposition varied from legislator to legislator. Conservative lawmakers found Vardaman too progressive, noting that he stood for all the things the Populist Party had stood for. Some legislators feared that Vardaman's constant agitation of racial issues might lead Congress to begin enforcing the dormant constitutional promises of racial equality. Legislators of aristocratic background sneered at Vardaman's humble beginnings and said they did not want to send a buffoon to the halls of the Senate.

Vardaman's enemies devised an elaborate strategy to ensure his defeat. First, they encouraged a large number of candidates to run for the Senate seat. Each of these candidates was known and respected in his own region of the state. Second, each of the anti-Vardaman candidates agreed not to drop out of the race without steering his supporters to another anti-Vardaman candidate. Third, the legislature would select the new senator in the Democratic caucus, then simply ratify that selection in the legislature itself. Vardaman's opponents strongly wanted to vote by a secret ballot, and use of a secret ballot was permitted in the Democratic caucus but not in an actual meeting of the legislature. The secret ballot was important to plans of the anti-Vardaman crowd because they risked the anger of a large number of their constituents if they publicly voted against the popular Vardaman.[29]

The strategy unfolded with ease. Opposing Vardaman were LeRoy Percy, Charlton H. Alexander, Frank A. Critz, John C. Kyle, Adam Byrd, and Hugh M. Street. Each candidate got a chance to address the caucus. In his address, Vardaman denounced U.S. imperialism, saying the nation should not be in "the business of owning peoples." He advocated a low tariff and an income tax on the wealthy. He also vowed to fight racial equality in every way he could. LeRoy Percy, who emerged as Vardaman's chief opponent, was unknown outside the Delta, and he had never held elective office. In his speech to the caucus, he made clear his conservatism. Like any good Delta candidate, he promised to work for levees and dredging. He warned that anyone who advocated repeal of the Civil War amendments would only stir up trouble where there was none and as such was "an enemy to the welfare of the state."[30]

Eighty-six votes were required for election. Vardaman had seventy-one on the first ballot and soon increased that number to seventy-eight. Yet his enemies' plans proved unstoppable. Gradually candidates withdrew, throwing their support to another anti-Vardaman candidate. January gave way to February, and finally on February 18 a "caucus within a caucus" met and determined that the strongest anti-Vardaman candidate was Percy. On February 22 the Democratic caucus met for the last time and elected Percy U.S. senator by a vote of eighty-seven to eighty-two, on the fifty-eighth secret ballot. The more conservative element won, but Vardaman and his supporters were livid. Vardaman promised his backers they would win the seat when the people had a chance to choose the U.S. senator in the primary election of 1911. Vardaman's friends attacked the well-planned scheme that had denied their candidate his election. They denounced especially the "secret caucus," and for several years in Mississippi politics "secret caucus" was a powerful and emotional phrase. The term led voters to believe that secret meetings had elected a Delta aristocrat to the U.S. Senate. Actually, the meetings had been open and the press reports quite thorough. Only the balloting was secret. Still, few Mississippi voters would respect politicians who hid their actions behind a secret ballot.[31]

During the long weeks of the caucus, and especially afterward, it became clear the caucus was a body of which no one was proud. Liquor lobbyists sponsored a "hospitality room," at which legislators imbibed while hearing why the driest candidates, Vardaman and Alexander, should not be elected. Journalists reported seeing mysterious well-dressed women arrive by train and disappear into legislators' hotel rooms. Others reported that Governor Noel was dangling patronage plums in front of legislators who agreed to vote against Vardaman. The *Issue* alleged railroad lobbyists were especially active on Percy's behalf.[32]

Another hot controversy swirled around legislator Walter W. Robertson. Robertson was known to have a drinking problem, and the Vardaman camp alleged Percy's supporters took advantage of Robertson's weakness. In the pages of his prohibitionist newspaper, editor Benjamin T. Hobbs alleged that Percy had gotten Robertson drunk to the point of delirium tremens. In a published reply, Robertson admitted the delirium tremens but said that actually the condition had been caused by cheap Vardaman whiskey. Vardaman supporters doubted Robertson had written his own reply. Following further allegations about Robertson's drunkenness and his support of Percy, Robertson published a defense that said the allegations came from (in the words of the headline) "An Infamous Liar. Some Unknown Vile and Infamous Wretch Pukes His Filthy Slime into the Faces of Decent and Civilized People." Robertson, engaged now in writing as spicy as that of editor Vardaman, said of his anonymous accuser that "I do not believe it would be safe for his own mother to stay under the same roof with him without a body guard."[33]

Yet the most sensational issue was the allegation made by a hitherto unknown state senator, Theodore G. Bilbo. Bilbo accused a Percy supporter named L. C. Dulaney of paying him $645 to vote for Percy. Bilbo claimed to have attempted a sting operation to catch one of the many bribers alleged to be operating around the capitol. At the Senate investigation that followed, several legislators and a police officer testified that Bilbo had discussed his plans with them in advance. A woman named Coral Johnson Neil testified that she had earned some easy money by steering Bilbo and other legislators to Dulaney and other men prepared to offer bribes. Dulaney himself testified at the Senate investigations, where he denied that he had given Bilbo money but admitted offering liquor. He said that Bilbo seemed to have quite a taste for whiskey and that the senator carried whole bottles back to his room.[34]

At the conclusion of the investigation, more than half of the senators voted to expel Bilbo for taking a bribe. Since those who wanted to do so could not muster the required two-thirds vote, Bilbo was not expelled, but his supporters stormed out of the Senate chamber after the vote. In their absence, the Senate passed a resolution by a vote of twenty-eight to one, declaring Bilbo "unfit to sit with honest, upright men." Both the Senate and the House of Representatives passed resolutions saying Percy's election had been an honest one, although a minority report in the House found that patronage and whiskey were both used to win votes for Percy. A Hinds County grand jury indicted Dulaney on bribery charges, but the trial jury acquitted him. Still, most observers recognized Dulaney had abundant reason for spending two months in Jackson, using liquor if not dollars to defeat Vardaman's candidacy. Dulaney was a wealthy Delta planter who had grown rich by leasing convicts. He had also enjoyed some political successes under the old convention system. Dulaney was bitter about Vardaman because Vardaman symbolized both the abolition of the convict lease system and the end of the convention system of making nominations. Further, Dulaney admitted he feared Vardaman's race-baiting would cause a black exodus and a labor shortage in the Delta. Thus the great number of Vardaman supporters in the state only felt reinforced in their belief that their candidate was defeated by political stratagems and secrecy and by liquor, bribes, and patronage. Many voters vowed to punish the anti-Vardaman politicians by voting in 1911 to take the Senate seat away from Percy and to give it to Vardaman.[35]

The 1911 election featured races for governor and other state offices and a U.S. Senate seat. The governor's race was anticlimactic. Four years earlier, candidate Earl Brewer had won more than 49 percent of the vote in the second primary, barely losing to Edmund F. Noel. Brewer now was unopposed in his second run for governor. He was a Progressive, but he had managed the miracle of alienating neither Delta conservatives, the old McLaurin machine, nor Vardaman's followers. Most attention focused on the race for lieutenant governor, where Theodore G. Bilbo was running against Wiley Nash and T. O. Yewell. Also capturing voters' attention was the Senate race, where Senator Percy was facing the electorate for the first time in his life. Opposing Percy was Vardaman and another candidate from the so-called secret caucus, Charlton H. Alexander.

The incumbent Percy was out of his element. While undoubtedly his business acumen, broad education, and command of the law served him well in Washington, he was now forced to present his credentials to the people of Mississippi. He argued that Vardaman's recklessness on racial issues would only stir up strife and tempt the federal government to interfere in the state's affairs. At times Percy tried to interest his audiences in the intricacies of the tariff, including the pros and cons of Canadian reciprocity. Over and over, however, angry Vardamanites challenged Percy to prove his elevation to the Senate had been legitimate. Even at the most orderly campaign meetings, Percy's opponents handed him a list of questions they wanted him to answer. Was it true he hunted and fished on Sundays? Was it true his wife was a Catholic? For Percy, the campaign

LeRoy Percy's 1911 bid to win reelection to the U.S. Senate turned into a class conflict, with "redneck" farmers of modest means leading the attacks against him. Many small farmers resented Percy's wealth and his polished manner. (Photo courtesy of the Library of Congress.)

deteriorated into a class battle in which his economic class was hopelessly outnumbered. Farmers with their rudimentary education and callused hands resented the polished and articulate Percy.[36]

At a campaign meeting at Godbold's Wells in Pike County, attended by trainloads of voters, Percy was unable to speak because the crowd was hurrahing for Vardaman and Bilbo. Percy began shouting back at the crowd, meeting their taunts with taunts of his own. Finally, in anger he shouted a new epithet at the crowd—"Cattle!" Presumably he meant that members of the audience were following Vardaman unthinkingly. Vardaman's supporters accepted the cattle and redneck epithets and used them on campaign banners. Percy's epithet helped unify the state's white small farmers and lower middle classes even more than they were already unified.[37]

Later, the senator's son, William Alexander Percy, wrote a description of the campaign. The account shows some of the aristocratic attitudes of the Percy family, while also documenting the class hatred they encountered. The younger Percy recalled surveying the crowd at a political meeting at Black Hawk. He found them "an ill-dressed, surly audience, unintelligent and slinking." The crowd proved uninterested in Senator Percy's discussion of the Panama Canal and tariff revision.

Will Percy described the audience that day as "the sort of people that lynch Negroes, that mistake hoodlumism for wit, and cunning for intelligence, that attend revivals and fight and fornicate in the bushes afterwards." They were, the writer concluded, "undiluted Anglo-Saxons. They were the sovereign voter. It was so horrible it seemed unreal."[38]

Vardaman's hopes of an easy first primary win were dimmed by an unexpected accusation by *Jackson Daily News* editor Fred Sullens. Sullens accused Vardaman of accepting a pass from the Gulf and Ship Island Railroad and using it for free passage to Biloxi. This was a serious charge against a man who accused Percy of being a tool of the railroads and who promised as U.S. senator he would bring national ownership or at least genuine regulation to the railroad industry. Vardaman's managers called upon Sullens to produce his evidence, and when he did not produce it they denied the truth of his charges. Sullens finally produced the pass, however, and provided a rotogravure illustration of it to any newspaper that chose to run it. Sullens also produced an affidavit from the conductor who had accepted the pass for free passage. The charges undoubtedly hurt Vardaman, but many of his allies continued to protest his innocence.[39]

Vardaman told his audiences that on the trip in question his aides had made all the arrangements, and he protested that if a pass had been used, he had not been aware of it. Sullens, however, produced the pass that had Vardaman's signature on it. Vardaman argued that even if a pass had been used, the trip in question had been an inspection trip to the home for aged Confederate veterans at Biloxi, so the railroad really had presented the pass "to the old veterans in gray." Finally, Vardaman pointed out that the pass in question must have been passed on to Sullens by the railroad company, thus proving powerful corporate interests feared the election of Vardaman, the people's candidate.[40]

Vardaman did not agitate racial issues as much in the 1911 canvass as he had in earlier campaigns. He did not need to. With a majority of Mississippi voters believing that the aristocratic Percy had stolen the Senate seat from him, it was not necessary for Vardaman to do much race-baiting. Yet Vardaman sometimes returned to his earlier proposals for ensuring white supremacy. Audiences seemed to expect racist content in Vardaman speeches. So he discussed so-called scientific proofs of white superiority, including the supposed fact that the sutures in the skulls of persons of color close up at an early age, hindering further mental development. Vardaman repeated the story that black southerners were resistant to malaria because mosquitoes found whites to be superior. On the occasions when Vardaman addressed the Fourteenth and Fifteenth amendments, he seemed unaware of the

This photograph shows some of the twenty yoke of oxen that drew Vardaman into the town of Kosciusko for a campaign rally on June 22, 1911. Vardaman stands hatless on the wagon to the right of center of the photo.

constitutional convention of 1890. Vardaman warned that white dominance in the state would never be safe until black voters were disfranchised. "When we drive negroes away from the polls with shotguns," Vardaman intoned, "we suffer moral deterioration. When we falsify returns, we suffer the same way." The candidate therefore revived his calls for repeal of the Fifteenth Amendment. To the Percy and Alexander camps, it was clear white supremacy was not in any danger and that Vardaman was simply a demagogue.[41]

Vardaman enjoyed mass support that few politicians experience. On July 4 he was borne to Meridian on a log wagon drawn by eighty oxen. Citizens pushed each other out of the way to touch their champion's garments or the wagon on which he rode. He was dressed in his usual white attire, and as in earlier campaigns, he still sported strikingly long hair, now becoming streaked with gray. In the evening, members of Vardaman Clubs 1,000 strong marched in a torchlight procession. Vardaman himself was again drawn by oxen, a fitting symbol (as the Vardaman press noted) for the "cattle" that would pull Vardaman into office. After Vardaman's speech at the state fair just before Election Day, his supporters stormed the platform and carried the candidate off on their shoulders. Some managed to grab his hat and carved it up for mementos. Senator John Sharp Williams had once been Vardaman's friend and supporter, but he now was horrified at a candidate he saw as the worst kind of demagogue. In a letter to a friend, Williams wrote, "When men get to fighting about who shall touch the stupid car, upon which a man almost as stupid is riding, there enters into it a factor of fanaticism that I don't understand and am not capable of measuring." Williams was repelled by the idea of having Vardaman as his Senate colleague, and he stumped hard for Percy, but Percy's candidacy was a lost cause.[42]

In many ways the race for lieutenant governor paralleled the senatorial contest. The candidates and their editorial supporters employed bitter invective. The *Jackson Daily Clarion-Ledger* called Bilbo a "repudiated man with no reputation to protect." The *Daily News* called him a "frequenter of lewd houses." Bilbo replied that the *Clarion-Ledger* editor was a "dunghill cock," while *Daily News* editor Fred Sullens was "a degenerate by birth, a carpetbagger by inheritance, a liar by instinct, a slanderer and assassin of character by practice, and a coward by nature." When Bilbo attacked Washington Gibbs (a Percy ally) as a "renegade Confederate soldier," the old veteran stalked Bilbo and gave him a severe caning on the streets of Yazoo City. Sullens's headline: "War Horse of Yazoo Broke Good Walking Stick Over Head of Poplarville Pervert."[43]

Bilbo's most memorable speech in the campaign was at Blue Mountain on April 4, 1911. He attacked former penitentiary warden John J. Henry for having penned a scurrilous anti-Bilbo leaflet. (Henry, who was not present at the speech, later denied having written the pamphlet.) Bilbo described Henry in language that was shocking even for this no-holds-barred contest. Henry was "a cross between a hyena and a mongrel, begotten in a nigger graveyard at midnight, suckled by a sow and educated by a fool." The *Memphis Commercial-Appeal* branded Bilbo's words "horribly repulsive, disgusting, and shocking." Several women got up and left the audience. Afterward, many prominent Mississippians wrote to Henry, urging forbearance. Former governor Longino asked Henry not to retaliate against Bilbo, since "if in an altercation you should have to kill him it would bring untold trouble to you and your friends and in all likelihood prove advantageous toward Vardaman's election." Local Bilbo supporters promised they would get a retraction from the candidate, but a couple of months later Bilbo attacked Henry again, using the same language.[44]

As Bilbo was en route to speak at Sturgis, Henry boarded the train and beat Bilbo savagely on the head with the butt of his pistol. Given the highly charged political climate at the time, accounts of the attack differ greatly. Stories in the Bilbo press said Henry had three accomplices and struck Bilbo from behind. Anti-Bilbo descriptions of the attack said Henry acted alone and hit Bilbo only after asking for an apology and being refused. The first report from Bilbo's doctor said the candidate's wounds were "not serious," but later reports described Bilbo as in critical condition. John J. Henry became a hero in many circles. From New Albany, one man wrote, "I see from the papers that you have knocked Old Bilbo on the head. Hit him again it will do him good." Others took Henry to task for not finishing the job. A correspondent from Sandy Bayou wrote that he could not understand why Henry did not kill Bilbo when he had the chance, adding, "If you put your gun out of commission I have a .45 that's at your disposal."[45]

Henry grew increasingly irritated, however, when his trial for assaulting Bilbo was repeatedly postponed. He suspected that Bilbo supporters would prefer not to have a trial, since Bilbo seemed more of a martyr if no one was punished for the attack. Bilbo was growing adept at turning criticism into sympathy. In this first part of his political career, he was occasionally accused of having cheated at college, of having romanced one of his students during his career as a teacher, and of having lied about the bribery incident. Yet he was always able to turn the criticisms to his favor. Corporate interests and wealthy Mississippians were trying to destroy him, the candidate claimed, to stop him from doing the people's work. His opponents had tried to expel him from the state Senate and had failed. Such people were even willing to use brutal violence to try to silence him. Bilbo's use of the attacks on him to gain sympathy clearly worked. State senator G. A. Hobbs, for example, later told how "after Mr. Bilbo had been assaulted at Starkville, I resolved all doubts in his favor, and being in sympathy with him, I decided to support him."[46]

While Bilbo and Vardaman were not formally allied in 1911, they cooperated in a loose way. Both claimed that a plot was afoot to deny to the citizens of Mississippi the election of people's candidates. The plot could involve liquor and bribery, as in the "secret caucus," or it could involve the butt of a pistol, as in Henry's attack. The people must rally, urged Vardaman and Bilbo, and overturn the wishes of men like Percy, Dulaney, and Henry. The 1911 election was important because it divided voters clearly along class lines. In earlier contests, such as those during the Populist revolt, some small farmers sided with the rebellious element, while some remained loyal to traditional party leaders such as James Z. George. In the 1903 election that brought Vardaman to power, many agrarians and reformers voted for Vardaman, but many others from these groups voted for Edmund F. Noel, the architect of Mississippi's primary election system. In 1911, however, the voters faced a clear choice between candidates who attacked corporations and bankers, on the one hand, and wealthy, conservative leaders such as Percy, on the other.

The 1911 election was a major victory for the Vardaman-Bilbo wing of the party. LeRoy Percy carried only five of the state's seventy-nine counties. Vardaman won 60 percent of the vote in the three-way race, making a second Senate primary unnecessary. Bilbo also won in the first primary, winning nearly as many votes as Vardaman. Yet just prior to the general election, a number of Delta leaders urged their neighbors to go to the polls and vote for the Socialist candidate for lieutenant governor. Socialist candidate James T. Lester, a retired teacher and grandson of the state's second governor, was hardly a wild-eyed radical, and Delta leaders found the Socialist far preferable to Bilbo. Accordingly, Lester won 19 percent of the vote, compared with only 5 percent for the Socialist gubernatorial nominee, Sumner W. Rose. Lester actually carried two Delta counties, and a change of four votes would have given him two counties more. Still, the voters had spoken, and the voters wanted Bilbo and Vardaman. Earl Brewer won his election as governor unopposed and in his inaugural address urged reconciliation.[47]

In Washington, Senator Vardaman earned the reputation of a true Progressive. He often clashed with his colleague John Sharp Williams and with the new Democratic president, Woodrow Wilson. The Senate Finance Committee (chaired by Williams) reported an income tax bill with a maximum tax of only 3 percent even on the wealthiest Americans. Williams and other Democratic leaders attempted to hold Progressive Democrats in line. Vardaman, however, bolted and supported the alternative proposal of Republican senator Robert La Follette, which would tax large incomes at a rate of 10 percent. When other Democrats threatened to follow Vardaman, Williams was forced to compromise, making the highest tax rate 6 percent. The two men had fundamental differences on this new American institution, the income tax. Williams believed the tax would be useful in raising revenue but that it must not make "war upon great fortunes." Vardaman saw the income tax as a way of taking some of the great fortunes and using them to advance the general welfare.[48]

John Sharp Williams voted for some Progressive reforms, but Vardaman supported bold federal activism for the people's benefit. Vardaman wanted a federal child labor law, and he advocated investigation of the terrible conditions faced by miners in West Virginia. He supported the Warehouse Act, which would have launched a system much like the Populist Party's subtreasury system. Like the Populists, Vardaman supported federal ownership of railroads. Like most Progressives, Vardaman favored restriction of immigration, believing that unrestricted immigration contributed to existing urban problems. On the floor of the

Although during his campaigns many observers found Bilbo to be a demagogue, he proved to be a constructive, progressive governor.

Senate, Vardaman curbed his usual racist language. Only occasionally did he turn to racial issues at all.[49]

Meanwhile, Bilbo found the lieutenant governor's office a poor pulpit. As the 1915 election approached, he announced he would run for governor. When the campaign got under way, his opponents sought to make Bilbo's character the single issue of the campaign. Governor Earl Brewer produced new evidence suggesting that Bilbo had been actively involved in soliciting bribes in the so-called secret caucus. In raising character issues, his opponents again gave Bilbo the opportunity to paint a picture of a conspiracy of wealthy Mississippians out to destroy his career. Bilbo defended himself against the new charges but surprisingly did little character assassination of his own. He also refrained from the kind of race-baiting that had served Vardaman so well. In the 1915 campaign, Bilbo advocated Progressive reforms such as the initiative and referendum, tax reform, and increased funding for education. He stressed class rather than race and spoke of wealthy predators who stalked his candidacy, hoping to deny small farmers their victory. Bilbo was disappointed not to have Vardaman's endorsement, but in fact four of the five candidates were Vardamanites. As it turned out, Bilbo won a majority in the first primary even in this five-way race.[50]

As governor, Bilbo surprised those who suspected he would accomplish little that was constructive. In fact, he had the most successful administration of all the governors who served between 1877 and 1917. He had promised to put the state's finances in order, but on taking office he was horrified to discover the state was $1.25 million in the red. Nevertheless, Bilbo and the legislature in four years were able to put the state's finances on a sound footing. No longer would state employees' paychecks be delayed. Correcting the state's financial problems required additional taxes, but true to his campaign promises, Bilbo and his legislative allies shielded small farmers from the new revenue measures. Other campaign pledges the new governor redeemed were the founding of the State Highway Commission and a juvenile reformatory. State agencies established during the Bilbo administration also included a board of pardons, a board of bank examiners, and a new charity hospital. The founding of the Livestock Sanitary Board gave cattle farming a boost. The board would oversee the dipping of cattle to eliminate ticks that caused disease—sickness that in many instances had made Mississippi cattle unsalable. Education funding was put on a firmer footing. The state's first compulsory school attendance law passed, and night classes for adults were initiated.[51]

Three issues were especially important to Mississippi Progressives—woman suffrage, prohibition, and improvements in education. In the case of woman suffrage, Mississippians were surprisingly active at an early date. Around 1880 a friend wrote to Lucy Treadway, a young Mississippi farm woman, that "the Woman's Rights Society is blooming and meets to-night week at Sister Susans." The state surprised the nation in 1890 when the constitutional convention gave serious consideration to woman suffrage and at one point seemed on the verge of enacting it. Although woman suffrage failed to find a place in Mississippi's new constitution, the proposal received such a respectful hearing that national woman suffrage leaders began organizing in the South.[52]

The Mississippi Woman Suffrage Association (MWSA) was founded at Meridian in 1897. Its two most prominent advocates were the masterful public speaker Belle Kearney (noted leader of the WCTU) and Nellie Nugent Somerville, a member of a prominent Delta family who brought great organizational skill to the MWSA. Across the South, woman suffrage leaders recruited heavily among the wives and daughters of the wealthy and influential. These women were more likely to have the time available to devote to organizing and lobbying. Also, newspapers and politicians were less likely to criticize members of respected families. Kearney, Somerville, and other key leaders of the Mississippi woman suffrage movement all came from the state's "first families."[53]

Nellie Nugent Somerville campaigned tirelessly for the right of women to vote in Mississippi. She was persuasive in both her writing and public speaking.

For men who suggested that a woman's place was in the home, Nellie Nugent Somerville had some ready answers. In 1915 she produced a broadside with the bold headline, "Who Takes Care of Mississippi Women?" In it, Somerville proved that one-fifth of all Mississippi women were wage earners. She pointed out that several thousand Mississippi women taught school but were denied any voice in choosing the legislators who enacted educational policy. Hundreds of women in the state were stenographers, but Somerville noted that, unlike male clerks, they could not be notaries—and could not help choose legislators who would allow women to become notaries. Thousands of Mississippi women worked in factories, Somerville argued, but had no influence with state lawmakers over matters of workplace safety. To those who urged that women stick to their traditional interests, Somerville in an 1898 speech at Clarksdale said that women would be happy to maintain their traditional roles. One traditional role was raising children, but women had no voice in shaping child labor legislation or education statutes. Women traditionally prepared food for the family but could not influence the legislature in matters of meat inspection. Women traditionally helped the less fortunate but could have no role in guiding the state's policies on charity hospitals and institutions for those who were deaf or blind.[54]

Just as Mississippi had captured national attention when the state considered woman suffrage in 1890, so in 1907 the nation watched as the MWSA made another novel proposal. Belle Kearney drafted a proposal that would give the right to vote in presidential elections to educated and property-owning Mississippi women. Kearney believed that her proposal would enfranchise mostly white women and thus would be an added guarantee of white political domination in the state. Soon, however, two regional suffrage leaders modified the proposal. Kate Gordon of Louisiana and Laura Clay of Kentucky believed Mississippi was so proud of its record in disfranchising black citizens that the state would never approve a suffrage plan that even theoretically allowed black women to vote. Gordon and Clay's counterproposal explicitly limited female suffrage to white women only. Their counterproposal also dropped Kearney's idea that this initial grant of woman suffrage should be for presidential elections only. Kearney believed this might be an easy first step for legislators who cared most strongly about state and local races, but Gordon and Clay pointed out that in the one-party South, presidential races were anticlimactic.[55]

Kearney and Somerville believed the Gordon-Clay proposition was tragically flawed, particularly where it limited the vote to white women. They pointed out that Mississippi had already disfranchised African Americans; thus it was not necessary to say suffrage would be for white women only. If suffrage leaders explicitly excluded black women, the U.S. Supreme Court would almost certainly declare the new enactment unconstitutional under the Fourteenth and Fifteenth amendments. The MWSA leaders were outvoted, however, by the rank-and-file state membership, and the Gordon-Clay proposal went forward. The 1907 movement in Mississippi fell apart after the National Woman Suffrage Association declined to endorse it and after the MWSA could not find a single prominent judge or attorney in the state who would issue his opinion of the proposal's constitutionality.[56]

Yet the national, regional, and state leaders did not lose heart. Perhaps the most promising thing about proposed woman suffrage in Mississippi was the large number of politicians who endorsed the idea. These included U.S. senator John Sharp Williams and former governor Edmund F. Noel. James K. Vardaman opposed some early woman suffrage proposals because they included black women in the grant of the franchise. Later, however, Vardaman announced that since woman suffrage could help the cause of prohibition, he supported it.[57]

At its 1913 meeting, the MWSA resolved to ask the legislature to vote directly on woman suffrage, stripped of the explicit limitation to white women only. The *Jackson Daily News* and several other prominent newspapers endorsed the proposal. Legislator N. A. Mott of Yazoo County introduced a resolution calling for a woman suffrage amendment to the state constitution. The House Committee on the Constitution heard testimony from Somerville, Kearney, and several others, then rejected the proposed amendment by one vote. They invited MWSA leaders to defend their proposal before the full House the following day, and members of the state Senate came over to listen as well. The House of Representatives then defeated the proposal by a vote of eighty-eight to forty-three.[58]

When the national suffrage movement was able to get Congress to pass the Nineteenth Amendment and send it on to the states for ratification, Mississippi suffragists experienced mixed emotions. While the new amendment seemed promising, state suffrage leaders still had not given up hope of enacting suffrage at the state level. The Mississippi legislature, however, continued to be inhospitable toward suffrage proposals. Not content simply to fail to ratify the Nineteenth Amendment, Mississippi lawmakers actually framed and passed an unusual resolution explicitly rejecting the amendment. Mississippi woman suffrage leaders were caught by surprise when, with only one state's ratification still needed for the amendment to become law, the state Senate ratified it by a one-vote margin. There is evidence senators acted under pressure from the national leadership of the Democratic Party. At any rate, the state House of Representatives voted one final time to reject the amendment, again by a lopsided vote. Not content simply to reject the Nineteenth Amendment, Mississippi (like Georgia and Virginia) declined to call a special session of the legislature to enable registration of women voters in time for the 1920 election. For good measure, the 1920 state ballot included a referendum on woman suffrage. Thus in November 1920, while in all but three states women were casting their votes for the first time under the Nineteenth Amendment, in Mississippi only male voters voted, overwhelmingly defeating the woman suffrage referendum.[59]

Thus the worst fear of southern woman suffrage leaders had become a reality. Woman suffrage, like African American suffrage, had been imposed upon Mississippi from outside. The woman suffrage movement in Mississippi was driven by extraneous issues. It was both aided and hindered by the movement for guaranteeing white political supremacy in the state and also by the prohibition movement. In 1890, for a few weeks anyway, the state seemed close to enacting woman suffrage in a form that would swell the number of white voters and thus add one additional assurance of white political supremacy in the state. On other occasions, lawmakers would not listen to woman suffrage proposals out of concerns that such plans would add to the number of black voters by enfranchising some black women. The movement for woman suffrage was greatly aided by the prohibition movement, and many of the most influential prohibition leaders came to support woman suffrage. On the other hand, those who opposed prohibition vowed to block any plan to give women the vote. Although MWSA leaders were keenly disappointed by the

MISS BELLE KEARNEY
Candidate for the United States Senate

Belle Kearney campaigned hard for woman suffrage in Mississippi in the first two decades of the twentieth century. Shortly after approval of the Nineteenth Amendment, she ran unsuccessfully for a U.S. Senate seat, then was elected to the state Senate.

legislature's refusal to enact woman suffrage in any form and by its refusal to ratify the Nineteenth Amendment, Mississippi did come to accept a new role for women. White women across the state voted for the first time in the congressional elections of 1922. In state races in 1923, both Belle Kearney and Nellie Nugent Somerville not only voted but ran for—and won—seats in the legislature.[60]

Like the woman suffrage movement, the prohibition cause had a strong, statewide, women-led organization behind it. The state's WCTU had thousands of active members and a number of articulate leaders, including Belle Kearney and Harriet Kells. The group aimed to educate citizens on the evils of alcohol and to lobby city and county officials and state lawmakers. The WCTU lobbied at the county level for local option prohibition, at the state level for statewide prohibition, and at the national level for a constitutional amendment outlawing the manufacture of alcoholic beverages.[61]

As with the issue of woman suffrage, so was the prohibition cause entangled with racial questions. While hundreds of thousands of black church members in the state denounced the evils of drink, white prohibition leaders discovered the effective tactic of linking drinking with black Mississippians. Thus an additional way to guarantee white control of the black population was to outlaw liquor. WCTU leaders described the rage and aggression sometimes found in black men

Methodist bishop Charles B. Galloway was among the state's most important leaders of the prohibition movement. He stressed local-option prohibition, seeking to persuade counties to vote themselves dry.

who had been drinking. In order to make Mississippi's black underclass more easily controlled, alcohol must be outlawed, they argued. This linking of prohibition with promises of race control was the most effective argument WCTU leaders made with state legislators.[62]

State prohibitionists were hindered, however, by internal divisions. Baptist prohibitionists tended to believe the existing local option system was not enough and that the legislature must inaugurate statewide prohibition. Many Methodists thought that local option prohibition was successful and that the state's prohibitionists should simply push for additional counties to go dry, while also insisting on stronger enforcement of existing laws. The chief proponent of this latter local option view was Methodist bishop Charles B. Galloway. For a time, Galloway's stand seemed reasonable, as county after county marched into the dry column. By early 1908 only nine counties still permitted alcohol sales. Unfortunately for Galloway and his supporters, it was clear that these nine counties (including Adams and Warren with their important cities of Natchez and Vicksburg) were unlikely ever to outlaw alcohol.[63]

Proposals in the legislature for initiating statewide prohibition did better with each passing year. In 1903 WCTU leaders and others convened a statewide prohibition convention in Jackson. Delegates vowed to work hard to secure the election of legislators committed to prohibition. During the 1903 campaign, the convention's executive committee sent a questionnaire to all legislative candidates, asking their views on prohibition. More than 150 responded, and all but three of these candidates declared their support for prohibition. Thus, starting in 1904, the legislature had a large number of prohibitionist members. The new governor, James K. Vardaman, was a strong supporter of local option prohibition but avoided endorsing statewide prohibition. The 1904 legislature debated prohibition extensively, and the final vote in the House of Representatives was sixty-six to forty-three in favor of statewide prohibition. This was short of the two-thirds vote required for a state constitutional amendment.[64]

In 1907 outgoing governor Vardaman asked the legislature to do something about the whiskey evil, and newly elected governor Noel urged passage of a statewide prohibition statute. Noel was a Progressive, and prohibition was part of a larger program he sought, together with a child labor law, food inspection laws, and an elected judiciary. Charlton H. Alexander drafted Mississippi's prohibition statute. The law simply revoked all state liquor licenses effective on the last day of 1908. The law was not as severe as it might have been, since possession of a quart or less of alcohol was not a crime. Druggists were still permitted to sell alcohol for use as medicine or wine for church sacraments. Citizens were still permitted to make wine at home. The law passed the House of Representatives without a dissenting vote, although a number of Delta lawmakers were conspicuously absent. All but four state senators voted for the law.[65]

December 31, 1908, was the last day of legal liquor sales in Mississippi. It was a day of great hilarity in those cities that did not have local option prohibition. Revelers filled the streets, and retail liquor dealers did a booming business. The next day, saloons and liquor stores closed down. The *Natchez Democrat* noted with disgust that the city would be losing $26,000 per year in liquor license fees. The *Democrat* predicted prohibition would have only a short reign in Mississippi after lawmakers found out how costly it was to find and close down illegal drinking establishments.[66]

Making Mississippi a dry state in fact as well as law proved difficult. Citizens could still have liquor shipped in from wet states. Many observers believed the Mississippi legislature could do nothing about such shipments, since to do so would be to interfere with interstate commerce or with the U.S. Post Office. Finally, lawmakers passed a law that made it a crime to move a shipment of liquor more than one hundred feet from the point of original delivery (usually a post office or express station). Another problem in making the state truly dry was entrepreneurs who set up drinking establishments within a few thousand yards of Natchez and Vicksburg. Some Mississippi saloon operators purchased floating saloons that could ply the waters of the Mississippi River. Others moved their operations to islands in the Mississippi River or to the Louisiana shore. After the town of Gainesville, Mississippi, dried up, for example, enterprising entrepreneurs built a new saloon called the Blue Goose on the Louisiana side of the river. Saloon owners provided a fleet of rowboats by which Mississippi patrons could row themselves to the Blue Goose. If, after an evening at the Goose, a Mississippi patron was too intoxicated to row, an employee of the saloon would row the patron back to Mississippi. With some justification, the leaders of Adams and Warren counties wondered why they should be deprived of their liquor license fees if saloons were going to be nearby anyway.[67]

Another problem with enforcement of prohibition in Mississippi was that illegal liquor retailers were legion. In the town of Amory, the standard joke was "Who could be buying all this illegal liquor? After all, everyone in town is selling it!" Governor Noel sent a private detective named P. B. French into Amory in 1910. The detective arrived in Amory posing as a sheep buyer, having first "spattered his mustache and clothing with whiskey." French was admitted without question "into any dive in town." Thirty prosecutions resulted, with thirty convictions. Noel's efforts to get the new laws enforced in Warren County were not so successful. The governor wrote the local judge urging strict enforcement of the law. Judge H. C. Mounger, however, replied by admitting there was widespread violation of the law in Vicksburg, then saying that there was nothing he could do about it. The problem, he alleged, was not with the judge or prosecutor but with the citizens. He reported the last grand jury had examined 170 witnesses on matters of illegal liquor sales but had returned no indictments. "From what I can learn," Mounger explained to the governor, "public sentiment is not in favor of the enforcement of the liquor laws," and in such cases prosecution was useless.[68]

Some of Mississippi's problems with liquor law enforcement would have been lessened if the entire nation were living under prohibition. In that case, legal shipments of liquor into Mississippi would be a thing of the past, as would floating saloons. When Congress passed the Eighteenth Amendment in 1919 bringing national prohibition, Mississippi was the first state to ratify it. The vote was ninety-three to three in the lower house of the legislature and twenty-nine to five in the state Senate. With ratification of the amendment, Mississippi became even drier, as nearby states could no longer contaminate Mississippi's prohibition program. The state never was, of course, "bone-dry," since illegal liquor sales continued.[69]

The prohibition movement in Mississippi was fueled by various other movements. White supremacists argued that black Mississippians would work harder and be less rebellious if liquor were outlawed. Baptists, Methodists, Presbyterians, and others believed the state would be less sinful and would have more church-centered homes if alcoholic beverages were eliminated. Woman suffrage leaders such as Belle Kearney believed the prohibition movement was an allied reform that would make women's lives better in the state of Mississippi as the phenomenon of alcoholic and abusive husbands declined. Progressives believed prohibition was just one more area where government could get involved to institutionalize a scientific truth—that the consumption of alcoholic beverages was medically damaging and detrimental to social institutions.

Progressives and women's groups were also active in educational reform in Mississippi. Mississippi faced serious disparities in the quality of its schools. White schools were better than black schools, while urban schools were better than rural schools. Schools of each race in black-majority counties were better funded than the schools of each race in white-majority counties. All counties received funds from the poll tax, as well as a share of the modest state appropriation for education. Some counties levied extra taxes to support local schools, while some did not. Most cities ran their own separate school systems and appropriated funds for these systems in a relatively generous way. In some Mississippi cities, the school year lasted 150 days, while in many rural counties the school year lasted only 65 days and was sometimes cut short by lack of funds.[70]

James K. Vardaman's rise to power was based largely on his promise to "segregate" taxes, or, in other words, to spend on black education only the funds remitted by black taxpayers. While this system never became a reality, the state did take a few steps in that direction, deciding, for example, that poll taxes should remain in the counties where they were collected rather than go into the state's general education fund. This meant, for instance, that a white-majority county like Harrison, with many white payers of the poll tax, would not see some of these poll-tax dollars used in black-majority counties like Issaquena, where few persons paid the poll tax. Agrarian leaders like Frank Burkitt for many years pushed for frugality in education, but Mississippi schools were so obviously inadequate that in 1910 the Burkitt School Act increased educational funding by 10 percent in one year.[71]

In 1910 the legislature authorized counties to build consolidated schools, larger than the old schools but more widely scattered. Recognizing the distance many students would have to travel to the new schools, the legislature authorized counties to provide pupils' transportation to school. Studies by Progressive educators showed that these larger schools could offer a superior education to the students who attended them. Many counties rushed to take advantage of the new system. Holmes County, for example, closed four schools and built a modern consolidated school, providing transportation (by wagon) for the pupils.[72]

State educators and lawmakers were shocked by the public reaction to school consolidation. Many parents viewed the consolidation movement as a personal affront. One-room schools had been good enough for them, so why was it now necessary to change? Many suspected taxes would rise sharply to pay for the new schools as well as for transportation. Some feared the well-educated graduates of these schools would leave the state looking for new opportunities. Some objected to the loss of local control, as the community school gave way to the more distant and bureaucratic school. Tensions ran high. At East Lincoln Consolidated School, a student shot and killed principal A. K. Watkins. Arsonists torched a number of the new school buildings, some more than once.

The citizen reaction to consolidated schools was one of several such rebellions against increasingly centralized authority in this period. Others included the rebellion of many farmers against compulsory cattle dipping (and their dynamiting of dipping vats) and parents' refusal to accept the decisions of many county textbook commissions to require students to purchase new texts. In the case of school consolidation, the state's educators finally won the battle of public opinion, and the quality of the state's schools began to increase.[73]

In the 1915 election, the Vardaman-Bilbo faction proved itself incredibly strong. Four of the five gubernatorial candidates were Vardaman supporters, and Vardamanite Theodore G. Bilbo was elected governor by carrying all but five counties. Within three years the careers of both Vardaman and Bilbo were in shambles. The faction's problems began when Europe erupted into war. Senator Vardaman became especially concerned at Britain's interference with ships carrying American cotton. In his speeches, Vardaman began to treat Britain as somewhat of an enemy of the United States, while a majority of politicians considered Britain a key ally. President Wilson was pushing a military preparedness program. Vardaman denounced it, while his colleague John Sharp Williams praised it.

As the North Atlantic sea-lanes became increasingly dangerous, Senator Thomas P. Gore, Democrat from Oklahoma, coauthored the Gore-McLemore Resolutions. These resolutions advised American citizens not to travel on ships owned by warring nations. Gore was the former "boy orator" of the Populist Party in Webster County, Mississippi. Now an Oklahoma Democrat, Gore found a ready supporter in James K. Vardaman. Vardaman had the foresight to predict that American civilian deaths in the war zone could lead the nation to a declaration of war. Vardaman tried to prevent the tabling of the Gore-McLemore Resolutions, but he failed. When the Germans resumed unrestricted submarine warfare, the Wilson administration broke off relations, and the Senate passed a resolution praising the president's action. This resolution passed seventy-eight to five, with Vardaman on the losing side. A bill to arm merchant ships was filibustered to death in the Senate, leading President Wilson to denounce Vardaman as one of a "little group of willful men" who had left American ships vulnerable. Vardaman admitted opposing the bill but denied he had filibustered. When finally the Senate voted to declare war on Germany and its allies, the vote was eighty-two to six, with Vardaman again part of a decided minority.[74]

Back home, Vardaman's enemies had a field day. A Biloxi blacksmith constructed a huge iron cross for Vardaman, a replica of Germany's famous military decoration. Citizens hung the senator in effigy in Clarksdale. Vardaman must have been chagrined when only a week after the declaration of war the Socialist newspaper *Appeal to Reason* praised him as an exponent of peace. Socialist praise would be of little use to him in Mississippi. It was true that once Congress declared war, Vardaman supported the commander-in-chief on most issues. Still, he opposed the draft, preferring that the war be fought with volunteers. He also opposed the Sedition Act and other laws limiting free speech. In opposing the United States' entry into World War I and in opposing laws initiating the draft and limiting dissent, Vardaman provided the best evidence he was not a demagogue. If a demagogue is one who uses the emotions of the people for political advantage, Vardaman certainly failed to act the part here. As citizens in Mississippi grew feverishly patriotic and furiously anti-German, Vardaman refused to become a war hawk. While eventually supporting the president on most issues, Vardaman was always cautious on war matters, never a saber rattler, and President Wilson always considered him weak in his support of the nation's soldiers.[75]

The 1918 election for U.S. senator and members of Congress would provide an important test of the strength of Vardaman and Bilbo. Bilbo announced he would run for a seat in the U.S. House of Representatives, even though his term as governor would not expire until after the 1919 election. Vardaman would be running for reelection to the Senate, opposed by former governor Noel and Congressman Pat Harrison. Harrison proved to be the stronger candidate, and he hit Vardaman hard for his alleged lack of patriotism. Harrison announced his candidacy at the 1917 Neshoba County fair, saying that if the voter felt true patriotism, "you cannot reward the man who gives aid and comfort to the enemies of the government." Vardaman encountered hecklers and more than once had to speak from a podium that had been spattered with yellow paint to symbolize cowardice. Yet the senator was not without his supporters. Many wondered, if Harrison was so patriotic, why he had not volunteered for military service. Harrison was thirty-six years old, while Vardaman had been thirty-seven when he had volunteered for military service in 1898. Others wondered why Harrison offered no new issues or new proposals but only criticized Vardaman's voting record.[76]

Vardaman at this time was suffering from high blood pressure and had probably suffered minor strokes. Medical problems occasionally forced him to stop campaigning and rest at his sister's home in Alabama. When he did speak, Vardaman said he was incredulous people could accuse him of a lack of patriotism, since, unlike his opponent, he was a war veteran. He also denied Harrison was an invariable Wilson supporter. Vardaman pointed out Harrison had voted against Wilson's child labor bill and wondered how any member of Congress could fail to support a law to protect children. But to Mississippi voters, the old Progressive issues like child labor were fading away, as war became the only issue.[77]

In Bilbo's congressional race against Paul B. Johnson Sr., both candidates supported the president and his preparedness policy. Since war policy would not help differentiate himself from Bilbo, Johnson seized instead upon an issue important to thousands of farmers. The 1916 legislature had passed a law requiring farmers to dip their cattle every two weeks to control cattle tick fever. Governor Bilbo had supported the law. Now Johnson raised the issue, pointing out that cattle were sometimes injured in the dipping vats and sometimes poisoned. Johnson argued that it was not even clear that dipping was effective in eliminating ticks. Johnson's use of a cowbell from the podium delighted farmers, and increasingly the state's farmers were heard to say, "I'm fer Bilbo but I'm agin' dippin'." As Bilbo later put it, "I was crucified on a cross of ticks."[78]

The August 19 primary resulted in a decisive victory for Johnson; a second primary would not be needed. Not only Bilbo but Vardaman also went down to defeat, as Harrison won with 56,715 votes for U.S. senator while Vardaman received 44,154 and Noel 6,730 votes. Only fifteen years after his dramatic rise to power, Vardaman had met an emphatic rebuke from the voters. He never held office again. Bilbo, too, met an impressive defeat. Many had felt certain the incumbent governor would easily win a seat in Congress, but such was not the case. Bilbo tried for a second term as governor in the 1923 election but met another defeat. Eventually, he would win a second governor's term in 1927 and later was a U.S. senator famous for his racist statements and actions. The entry of the United States into World War I provided a watershed, as the era of Vardaman and Bilbo gave way to a period when business interests exerted more control over state government. Progressivism entered a decline, as it also did at the national level.[79]

Writers who have examined the era of Vardaman and Bilbo have disagreed over how to interpret this stormy period of Mississippi politics. Thomas Boschert asserted that the state's new political leaders relied on small farmers' votes but "did little to relieve the plight of the poor white farmers." John R. Skates agreed that despite all the political agitation, Mississippians by the time of World War II were living much as their great-grandparents had lived. Nannie Pitts McLemore argued that Mississippi experienced true Progressivism but that the state's greatest Progressive was neither Vardaman nor Bilbo but the less famous Edmund F. Noel. Vincent Giroux found Theodore Bilbo petty and vindictive, more style than substance, and one who failed to deliver on his promises. On the other hand, William D. McCain believed that the election of Bilbo as governor in 1915 marked the "triumph of democracy," as masses triumphed over the elites. William F. Holmes, Vardaman's biographer, maintained that his subject was one of the nation's great Progressives. Holmes mused that Vardaman is not respected as much as northern Progressives because of his racial beliefs and statements, but he noted that these racial beliefs were typical of early-twentieth-century Americans. Holmes argued that while Vardaman may have exploited racial issues, he did not create the climate of racial hatred.[80]

Charges that Vardaman was a racist demagogue are most assuredly true. While his biographer is correct in saying that Vardaman's racist rhetoric reflected views that were widespread among white Mississippians, his rhetoric went beyond what we might reasonably expect of a governor or a U.S. senator. In running for governor, Vardaman said he could not denounce the work of lynch mobs and added that as a private citizen, he would not shrink from participating in such a mob. Vardaman's defenders are justified in saying that as governor he did exert himself to prevent lynchings. On the other hand, his campaign rhetoric supporting lynching helped create a climate where members of lynch mobs felt justified, even heroic, in their actions. Other Mississippi politicians of this era, such as Earl Brewer, Frank A. Critz, and Edmund F. Noel, adopted a more statesmanlike tone, and they enjoyed political success. Vardaman lacked the paternalistic solicitude demonstrated by so many Delta leaders toward black Mississippians. Under the tutelage of his older friend Dr. B. F. Ward, Vardaman developed a dim view of the character and characteristics of African Americans.

Was Mississippi a Progressive state in this period? Emphatically, yes. Under Governors Longino, Vardaman, Noel, Brewer, and Bilbo, the state enacted a whole array of Progressive reforms. These included passage of a pure food and drug law and the founding of the state Department of Health, which battled yellow fever, hookworm, pellagra, tuberculosis, and other diseases. Mississippi's Progressives passed a strong child labor law and stopped sending youths to adult prisons. Legislators ended convict leasing, and the convict death rate fell. State agricultural agencies gathered data the state's farmers needed, helped them fight the boll weevil, and aided diversification into animal husbandry and new crops. Innovations such as the initiative, referendum, and election of judges made government more democratic. Mississippi was the first state in the nation to bring two important Progressive reforms: a statewide primary to elect its state and county officers and the ratification of the Eighteenth Amendment bringing national prohibition.

To call Mississippi a Progressive state in these years is not to say that all policies pursued by the state and county governments were just. Few, if any, states could match Mississippi's institutionalized racial injustice. Arrest and brutal imprisonment of black citizens for trivial offenses such as vagrancy exemplify this institutionalized racism. Black citizens' exclusion from the voter rolls and the inadequate funding of black schools are further examples. Still, Mississippi's leading politicians of this period meet the standard definition of Progressives. They drew attention to the state's problems and sought legislation to eliminate those problems. The state's leading politicians had a blind spot when it came to racial injustice, not recognizing it as a problem.

Some have suggested that despite all the allegations of a successful "revolt of the rednecks" in Mississippi, in fact the state's politicians did little to help the average citizen. Yet the early twentieth century brought important political changes to the state. Voters of modest means, including small farmers, had a much stronger voice in government after 1903 than they had in the late nineteenth century. While few small farmers served in important offices, they helped elect the candidates who did, choosing persons who spoke to their wants and needs, including Vardaman, Noel, and Bilbo. Gone were days when a small clique handpicked conservative nominees at party conventions. While it is true Mississippi continued to face problems of poverty, lack of industrialization, and a weak educational system, the Progressive politicians did not cause these problems, and in fact they brought improvements. Progressives increased school funding, made factories safer, nearly eliminated a number of diseases, and helped bring improved roads, railroads, and rural mail service.

Two great shortcomings in the state's political system would be left for future generations to solve. One was the lack of a two-party system, which left Mississippi far out of the mainstream of national politics. Despite its devotion to the Democratic Party, the Democratic administrations of Grover Cleveland and Woodrow Wilson bestowed upon Mississippi little in the way of patronage rewards or funds for state projects, since other states such as Indiana and Ohio were closely contested, and in those states government jobs and federal contracts earned political dividends for the national Democratic Party. The other legacy left for another generation to solve was the tendency to racial demagoguery. Politicians recognized that they needed to use emotional issues to win over the voters and to motivate them to turn out on Election Day. No issue was more certain to pique the interest of Mississippi's white electorate than warnings that—in this black-majority state—black citizens might rise up in rebellion from the place Mississippi's laws and customs had assigned to them. Vardaman's horrific speeches about black rapists and white lynch mobs attracted crowds and converted his listeners into loyal voters who could be counted on to vote. Unfortunately, the rhetoric of Vardaman and Bilbo did not simply reflect the state's prevailing racism but also encouraged it. When the governor himself refused to denounce the practice of lynching, lynching became an even more socially acceptable practice than it otherwise would have been. Not until the 1960s would two-party politics begin to show any promise in the state, and not until 1970 and beyond would politicians finally come to believe racial conciliation might in some cases be politically useful. Until then, Mississippi politics would continue in its one-party, white supremacist track.

CHAPTER TWELVE

Change and Continuity in Mississippi

Was Mississippi's history—and the history of the South generally—a story of continuity or change? Historians have been wrestling with this question for more than half a century. Wilbur Cash, in his 1941 book *The Mind of the South*, presented the region's history as one of remarkable continuity. Concerning the rise of demagogues like James K. Vardaman, for example, Cash argued that "the politics of the South went right on serving only the interests of the upper orders quite as though the demagogues had never been elected at all." C. Vann Woodward, on the other hand, presented southern history as a story of change. He asserted that Jim Crow segregation, for example, was a new system inaugurated just before 1900, replacing a much more relaxed system of race relations. Woodward treated the Populists and the agrarian Democrats as players who brought real change to the southern political scene. Edward L. Ayers, in his 1992 book *The Promise of the New South: Life after Reconstruction*, emphasized new beginnings, ranging from industrialization to the rise of blues music, although he admits "some Southerners tested new ways only to return to the old."[1]

Looking at Mississippi specifically, Albert D. Kirwan, in his 1951 classic *Revolt of the Rednecks*, argued that small farmers won a great victory with the advent of statewide primaries in 1903—a victory that ushered in an era of change. Most recent writings on Mississippi's history, however, have emphasized continuity. John R. Skates, for example, observed that "in 1940 Mississippi's institutions were the same ones that had developed a hundred years earlier." Skates found that important changes did not come until the period of World War II and afterward. Similarly, writing about the politics of this era, historian Thomas Boschert was unimpressed with agrarian political victories. Of the legislators who passed the 1902 primary election law, for instance, Boschert wrote that "there were hardly any poor, struggling plowhands in the bunch," but on the contrary, then as earlier, the legislature was made up of economic elites. Of course it is possible that elites dominated the legislature but still felt forced by strong agrarian sentiment to pass new laws of interest to the small farmers. Yet for Boschert, the new generation of leaders including Vardaman and Bilbo "did little to relieve the plight of the poor white farmers."[2]

Mississippi in the four decades after Reconstruction saw marked change in agriculture. While cotton was overwhelmingly the state's chief crop during the forty years after 1877, other agricultural products increased sharply in importance as evangelists spread the diversified farming gospel. Milk production in Mississippi tripled between 1879 and 1919, while the state produced fifty times as much hay in the latter year as in the former. Production of corn, sweet potatoes, poultry, and other farm products increased sharply over the four decades. Diversification helped the state's farmers in many ways. Growing clover and vetch for hay rebuilt the soil. Raising food crops helped ease farmers' indebtedness, since they did not have to borrow money to feed their families. Diversification helped alleviate perhaps the greatest problem facing Mississippi farmers: the rapid expansion of cotton production in the world, which led to a sharp decline in cotton prices. There were almost no negatives to farmers' diversifying, except that in some years they would have earned more cash if they had raised cotton exclusively.

Yet diversification proved difficult for many farmers. Cotton was a crop they knew well, a crop for which Mississippi's soil and climate were ideally suited. Mississippi, like other southern states, had been subjected to a second Yankee invasion, this one of northern factory goods. Farmers and their families longed for printed cloth and Singer sewing machines, mechanized corn shellers and decorative parlor lamps. Raising food crops could help lead to independence from indebtedness, but only a cash crop could give farm families the benefits of factory goods in the new consumer economy. Finally, diversification proved especially difficult on the small farms typical in Mississippi. As historian John Boles has noted, if a farmer had only twenty-three acres, it would not make sense to plant three or four food crops in addition to cotton. The latest scientific methods and farm machinery were also difficult to use on the smallest farms. Allowing acreage to lie fallow was an unaffordable luxury for the farmer who had only two dozen acres. And if a farmer owned only three hogs and two cows, asked Boles, "How could such a farmer selectively breed his livestock?"[3]

Mississippi farmers sought to band together for the common good. With almost no history of organizing to build upon, Mississippi farmers organized branches of several important agricultural organizations, including the Grange, the Farmers' Alliance, and the Farmers' Union. These organizations enjoyed a rapid rise in membership, and they lobbied the legislature and launched farmers' cooperatives. Yet in the long run they failed. Farmers' independent natures meant they objected to being told where to shop, what to grow or how to grow it, or to whom to sell their crop. Dependent on credit, farmers lacked the freedom to patronize the cash-only farmers' co-ops. They often had to disregard the diversification gospel since lenders insisted on a lien on a cotton crop. Within a year or two of the demise of the large Grange and Farmers' Alliance organizations, it was almost as if these groups had never existed, with farmers following their traditional practices without the benefit of a large and influential organization. By 1917 no state in the Union had a less impressive record of farmer involvement in cooperative stores and cooperative marketing. No large farm organization remained in Mississippi except for the children's Corn Clubs and Tomato Clubs.

The greatest continuity in Mississippi agriculture was farmers' continued reliance on cotton. While it was true that acreage devoted to corn and truck crops and hay increased, cotton acreage increased, too. The state's cotton production doubled between 1870 and 1920. So dependent was the state upon cotton production that a bad cotton year was devastating for state and county tax receipts and for merchants' sales. A good year for cotton led to a temporary boom in the state's economy, a boom that ended if the next year's cotton prices were low.

By several measures Mississippi farms were characterized more by change than continuity. As Mississippi's population increased (primarily by births), demand for land to farm also increased. This led enterprising Mississippians to bring new lands into production, and the percentage of the state's land area that was in farms increased. Part of this increase involved newly cleared land in the Delta, and the soil on these new plantations was extraordinarily rich. Yet the sandy soils of the Piney Woods and the rocky and hilly soils of parts of the northeast were also brought into production, even though they had been rejected earlier as inferior. At the same time these marginal lands were being brought into agricultural production, the average farm size was falling. This was a result of an increasingly large population seeking farmland. Landlords rented small plots to sharecropper families, knowing that because of the small farm size, the lands would be intensively cultivated.

The period between 1880 and 1920 saw a substantial drop in average farm size, from 156 acres to 67 acres. Increasingly, Mississippi farmers were farming poor lands, but they were unable to afford the fertilizer or fallow periods that would have helped marginal lands to produce. The final tragedy was small farmers' loss of their lands to planters, merchants, and bankers. The percentage of Mississippi farms that were run by their owners fell sharply between 1880 and 1920, from 56 percent to 33 percent. This decline of farm ownership over four decades affected both black and white Mississippi yeomen farmers, who increasingly fell into the ranks of tenants. Many years these tenants had no cash income, earning nothing beyond the cost of their "furnish." The poverty of Mississippi's farmers helped keep tax receipts low, limiting the kinds of services state and local governments could offer. Inadequate schools and impassable roads could not be improved while the people of the state were so impoverished, nor would railroad companies invest in communities too poor to support freight or passenger services.

The Mississippian of 1917, transported back to his or her great-grandparents' farm, would have felt very much at home, for the methods of farming and household management had not changed. Agriculture was based on mules and hoes. Modern conveniences like electric appliances, indoor plumbing, and iceboxes had not reached Mississippi farms. In 1917 as in the antebellum period, Mississippi agriculture was based largely on the labor of a rigidly controlled African American population. Some of the black laborers toiled for wealthy planters, while others worked singly or in pairs with white small farmers. Black labor was so inexpensive, and black workers so unlikely to find alternative employment in a northern (or Mississippi) factory, that it made no sense for landowners to invest in tractors or other mechanization. Not until the great exodus of black farmworkers to northern cities during World War II would Mississippi farms finally see the arrival of the tractor, three-quarters of a century after the farmers in the Great Plains states had begun to mechanize.

White planters and yeomen farmers recognized the importance of having a dependable black labor force. After the Civil War, planters reluctantly agreed that black families could work their own plots rather than work in gangs as had been the practice under slavery. Black laborers agreed they would sign an annual contract, not seeking to move on until a crop had been harvested. While some have suggested that under the sharecropping system, planters and laborers cooperated together to achieve shared successes (a large crop), actually landowners and sharecroppers had markedly different goals. The planter, unlike the sharecropper, favored the idea of families working very small plots of land intensively, while the sharecroppers preferred larger plots. Planters ran their own commissaries, charging high prices and exorbitant interest, while the sharecroppers hoped to limit their indebtedness. Estimates suggest that sharecroppers kept only about 12 percent more of the wealth they produced than had the slaves.

For black sharecroppers, change since emancipation seemed modest. While they could obtain clothes and food at the plantation store, they had received similar allotments under slavery. Some planters still called the sharecroppers to work with the same morning bell used in slavery times, and many still insisted on their supposed right to punish black sharecroppers with the lash. The planter's economic situation in some ways was much improved in the decades after the Civil War. Planters now earned a great deal of money selling goods to tenants at high prices and high interest rates. For many planters, the income from the commissary surpassed the income from cotton production.

To keep the black laborers in place and ready to work, planters employed a variety of laws and customs. Workers were punished if they left employment before the end of the crop year. The legal punishment was typically a prison sentence, and prisoners would see their labor leased to the highest bidder. Convicts were so brutalized that most black laborers did all in their power to avoid running afoul of the labor and vagrancy laws. Outside the legal system, the practice of lynching reminded African Americans in Mississippi that they were expected to acquiesce to the state's system of race control and that failure to do so could be fatal. Finally, informal practices of segregation reserved the best jobs for whites. Black workers could not escape sharecropping and find work at the state's textile mills or canneries, because such jobs were reserved for whites. With unemployment a crime that meant hellish imprisonment, most black Mississippians toiled in the fields of white landowners, avoiding confrontation with whites who depended upon their labor.

African Americans in Mississippi occasionally confronted the system of race control head-on, refusing to accept the lower caste status prescribed by law and custom. Those who challenged the system were driven from the state or killed. In Leflore County in 1889, black farmers and laborers joined the Colored Farmers' Alliance and made plans to bypass local planters and merchants. They ordered goods instead from a Farmers' Alliance cooperative store at Durant. Brutal suppression of the group's leaders followed. Whites called such instances of black resistance "race riots," and their suppression of the riots served notice on black residents that resistance to the system of race control would be crushed. Given the utter white control of the state's power structure—of land, jobs, credit, courts, police, and militia—the most remarkable thing is how widespread black resistance to the system was.

If Mississippi's black citizens preferred to avoid violent clashes with the state's white power structure, they found other ways of resisting. One was to work incredibly hard and overcome almost insuperable obstacles to find economic and professional success. Given the biases of law and custom, it is surprising that in 1900 some sixteen in one hundred black farm families in Mississippi worked land that they owned. Others operated successful businesses and helped build up the black communities of their cities. Black physician and lawyer S. D. Redmond rose from humble beginnings to own two drugstores and more than a hundred houses in the state capital and was a successful bank president—all by the age of thirty-six. In Mound Bayou, Isaiah T. Montgomery and Benjamin T. Green built up one of the most prosperous all-black towns in the nation. While Mound Bayou entered some hard times just before World War I, in its heyday the town was the pride of black Mississippians.

The Democratic Party had unbroken control of Mississippi's government, and it crushed any political opposition that appeared. Politicians like James K. Vardaman reminded voters that the Democratic Party was the party of white control and that to vote for any other party was to divide whites and to leave the state open to black domination. Thus, while the state did see the rise of new agrarian and farmer-labor parties in this period, such parties were beaten back by Democrats drawing the color line—their insisting it was the duty of every white man to vote Democratic. While the Greenback Party of the late 1870s and early 1880s included black members and occasionally fielded black candidates, the later Populist Party did not. Nevertheless, Democrats alleged that the Populists threatened the state's system of white domination, and voters tended to agree.

Political continuities over the decades were apparent. The Democratic Party was in control in the state in 1877, and it was still in firm control in 1917. In 1917 as in 1877, the state's lawmakers and governors were mostly lawyers, planters, merchants, and larger farmers. Successful politicians preached white unity and white domination of all facets of life in Mississippi. Yet even the Democratic Party fostered divisions among whites, and as a result of these political battles, some change came to Mississippi. Democratic divisions pitted the politicians of the black-majority counties against those of the white-majority counties. Agrarian Democrats battled town boosters and urban reformers. Dry Democrats battled party members who were wets. While no dirt farmer was elected to the highest offices in Mississippi, state lawmakers enacted laws that helped small farmers, including the funding of agricultural experiment stations, farmers' institutes, and agricultural high schools.

Among the clear changes in Mississippi politics were revisions of the state's system of voter qualifications. Prior to 1890, black voting had fallen off considerably, and despite the state's black majority, black voters had tended to play a minor role in state politics. Yet in the 1888 election presidential candidate Benjamin Harrison won more than 30,000 votes in Mississippi, better than one out of every four votes cast—it was clear that most of these votes had been cast by black voters. After 1890, however, with the new poll tax, literacy test, and other instruments of disfranchisement, black voting was almost completely eliminated in the state.

Early in the twentieth century Mississippi's government officials embraced a national movement called Progressivism. Governors James K. Vardaman, Edmund F. Noel, Earl L. Brewer, and Theodore G. Bilbo urged upon state lawmakers a detailed program for an activist government that would help solve Mississippi's problems. Under these Progressive leaders, Mississippi outlawed child labor and attacked diseases such as pellagra and hookworm. New state agencies helped eradicate cattle ticks, prevent bank failures, and protect consumers. In Congress, Mississippi Progressives sought strong government action to regulate railroads and to ensure the safety of the nation's food supply. Mississippi's involvement in Progressivism shows discontinuity in state politics. The Progressives replaced an earlier generation of state political leaders who had been largely content to protect the status quo and to aid merchants, bankers, planters, and railroads.

Another good example of political change was the movement for prohibition. A weak and amorphous movement in 1877, it was extremely strong and well organized by the time of the United States' entry into World War I. Many—though not all—of Mississippi's Progressive leaders favored prohibition. Public health officials argued that alcohol left the body weak and vulnerable to illness. Church leaders saw drinking as a sin, while leaders of a number of women's groups pointed out how many Mississippi wives were terrorized by a drunkard husband. Whites generally believed alcohol encouraged blacks to "forget their place" and to lash out dangerously at the system (and perhaps it did). Thus, for the health of the state, for its economic betterment, for happier Christian families, and for the cause of white supremacy, the drys believed alcohol should be outlawed.

On a county-by-county basis, prohibition marched across Mississippi in the 1880s and 1890s. By 1908 all but nine counties had banned the sale of alcoholic beverages. The legislature brought statewide prohibition to Mississippi beginning on January 1, 1909. Mississippi prohibitionists vowed not to rest until alcoholic beverages were prohibited across the nation, and in 1917 Congress passed the Eighteenth Amendment to the U.S. Constitution. Mississippi was the first state to ratify the amendment, doing so by lopsided margins in both houses of the legislature. While illegal liquor sales did occur, Mississippi was one of the driest states in the nation, and prohibition is an important example of real change coming to the state by the action of its political leaders.

Perhaps the greatest discontinuity in the history of Mississippi in the four decades after Reconstruction was in the area of industrialization. Mississippi in 1877 had few industrial establishments, and most of the ones counted by the 1880 census takers were gristmills, small harness shops, and the like. Yet forty years later the state had a number of factories, offering an alternative to agriculture for state workers—one that had not really been available in the immediate aftermath of the Civil War. While the total number of manufacturing establishments less than doubled, it is clear the new manufacturing establishments were on a new scale. The horsepower employed in manufacturing in 1920 was about ten times that of four decades earlier, while the number of workers employed was also about ten times as great. The value of the products manufactured in 1920 was more than twenty-five times as great as in 1880. In a period when agriculture was also expanding, the percent of the workforce engaged in manufacturing more than quadrupled in Mississippi. Industry provided tens of thousands of jobs for Mississippians, giving citizens employment options outside agriculture. By reducing Mississippi's dependence upon farming, the state's economy was better able to weather those years when droughts or low cotton prices spelled hard times.

The unfortunate aspect of Mississippi's industrialization is that the state was only processing the raw materials produced locally. It made sense to make turpentine and lumber and cottonseed oil locally, rather than ship bulky raw materials out of state for processing. Yet few investors either inside or outside of Mississippi were interested in building factories in the state that did more than process raw products. One problem was that local investors could get such a good return on their money by running plantations and operating commissaries that there was little temptation to launch untested enterprises such as clothing factories or furniture mills. Outside investors seldom thought of Mississippi when they were selecting locations for new factories. The state was overwhelmingly rural, while most factories were located in cities. The state had an inadequate school system, and relatively few Mississippians managed to acquire skills as machinists, tool and die makers, or lathe operators. In the 1870s, 1880s, and 1890s many northerners thought of Mississippi as a place subject to terrifying illnesses such as yellow fever and knew that diseases all too often brought the state's economy to a standstill.

Mississippi towns and cities had their boosters who tried to modernize their localities, improve education, and attract new residents. The growth of the river cities Natchez and Vicksburg was impressive, but Jackson, Meridian, and

Hattiesburg grew even faster, benefiting from new lumber mills and the completion of railroads that made these cities important hubs. Mississippi cities also modernized. Electric and natural gas utilities, streetcars, ice delivery, and water and sewer service brought many Mississippians into the modern age. Town and city governments used local taxation to improve education. The better schools and the availability of utility service helped towns and cities attract some new industries.

Mississippi's conquest of public health menaces also made the state more attractive to northern investors. National public health activists used Mississippi as a kind of laboratory for studying diseases, including yellow fever, pellagra, and hookworm. As the state's workforce grew healthier, there was less reason for the nation's investors to shun the state. After the crushing of several Knights of Labor lumber mill strikes, the 1911 Harriman railroad strike, and the 1915 shrimp fishermen's strike, Mississippi also seemed to offer investors a locale where union organizing was unlikely to succeed. Finally, an aggressive program of rail development, followed by a campaign to upgrade the state's roads, provided still other incentives for factories to locate in Mississippi.

But there was one fact the state's leaders simply could not overcome. Nature had seemingly foreordained that Mississippi should be only a farm state. While Tennessee had abundant coal to help power factories and Alabama had iron ore that would lead to the rise of the great city of Birmingham, Mississippi lacked important mineral resources. Successful oil strikes would not come until the 1930s. In an era when the majority of American factories were powered by water, Mississippi lacked the fast-moving streams that could successfully power large manufacturing establishments. Though the Mississippi River was powerful, it was hardly appropriate for the building of water wheels. Other rivers were sluggish.

The United States' entry into World War I in 1917 accelerated the pace of change in Mississippi. The European war began in 1914, and Mississippians watched it with interest. In a state where the great majority of white people were descended from immigrants from the British Isles, Mississippians recognized early that their sympathies lay with the nations fighting Germany. In his memoir of growing up in Ocean Springs, Thomas Park recalled that someone painted obscene slogans about the Kaiser all around the town. "This 'graffiti,'" Park wrote, "so rare then, so common today, was permitted to remain in place for some time—a remarkable reverse of the tidiness that characterized our town." Park recalled how barbershop conversation shifted from local gossip to international events and was all "profanity, obscenity, and braggadocio."[4]

Park remembered with great vividness how a mob in Ocean Springs dragged a suspected German sympathizer by his heels, while shouting "Pro German! Pro German!" The mob stripped the unfortunate man to his underwear, then held an American flag up to "his flushed and terrified face" and forced him to kiss it. As Germany made overtures to Mexico for an alliance, rumors were rife that Mexico was on the verge of attacking across the Gulf. Thomas Park's father worried that Ocean Springs would be on the front lines of this conflict, and he took his guns out to a shed and began cleaning them. "His expression," his son recalled, "was grim." By the time the United States declared war on Germany in April 1917, the great majority of Mississippians were ready to fight.[5]

Near Hattiesburg, the U.S. Army opened a training base named Camp Shelby in the late summer of 1917. By October the camp was consuming 300,000 pounds of potatoes per month, 400,000 pounds of bread, 21 tons of beans, and 29,000 large cans of tomatoes. About 30,000 men were stationed at Camp Shelby. To occupy their spare time, soldiers took French lessons or went on special railroad excursions to Gulfport. Moving pictures were a real novelty for soldiers from rural areas. About one hundred soldiers per week answered the altar call at revival meetings. Sports also helped fill the odd hours for Camp Shelby enlisted men. In October 1917 the men organized Democratic and Republican baseball teams. In the first match, the Republicans beat the Democrats by a score of 11-1, handing the Republicans a rare victory on Mississippi soil. The soldiers, of course, hailed from all over the United States, making a Republican victory possible.[6]

Camp Shelby was home to the newspaper the *Trench and Camp*. The paper included local coverage of activities at the camp and carried syndicated articles giving war news. The *Trench and Camp* was in part a propaganda organ, preparing psychologically the young soldiers training in Mississippi. The 1917 headlines of this camp newspaper were nothing short of remarkable, revealing the things the national government wanted the soldiers to know and believe. One article profiled an American soldier injured on the battlefields of France; its headline read "Laughs at the Loss of Both Legs, Still Eager to Serve." Another headline read "Submarines Have Very Little Chance to Sink American Troopships." Yet another article had the silly headline, "'Shell Shock' Nothing but a State of Mind, Says Noted Authority." Perhaps the most amazing piece of indoctrination was the *Trench and Camp* article headlined "Wounds from Bullets of Modern Rifle Heal Easily." This article explained there was so much heat and pressure in a rifle barrel that bullets "are literally sterilized by the heat, and they enter the body almost as clean and antiseptic as a surgeon's knife." Indeed, according to the article, unless a bullet struck a particularly vulnerable spot, such as an artery, bullet wounds "are regarded almost as a trifle."[7]

The United States' entry into World War I brought important changes to race relations in Mississippi. More marked changes would come with World War II and would finally culminate in the civil rights movement of the 1950s and 1960s. World War I saw an exodus of African Americans to northern cities. The departure of northern factory workers to the war had created a severe labor shortage. This exodus affected the entire South, but Mississippi saw by far the largest out-migration. In the South, some 7 percent of the black population left between 1910 and 1920; in Mississippi, the figure was 15 percent.[8] All told, nearly 150,000 African Americans left Mississippi during the decade, most of them during the years of World War I. Delta planters were especially hard hit. The U.S. government estimated that in Lowndes County, 60 percent of the black labor force departed for northern factory jobs, leaving the cotton crop unpicked. Some planters responded by offering more generous contracts, but their offers often came too late. The *Meridian Star* explained that "the blacks are leaving in large numbers daily," and "it has been impossible to check the exodus." Similarly, in early 1917 the *Jackson Clarion-Ledger* was of the opinion that unless quick action was taken, "the railroads soon will have hauled all the negroes out of Jackson."[9]

Several agencies of the U.S. government sent investigators into Mississippi to discover the reason for this great black migration. New availability of northern factory jobs was only part of the explanation. Another stimulus was the poverty in Mississippi—meatless diets, chronic illnesses, endless toil under the hot sun, and scarcity of cash income. Even more important than economic factors was black residents' anger at the treatment they received from whites. The "matter of treatment," summarized one government interviewer, was the "all-absorbing, burning question." Many black residents of the state contrasted their poverty and fear with the prospect of life in a northern city, where they could earn a cash paycheck, vote and serve on juries, join unions, and enjoy parks and libraries.[10]

Early on, some newspapers that commented on the 1916 and 1917 exodus suggested that it was a good thing for blacks to leave the state. The *Vicksburg Herald* believed such an exodus would help reduce crowding on the land and would teach Yankees that race relations were not a simple matter. But as the months went by and the exodus showed no signs of abating, white Mississippians started to worry. Some forced black passengers off northbound trains, while others harassed the labor agents who were recruiting workers for northern manufacturers. Mississippi journalists tried to convince black residents that life in northern states had its drawbacks.

After a race riot in East St. Louis in 1917, a Mississippi newspaper ran a headline that read "Many Killed in Riots" and "Negroes Learning a Valuable Lesson." The death toll at the East St. Louis riot was about 40, but one Mississippi newspaper reported nearly 500 casualties, while another claimed 600 deaths. Despite these journalistic exaggerations, the exodus continued unabated.[11]

Nationwide and in Mississippi, black veterans returned home from World War I with a new belief in the many wrongs done to African Americans. Wartime propaganda had spoken of American soldiers making the world safe for democracy, but black veterans found little democracy in white-run Mississippi. Baldwin Dansby, president of Jackson College, later stated his belief that the return of black veterans from World War I marked the beginning of the twentieth-century civil rights movement. The soldier "got the idea in World War I that he was a citizen, fighting for the country just like everyone else," and had earned certain basic rights and a level of respect. In the 1920s and 1930s Mississippi saw the founding of chapters of the NAACP and Marcus Garvey's Universal Negro Improvement Association. While bolder civil rights actions would not come until the 1960s, World War I did plant seeds of change.[12]

Mississippi saw impressive growth between 1877 and 1917. Cotton production increased sharply, as did the production of dozens of other agricultural products. The number of workers employed in manufacturing similarly increased, and the state saw a very large jump in the value of manufactured products. Cities grew rapidly. Yet all this growth is impressive only when we compare Mississippi in 1877 with Mississippi in 1917. The positive changes are much less impressive when we compare Mississippi's statistics in 1917 or 1920 with other states in the region and nation. The forty-year period 1877 to 1917 saw astounding growth of the nation's agriculture, manufacturing, mining, and commerce. The population of the country burgeoned with the arrival of millions of European immigrants, who were soon hard at work in the nation's factories.

By a host of measures Mississippi in 1920 was out of the national mainstream. Mississippi's nonconformity is most easily seen by looking at its rank among the forty-eight states. Mississippi ranked first in the nation in percentage of the population that was rural and first in the percentage of workers who were engaged in farming. It also ranked first in the percentage of the population that was African American. It ranked second or third in the nation in the percentage of the population that was born in the United States, the percentage of farms run by tenants, and the percentage of the population that was illiterate. It ranked last in the nation in percent of farms that employed a tractor. It ranked among the bottom two or three states in the size of the average farm and in the length of the school year.

While the state's rankings on some of these measures—such as race and nativity—were not inherently good or bad, they did help lead the rest of the nation to perceive Mississippi as an unusual, hard-to-fathom place, perhaps a risky place for investment. Factories were usually an urban phenomenon, but no state was less urban than Mississippi. Immigrants were a proven source of factory laborers, but only two other states had a smaller percentage of immigrants in the population. African Americans were largely untested as factory workers before 1917, yet this group made up the largest segment of Mississippi's population. Coupled with the lack of mineral resources and the lack of waterpower, Mississippi's unusual demographics helped stunt industrialization.

By a host of measures, Mississippi by 1917 had experienced some four decades of impressive absolute growth, but relative to the rest of the nation, the degree of change was small. Why did Mississippi not keep pace with the other states in terms of economic growth? One reason was that an economic and political elite ran the state and fostered a system of labor and race control that worked to their own benefit but not to the overall development of the state. To planters and merchants in the Delta, the Black Belt, and elsewhere in the state, it was advantageous to have a poor and dependent labor supply that had few economic options other than to raise cotton on rented lands on borrowed living expenses. Plantations offered large profits, and few wealthy Mississippians were tempted to try something untested, such as opening a textile mill. Northerners generally were as ignorant of investment possibilities in Mississippi as they were about such opportunities in Venezuela or Angola. While northerners occasionally stumbled across obvious opportunities in Mississippi, such as timbering, generally they stayed away from Mississippi with its legendary fevers, its largely African American labor force jealously guarded by employers, its poor schools, and its lack of urban places.

Mississippi continued as the most rural, agricultural state in the nation, and that fact had terrible consequences in some years. Droughts or floods or other agricultural calamities spelled disaster not only for farmers but also for merchants and for state government as well. Mississippi's large dependence upon agriculture made for an uncertain tax base, and after Reconstruction ended, politicians' most trumpeted promise was to keep tax rates low. Tax revenues were made even more precarious when the state enacted prohibition, since the tax on liquors had been of great importance to Mississippi. Low tax receipts meant that substantial aid to railroads, successful modernizing of the state's roads, state-sponsored flood control, and improving the public schools were unlikely.

Across America, education offered one possible way out of poverty. In Mississippi, this was less true, partly because the low tax rates and irregular tax collections kept public education woefully underfunded. Mississippi in 1920 ranked next to last of the states in the length of its school year, and only two states had a lower literacy rate. With a high illiteracy rate for both whites and blacks, compared with other states, it was clear that education could do little to lift the state out of poverty or out of the economic doldrums.

A number of factors in the decades after 1917 would help Mississippi's absolute development and make it a place not so unlike the rest of the United States. Several new taxes helped lead to increasing modernization, including the building of an impressive system of highways. The state's Balance Agriculture with Industry program initiated in the 1930s helped increase the state's manufacturing payroll, though admittedly such industrial jobs were often in low-paying industries. Increased economic diversification finally ended the rule of cotton as undisputed king. This diversification included the growing of soybeans, the development of the cattle industry, and the successful drilling of oil wells. The Tennessee Valley Authority (TVA) helped modernize the northeastern counties, a region of the state that had long needed economic development. The exodus of thousands of black Mississippians in the World War II period led to the end of mule-based agriculture and of the cultivation of tiny plots of land. The settling of civil rights questions in the 1960s and 1970s encouraged new economic development. Programs of Franklin Roosevelt's New Deal and Lyndon Johnson's Great Society helped alleviate poverty in Mississippi, while members of Congress, including Jamie Whitten and John Stennis, helped steer federal projects and installations to the state. Poverty—and a vast gulf between rich and poor—would nevertheless prove persistent and hard to conquer, providing one more example of the great continuities that have characterized Mississippi's history.

Notes

Chapter 1

1. Mississippi Department of Archives and History, *Official and Statistical Register of the State of Mississippi, 1920–1924* (Jackson, Miss.: Hederman Brothers, 1923), 649 (hereafter MDA&H, *Official and Statistical Register, 1920–1924*).
2. James S. Ferguson, "Agrarianism in Mississippi, 1871–1900: A Study in Nonconformity" (Ph.D. diss., University of North Carolina at Chapel Hill, 1952).
3. Stephen Cresswell, *Mormons and Cowboys, Moonshiners and Klansmen: Federal Law Enforcement in the South and West, 1870–1893* (Tuscaloosa: University of Alabama Press, 1991), 19–78; William Gillette, *Retreat from Reconstruction, 1869–1879* (Baton Rouge: Louisiana State University Press, 1979), 157.
4. Albert D. Kirwan, *Revolt of the Rednecks: Mississippi Politics, 1876–1925* (Lexington: University of Kentucky Press, 1951), 24–25; James L. Sledge III, "The Chisholm Massacre: Politics and Violence in East Mississippi," *Journal of Mississippi History* 40 (1993): 203–15; James M. Wells, *The Chisholm Massacre: A Picture of "Home Rule" in Mississippi*, 3rd ed. (Washington, D.C.: Chisholm Monument Association, 1878); James D. Lynch, *Kemper County Vindicated, and a Peep at Radical Rule in Mississippi* (New York: E. J. Hale and Son, 1879).
5. Kirwan, *Revolt*, 24–25; *New York Tribune*, quoted in Sledge, "Chisholm Massacre," 211.
6. Kirwan, *Revolt*, 45–46.
7. W. W. Graham to John M. Stone, November 15, 1877, with enclosed copy of speech, Governor's Papers, Record Group 27, Mississippi Department of Archives and History, Jackson (hereafter MDA&H).
8. MDA&H, *Official and Statistical Register, 1920–1924*, 649.

Chapter 2

1. *Compendium of the Ninth Census* (Washington, D.C.: Government Printing Office, 1872), 698; MDA&H, *Official and Statistical Register, 1920–1924*, 560–61.
2. *Report on the Productions of Agriculture as Returned at the Tenth Census, June 1, 1880, Embracing General Statistics* (Washington, D.C.: Government Printing Office, 1883), 4–5; Gavin Wright, *Old South, New South: Revolutions in the Southern Economy since the Civil War* (New York: Basic Books, 1986), 36.
3. *Report on the Productions of Agriculture*, 66, 100; MDA&H, *Official and Statistical Register, 1920–1924*, 539.

4. James C. Cobb, *The Most Southern Place on Earth: The Mississippi Delta and the Roots of Regional Identity* (New York: Oxford University Press, 1992), 76.
5. Cobb, *The Most Southern Place*, 76.
6. U.S. Congress, Senate, *Report of the Committee on Agriculture and Forestry on the Condition of Cotton Growers*, S. Rept. 986, 53rd Congress, 3rd sess. (1895): 335.
7. Poe quoted in Gilbert C. Fite, *Cotton Fields No More: Southern Agriculture, 1865–1980* (Lexington: University Press of Kentucky, 1984), 7; Arthur Palmer Hudson, "An Attala Boyhood," *Journal of Mississippi History* 4 (1942): 127, 145; L. N. Treadway to Lucy Treadway, December 3, 1877, Aldrich Family Papers, Special Collections, University of Mississippi Library, Oxford (hereafter SC-UM).
8. Gavin Wright and Howard Kunreuther, "Cotton, Corn, and Risk in the Nineteenth Century," *Journal of Economic History* 15 (1975): 526–51.
9. Fite, *Cotton Fields No More*, 6–7.
10. U.S. Bureau of the Census, *Census Reports: Twelfth Census of the United States, Taken in the Year 1900: Agriculture* (Washington, D.C.: Government Printing Office, 1901), lxix–lxxi.
11. Bradley G. Bond, *Political Culture in the Nineteenth-Century South: Mississippi, 1830–1900* (Baton Rouge: Louisiana State University Press, 1995), 147–49, 264–65; Stephen Cresswell, *Multiparty Politics in Mississippi, 1877–1902* (Jackson: University Press of Mississippi, 1995), 9–11, 37, 59.
12. U.S. Bureau of Census, *Fourteenth Census of the United States, Taken in the Year 1920: Population* (Washington, D.C.: Government Printing Office, 1921), 31.
13. Fite, *Cotton Fields No More*, 26–27.
14. Ferguson, "Agrarianism," 52.
15. Ferguson, "Agrarianism," 37.
16. Ferguson, "Agrarianism," 57–68, 126–36.
17. Ferguson, "Agrarianism," 136.
18. Minute Books, entry for May 21, 1881, Papers of the Bowling Green Grange, MDA&H.
19. Ferguson, "Agrarianism," 91–97.
20. Fite, *Cotton Fields No More*, 38.
21. Thomas N. Boschert, "'A Family Affair': Mississippi Politics, 1882–1932" (Ph.D. diss., University of Mississippi, 1995), 62–67.
22. Ferguson, "Agrarianism," 143.
23. *Winona Times*, July 13, 1888.
24. Ferguson, "Agrarianism," 150, 156.
25. Ferguson, "Agrarianism," 160.
26. *Biographical Directory of the American Congress* (Washington, D.C.: Government Printing Office, 1971), 573, 1286.
27. Ferguson, "Agrarianism," 115.
28. Cresswell, *Multiparty Politics*, 111.
29. Cresswell, *Multiparty Politics*, 112; *Grenada Sentinel*, November 21, 1891.
30. Cresswell, *Multiparty Politics*, 111–13.
31. Fite, *Cotton Fields No More*, 62–67.

NOTES

32. U.S. Bureau of Census, *Fourteenth Census of the United States, Taken in the Year 1920: Agriculture* (Washington, D.C.: Government Printing Office, 1922), 49; Fite, *Cotton Fields No More*, 54.
33. U.S. Bureau of the Census, *Report on Cotton Production in the United States* (Washington, D.C.: Government Printing Office, 1884).
34. Cobb, *Most Southern Place*, 5–6.
35. Mary Hamilton, *Trials of the Earth: The Autobiography of Mary Hamilton*, edited by Helen Dick Davis (Jackson: University Press of Mississippi, 1992), 65–86. The author's ancestors farmed at Cresswell's Deadening, a community on Honey Island.
36. William L. Giles, "Agricultural Revolution, 1890–1970," in *A History of Mississippi*, ed. Richard Aubrey McLemore, 2:177, 190–91 (Jackson: University and College Press of Mississippi, 1973).
37. *Laurel Chronicle*, July 14, 1911; *Hattiesburg News*, August 25, 1915.
38. Fite, *Cotton Fields No More*, 77; Giles, "Agricultural Revolution," 192–94.
39. *Wesson Enterprise*, April 1, 1910; *Hattiesburg News*, August 25, 1915; Giles, "Agricultural Revolution," 189–90.
40. U.S. Congress, *Report of the Committee on Agriculture*, 340.
41. Fite, *Cotton Fields No More*, 60–70.
42. *Batesville Blade*, March 18, 1881; *Wesson Mirror*, October 31, 1891; *Vicksburg Evening Post*, May 20, 1905.
43. *Summit Sentinel* quoted in *Vicksburg Daily Herald*, December 27, 1908; *Gloster Record* quoted in *Vicksburg Daily Herald*, December 27, 1908; *Wesson Herald*, December 9, 1882.
44. Mississippi Department of Archives and History, *Official and Statistical Register of the State of Mississippi, 1912* (Nashville, Tenn.: Brandon Printing, 1912), 272–73; James L. McCorkle Jr., "The Illinois Central Railroad and the Mississippi Commercial Vegetable Industry," *Journal of Mississippi History* 39 (1977): 155–72; *Wesson Enterprise*, June 16, 1905.
45. James G. Revels, "Redeemers, Rednecks, and Racial Integrity," in McLemore, *History of Mississippi*, 1:590, 605.
46. These statements are all based on the array of statistics given in the agricultural reports of the Census Bureau for the tenth and fourteenth censuses.
47. Wright, *Old South, New South*, 59.

Chapter 3

1. *Statistical Abstract of the United States, 1912* (Washington, D.C.: Government Printing Office, 1913), 2–25.
2. Julie Saville, *The Work of Reconstruction: From Slave to Wage Laborer in South Carolina, 1860–1870* (Cambridge: Cambridge University Press, 1994).
3. Fite, *Cotton Fields No More*, 5–6; Cobb, *Most Southern Place*, 55–100.
4. See Wright, *Old South, New South*, ch. 2.
5. Neil R. McMillen, *Dark Journey: Black Mississippians in the Age of Jim Crow* (Champaign: University of Illinois Press, 1989), 129.

6. LeRoy Barry Allen, "Autobiography of LeRoy Barry Allen," typescript, SC-UM, 118; Cobb, *Most Southern Place*, 104.
7. Allen, "Autobiography," 117.
8. Allen, "Autobiography," 209; Cobb, *Most Southern Place*, 76.
9. Cobb, *Most Southern Place*, 105; McMillen, *Dark Journey*, 125.
10. Cobb, *Most Southern Place*, 103.
11. Ferguson, "Agrarianism," 20; McMillen, *Dark Journey*, 131.
12. William H. Holtzclaw, *Black Man's Burden* (New York: Neale Publishing, 1915), 17.
13. Cobb, *Most Southern Place*, 108.
14. McMillen, *Dark Journey*, 134.
15. Wright and Kunreuther, "Cotton, Corn, and Risk," 526, 548–49.
16. Roger L. Ransom and Richard Sutch, *One Kind of Freedom: The Economic Consequences of Emancipation* (Cambridge: Cambridge University Press, 1977), 163–65; Wright and Kunreuther, "Cotton, Corn, and Risk," 548–49.
17. William Cohen, *At Freedom's Edge: Black Mobility and the Southern White Quest for Racial Control, 1865–1915* (Baton Rouge: Louisiana State University Press, 1991), 226–32; Pete Daniel, *The Shadow of Slavery: Peonage in the South, 1901–1969* (Urbana: University of Illinois Press, 1972).
18. Cohen, *At Freedom's Edge*, 292–96.
19. Cohen, *At Freedom's Edge*, 284.
20. McMillen, *Dark Journey*, 147.
21. Cohen, *At Freedom's Edge*, 220–26.
22. *Report on Crime, Pauperism, and Benevolence in the United States at the Eleventh Census: 1890* (Washington, D.C.: Government Printing Office, 1896), 125–27; Hamilton, *Trials of the Earth*, 200–202.
23. James H. Lemley, *The Gulf, Mobile, and Ohio: A Railroad That Had to Expand or Expire* (Homewood, Ill.: Richard D. Irwin, 1953), 290.
24. David M. Oshinsky, *"Worse Than Slavery": Parchman Farm and the Ordeal of Jim Crow Justice* (New York: Free Press, 1996), vii.
25. Cobb, *Most Southern Place*, 106; McMillen, *Dark Journey*, 150.
26. Cohen, *At Freedom's Edge*, xv–xvi, 232–47.
27. William F. Holmes, "Labor Agents and the Georgia Exodus, 1899–1900," *South Atlantic Quarterly* 79 (1980): 436–48.
28. Cohen, *At Freedom's Edge*, 272.
29. Cobb, *Most Southern Place*, 82–83.
30. U.S. Congress, *Report of the Committee on Agriculture*; *Vicksburg Herald* quoted in *Wesson Enterprise*, July 7, 1905; James W. Loewen, *The Mississippi Chinese: Between Black and White* (Cambridge, Mass.: Harvard University Press, 1971); Robert Seto Quan and Julian B. Roebuck, *Lotus among the Magnolias: The Mississippi Chinese* (Jackson: University Press of Mississippi, 1982).
31. *Greenville Times*, October 15, 1881; *Vicksburg Herald* quoted in *Wesson Enterprise*, July 7, 1905; Cobb, *Most Southern Place*, 110–11.
32. Cobb, *Most Southern Place*, 110.

Chapter 4

1. McMillen, *Dark Journey*, 7.
2. Vernon Lane Wharton, *The Negro in Mississippi, 1865–1890* (Chapel Hill: University of North Carolina Press, 1947), 230–33; McMillen, *Dark Journey*, 5–7; Cobb, *Most Southern Place*, 90.
3. Stanley J. Folmsbee, "The Origin of the First 'Jim Crow' Law," *Journal of Southern History* 15 (1949): 243–47; *Louisville, New Orleans, and Texas Railway Company v. Mississippi*, 133 U.S. 587 (1890).
4. McMillen, *Dark Journey*, 8.
5. McMillen, *Dark Journey*, 23–25.
6. Horace S. Fulkerson, *The Negro: As He Was; As He Is; As He Will Be* (Vicksburg, Miss.: Commercial Herald, 1887), 103, 106, 108.
7. Chandler's 1888 pamphlet was entitled "The Negro in Politics: The Paramount Political Question of the Day" and is reprinted in Greene C. Chandler, *Journal and Speeches of Greene Callier Chandler* (N.p., 1953), 227.
8. *Southern Light and Traction Company v. Charlotte Compton*, 86 Miss. 269 (1905).
9. *Vicksburg Evening Post*, May 24, 1905.
10. Willard Faroe Bond, *I Had a Friend: An Autobiography* (N.p., 1958), 60.
11. U.S. Bureau of the Census, manuscript census returns for the 1880, 1900, and 1910 censuses, Jasper County, Beat Four. For 1880: enumeration district 111, sheet 11. For 1900: enumeration district 53, page 7. For 1910: enumeration district 19, page 25. See also Victoria E. Bynum, " 'White Negroes' in Segregated Mississippi: Miscegenation, Racial Identity, and the Law," *Journal of Southern History* 64 (1998): 247–77; Victoria E. Bynum, *The Free State of Jones: Mississippi's Longest Civil War* (Chapel Hill: University of North Carolina Press, 2003).
12. U.S. Bureau of the Census, manuscript census returns, 1900, Warren County, City of Vicksburg.
13. Charles L. Dyer, *Along the Gulf: An Entertaining Story of an Outing among the Beautiful Resorts on the Mississippi Sound* (N.p., 1895), 63; *McComb City Enterprise*, September 23, 1893.
14. *Magnolia Gazette* quoted in William F. Holmes, "Whitecapping: Anti-Semitism in the Populist Era," *American Jewish Historical Quarterly* 63 (1974): 244–61.
15. Frances Williams Griffith, *True Life Story of Will Purvis* (Purvis, Miss.: Booster, 1935), 4; Allie Stokes to John J. Stokes, February 6, 1893, Stokes Papers, Special Collections, Louisiana State University Library, Baton Rouge (hereafter SC-LSU).
16. Holmes, "Whitecapping: Anti-Semitism," 252.
17. *New Orleans Times-Democrat* quoted in Holmes, "Whitecapping: Anti-Semitism," 252.
18. Holmes, "Whitecapping: Anti-Semitism," 250–54.
19. William F. Holmes, "Whitecapping: Agrarian Violence in Mississippi, 1902–1906," *Journal of Southern History* 35 (1969): 165–85; Holmes, "Whitecapping: Anti-Semitism," 260.
20. *Macon Beacon*, November 12, 1881; Cresswell, *Multiparty Politics*, 69–70.
21. McMillen, *Dark Journey*, 226.
22. *Boise (Idaho) Daily Statesman*, October 25, 26, 1892; *New York Times*, October 25, 1898.

23. William F. Holmes, "The Leflore County Massacre and the Demise of the Colored Farmers Alliance," *Phylon* 34 (1973): 267–74.
24. Holmes, "Leflore County Massacre," 272–74.
25. William I. Hair, "Lynching," in *Encyclopedia of Southern Culture*, ed. Charles Reagan Wilson and William Ferris, 174–75 (Chapel Hill: University of North Carolina Press, 1989); Mary Elizabeth Hines, "Death at the Hands of Persons Unknown: The Geography of Lynching in the Deep South, 1882 to 1910" (Ph.D. diss., Louisiana State University, 1992), 148–49.
26. *Jackson Weekly Clarion*, February 14, 1877; McMillen, *Dark Journey*, 224.
27. Charles B. Galloway, "Some Thoughts on Lynching," *South Atlantic Quarterly* 5 (October 1906): 351–53.
28. *Inaugural Addresses of the Governors of Mississippi, 1890–1980* (University, Miss.: Bureau of Commercial Research, 1980), 16.
29. *Inaugural Addresses*, 16; McMillen, *Dark Journey*, 247.
30. McMillen, *Dark Journey*, 197, 202.
31. McMillen, *Dark Journey*, 197, 202–5.
32. Hines, "Death at the Hands," 186.

Chapter 5

1. McMillen, *Dark Journey*, 288.
2. McMillen, *Dark Journey*, 116–19, 283–92.
3. Sydney Nathans, "'Gotta Mind to Move, a Mind to Settle Down': Afro-Americans and the Plantation Frontier," in *A Master's Due: Essays in Honor of David Herbert Donald*, ed. William J. Cooper, Michael Holt, and John McCardell (Baton Rouge: Louisiana State University Press, 1985), 211–16.
4. Nathans, "'Gotta Mind,'" 209, 221.
5. Nell Irvin Painter, *Exodusters: Black Migration to Kansas After Reconstruction* (New York: Knopf, 1977), 142–44.
6. Painter, *Exodusters*, 154, 156.
7. *Raymond Hinds County Gazette*, February 26, 1879; Painter, *Exodusters*, 193.
8. Cohen, *At Freedom's Edge*, 176–77.
9. U.S. Congress, Senate, *Report and Testimony of the Select Committee of the United States Senate to Investigate the Causes of the Removal of the Negroes from the Southern States to the Northern States*, 3 vols., S. Rpt. 693, 46th Cong., 2nd sess. (1880), 3: 223–24, 501.
10. Cohen, *At Freedom's Edge*, 180–81; Painter, *Exodusters*, 229.
11. Rebecca Safstrom Basko, "The Exoduster Experience: During and after the Migration," *Journal of Mississippi History* 59 (1997): 141–44.
12. Norman L. Crockett, *The Black Towns* (Lawrence: Regents Press of Kansas, 1979), 12.
13. *Greenville Times*, February 18, 1882.
14. Cobb, *Most Southern Place on Earth*, 80–81; Crockett, *Black Towns*, 12–13.
15. Crockett, *Black Towns*, 116–117. Gaither's name is given in some records as Gaiter.

NOTES

16. Crockett, *Black Towns*, 12–15, 60–67, 116, 126. Rosenwald was president of Sears, Roebuck and a noted philanthropist.
17. Kevin Martin Hamilton et al., *Black Towns and Profit: Promotion and Development in the Transappalachian West, 1877–1915* (Urbana: University of Illinois Press, 1991), 1–4, 73–78; Crockett, *Black Towns*, 84, 130–31.
18. Crockett, *Black Towns*, 178, 188.
19. Crockett, *Black Towns*, 15, 121.
20. *Moorhead, Mississippi: A Prohibition Industrial Colony in the Heart of the Famous Cotton Delta of Mississippi* (Chicago: Rand, McNally, n.d.); Dunbar Rowland, *Mississippi: Comprising Sketches of Counties, Towns, Events, Institutions, and Persons, Arranged in Cyclopedic Form*, 4 vols. (Atlanta: Southern Historical Publishing Association, 1907), 2: 282.
21. Holtzclaw, *Black Man's Burden*, 76; Arnie Cooper, "'We Stand Upon the Structure We Ourselves Have Builded': William H. Holtzclaw and Utica Institute, 1903–1915," *Journal of Mississippi History* 47 (1985): 15–33; Alferdteen Harrison, *Piney Woods School: An Oral History* (Jackson: University Press of Mississippi, 1982).
22. Julius E. Thompson, *The Black Press in Mississippi, 1865–1985* (Gainesville: University Press of Florida, 1993).
23. George S. Schuyler, "Freedom of the Press in Mississippi," *Crisis* 43 (October 1936): 302; McMillen, *Dark Journey*, 175.
24. Jacqueline Jones Royster, ed., *Southern Horrors and Other Writings: The Anti-Lynching Campaign of Ida B. Wells, 1892–1900* (Boston: Bedford Books, 1997), 1–4, 14–19.
25. Ida B. Wells, *A Red Record*, in Royster, *Southern Horrors*, 73–157; Wells, *Mob Rule in New Orleans*, in Royster, *Southern Horrors*, 158–208.
26. Wells, *Red Record*, 73, 111, 112.
27. Royster, *Southern Horrors*, 57–58.
28. Royster, *Southern Horrors*, 53.
29. Noel's first name is spelled both Edmond and Edmund in various primary and secondary historical sources. For his signature, Noel used E. F. Noel.
30. Holtzclaw, *Black Man's Burden*, 207–9.
31. Samuel Alfred Beadle, *Sketches from Life in Dixie* (Chicago: Scroll Publishers and Literary Syndicate, 1899), 75–82.
32. Beadle, *Sketches*, 64, 66, 100.
33. *Aberdeen Weekly* and *Natchez Daily Democrat* quoted in McMillen, *Dark Journey*, 294–95.
34. A. T. Morgan, *Yazoo, or on the Picket Line of Freedom in the South* (1884; repr., New York, Russell and Russell, 1968), 208, 494–95; Cresswell, *Multiparty Politics*, 92.
35. Morgan, *Yazoo*, 501.

Chapter 6

1. On the groups that opposed the Democrats, see Cresswell, *Multiparty Politics*.
2. For a good overview of political ideologies in this period, see Bond, *Political Culture*. Another good treatment of state politics in this era is Boschert, "'Family Affair.'"

3. *Biographical Directory of the American Congress*, 994.
4. Richard Aubrey McLemore, *A History of Mississippi*, 2 vols. (Jackson: University and College Press of Mississippi, 1973), 1: 588–606; Bond, *Political Culture*, 126.
5. McLemore, *History of Mississippi*, 1: 613–19, 2: 8–24; Bond, *Political Culture*, 245–82; Cresswell, *Multiparty Politics*, 102–13.
6. *Biographical Directory of the American Congress*, 1257.
7. McLemore, *History of Mississippi*, 1:435, 592–98; Bond, *Political Culture*, 171–82, 272–74.
8. Bond, *Political Culture*, 272; *Biographical Directory of the American Congress*, 1256–57.
9. *Biographical Directory of the American Congress*, 1876; McLemore, *History of Mississippi*, 1: 599–600; Cresswell, *Multiparty Politics*, 110–12; Bradley G. Bond, "Edward C. Walthall and the 1880 Senatorial Nomination: Politics of Balance in the Redeemer Era," *Journal of Mississippi History* 50 (1988): 1–20.
10. Cresswell, *Multiparty Politics*, 88, 110–12.
11. Lilibel Broadaway, "Frank Burkitt: The Man in the Wool Hat" (M.A. thesis, Mississippi State University, 1948); Cresswell, *Multiparty Politics*, 114–16.
12. Cresswell, *Multiparty Politics*, 107, 119–20, 143–55.
13. *Yazoo Herald* quoted in *Greenville Times*, November 19, 1881.
14. Kirwan, *Revolt*, 18.
15. Kirwan, *Revolt*, 27–28; Jones quoted in Boschert, " 'Family Affair,' " 98.
16. Kirwan, *Revolt*, 105–8.
17. Harris Dickson, *An Old Fashioned Senator: A Story-Biography of John Sharp Williams* (New York: Frederick A. Stokes, 1925), 64, 66.
18. *Ackerman Choctaw Plaindealer*, November 21, 1890; *Durant News* quoted in *Ackerman Choctaw Plaindealer*, November 28, 1890.
19. Kirwan, *Revolt*, 44–45.
20. *Batesville Blade*, May 18, June 17, 1881; *Greenville Times*, October 29, 1881; Bond, *Political Culture*, 259–65.
21. Daniel Vogt, "Problems of Government Regulation: The Mississippi Railroad Commission, 1884–1956" (Ph.D. diss., University of Southern Mississippi, 1980), 22–24.
22. Kirwan, *Revolt*, 55.
23. *Wesson Herald*, July 14, 1883.
24. Vogt, "Problems," 59–60.
25. Bond, *Political Culture*, 274–79; Vogt, "Problems," 83–85.
26. Vogt, "Problems," 208–16.
27. William Graham Davis, "Attacking the 'Matchless Evil': Temperance and Prohibition in Mississippi, 1817–1908" (Ph.D. diss., Mississippi State University, 1975); Todd Ashley Herring, "Saloons and Drinking in Mississippi from the Colonial Era to Prohibition" (M.A. thesis, Mississippi State University, 1991).
28. *Mississippi Baptist Record*, April 10, 1879, December 16, 1880.
29. *Wesson Herald*, July 14, 1883.
30. *Vicksburg Herald* quoted in *Greenville Times*, February 18, 1882; Kirwan, *Revolt*, 108–9; Cresswell, *Multiparty Politics*, 133.
31. Louisa Taylor diary, July 21, 1889, Calvin Taylor Family Papers, SC-LSU.

32. Lillie Stokes's postscript appended to C. L. Stokes to My Dear Boy, November 7, 1891, Joel A. Stokes Family Papers, SC-LSU; *New Orleans Daily Picayune*, July 6, 1890; *Batesville Blade*, February 25, 1881.
33. Davis, "Attacking the 'Matchless Evil,'" 115–35, 143–44.
34. Davis, "Attacking the 'Matchless Evil,'" 145–46, 153–56.
35. Davis, "Attacking the 'Matchless Evil,'" 157–67.
36. *New Orleans Daily Picayune*, March 7, 1888.
37. *Jackson New Mississippian*, June 5, July 27, 1886.
38. Herring, "Saloons and Drinking," 123–24; Davis, "Attacking the 'Matchless Evil,'" 178–79.
39. Kirwan, *Revolt*, 61–64.
40. Vogt, "Problems," 83–85.
41. Cohen, *At Freedom's Edge*, 220–26.
42. Vogt, "Problems," 85–88.
43. The committee report is quoted in John D. M. Griffiths, "A State of Servitude Worse Than Slavery: The Politics of Penal Administration in Mississippi, 1865–1900," *Journal of Mississippi History* 55 (1993): 9.
44. Vogt, "Problems," 91–93.
45. Griffiths, "State of Servitude," 1–2.
46. *Jackson Weekly Clarion*, February 3, 1898; Vogt, "Problems," 92–93.
47. Bond, *Political Culture*, 274–79.

Chapter 7

1. Bond, *Political Culture*, 280–81.
2. Kirwan, *Revolt*, 60.
3. *Congressional Quarterly's Guide to U.S. Elections*, 2nd ed. (Washington, D.C.: Congressional Quarterly, 1985), 442; *Journal of the Senate, of the State of Mississippi, at a Regular Session Thereof, Convened in the City of Jackson, Jan. 7, 1890* (Jackson, Miss.: R. H. Henry, State Printer, 1890), 499–504.
4. *Greenville Times*, November 19, 1881.
5. Solomon S. Calhoon, "The Causes and Events That Led to the Calling of the Constitutional Convention of 1890," *Publications of the Mississippi Historical Society* 6 (1902): 107–9.
6. Calhoon, "Causes," 105–18; Cresswell, *Mormons and Cowboys*, 40–41; Cresswell, *Multiparty Politics*, 94–96.
7. Kirwan, *Revolt*, 60–63; Cresswell, *Multiparty Politics*, 100–103.
8. Cresswell, *Multiparty Politics*, 102–4. Delegate L. W. Magruder is sometimes erroneously omitted from the list of at-large delegates.
9. Cresswell, *Multiparty Politics*, 103–5.
10. *New Orleans Daily Picayune*, July 21, 1890.
11. *New Orleans Daily Picayune*, July 6, 1890; *Ellisville Alliance Eagle*, October 16, 1890.
12. Cresswell, *Multiparty Politics*, 104–6. Cresswell, *Multiparty Politcs*, 103–5; modern histories sometimes erroneously identify Cook as black.

13. *Journal of the Proceedings of the Constitutional Convention of the State of Mississippi . . . 1890* (Jackson, Miss: E. L. Martin, 1890), 704–8 (hereafter *Proceedings*).
14. Statements on agrarian delegates based on a broad review of the roll calls contained in the *Proceedings*. On People's Party personnel, see Stephen Cresswell, "Who Was Who in Mississippi's Opposition Political Parties, 1878–1963," unpublished 1994 typescript, Mississippi Department of Archives and History, Jackson.
15. *Proceedings*, 9–11.
16. Kirwan, *Revolt*, 67.
17. Bond, *Political Culture*, 249; *Proceedings*, 203.
18. Edward L. Ayers, *The Promise of the New South: Life After Reconstruction* (New York: Oxford University Press, 1992), 317; *Ackerman Choctaw Plaindealer*, September 5, 1890.
19. *Proceedings*, 78–87.
20. *Proceedings*, 86–87, 303–4.
21. Isaiah T. Montgomery, *"What Answer?" Speech in Support of Franchise Committee Report, Mississippi Constitutional Convention, 1890*. Ed. Matthew Holden Jr. (Charlottesville, Va.: Isaiah T. Montgomery Studies Project, 2004), 31, 32, 34.
22. Montgomery, *"What Answer?"* 34.
23. Kirwan, *Revolt*, 82; McMillen, *Dark Journey*, 56–57, 296–97.
24. Kirwan, *Revolt*, 70–72.
25. Albert D. Kirwan, "Apportionment in the Mississippi Constitution of 1890," *Journal of Southern History* 14 (1948): 238.
26. These statements are based on my use of the rosters bound at the back of the legislative journals for each session. The 1885 figures are based on county population figures from the 1880 census, while the 1895 numbers are based on census figures from 1890.
27. Kirwan, *Revolt*, 140–42.
28. *Proceedings*, 392, 399.
29. *Proceedings*, 685–96.
30. *Proceedings*, 550, 637–38, 701.
31. *Ackerman Choctaw Plaindealer*, August 15, 1890; *Ellisville Alliance Eagle*, October 16, 1890; *Natchez Democrat* quoted in Kirwan, "Apportionment," 238.
32. James H. Stone, "A Note on Voter Registration Under the Mississippi Understanding Clause, 1892," *Journal of Southern History* 38 (1972): 293–96; W. Dean Burnham, *Presidential Ballots, 1836–1892* (Baltimore: Johns Hopkins University Press, 1955), 552–71.
33. Stone, "Note on Voter Registration," 293–96.
34. J. Morgan Kousser, *The Shaping of Southern Politics: Suffrage Restriction and the Establishment of the One-Party South, 1880–1910* (New Haven, Conn.: Yale University Press, 1974), 3–5, 243.
35. *Williams v. Mississippi*, 170 U.S. 213, 222 (1898).
36. Although Republican leader George Sheldon served in the legislature in the early twentieth century, he was nominated by his Democratic neighbors and was not a Republican nominee. For the original statement of the fait accompli theory, see V. O. Key, with Alexander Heard, *Southern Politics in State and Nation* (New York: Knopf, 1949), 531–33.
37. William F. Holmes, *The White Chief: James Kimball Vardaman* (Baton Rouge: Louisiana State University Press, 1970), 82–83.

38. Cresswell, *Multiparty Politics*, 73–141.
39. Thomas N. Boschert, "The Politics of Expediency: Fusion in the Mississippi Delta, Late Nineteenth-Century" (M.A. thesis, University of Mississippi, 1985).
40. Cresswell, *Multiparty Politics*, 221–27.
41. *Jackson Daily Times* quoted in Kirwan, *Revolt*, 23; *New York Times*, September 11, 1885; *Greenville Times*, November 12, 1881.
42. *New Orleans Daily Picayune*, August 1, 1890; *Jackson Clarion-Ledger*, March 15, 22, 1894.
43. Cresswell, *Mormons and Cowboys*, 71–78.
44. Cresswell, *Multiparty Politics*, 151–54.

Chapter 8

1. Hudson, "Attala Boyhood," 134–35.
2. U.S. Bureau of the Census, *Report on the Manufactures of the United States at the Tenth Census* (Washington, D.C.: Government Printing Office, 1883), 5–8.
3. *Hattiesburg News*, August 25, 1915.
4. Smith quoted in S. G. Thigpen, *A Boy in Rural Mississippi and Other Stories* (Picayune, Miss.: privately printed, 1966), 155; *Biloxi Daily Herald*, February 18, 1888.
5. *Southern Lumberman*, December 23, 1911.
6. Allen, "Autobiography," 20–31; Hamilton, *Trials of the Earth*, 51–66, 83–86, 93; *Greenville Times*, December 8, 1883.
7. Sammy Orren Cranford, *The Fernwood, Columbia, and Gulf: A Railroad in the Piney Woods of South Mississippi* (New York: Garland, 1989), 4–6; Nollie Hickman, *Mississippi Harvest: Lumbering in the Long Leaf Pine Belt, 1840–1915* (University: University of Mississippi, 1962), 2–3, 57–60; Bond, *I Had a Friend*, 207–11.
8. Hickman, *Mississippi Harvest*, 58–61, 102–14, 155–56.
9. Noel Polk, ed., *Mississippi's Piney Woods: A Human Perspective* (Jackson: University Press of Mississippi, 1986), 81–82.
10. Polk, *Mississippi's Piney Woods*, 82.
11. Hickman, *Mississippi Harvest*, 114–17.
12. Bond, *I Had a Friend*, 207–11; Hickman, *Mississippi Harvest*, 64–65, 118–20, 215.
13. Hickman, *Mississippi Harvest*, 46–47, 161–62, 166.
14. U.S. Bureau of the Census, *Statistical Abstract of the United States, 1922* (Washington, D.C.: Government Printing Office, 1923), 162–68, 222–40.
15. Eva Davis Beets, "Growing Up in Marion County: A Memoir by Eva Davis Beets," ed. Christine Wilson, *Journal of Mississippi History* 48 (1986): 199, 211.
16. Annie Louise D'Olive, "Reminiscences of Ten Mile: A South Mississippi Saw Mill Town," *Journal of Mississippi History* 39 (1977): 173–84; Cranford, *Fernwood*, 15–26, 51–61.
17. *Biloxi Daily Herald*, August 26, 1915; Jo Dent Hodge, "The Lumber Industry in Laurel, Mississippi, at the Turn of the Century," *Journal of Mississippi History* 35 (1973): 361–79.
18. Cranford, *Fernwood*, 51–61, 82–135.
19. Hickman, *Mississippi Harvest*, 121–31.

20. Thigpen, *Boy in Rural Mississippi*, 176–80; Hickman, *Mississippi Harvest*, 122–35.
21. Thigpen, *Boy in Rural Mississippi*, 176–81; Hickman, *Mississippi Harvest*, 139–51.
22. Hickman, *Mississippi Harvest*, 263–65; Cranford, *Fernwood*, 79–81.
23. *Wesson Herald*, October 21, 1882, July 21, 1883.
24. *Wesson Herald*, May 26, 1883; Durr Walker and David Higgs, *Wesson: Industrial City of the South* (N.p., n.d. [1994?]), 22–23.
25. Walker and Higgs, *Wesson*, 25; *Wesson Herald*, January 14, 1882, May 26, 1883.
26. Walker and Higgs, *Wesson*, 25.
27. U.S. Census Bureau Records, Record Group 29, Census of Population, 1880, manuscript census returns for Copiah County Mississippi.
28. U.S. Census Bureau Records, Record Group 29, Census of Population, 1880, manuscript census returns for Copiah County Mississippi; Walker and Higgs, *Wesson*, 25–34.
29. *Wesson Enterprise*, March 4, April 22, 29, 1910.
30. *Wesson Enterprise*, March 4, 11, April 15, 1910.
31. U.S. Congress, *Report of the Committee on Agriculture*, 334–35.
32. McCorkle, "Illinois Central Railroad," 155, 160–72; Carlton J. Corliss, *Main Line of Mid-America: The Story of the Illinois Central* (New York: Creative Age Press, 1950), 297–98; *Wesson Herald*, May 26, 1883; *Wesson Argosy*, November 1887.
33. Dyer, *Along the Gulf*, 59–63; U.S. Bureau of the Census, *Fisheries of the United States, 1908* (Washington, D.C.: Government Printing Office, 1911), 41; MDA&H, *Official and Statistical Register, 1920–1924*, 720.
34. *Statistical History of the United States, from Colonial Times to the Present* (New York: Basic Books, 1976), 127, 138.
35. Hickman, *Mississippi Harvest*, 266–67; Ransom and Sutch, *One Kind of Freedom*, 188; Todd L. Savitt and James Harvey Young, eds., *Disease and Distinctiveness in the American South* (Knoxville: University of Tennessee Press, 1988), 8; Eric C. Clark, "Industrial Development and State Government in Mississippi, 1890–1980" (Ph.D. diss., Mississippi State University, 1989), 3–5.
36. Anthony M. Muckenfuss, "The Development of Manufacturing in Mississippi," *Publications of the Mississippi Historical Society* 10 (1909): 176–77.
37. John H. Ellis, *Yellow Fever and Public Health in the New South* (Lexington: University Press of Kentucky, 1992), 147.
38. U.S. Bureau of the Census, *Reports on Waterpower of the United States*, Part 2 (Washington, D.C.: Government Printing Office, 1887), 141, 147; U.S. Bureau of the Census, *Report on the Manufactures of the United States*, 9.
39. Clark, "Industrial Development," 5–7.

Chapter 9

1. Hickman, *Mississippi Harvest*, 249–53.
2. D'Olive, "Reminiscences," 175–77; *Wesson Times*, August 8, 1885.
3. MDA&H, *Official and Statistical Register, 1920–1924*, 718–22.

4. Telegram quoted in Holmes, "Whitecapping: Anti-Semitism," 260; Polk, *Mississippi's Piney Woods*, 83.
5. Elizabeth H. Davidson, *Child Labor Legislation in the Southern Textile States* (Chapel Hill: University of North Carolina Press, 1939), 238, 242.
6. *Wesson Mirror*, May 26, July 14, 1883.
7. Davidson, *Child Labor*, 16–17.
8. Davidson, *Child Labor*, 239–40.
9. Davidson, *Child Labor*, 16–17, 238–41.
10. *Wesson Enterprise*, September 30, 1910.
11. Hickman, *Mississippi Harvest*, 234–45.
12. Donald C. Mosley, "The Labor Union Movement," in McLemore, *History of Mississippi*, 2:250, 257; D. W. Woodward, *Negro Progress in a Mississippi Town, Being a Study of Conditions in Jackson, Mississippi* (Cheyney, Pa.: Biddle Press, n.d. [1907?]), 7–8.
13. *New Orleans Daily Picayune*, July 22, 1890; Frederic Meyers, "The Knights of Labor in the South," *Southern Economic Journal* 6 (1940): 479–87; *New Orleans Daily Picayune*, July 20, 22, 1890.
14. *Vicksburg Daily Commercial Herald*, July 2, 5, 1890; *New Orleans Daily Picayune*, July 16, 1890.
15. *McComb City Enterprise*, September 28, 1911; *Hattiesburg News*, October 2, 1911; Ronald L. Filippelli, ed., *Labor Conflict in the United States: An Encyclopedia* (New York: Garland, 1990), 253.
16. *Laurel Chronicle*, October 6, 1911; *McComb City Enterprise*, October 5, 1911; *Hattiesburg News*, October 4, 5, 1911; Filippelli, *Labor Conflict*, 254.
17. *McComb City Enterprise*, October 5, 1911.
18. *Hattiesburg News*, October 5, 6, 1911; Donald C. Mosley, "A History of Labor Unions in Mississippi" (Ph.D. diss., University of Alabama, 1965), 79–81.
19. *Hattiesburg News*, October 7, 1911.
20. *Hattiesburg News*, October 6, 10, 1911; *McComb City Enterprise*, February 8, 1912.
21. *Journal of the House of Representatives of the State of Mississippi, at a Special Session Thereof in the City of Jackson, Commencing Nov. 1, 1911* . . . (Nashville, Tenn., 1911), 11, 24–55.
22. *Journal of the House of Representatives of the State of Mississippi, at a Special Session*, 67–86; *Hattiesburg News*, November 3, 1911.
23. *Hattiesburg News*, October 19, November 3, 1911; *McComb City Enterprise*, November 23, 30, 1911.
24. *Hattiesburg News*, October 4, 12, 1911; *McComb City Enterprise*, October 5, 12, November 9, 1911.
25. *Hattiesburg News*, October 5, 6, 1911; Filippelli, *Labor Conflict*, 253–54.
26. Mosley, "History of Labor Unions," 78; Filippelli, *Labor Conflict*, 254.

Chapter 10

1. U.S. Bureau of the Census, *Twelfth Census of the United States, Taken in the Year 1900: Manufactures* (Washington, D.C.: Government Printing Office, 1900), 216–32, 276–79, 297, 311; *Wesson Argosy*, November 5, 1887; *Batesville Blade*, May 27, 1881.

2. Thomas Park, "Recollections of Ocean Springs," 1982 typescript, SC-UM, 15; Laura Taylor Diary, December 8, 1896, Calvin Taylor Family Papers, Special Collections, Louisiana State University (hereafter SC-LSU).
3. Corliss, *Main Line*, 238–39; Thomas D. Clark, "Changes in Transportation," in McLemore, *History of Mississippi*, 2:274, 309–11.
4. John F. Stover, *The Railroads of the South, 1865–1900: A Study in Finance and Control* (Chapel Hill: University of North Carolina Press, 1955), 499–505; Corliss, *Main Line*, 175–207.
5. Cobb, *Most Southern Place*, 79–82; Corliss, *Main Line*, 239–44; Bond, *Political Culture*, 195–203; Clark, "Changes in Transportation," 306–7.
6. Corliss, *Main Line*, 375–84; Hickman, *Mississippi Harvest*, 213.
7. Hickman, *Mississippi Harvest*, 214; Corliss, *Main Line*, 385–400; Lemley, *Gulf, Mobile, and Ohio*, 290–92; Clark, "Changes in Transportation," 307–9.
8. Lemley, *Gulf, Mobile, and Ohio*, 284–89.
9. Corliss, *Main Line*, 312–14.
10. *Vicksburg Evening Post*, June 10, 1905; Dale L. Flesher and Jalal Soroosh, "Riverboat Accounting and Profitability: *The Betsey Ann*," *Journal of Mississippi History* 49 (1987): 23–33; Thigpen, *Boy in Rural Mississippi*, 103–4; Cobb, *Most Southern Place*, 79–80; Clark, "Changes in Transportation," 302–4.
11. Joseph Hyde Pratt, "The Good Roads Movement in the South," *Annals of the American Academy of Political and Social Science* 35 (1910): 105–13; Corey T. Lesseig, "'Out of the Mud': The Good Roads Crusade and Social Change in Twentieth Century Mississippi," *Journal of Mississippi History* 40 (1998): 51–72; Fite, *Cotton Fields No More*, 32.
12. Thigpen, *Boy in Rural Mississippi*, 27, 49.
13. *Official Good Roads Yearbook of the United States: 1912* (Washington, D.C.: American Association for Highway Improvement, 1912), 91–92; Howard L. Preston, *Dirt Roads to Dixie: Accessibility and Modernization in the South, 1885–1935* (Knoxville: University of Tennessee Press, 1991), 20–21; Bond, *Political Culture*, 30–33; Hudson, "Attala Boyhood," 127, 141–42; Clark, "Changes in Transportation," 280–83.
14. Clark, "Changes in Transportation," 274–80.
15. Park, "Recollections," 16–18.
16. *Biloxi Daily Herald*, August 24, September 15, 1915; *Hattiesburg News*, August 26, 1915.
17. *Hattiesburg News*, August 24, 26, 1915; Preston, *Dirt Roads*, 14–15.
18. Preston, *Dirt Roads*, 26–27.
19. Pratt, "Good Roads Movement," 105–7; Preston, *Dirt Roads*, 14–15.
20. Pamphlet title quoted in Giles, "Agricultural Revolution" 188; Pratt, "Good Roads Movement," 110–13.
21. *Official Good Roads Yearbook*, 186.
22. *Hattiesburg News*, August 6, 26, 1915; Preston, *Dirt Roads*, 4–5.
23. *Official Good Roads Yearbook*, 350; Hudson, "Attala Boyhood," 141–42; Virginia Estes Causey, "Glen Allen, Mississippi: Change and Continuity in a Delta Community, 1900 to 1950" (Ph.D. diss., Emory University, 1983), 78–82; Bond, *Political Culture*, 30–33; Clark, "Changes in Transportation," 280–83.

24. Clark, "Changes in Transportation," 283–95.
25. Stephen Cresswell, "Grassroots Radicalism in the Magnolia State: Mississippi's Socialist Movement at the Local Level, 1910–1919," *Labor History* 33 (1992): 81, 91–93.
26. Ordinance 419 (March 2, 1909), Minute Books of Biloxi City Council, 7:521; *Biloxi Daily Herald*, February 2, 3, 7, 11, 25, 27, March 13, 15, 1911; *Bay St. Louis Gulf Coast Progress*, March 22, 1911.
27. *Batesville Blade*, May 6, 1881; Thigpen, *Boy in Rural Mississippi*, 47; U.S. Bureau of the Census, *Telephones and Telegraphs, 1902* (Washington, D.C.: Government Printing Office, 1906), 9–85.
28. *Hattiesburg News*, September 26, 1912; George E. Waring, comp., *Report on the Social Statistics of Cities* (Washington, D.C.: Government Printing Office, 1887), 210; *Wesson Herald*, May 26, 1883; U.S. Bureau of the Census, *Telephones and Telegraphs*, 130; U.S. Bureau of the Census, *Central Electric and Light Power Stations, 1902* (Washington, D.C.: Government Printing Office, 1905), 13, 106–7.
29. Leo E. Turitz and Evelyn Turitz, *Jews in Early Mississippi* (Jackson: University Press of Mississippi, 1983), 91–95.
30. *Hattiesburg News*, July 28, 31, November 15, 1915.
31. Ayers, *Promise of the New South*, 56, 198.
32. Khaled J. Bloom, *The Mississippi Valley's Great Yellow Fever Epidemic of 1878* (Baton Rouge: Louisiana State University Press, 1993), 1–7.
33. Bloom, *Mississippi Valley's Great Yellow Fever Epidemic*, 3–5; Ellis, *Yellow Fever*, 75–81.
34. Samuel Agnew diary, October 12, 13, 1878, Southern Historical Collection, University of North Carolina Libraries, Chapel Hill, photocopy at SC-UM.
35. Agnew diary, October 13, 1878.
36. *New Orleans Daily Picayune*, October 4, 1878.
37. Emily Douglas Autobiography, manuscript, Emily Caroline Douglas Papers, SC-LSU, 314, 317, 325.
38. Bloom, *Mississippi Valley's Great Yellow Fever Epidemic*, 7–11, 181.
39. Bloom, *Mississippi Valley's Great Yellow Fever Epidemic*, 7–11.
40. *New Orleans Daily Picayune*, October 13, 1878; Ellis, *Yellow Fever*, 147.
41. Bloom, *Mississippi Valley's Great Yellow Fever Epidemic*, 146–47; *New Orleans Daily Picayune*, October 4, 6, 13, 1878.
42. Bloom, *Mississippi Valley's Great Yellow Fever Epidemic*, 11–19, 146–47.
43. Margaret Humphreys, *Yellow Fever and the South* (Baltimore: Johns Hopkins University Press, 1999), 137–38, 174; Bloom, *Mississippi Valley's Great Yellow Fever Epidemic*, 92–99, 129, 146, 151.
44. Bloom, *Mississippi Valley's Great Yellow Fever Epidemic*, 19–20.
45. Ellis, *Yellow Fever*, 75–81.
46. Humphreys, *Yellow Fever and the South*, 137–44.
47. *Jackson Daily Clarion-Ledger*, November 1, 1898; Bloom, *Mississippi Valley's Great Yellow Fever Epidemic*, 247–54, 262.
48. Humphreys, *Yellow Fever and the South*, 138–44.
49. Bloom, *Mississippi Valley's Great Yellow Fever Epidemic*, 255–56.

50. Bloom, *Mississippi Valley's Great Yellow Fever Epidemic*, 256–64.
51. Bloom, *Mississippi Valley's Great Yellow Fever Epidemic*, 264.
52. Laura D. S. Harrell, "Medical Services in Mississippi, 1890–1970," in McLemore, *History of Mississippi*, 2:516, 536–37.
53. Humphreys, *Yellow Fever and the South*, 173.
54. Daphne Roe, *A Plague of Corn: The Social History of Pellagra* (Ithaca, N.Y.: Cornell University Press, 1973), 1–76.
55. Roe, *Plague*, 1–76, 95–97.
56. Elizabeth W. Etheridge, *The Butterfly Caste: A Social History of Pellagra in the South* (Westport, Conn.: Greenwood, 1972), 72–75.
57. Roe, *Plague*, 99–101.
58. Dr. Joseph Goldberger to Mary Goldberger, April 19, 1915, Goldberger Papers, SC-UM.
59. Dr. Joseph Goldberger to Mary Goldberger, October 30, 1915, Goldberger Papers, SC-UM; Etheridge, *Butterfly*, 93–94.
60. Mary Goldberger, "Science Pigeonholed—Pellagra," typescript of a speech delivered by Mary Goldberger [circa 1954?], Goldberger Papers, SC-UM; Etheridge, *Butterfly*, 101.
61. Etheridge, *Butterfly*, 104–5.
62. Roe, *Plague*, 104–71; Etheridge, *Butterfly*, 71, 89, 113.
63. Etheridge, *Butterfly*, 111–12, 144.
64. Harry Frank Farmer, "The Hookworm Eradication Program in the South, 1909–1925" (Ph.D. diss., University of Georgia, 1970), 20–101.
65. Etheridge, *Butterfly*, 13–15; Farmer, "Hookworm," 101–3.
66. Savitt and Young, *Disease and Distinctiveness*, 14; Etheridge, *Butterfly*, 13–15; Farmer, "Hookworm," 65–66.
67. Farmer, "Hookworm," 101–3.
68. The best essays on the effects of disease upon the southern economy are found in Savitt and Young, *Disease and Distinctiveness*.

Chapter 11

1. For a good overview of these divisions, see Boschert, "'Family Affair.'"
2. Kirwan, *Revolt*, 140–42.
3. John R. Skates, *Mississippi's Old Capitol: Biography of a Building* (Jackson: Mississippi Department of Archives and History, 1990).
4. William Alexander Percy, *Lanterns on the Levee: Recollections of a Planter's Son* (New York: Knopf, 1941), 19.
5. Chester M. Morgan, *Redneck Liberal: Theodore G. Bilbo and the New Deal* (Baton Rouge: Louisiana State University Press, 1985), 11–15.
6. Bond, *Political Culture*, 287–92; Holmes, *White Chief*, 95–97.
7. Bond, *Political Culture*, 292; Kirwan, *Revolt*, 134–35.
8. Holmes, *White Chief*, 23; *New Orleans Daily Picayune*, August 1, 1890.

NOTES

9. Holmes, *White Chief*, 32, 39.
10. Holmes, *White Chief*, 47–51.
11. Holmes, *White Chief*, 58, 89.
12. Boschert, "'Family Affair,'" 175–85.
13. Boschert, "'Family Affair,'" 183–87.
14. Holmes, *White Chief*, 109.
15. *Jackson Clarion-Ledger* quoted in Boschert, "'Family Affair,'" 192; Holmes, *White Chief*, 102–4.
16. Holmes, *White Chief*, 112–13.
17. *Inaugural Addresses*, 29.
18. Holmes, *White Chief*, 122.
19. Clark, "Industrial Development," 55, 56–57.
20. Boschert, "'Family Affair,'" 200, 212.
21. Holmes, *White Chief*, 134.
22. Boschert, "'Family Affair,'" 183, 240; Holmes, "Whitecapping: Agrarian Violence," 165–85.
23. Holmes, *White Chief*, 283–87.
24. Boschert, "'Family Affair,'" 217–27.
25. Nannie Pitts McLemore, "The Progressive Era," in McLemore, *History of Mississippi*, 2:29, 42–43.
26. Holmes, *White Chief*, 188.
27. Holmes, *White Chief*, 190–93.
28. Holmes, *White Chief*, 197–99.
29. Morgan, *Redneck Liberal*, 32–33.
30. McLemore, "Progressive Era," 2:50.
31. Morgan, *Redneck Liberal*, 246.
32. Holmes, *White Chief*, 212–13.
33. *Wesson Enterprise*, May 13, 1910.
34. Morgan, *Redneck Liberal*, 34; Holmes, *White Chief*, 222.
35. Morgan, *Redneck Liberal*, 33.
36. Percy, *Lanterns*, 147–48.
37. Holmes, *White Chief*, 238–39.
38. Percy, *Lanterns*, 149.
39. *Biloxi Daily Herald*, January 25, 1911.
40. *Biloxi Daily Herald*, March 7, 1911.
41. *Biloxi Daily Herald*, March 8, 1911.
42. Holmes, *White Chief*, 249–50.
43. Morgan, *Redneck Liberal*, 34.
44. *Issue*, July 7, 14, 1911; Wilmuth Saunders Rutledge, "The John J. Henry-Theodore Bilbo Encounter, 1911," *Journal of Mississippi History* 34 (1972): 357, 361.
45. Rutledge, "John J. Henry," 364–67.
46. Rutledge, "John J. Henry," 365; Morgan, *Redneck Liberal*, 29, 34–36.
47. MDA&H, *Official and Statistical Register, 1920–1924*, chart opposite page 130; *Issue*, November 10, 1911.

48. Holmes, *White Chief*, 275.
49. Holmes, *White Chief*, 278–85.
50. Holmes, *White Chief*, 328–36.
51. Morgan, *Redneck Liberal*, 37.
52. C. F. R. to Lucy Treadway, n.d. [circa 1880], Aldrich Family Papers, SC-UM; Marjorie Spruill Wheeler, *New Women of the New South: The Leaders of the Woman Suffrage Movement in the Southern States* (New York: Oxford University Press, 1993), 76–115.
53. Nellie Nugent Somerville, "History of the Mississippi Woman Suffrage Association, 1897–1919," undated typescript, Nellie Nugent Somerville Papers, MDA&H.
54. "Who Takes Care of Mississippi Women," broadside, Somerville Papers, MDA&H; "Address of the State President Before the Woman Suffrage Club of Clarksdale, Mississippi . . . November 18, 1898," Somerville Papers, MDA&H.
55. Wheeler, *New Women*, 120–25.
56. Wheeler, *New Women*, 122–25.
57. Holmes, *White Chief*, 290.
58. Somerville, "History of the Mississippi Woman Suffrage Association."
59. Wheeler, *New Women*, 181–82.
60. Wheeler, *New Women*, 181, 191–94.
61. *Mississippi Women's Christian Temperance Union, 1913. Report of the Thirteenth Annual Convention*, 55–57, SC-UM.
62. Herring, "Saloons and Drinking," 123–31.
63. Davis, "Attacking 'The Matchless Evil,' " 221–22.
64. Davis, "Attacking 'The Matchless Evil,' " 233–46.
65. Davis, "Attacking 'The Matchless Evil,' " 252–56.
66. *Natchez Daily Democrat*, December 31, 1908.
67. Boschert, " 'Family Affair,' " 231; Thigpen, *Boy in Rural Mississippi*, 103–4.
68. Rev. J. F. Hailey to Edmund F. Noel, January 13, 1911, Governor's Papers, Record Group 27, MDA&H; Judge H. C. Mounger to Noel, November 29, 1910, Governor's Papers, MDA&H.
69. Davis, "Attacking 'The Matchless Evil,'" 252–56.
70. Bond, *I Had a Friend*, 101–5.
71. Kirwan, *Revolt*, 137–40; *Wesson Enterprise*, February 25, 1910.
72. Bond, *I Had a Friend*, 96–98.
73. Bond, *I Had a Friend*, 99–100.
74. Holmes, *White Chief*, 311–16.
75. Holmes, *White Chief*, 316–25; *Girard (Kans.) Appeal to Reason*, April 14, 1917.
76. Holmes, *White Chief*, 349.
77. Holmes, *White Chief*, 349.
78. Morgan, *Redneck Liberal*, 39.
79. Holmes, *White Chief*, 361–81.
80. Boschert, " 'Family Affair,' " 401. On pages 12–16, Boschert has an excellent historiographical overview of the writers mentioned here.

Chapter 12

1. Wilbur Cash, *The Mind of the South* (New York: Knopf, 1941); C. Vann Woodward, *Origins of the New South, 1877–1913*, rev. ed. (Baton Rouge: Louisiana State University Press, 1951); Ayers, *Promise of the New South*.
2. Kirwan, *Revolt*; John R. Skates, "Mississippi," in *Encyclopedia of Southern History*, ed. David C. Roller and Robert W. Twyman, 825–36 (Baton Rouge: Louisiana State University Press, 1979); Boschert, " 'Family Affair,' " 173, 402.
3. John B. Boles, *The South Through Time: A History of an American Region* (Englewood Cliffs, N.J.: Prentice Hall, 1995), 413; Wright, *Old South, New South*, 3–42; Roger L. Ransom and Richard Sutch, *Conflict and Compromise: The Political Economy of Slavery, Emancipation, and the Civil War* (Cambridge: Cambridge University Press, 1977); Fite, *Cotton Fields No More*, 28–31.
4. Park, "Recollections," 27.
5. Park, "Recollections," 28–29.
6. *Camp Shelby Trench and Camp*, October, November, and December 1917.
7. *Camp Shelby Trench and Camp*, October 17, 24, November 14, December 18, 1917.
8. Cohen, *At Freedom's Edge*, 292–96.
9. McMillen, *Dark Journey*, 263.
10. McMillen, *Dark Journey*, 264.
11. McMillen, *Dark Journey*, 273, 408–56.
12. McMillen, *Dark Journey*, 303, 305–18.

BIBLIOGRAPHY

Books

Abney, F. Glenn. *Mississippi Election Statistics: 1900–1967.* University, Miss.: Bureau of Governmental Research, 1968.
Ayers, Edward L. *The Promise of the New South: Life after Reconstruction.* New York: Oxford University Press, 1992.
Beadle, Samuel Alfred. *Sketches from Life in Dixie.* Chicago: Scroll Publishers and Literary Syndicate, 1899.
Biographical and Historical Memoirs of Mississippi. 2 vols. Chicago: Goodspeed, 1891.
Biographical Directory of the American Congress. Washington, D.C.: Government Printing Office, 1971.
Bloom, Khaled J. *The Mississippi Valley's Great Yellow Fever Epidemic of 1878.* Baton Rouge: Louisiana State University Press, 1993.
Boles, John B. *The South Through Time: A History of an American Region.* Englewood Cliffs, N.J.: Prentice Hall, 1995.
Bolton, Charles. *Poor Whites of the Antebellum South: Tenants and Laborers in Central North Carolina and Northeast Mississippi.* Durham, N.C.: Duke University Press, 1994.
Bond, Bradley G. *Political Culture in the Nineteenth-Century South: Mississippi, 1830–1900.* Baton Rouge: Louisiana State University Press, 1995.
Bond, Willard Faroe. *I Had a Friend: An Autobiography.* N.p., 1958.
Brandfon, Robert L. *Cotton Kingdom of the New South: A History of the Yazoo Mississippi Delta from Reconstruction to the Twentieth Century.* Cambridge, Mass.: Harvard University Press, 1967.
Burnham, W. Dean. *Presidential Ballots, 1836–1892.* Baltimore: Johns Hopkins University Press, 1955.
Bynum, Victoria E. *The Free State of Jones: Mississippi's Longest Civil War.* Chapel Hill: University of North Carolina Press, 2003.
Carpenter, Barbara, ed. *Ethnic Heritage in Mississippi.* Jackson: University Press of Mississippi, for the Mississippi Humanities Council, 1992.
Cash, Wilbur. *The Mind of the South.* New York: Knopf, 1941.
Chandler, Greene C. *Journal and Speeches of Greene Callier Chandler.* N.p., 1953.
Claiborne, John Francis Hamtrack, and C. M. Lagrone, comps. *Mississippi, as a Province, Territory, and State, with Biographical Notices of Eminent Citizens.* Jackson, Miss.: Power and Barksdale, 1880.
Clark, Thomas D. *A Pioneer Southern Railroad from New Orleans to Cairo.* Chapel Hill: University of North Carolina Press, 1936.

Cobb, James C. *The Most Southern Place on Earth: The Mississippi Delta and the Roots of Regional Identity*. New York: Oxford University Press, 1992.
Cohen, William. *At Freedom's Edge: Black Mobility and the Southern White Quest for Racial Control, 1865–1915*. Baton Rouge: Louisiana State University Press, 1991.
Congressional Quarterly's Guide to U.S. Elections. 2nd ed. Washington, D.C.: Congressional Quarterly, 1985.
Cooper, William J., Michael Holt, and John McCardell, eds. *A Master's Due: Essays in Honor of David Herbert Donald*. Baton Rouge: Louisiana State University Press, 1985.
Corliss, Carlton J. *Main Line of Mid-America: The Story of the Illinois Central*. New York: Creative Age Press, 1950.
Cranford, Sammy O. *The Fernwood, Columbia and Gulf: A Railroad in the Piney Woods of South Mississippi*. New York: Garland, 1989.
Cresswell, Stephen. *Mormons and Cowboys, Moonshiners and Klansmen: Federal Law Enforcement in the South and West, 1870–1893*. Tuscaloosa: University of Alabama Press, 1991.
———. *Multiparty Politics in Mississippi, 1877–1902*. Jackson: University Press of Mississippi, 1995.
Crockett, Norman L. *The Black Towns*. Lawrence: Regents Press of Kansas, 1979.
Daniel, Pete. *The Shadow of Slavery: Peonage in the South, 1901–1969*. Urbana: University of Illinois Press, 1972.
Davidson, Elizabeth H. *Child Labor Legislation in the Southern Textile States*. Chapel Hill: University of North Carolina Press, 1939.
Dickson, Harris. *An Old Fashioned Senator: A Story-Biography of John Sharp Williams*. New York: Frederick A. Stokes, 1925.
Dyer, Charles L. *Along the Gulf: An Entertaining Story of an Outing Among the Beautiful Resorts on the Mississippi Sound*. N.p., 1895.
Ellis, John H. *Yellow Fever and Public Health in the New South*. Lexington: University Press of Kentucky, 1992.
Etheridge, Elizabeth W. *The Butterfly Caste: A Social History of Pellagra in the South*. Westport, Conn.: Greenwood, 1972.
Fickle, James E. *Mississippi Forests and Forestry*. Jackson: University Press of Mississippi, 2001.
———. *Timber: A Photographic History of Mississippi Forestry*. Jackson: University Press of Mississippi, 2004.
Filippelli, Ronald L., ed. *Labor Conflict in the United States: An Encyclopedia*. New York: Garland, 1990.
Fite, Gilbert C. *Cotton Fields No More: Southern Agriculture, 1865–1980*. Lexington: University Press of Kentucky, 1984.
Foner, Eric. *Reconstruction: America's Unfinished Revolution, 1863–1877*. New York: Harper and Row, 1988.
Fulkerson, Horace S. *The Negro: As He Was; As He Is; As He Will Be*. Vicksburg, Miss.: Commercial World, 1887.
Gentry, Claude. *Private John Allen: Gentleman, Statesman, Sage, Prophet*. Baldwyn, Miss.: n.p., 1951.
Gillette, William. *Retreat from Reconstruction, 1869–1879*. Baton Rouge: Louisiana State University Press, 1979.

Grantham, Dewey. *Southern Progressivism: The Reconciliation of Progress and Tradition.* Knoxville: University of Tennessee Press, 1983.
Green, Adwin Wigfall. *The Man Bilbo.* Baton Rouge: Louisiana State University Press, 1963.
Griffith, Frances Williams. *True Life Story of Will Purvis.* Purvis, Miss.: Booster, 1935.
Hamilton, Kenneth Marvin. *Black Towns and Profit: Promotion and Development in the Transappalachian West, 1877–1915.* Urbana: University of Illinois Press, 1991.
Hamilton, Mary. *Trials of the Earth: The Autobiography of Mary Hamilton.* Edited by Helen Dick Davis. Jackson: University Press of Mississippi, 1992.
Harris, William C. *The Day of the Carpetbagger: Republican Reconstruction in Mississippi.* Baton Rouge: Louisiana State University Press, 1979.
Harrison, Alferdteen. *Piney Woods School: An Oral History.* Jackson: University Press of Mississippi, 1982.
Harrison, Robert W. *Levee Districts and Levee Building in Mississippi: A Study of State and Local Efforts to Control Mississippi River Floods.* Stoneville, Miss.: Delta Council, 1951.
Hickman, Nollie. *Mississippi Harvest: Lumbering in the Long Leaf Pine Belt, 1840–1915.* University: University of Mississippi, 1962.
Holmes, William F. *The White Chief: James Kimball Vardaman.* Baton Rouge: Louisiana State University Press, 1970.
Holtzclaw, William H. *Black Man's Burden.* New York: Neale Publishing, 1915.
Humphreys, Margaret. *Yellow Fever and the South.* Baltimore: Johns Hopkins University Press, 1999.
Hyman, Michael R. *The Anti-Redeemers: Hill-Country Political Dissenters in the Lower South from Redemption to Populism.* Baton Rouge: Louisiana State University Press, 1990.
Inaugural Addresses of the Governors of Mississippi, 1890–1980. University, Miss.: Bureau of Governmental Research, 1980.
Jackson, David H. *A Chief Lieutenant of the Tuskegee Machine: Charles Banks of Mississippi.* Gainesville: University Press of Florida, 2002.
Key, V. O., with Alexander Heard. *Southern Politics in State and Nation.* New York: Knopf, 1949.
Kirwan, Albert D. *Revolt of the Rednecks: Mississippi Politics, 1876–1925.* Lexington: University of Kentucky Press, 1951.
Kousser, J. Morgan. *The Shaping of Southern Politics: Suffrage Restriction and the Establishment of the One-Party South, 1880–1910.* New Haven, Conn.: Yale University Press, 1974.
Kraut, Alan M. *Goldberger's War: The Life and Work of a Public Health Crusader.* New York: Hill and Wang, 2003.
Lemley, James H. *The Gulf, Mobile and Ohio: A Railroad That Had to Expand or Expire.* Homewood, Ill.: Richard D. Irwin, 1953.
Link, William A. *The Paradox of Southern Progressivism, 1880–1930.* Chapel Hill: University of North Carolina Press, 1992.
Loewen, James W. *The Mississippi Chinese: Between Black and White.* Cambridge, Mass.: Harvard University Press, 1971.
Lowry, Robert, and William H. McCardle. *A History of Mississippi, from the Discovery of the Great River by Hernando DeSoto . . . to the Death of Jefferson Davis.* Jackson: R. H. Henry, 1891.

Lynch, James D. *Kemper County Vindicated, and a Peep at Radical Rule in Mississippi*. New York: E. J. Hale, 1879.
Lynch, John Roy. *The Facts of Reconstruction*. 1913. Reprint, New York: Arno Press, 1968.
———. *Reminiscences of an Active Life: The Autobiography of John Roy Lynch*. Edited and with an introduction by John Hope Franklin. Chicago: University of Chicago Press, 1970.
Mayes, Edward. *Lucius Q. C. Lamar: His Life, Times, and Speeches, 1825–1893*. Nashville: Publishing House of the Methodist Episcopal Church, South, 1896.
McLaurin, Melton Alonza. *The Knights of Labor in the South*. Westport, Conn.: Greenwood, 1978.
McLemore, Richard Aubrey, ed. *A History of Mississippi*. 2 vols. Jackson: University and College Press of Mississippi, 1973.
McMillen, Neil R. *Dark Journey: Black Mississippians in the Age of Jim Crow*. Urbana: University of Illinois Press, 1989.
Montgomery, Isaiah T. "What Answer?" Speech in Support of Franchise Committee Report, Mississippi Constitutional Convention, 1890. Ed. Matthew Holden Jr. Charlottesville, Va.: Isaiah T. Montgomery Studies Project, 2004.
Moorhead, Mississippi: A Prohibition Industrial Colony in the Heart of the Famous Cotton Delta of Mississippi. Chicago: Rand, McNally, n.d.
Morgan, A. T. *Yazoo, or On the Picket Line of Freedom in the South*. 1884. Reprint, New York: Russell and Russell.
Morgan, Chester M. *Redneck Liberal: Theodore G. Bilbo and the New Deal*. Baton Rouge: Louisiana State University Press, 1985.
Noble, Stuart G. *Forty Years of the Public Schools in Mississippi, with Special Reference to the Education of the Negro*. New York: Teachers College, 1918.
Nordin, D. Sven. *Rich Harvest: A History of the Grange, 1867–1900*. Jackson: University Press of Mississippi, 1974.
Official Good Roads Yearbook of the United States: 1912. Washington, D.C.: American Association for Highway Improvement, 1912.
Osborn, George C. *John Sharp Williams: Planter-Statesman of the Deep South*. Baton Rouge: Louisiana State University Press, 1943.
Oshinsky, David M. *"Worse Than Slavery": Parchman Farm and the Ordeal of Jim Crow Justice*. New York: Free Press, 1996.
Ownby, Ted. *Subduing Satan: Religion, Recreation, and Manhood in the Rural South, 1865–1920*. Chapel Hill: University of North Carolina Press, 1990.
Painter, Nell Irvin. *Exodusters: Black Migration to Kansas After Reconstruction*. New York: Knopf, 1977.
Percy, William Alexander. *Lanterns on the Levee: Recollections of a Planter's Son*. New York: Knopf, 1941.
Pereyra, Lillian A. *James Lusk Alcorn: Persistent Whig*. Baton Rouge: Louisiana State University Press, 1966.
Perman, Michael. *The Road to Redemption: Southern Politics, 1869–1879*. Chapel Hill: University of North Carolina Press, 1984.
———. *Struggle for Mastery: Disfranchisement in the South, 1888–1908*. Chapel Hill: University of North Carolina Press, 2001.

Polk, Noel, ed. *Mississippi's Piney Woods: A Human Perspective*. Jackson: University Press of Mississippi, 1986.
Preston, Howard L. *Dirt Roads to Dixie: Accessibility and Modernization in the South, 1885–1935*. Knoxville: University of Tennessee Press, 1991.
Quan, Robert Seto, and Julian B. Roebuck. *Lotus among the Magnolias: The Mississippi Chinese*. Jackson: University Press of Mississippi, 1982.
Ransom, Roger L., and Richard Sutch. *One Kind of Freedom: The Economic Consequences of Emancipation*. Cambridge: Cambridge University Press, 1977.
———. *Conflict and Compromise: The Political Economy of Slavery, Emancipation, and the Civil War*. Cambridge: Cambridge University Press, 1977.
Roe, Daphne. *A Plague of Corn: The Social History of Pellagra*. Ithaca, N.Y.: Cornell University Press, 1973.
Roller, David C., and Robert W. Twyman, eds. *Encyclopedia of Southern History*. Baton Rouge: Louisiana State University Press, 1979.
Rowland, Dunbar. *History of Mississippi: Heart of the South*. Chicago: S. J. Clarke, 1925.
———. *Mississippi: Comprising Sketches of Counties, Towns, Events, Institutions, and Persons, Arranged in Cyclopedic Form*. 4 vols. Atlanta: Southern Historical Publishing Association, 1907.
Royster, Jacqueline Jones, ed., *Southern Horrors and Other Writings: The Anti-Lynching Campaign of Ida B. Wells, 1892–1900*. Boston: Bedford Books, 1997.
Saville, Julie. *The Work of Reconstruction: From Slave to Wage Laborer in South Carolina, 1860–1870*. Cambridge: Cambridge University Press, 1994.
Savitt, Todd L., and James Harvey Young, eds. *Disease and Distinctiveness in the American South*. Knoxville: University of Tennessee Press, 1988.
Scott, Anne Firor. *The Southern Lady: From Pedestal to Politics, 1830–1930*. Chicago: University of Chicago Press, 1970.
Sewell, George Alexander, and Margaret L. Dwight. *Mississippi Black History Makers*. Rev. and enlarged ed. Jackson: University Press of Mississippi, 1984.
Skates, John R. *Mississippi: A Bicentennial History*. New York: Norton, 1979.
———. *Mississippi's Old Capitol: Biography of a Building*. Jackson: Mississippi Department of Archives and History, 1990.
Statistical History of the United States, from Colonial Times to the Present. New York: Basic Books, 1976.
Stover, John F. *The Railroads of the South, 1865–1900: A Study in Finance and Control*. Chapel Hill: University of North Carolina Press, 1955.
Swain, Martha H., Elizabeth Anne Payne, Marjorie Julian Spruill, and Susan Ditto, eds. *Mississippi Women: Their History, Their Lives*. Athens: University of Georgia Press, 2003.
Thigpen, S. G. *A Boy in Rural Mississippi and Other Stories*. Picayune, Miss.: privately printed, 1966.
Thompson, Julius E. *The Black Press in Mississippi, 1865–1985*. Gainesville: University Press of Florida, 1993.
Turitz, Leo E., and Evelyn Turitz. *Jews in Early Mississippi*. Jackson: University Press of Mississippi, 1983.

Underwood, Felix J., and R. N. Whitfield. *Public Health and Medical Licensure in the State of Mississippi, 1798–1947*. 2 vols. Jackson: Tucker Printing, 1938, 1951.

Walker, Durr, and David Higgs. *Wesson: Industrial City of the South*. N.p.: n.d. [1994?].

Waring, George E. comp. *Report on the Social Statistics of Cities*. Washington, D.C.: Government Printing Office, 1887.

Wells, James M. *The Chisholm Massacre: A Picture of "Home Rule" in Mississippi*. 3rd ed. Washington, D.C.: Chisholm Monument Association, 1878.

Wharton, Vernon Lane. *The Negro in Mississippi, 1865–1890*. Chapel Hill: University of North Carolina Press, 1947.

Wheeler, Marjorie Spruill. *New Women of the New South: The Leaders of the Woman Suffrage Movement in the Southern States*. New York: Oxford University Press, 1993.

Wilson, Charles Reagan, and William Ferris. *Encyclopedia of Southern Culture*. Chapel Hill: University of North Carolina Press, 1989.

Woodward, C. Vann. *Origins of the New South, 1877–1913*. Rev. ed. Baton Rouge: Louisiana State University Press, 1971.

———. *The Strange Career of Jim Crow*. 3rd rev. ed. New York: Oxford University Press, 1974.

Woodward, D. W. *Negro Progress in a Mississippi Town, Being a Study of Conditions in Jackson, Mississippi*. Cheyney, Pa.: Biddle Press, n.d. [1907?].

Wright, Gavin. *Old South, New South: Revolutions in the Southern Economy since the Civil War*. New York: Basic Books, 1986.

Articles, Theses, Dissertations

Basko, Rebecca Safstrom. "The Exoduster Experience: During and after the Migration." *Journal of Mississippi History* 59 (1997): 141–44.

Beets, Eva Davis. "Growing Up in Marion County: A Memoir by Eva Davis Beets." Edited by Christine Wilson. *Journal of Mississippi History* 48 (1986): 199–213.

Bettersworth, John K. "Mississippi State University: A Centennial Sketch." *Journal of Mississippi History* 41 (1979): 33–52.

Bond, Bradley G. "Edward C. Walthall and the 1880 Senatorial Nomination: Politics of Balance in the Redeemer Era." *Journal of Mississippi History* 50 (1988): 1–20.

Boschert, Thomas N. "'A Family Affair': Mississippi Politics, 1882–1932." Ph.D. diss., University of Mississippi, 1995.

———. "The Politics of Expediency: Fusion in the Mississippi Delta, Late Nineteenth-Century." M.A. thesis, University of Mississippi, 1985.

Broadway, Lilibel. "Frank Burkitt: The Man in the Wool Hat." M.A. thesis, Mississippi State University, 1948.

Bynum, Victoria. "'White Negroes' in Segregated Mississippi: Miscegenation, Racial Identity, and the Law." *Journal of Southern History* 64 (1998): 247–77.

Calhoon, Solomon S. "The Causes and Events That Led to the Calling of the Constitutional Convention of 1890." *Publications of the Mississippi Historical Society* 6 (1902): 105–10.

Causey, Virginia Estes. "Glen Allen, Mississippi: Change and Continuity in a Delta Community, 1900 to 1950." Ph.D. diss., Emory University, 1983.

Clark, Eric C. "Industrial Development and State Government in Mississippi, 1890–1980." Ph.D. diss., Mississippi State University, 1989.

———. "Legislative Apportionment in the 1890 Constitutional Convention." *Journal of Mississippi History* 42 (1980): 298–315.

———. "Regulation of Corporations in the Mississippi Constitutional Convention of 1890." *Journal of Mississippi History* 48 (1986): 31–42.

Clark, Thomas D. "The Furnishing and Supply System in Southern Agriculture Since 1865." *Journal of Southern History* 12 (1946): 24–44.

Coleman, James P. "The Origin of the Constitution of 1890." *Journal of Mississippi History* 19 (1957): 69–92.

Cooper, Arnie. "'We Stand Upon the Structure We Ourselves Have Builded': William H. Holtzclaw and Utica Institute, 1903–1915." *Journal of Mississippi History* 47 (1985): 15–33.

Crawford, Charles W. "A History of the R. F. Learned Lumber Company, 1864–1945." Ph.D. diss., University of Mississippi, 1968.

Cresswell, Stephen. "Grassroots Radicalism in the Magnolia State: Mississippi's Socialist Movement at the Local Level, 1910–1919." *Labor History* 33 (1992): 81–101.

———. "Red Mississippi: The State's Socialist Party, 1904–1922." *Journal of Mississippi History* 50 (1988): 153–71.

———. "Who Was Who in Mississippi's Opposition Political Parties, 1878–1963." Unpublished typescript, 1994. Copy at Mississippi Department of Archives and History, Jackson.

Davis, William Graham. "Attacking the 'Matchless Evil': Temperance and Prohibition in Mississippi, 1817–1908." Ph.D. diss., Mississippi State University, 1975.

D'Olive, Annie Louise. "Reminiscences of Ten Mile: A South Mississippi Saw Mill Town." *Journal of Mississippi History* 39 (1977): 173–84.

Edwards, Thomas S. "'Reconstructing' Reconstruction: Changing Historical Paradigms in Mississippi." *Journal of Mississippi History* 51 (1989): 165–80.

Ellem, Warren A. "The Overthrow of Reconstruction in Mississippi." *Journal of Mississippi History* 54 (1992): 175–201.

———. "Who Were the Mississippi Scalawags?" *Journal of Southern History* 38 (1972): 217–40.

Farmer, Harry Frank. "The Hookworm Eradication Program in the South, 1909–1925." Ph.D. diss., University of Georgia, 1970.

Ferguson, James S. "Agrarianism in Mississippi, 1871–1900: A Study in Nonconformity." Ph.D. diss., University of North Carolina at Chapel Hill, 1952.

Fickle, James E. "Comfortable and Happy? Louisiana and Mississippi Lumber Workers, 1900–1950." *Louisiana History* 40 (1999): 407–32.

———. "Forest Products: The South's 'Forgotten Industry.'" *Journal of Mississippi History* 66 (2004): 1–16.

Flesher, Dale L., and Jalal Soroosh. "Riverboat Accounting and Profitability: *The Betsey Ann*." *Journal of Mississippi History* 49 (1987): 23–33.

Folmsbee, Stanley J. "The Origin of the First 'Jim Crow' Law." *Journal of Southern History* 15 (1949): 243–47.

Futrell, Robert F. "Efforts of Mississippians to Encourage Immigration, 1865–1880." *Journal of Mississippi History* 20 (1958): 59–76.
Galloway, Charles B. "Some Thoughts on Lynching." *South Atlantic Quarterly* 5 (October 1906): 351–53.
Gardner, Bettye J. "William H. Foote and Yazoo County Politics, 1866–1883." *Southern Studies* (Winter 1982): 398–407.
Giroux, Vincent A. "The Rise of Theodore Bilbo (1908–1932)." *Journal of Mississippi History* 43 (1981): 180–209.
———. "Theodore G. Bilbo: Progressive to Public Racist." Ph.D. diss., Indiana University, 1984.
Griffiths, John D. M. "A State of Servitude Worse Than Slavery: The Politics of Penal Administration in Mississippi, 1865–1900." *Journal of Mississippi History* 55 (1993): 1–18.
Halsell, Willie D. "The Bourbon Period in Mississippi Politics, 1875–1890." *Journal of Southern History* 11 (1945): 519–37.
———. "Democratic Dissentions in Mississippi, 1878–1882." *Journal of Mississippi History* 2 (1940): 123–35.
Hamilton, Charles Granville. "Mississippi Politics in the Progressive Era, 1904–1920." Ph.D. diss., Vanderbilt University, 1958.
Handford, Charlene Jeanette. "Bishop Charles Galloway's Rhetoric, 1903–1908." *Journal of Mississippi History* 44 (1982): 217–25.
Hataway, Marsha P. "The Development of the Mississippi State Highway System, 1916–1932." *Journal of Mississippi History* 28 (1966): 286–303.
Herring, Todd Ashley. "Saloons and Drinking in Mississippi from the Colonial Era to Prohibition." M.A. thesis, Mississippi State University, 1991.
Hines, Mary Elizabeth. "Death at the Hands of Persons Unknown: The Geography of Lynching in the Deep South, 1882 to 1910." Ph.D. diss., Louisiana State University, 1992.
Hodge, Jo Dent. "The Lumber Industry in Laurel, Mississippi, at the Turn of the Century." *Journal of Mississippi History* 35 (1973): 361–79.
Holmes, William F. "Labor Agents and the Georgia Exodus, 1899–1900." *South Atlantic Quarterly* 79 (1980): 436–48.
———. "The Leflore County Massacre and the Demise of the Colored Farmers Alliance." *Phylon* 34 (1973): 267–74.
———. "Whitecapping: Agrarian Violence in Mississippi, 1902–1906." *Journal of Southern History* 35 (1969): 165–85.
———. "Whitecapping: Anti-Semitism in the Populist Era." *American Jewish Historical Quarterly* 63 (1974): 244–61.
Hudson, Arthur Palmer. "An Attala Boyhood." *Journal of Mississippi History* 4 (1942): 127–55.
Hurns, Walter McClusky. "Post-Reconstruction Municipal Politics in Jackson, Mississippi." Ph.D. diss., Kansas State University, 1989.
Hyman, Michael R. "Taxation, Public Policy, and Political Dissent: Yeoman Disaffection in the Post-Reconstruction Lower South." *Journal of Southern History* 55 (1989): 49–76.
Irwin, James R., and Anthony Patrick O'Brien. "Economic Progress in the Post-Bellum South? African American Incomes in the Mississippi Delta, 1880–1910." *Explorations in Economic History* 38 (2001): 166–80.

Jeffrey, Julie Roy. "Women in the Southern Farmers' Alliance: A Reconsideration of the Role and Status of Women in the Late Nineteenth-Century South." *Feminist Studies* 3 (1975): 348–71.

Kight, Lawrence Edward. " 'The State Is on Trial': Governor Edmund F. Noel and the Defense of Mississippi's Legal Institutions Against Mob Violence." *Journal of Mississippi History* 60 (1998): 191–222.

Kirwan, Albert D. "Apportionment in the Mississippi Constitution of 1890." *Journal of Southern History* 14 (1948): 234–46.

Jackson, David H. "Charles Banks: 'Wizard of Mound Bayou.' " *Journal of Mississippi History* 62 (2000): 269–92.

Jenkins, Robert L. "The Development of Black Higher Education in Mississippi (1865–1920)." *Journal of Mississippi History* 45 (1983): 272–86.

Latham, Robert C. "The Dirt Farmer in Politics: A Study of Webster County, Mississippi, during the Rise of Democratic Factionalism, 1880–1910." M.A. thesis, Mississippi State College, 1951.

Legan, Marshall Scott. "The Disappearance of Bronze John in Mississippi." *Journal of Mississippi History* 38 (1976): 33–46.

———. "The Evolution of Public Health Services in Mississippi, 1865–1910." Ph.D. diss., University of Mississippi, 1968.

———. "Mississippi and the Yellow Fever Epidemics of 1878–1879." *Journal of Mississippi History* 33 (1971): 199–217.

———. "The War of the Waters: The Louisiana-Mississippi Quarantine War of 1905." *Journal of Mississippi History* 50 (1988): 89–110.

Lesseig, Corey T. " 'Out of the Mud': The Good Roads Crusade and Social Change in Twentieth Century Mississippi." *Journal of Mississippi History* 60 (1998): 51–72.

Lucas, Aubrey K. "The Mississippi Legislature and Mississippi Public Higher Education: 1890–1960." Ph.D. diss., Florida State University, 1966.

Mabry, William. "Disfranchisement of the Negro in Mississippi." *Journal of Southern History* 4 (1938): 318–33.

McCorkle, James L., Jr. "Cotton, War, and Mississippi, 1914–1915." *Journal of Mississippi History* 45 (1983): 90–115.

———. "The Illinois Central Railroad and the Mississippi Commercial Vegetable Industry." *Journal of Mississippi History* 39 (1977): 155–72.

———. "Mississippi from Neutrality to War (1914–1917)." *Journal of Mississippi History* 43 (1981): 85–125.

McMillen, Neil R. "Black Journalism in Mississippi: The Jim Crow Years." *Journal of Mississippi History* 49 (1987): 129–38.

Meredith, Mary Louise. "The Mississippi Women's Rights Movement, 1889–1923: The Leadership Role of Nellie Nugent Somerville and Greenville in Suffrage Reform." M.A. thesis, Delta State University, 1974.

Miller, Clark Leonard. "'Let Us Die to Make Men Free': Political Terrorism in Post-Reconstruction Mississippi, 1877–1896." Ph.D. diss., University of Minnesota, 1983.

Mills, Gary B. "New Life for the River of Death: Development of the Yazoo River Basin (1873–1977)." *Journal of Mississippi History* 41 (1979): 287–300.

Moore, Danny. " 'To Make the Best Better': The Establishment of Girls' Tomato Clubs in Mississippi, 1911–1915." *Journal of Mississippi History* 63 (2001): 101–18.
Mosley, Donald C. "A History of Labor Unions in Mississippi." Ph.D. diss., University of Alabama, 1965.
Muckenfuss, Anthony M. "The Development of Manufacturing in Mississippi." *Publications of the Mississippi Historical Society* 10 (1909): 163–80.
———. "History of the Application of Science to Industry in Mississippi." *Publications of the Mississippi Historical Society* 3 (1900): 235–47.
Myers, Frederic. "The Knights of Labor in the South." *Southern Economic Journal* 6 (1940): 479–87.
Patton, W. H. "History of the Prohibition Movement in Mississippi." *Publications of the Mississippi Historical Society* 10 (1909): 181–201.
Pratt, Joseph Hyde. "The Good Roads Movement in the South." *Annals of the American Academy of Political and Social Science* 35 (1910): 105–13.
Rutledge, Wilmuth Saunders. "The John J. Henry–Theodore Bilbo Encounter, 1911." *Journal of Mississippi History* 34 (1972): 357–72.
Sallis, William Charles. "The Color Line in Mississippi Politics: 1865–1915." Ph.D. diss., University of Kentucky, 1967.
Schuyler, George S. "Freedom of the Press in Mississippi." *Crisis* 43 (October 1936): 302–4.
Schwartz, Michael H. "An Estimate of the Size of the Southern Farmers' Alliance, 1884–1890." *Agricultural History* 51 (1977): 765.
Scott, John W. "Yellow Fever Strikes Bay St. Louis: The Epidemic of 1897." *Journal of Mississippi History* 63 (2001): 119–28.
Shue, W. D. "The Cotton Oil Industry." *Publications of the Mississippi Historical Society* 8 (1904): 253–92.
Sledge, James L., III. "The Chisholm Massacre: Politics and Violence in East Mississippi." *Journal of Mississippi History* 40 (1993): 203–15.
Smith, Claude P. "Official Efforts of the State of Mississippi to Encourage Immigration, 1868–1886." *Journal of Mississippi History* 32 (1970): 327–40.
Stone, Alfred Holt. "The Negro in the Yazoo-Mississippi Delta." *Publications of the American Economic Association*, 3rd series, 3 (1902): 255–62.
Stone, James H. "A Note on Voter Registration Under the Mississippi Understanding Clause, 1892." *Journal of Southern History* 38 (1972): 293–96.
Taylor, Antoinette Elizabeth. "The Woman Suffrage Movement in Mississippi, 1890–1920." *Journal of Mississippi History* 30 (1968): 1–34.
Upchurch, Thomas Adams. "Why Populism Failed in Mississippi." *Journal of Mississippi History* 65 (2003): 249–76.
Vogt, Daniel C. "A Note on Mississippi Republicans in 1912." *Journal of Mississippi History* 49 (1987): 49–55.
———. "Problems of Government Regulation: The Mississippi Railroad Commission, 1884–1956." Ph.D. diss., University of Southern Mississippi, 1980.
Washington, Booker T. "A Cheerful Journey Through Mississippi." *World's Work* (February 1908): 11278–82.

Wright, Gavin, and Howard Kunreuther. "Cotton, Corn, and Risk in the Nineteenth Century." *Journal of Economic History* 15 (1975): 526–51.

Manuscript Government Records

National
U.S. Bureau of the Census. Census of Population, Record Group 29, National Archives, Washington, D.C. Returns for the tenth through fourteenth censuses, 1880–1920. Most returns for the 1890 census, including all those for Mississippi, were destroyed by fire.
U.S. Department of Justice. Source-Chronological File for the Northern and Southern Districts of Mississippi, Records of the Department of Justice, Record Group 60, National Archives, Washington, D.C.
U.S. District Court for Northern Mississippi. Record Books and Minute Books, Records of the District Court for Northern Mississippi, Federal Records Center, East Point, Georgia.

State
Mississippi. Auditor of Public Accounts. Official records, Record Group 29, Mississippi Department of Archives and History, Jackson.
Mississippi. Governor. Official records, Record Group 27, Mississippi Department of Archives and History, Jackson.
Mississippi. Secretary of State. Official records, Record Group 28, Mississippi Department of Archives and History, Jackson.

Published Government Documents

National
U.S. Bureau of the Census. *Abstract of the Twelfth Census of the United States, 1900.* Washington, D.C.: Government Printing Office, 1902.
———. *Census Reports: Twelfth Census of the United States, Taken in the Year 1900: Agriculture.* Washington, D.C.: Government Printing Office, 1901.
———. *Central Electric and Light Power Stations, 1902.* Washington, D.C.: Government Printing Office, 1905.
———. *Compendium of the Ninth Census, June 1, 1870.* Washington, D.C.: Government Printing Office, 1872.
———. *Fisheries of the United States, 1908.* Washington, D.C.: Government Printing Office, 1911.
———. *Historical Statistics of the United States, From Colonial Times to 1970*, 2 vols. Washington, D.C.: Government Printing Office, 1975.
———. *Report of the Industrial Commission on Agriculture and Agricultural Labor*, vol. 10. Washington, D.C.: Government Printing Office, 1901.

———. *Report on Cotton Production in the United States.* Washington, D.C.: Government Printing Office, 1884.
———. *Report on Crime, Pauperism, and Benevolence in the United States at the Eleventh Census: 1890.* Washington, D.C.: Government Printing Office, 1896.
———. *Report on the Manufactures of the United States at the Tenth Census.* Washington, D.C.: Government Printing Office, 1883.
———. *Report on the Productions of Agriculture as Returned at the Tenth Census, June 1, 1880, Embracing General Statistics.* Washington, D.C.: Government Printing Office, 1883.
———. *Report on the Statistics of Agriculture in the United States at the Eleventh Census, 1890.* Washington, D.C.: Government Printing Office, 1896.
———. *Report on Valuation, Taxation, and Public Indebtedness in the United States, as Returned at the Tenth Census.* Washington, D.C.: Government Printing Office, 1884.
———. *Report on Wealth, Debt, and Taxation at the Eleventh Census, 1890.* Washington, D.C.: Government Printing Office, 1892.
———. *Reports on Waterpower of the United States.* Part 2. Washington, D.C.: Government Printing Office, 1887.
———. *Statistical Abstract of the United States, 1912.* Washington, D.C.: Government Printing Office, 1913.
———. *Statistical Abstract of the United States, 1922.* Washington, D.C.: Government Printing Office, 1923.
———. *Statistics of the Population of the United States at the Tenth Census.* Washington, D.C.: Government Printing Office, 1883.
———. *Statistics of the Wealth and Industry of the United States.* Washington, D.C.: Government Printing Office, 1872.
———. *Street and Electric Railways, 1907.* Washington, D.C.: Government Printing Office, 1910.
———. *Telephones and Telegraphs, 1902.* Washington, D.C.: Government Printing Office, 1906.
———. *Twelfth Census of the United States, Taken in the Year 1900: Manufactures.* Washington, D.C.: Government Printing Office, 1900.
———. *Twelfth Census of the United States, Taken in the Year 1900: Population.* 2 vols. Washington, D.C.: Government Printing Office, 1901.
U.S. Congress. Senate. *Report of the Committee on Agriculture and Forestry on the Condition of Cotton Growers.* S. Rept. 986, 53rd Congress, 3rd sess. (1895).

State

Mississippi. Constitutional Convention [1890]. *Journal of the Proceedings of the Constitutional Convention of the State of Mississippi, Begun at the City of Jackson on August 12, 1890, and Concluded November 1, 1890.* Jackson, Miss.: E. L. Martin, 1890.
Mississippi. House of Representatives. *Journal of the House of Representatives of the State of Mississippi.* Imprint varies, 1878–1904.
Mississippi. Secretary of State. *Biennial Report of the Secretary of State to the Legislature of Mississippi.* Imprint varies, 1878–1904.
Mississippi. Senate. *Journal of the Senate of the State of Mississippi.* Imprint varies, 1878–1904.

Mississippi Agricultural Experiment Station. *Fifty-nine Years of Progress in Mississippi through Agricultural Research*. State College: Mississippi Agricultural Experiment Station, 1948.
Mississippi Department of Archives and History. *Official and Statistical Register of the State of Mississippi, 1912*. Nashville, Tenn.: Brandon Printing, 1912.
———. *Official and Statistical Register of the State of Mississippi, 1920–24*. Jackson, Miss.: Hederman Brothers, 1923.

Manuscripts

Agnew, Samuel A. Diary. Southern Historical Collection, University of North Carolina. Photocopy at University of Mississippi Library, Oxford.
Aldrich Family Papers. Special Collections. University of Mississippi Library, Oxford.
Allen, LeRoy Barry. Typescript, "Autobiography of LeRoy Barry Allen." Special Collections, University of Mississippi Library, Oxford.
Ball, Henry Waring. Diary. Southern Historical Collection, University of North Carolina, Chapel Hill.
Calhoon, Solomon S. Papers. Mississippi Department of Archives and History, Jackson.
Chapman Family Papers. Mississippi Department of Archives and History, Jackson.
Douglas, Emily Caroline. Papers. Louisiana State University Library, Baton Rouge.
Goldberger, Joseph A. Papers. Special Collections, Williams Library, University of Mississippi, Oxford.
Gray, Louella. Letters. Special Collections, Williams Library, University of Mississippi, Oxford.
Johnson, Margaret. Correspondence. Louisiana State University Library, Baton Rouge.
Koch, Christian D. Family Papers. Louisiana State University Library, Baton Rouge.
Longest, Christopher. Diary. Special Collections, University of Mississippi Library, Oxford.
Park, Thomas. "Recollections of Ocean Springs." 1982 Typescript, Special Collections, University of Mississippi Library, Oxford.
Pinson, Hamet. Family Papers. Louisiana State University Library, Baton Rouge.
Somerville, Nellie Nugent. Papers. Radcliffe College; microfilm copy at Mississippi Department of Archives and History, Jackson.
Stokes, Joel A. Family Papers. Louisiana State University Library, Baton Rouge.
Taylor, Calvin. Family Papers. Louisiana State University Library, Baton Rouge.
Walthall, William T. Diary. Walthall Papers. Mississippi Department of Archives and History, Jackson.

Index

Adams, Wirt, 106
Adams County, 49, 106, 114
Africa, 72
African Americans, 238–39; confront the system, 69–88, 232–33; as a labor force, 37–51, 231–32; newspapers published by, 79–80; and segregation, 52–58; as victims of violence, 57–68
Agnew, Samuel, 177
Agricultural and Mechanical College, 32–33, 93, 97, 171
Agricultural experiment stations, 31–32
Agricultural extension service, 33
Agricultural Wheel, 23
Agriculture, 12–36; diversification of crops in, 12, 15, 33–36, 43–44, 229–30; size of farms in, 12, 18–19, 230–31
Alabama and Vicksburg Railroad, 166, 181
Alcorn, James Lusk, 4, 114, 164
Alcorn Agricultural and Mechanical College, 199
Alcorn County, 115
Alexander, Charlton H., 203, 205, 219
Allen, John, 97, 197
Allen, LeRoy, 41
American Federation of Labor, 158
Ames, Adelbert, 5–6
Amite County, 58–60
Amory, 220
Anguilla, 42
Apportionment. *See* Reapportionment
Attala County, 126, 127, 130, 172
Automobiles, 169–71

Back to Africa movement, 72
Bailey, Claude, 158
Bailey, John A., 113

Baker, E. B., 158
Balance Agriculture with Industry program, 241
Banks, Charles, 77
Barksdale, Ethelbert, 28, 93, 192
Barto, 140
Batesville, 199
Bay Springs, 142
Beadle, Samuel Alfred, 84–86
Beeman, Joseph H., 27
Bilbo, Theodore G.: and 1910 secret caucus, 204–5; and 1911 election, 205; and 1915 election, 212; and 1918 election, 223–24; as governor, 212–13; and Progressivism, 225–26
Biloxi, 8, 167, 173
Black Hawk, 206
Blue Mountain, 209
Bolivar County, 53, 114, 123, 192
Boll weevil, 31–32, 49
Bond, Willard F., 56
Bowles, George F., 114
Bowling Green, 22–23
Breeland, Israel, 134
Brewer, Earl, 159, 170, 185, 225; and Bilbo, 212; and 1911 election, 205, 211
Brewington, J. T., 73
Brookhaven, 60, 80
Bruce, Blanche K., 70–73, 80, 90, 92
Bryan, Eugene N., 80
Burke, William, 62
Burkitt, Frank, 24–28, 93–94, 100, 160; and convict leasing, 108; and educational reform, 221; and 1890 Constitution, 112, 115, 116, 122; and prohibition, 102; and Vardaman, 194
Byrd, Adam, 203

275

Cable, George Washington, 107
Calhoon, Solomon S., 111, 115, 117, 122, 125
Calhoun County, 104
Camp Shelby, 237–38
Campbell, J. A. P., 100
Canneries, 146, 151
Capital punishment, 67
Carnegie, Andrew, 77
Carroll County, 23, 112
Carruth, Maggie, 139, 151
Carter, Henry R., 182–83
Carthage, 168
Catchings, Thomas, 108
Cattle, 35, 241; dipping of, 213, 224
Chalmers, H. H., 101
Chalmers, James R., 112, 127
Chandler, Greene C., 55
Charity hospitals, 213
Child labor, 145, 153–55, 198, 211, 224
Chinese laborers, 50
Chisholm, W. W., 6–7
Choctaw County, 98, 143
Chrisman, J. B., 60
Civil War, 3–4
Clark, Joe, 171
Clarksdale, 223
Clay, Laura, 215
Clay County, 8, 106
Coahoma County, 146
Cochran, J. T., 175
Cohay, 140
Collier, J. W., 170
Collins, George, 14, 42, 71–72
Columbus, 152, 175
Columbus and Greenville Railroad, 166
Commissaries, 43–44
Compton, Charlie, 55–56
Consolidated schools, 221–22
Constitution of 1890, 119–24; background of, 110–21
Constitution of 1868, 111–12
Convicts, 67, 213; leasing of, 46–47, 107–9

Cook, F. M. B., 114
Cooperative economic ventures, 20–26, 30, 62–63
Copiah County, 35, 127; whitecapping in, 58–60
Corinth, 142
Corn Clubs, 33, 230
Cotton bagging, 25–26
Cotton ties, 21
Cottonseed oil mills, 145–46, 151
Covington County, 8
Cresswell's Deadening, 244n35
Criminal justice system, 66–67
Crittenden, J. C., 53
Critz, Frank A., 195–97, 203, 225
Cromwell, Oliver, 62–63
Crop lien system, 17, 42, 98–99
Crystal Springs, 35
Cutrer, J. W., 127

Dansby, Baldwin, 129
Dantzler Lumber Company, 152
Darden, Putnam, 23, 93, 100, 192
Davis, Joseph, 76
Davis, Richard S., 138
Davis, Sidney Fant, 66–67
Davis Bend Plantation, 76
Dawes, S. O., 23
Delta, 30, 132, 165–66
Denny, Walter, 103, 115
Dickson, Harris, 198
Disfranchisement, 110–20, 123–24, 234
Diversification. *See* Agriculture, diversification of crops in
Dixon, Henry M., 127
D'Lo, 141
D'Olive, Annie Louise, 139, 150
Douglas, Emily, 178
Douglass, Frederick, 106
Dry Grove, 178
Du Bois, W. E. B., 66
Dulaney, L. C., 204–5

Eastman Gardiner Company, 139
Educational reform, 221, 241
Eighteenth Amendment, 220
Eldridge, W. B., 157
Elections: of 1875, 5; of 1877, 7; of 1881, 111; of 1888, 124; of 1890 for Congress, 27; of 1890 for constitutional convention delegates, 113–15; of 1891, 27–28; of 1892, 123; of 1903, 194–97, 210, 219; of 1907, 200–1; of 1911, 205–11; of 1915, 212; of 1918, 223–24
Elective judiciary. *See* Judiciary
Electrical service, 174–75
Embry, J. C., 72–74
Enochs Brothers, 138–40
Enterprise, 142
Exoduster movement, 72–75

Fairley, Wes, 134
Falkner, William C., 167
Farmers' Alliance, 23–30, 98–99, 112, 114, 230
Farmers' Alliance Exchange, 24–25
Farmers' and Workingmen's Clubs, 7, 156
Farmers' Educational and Cooperative Union, 29–30, 230
Farmers' institutes, 33
Farmers' Union, 29–30, 230
Featherston, W. S., 115
Federal Roads Act, 172
Federation of Women's Clubs, 154
Felder, Murray G., 34, 160
Fernwood, 138, 140, 151
Fernwood and Gulf Railroad, 140
Fertilizer, 13, 34
Fewell, John W., 116–17
Finkbine Lumber Company, 141
Finlay, Carlos, 180
Finley, George J., 33
Flagg, Robert, 71
Foote, William H., 86–87
Force Bill. *See* Lodge Election Bill
Forrest County, 170
Fowler, Ebenezer, 82

Franklin County, 58–60
French, P. B., 220
Fulkerson, Horace S., 55

Gainesville, 168, 220
Gaither, Simon, 76, 247n15
Galloway, Charles B., 65, 105, 218
Gambrell, John B., 102
Gambrell, Roderick, 105–8, 127
Garvey, Marcus, 239
George, James Z., 6, 15, 190, 210; biographical sketch of, 89–91; and 1890 Constitution, 112–17, 123; and 1891 election, 27–28
George County, 170
Gibbs, Washington, 209
Gilchrist-Fordney Lumber Company, 135–36
Glen Allen, 172
Godbold's Wells, 206
Goldberger, Joseph, 184–87
Goodwin, N. D., 170
Gordon, James, 202
Gordon, Kate, 215
Gore, John E., 115, 122
Gore, Thomas P., 222
Gore-McLemore Resolutions, 223
Graham, W. W., 8
Grange, 19–23, 30, 99, 230
Grant, Ulysses S., 6
Great Agricultural Relief, 23
Great Society, 241
Great Southern Lumber Company, 138
Green, Benjamin T., 76, 233
Green, E. W., 70
Greenback Party, 99, 115, 125, 153, 156, 233
Greene County, 170
Greenville, 14, 69, 178–79
Greenwood, 127, 193
Grenada, 104, 106, 179
Gulf and Chicago Railroad, 167
Gulf and Ship Island Railroad, 108, 164, 166, 207

277

Gulfport, 166
Gully, John, 6–7

Hamilton, Jones S., 105–8
Hamilton, Mary, 31, 132
Handy, W. C., 79
Hannah, T. L., 117
Hardy, John T., 143–44
Harperville, 62
Harris, Wiley P., 115, 117
Harrison, Benjamin, 111, 123, 124, 234
Harrison, Pat, 223–24
Hattiesburg, 8, 175, 236–37
Hayes, Rutherford B., 73, 91
Hazlehurst, 175
Heidelberg, 168
Henry, John J., 209–10
Henry, R. H., 170
Hinds County, 105–6
Hine, Lewis, 152, 155
Hobbs, Benjamin T., 204
Hobbs, G. A., 210
Holly Springs, 80, 179
Holly Springs Normal Institute, 198
Holmes County, 22, 33, 98
Holtzclaw, William H., 43, 78–79; on lynching, 83–84
Homelessness, 131
Hookworm, 187–88
Howard, Perry, 80
Hoyt, A. J., 45
Hudson, Arthur, 15, 130, 172
Hunter, W. D., 31
Huntington, Collis P., 165

Illinois Central Railroad, 165–66, 170; major strike on, 157–62
Illiteracy, 19
Imperialism, 52, 125, 203
Income tax (federal), 211
Independent candidates, 7–8, 115
Industrial accidents, 150–51, 167
Industrialization, 130–62, 235

Inflation, 17, 125
Interracial marriages and liaisons, 56–57, 81–82
Issaquena County, 37, 82
Italian laborers, 50–51

Jackson, 3, 86, 106, 113, 126, 175; in World War I era, 238; and yellow fever, 181
Jackson, Benjamin, 81
Jackson, S. A., 127
Jackson Automobile Association, 170
Jackson County, 152
January, Don, 45
Jasper County, 57, 114, 124
Jefferson County, 70, 126
Jews, 59–61
Johnson, Coral, 204
Johnson, Paul B., Sr., 224
Johnson, Stewart, 199
Jones, J. H., 47
Jones, Joseph T., 166
Jones, Laurence C., 78
Jones, Moze Hunt, 160
Jones, Richard, 72
Jones, Sam, 96
Jones County, 8, 35, 115
Judiciary, 101, 122
Jute bagging, 25–26
Juvenile Reformatory, 213

Kansas, 72–75
Kearney, Belle, 103, 213–17, 221
Kells, Harriet, 217
Kemper County, 6–7, 61–62
King, Benjamin, 125
Kirksville, 104
Knight, Newton, 57
Knight, Rachel, 57
Knight, Serena, 57
Knights of Labor, 156–57, 161
Kosciusko, 172, 208
Kyle, John C., 203

Labor Agent Licensing Act, 48
Labor unions, 156–62
Lafayette County, 21
Lake, 179
Lake Como, 168
Lamar, L. Q. C., 6, 94, 180–81; biographical sketch of, 91–92
Lamar Life Insurance Company, 189
Lamb-Fish Lumber Company, 137
Lampton, Edward W., 54
Lauderdale County, 61, 106, 113, 172
Laurel, 8, 135, 138, 164, 168
Lawrence County, 58
Lee, Stephen D., 27
Lester, James T., 211
Levees, 96, 125, 128
Leflore County, 193
Leflore County Massacre, 62–63, 112, 232
Lewis, Clarke, 27
Liberia, 72
Lincoln County, 58–60, 152
Lindenmeyer, Charles, 34
Lindsey Wagon Company, 164
Lippincott, J. T., 56
Literacy, 19
Livestock. *See* Cattle
Livestock Sanitary Commission, 213, 224
Local option. *See* Prohibition
Lodge Election Bill, 112–13
Longino, Andrew H., 60, 192, 194, 199; and lynching, 65–66
Louisville, New Orleans, and Texas Railroad, 76, 166
Louisville, New Orleans, and Texas Railway Company v. Mississippi, 53
Louisville and Nashville Railroad, 167
Love, R. T., 23
Love, William F., 115
Lowndes County, 106, 124, 238
Lowry, Robert, 93, 101, 107, 112
Lumber industry, 133–34, 137. *See also* Timbering
Luster, G. W., 105

Lynch, John R., 70, 80, 127
Lynching, 63–66, 80–84, 96, 196, 200, 225, 227

Macune, C. W., 23
Magnolia, 179
Mann, Emma, 151
Marion, 61
Marion County, 58, 115, 124, 188
Marshall County, 32, 80
Martin, E. J., 24
Martin, John H., 106
Martin, Will, 165
Matthews, Prentice "Print," 127
McComb, 158–61
McCool, James, 192–93
McHenry, 181
McLain, Frank A., 115
McLaurin, Anselm J., 62, 93, 103, 115, 205; and Vardaman, 194, 197, 201; death of, 190, 202
McNeil, J. W., 35
Melchoir, George P., 114
Memphis and Vicksburg Railroad, 164
Meridian, 171, 175, 200–1, 208
Mesa, 140
Mineral resources, 149, 236, 241
Miscegenation, 56–57, 81–82
Mississippi Central Railroad, 164
Mississippi Cotton Association, 29
Mississippi Highway Association, 170
Mississippi Highway Commission, 172–73, 213
Mississippi Livestock Association, 35
Mississippi Mills, 143–45, 151–56
Mississippi Readmission Act, 117–18
Mississippi Woman Suffrage Association, 213–16
Mitchell, Charles B., 24
Mobile, Jackson, and Kansas City Railroad, 166
Mobile and Ohio Railroad, 166
Money, Hernando D., 28
Montgomery, Isaiah T., 70, 193; and 1890 Constitution, 114–19; and Kansas

migration, 74–75; and Mound Bayou, 76–77, 233; and Vardaman, 198
Montgomery, W. B., 35
Moore, Margaret Carruth, 139, 151
Moorhead, 78
Moss Point, 134
Mott, N. A., 215
Mound Bayou, 75–78, 233
Mounger, H. C., 220
Muckenfuss, Anthony M., 148

Nash, Wiley, 205
Natchez, 3, 55, 126, 142, 219–20
National Association for the Advancement of Colored People, 239
National Child Labor Committee, 154
National Guard, 64, 158–60, 199
Natural gas service, 175
Naval stores industry, 140–41
Neely, Allen, 41
Neely, Rufus Polk, 164
New Deal, 241
New Orleans, Jackson, and Great Northern Railroad, 165
Nineteenth Amendment, 216–17
Noel, Edmund F., 83, 158–60, 205, 225; helps bring primary elections, 191–94; in 1903 election, 195–97, 210; and 1910 secret caucus, 202, 204; supports prohibition, 219; supports woman suffrage, 215
Norwood and Butterfield Lumber Company, 152
Noxubee County, 123

Oak Hall, 23
Ocala Demands, 27
Ocean Springs, 236–37
Odum, Charley, 171
Odum, Howard, 69
Ohr, George, 174
Oliver, William, 143–44
Orwood, 182
Osyka, 132

Panola County, 34
Parchman Penitentiary, 47
Park, Thomas, 164, 169, 236–37
Parker, Mack, 71
Pascagoula River, 134
Patrons of Husbandry. See Grange
Patty, Robert C., 115
Paxton, A. J., 116
Pearl River County, 131, 188
Pearlington, 168
Pellagra, 184–87
Peonage, 44–46
People's Party. See Populist Party
Percy, LeRoy, 197; and 1910 secret caucus, 203–5; and 1911 Senate election, 205–7; as a planter, 43, 50–51
Percy, William Alexander, 191, 206
Perry County, 134
Pig Law, 46, 108
Pike County, 138, 159–60, 206; whitecapping in, 58–59
Piney Woods, 131–33, 166
Piney Woods School, 70, 78–79
Plantation stores, 43–44
Planters, 13–14, 39–43, 49–50
Planters' Cotton Tie Association, 21
Poe, Clarence H., 15
Political violence, 126–28
Pond, Chester H., 78
Populist Party, 29, 156, 200, 211, 222, 233; birth of, 94; and child labor, 153; and 1890 constitution, 115, 128; victorious candidates, 125
Powell, Robert, 131
Primary election laws, 191–95
Prisoners. See Convicts
Progressivism, 10, 211–13, 225; summary of Mississippi's role in, 226, 234
Prohibition: in late nineteenth century, 102–7, 110, 126; in twentieth century, 217–21, 234–35, 240
Public health, 175–89
Purvis, Will, 58

280

Quarantines, 98
Quincy, 81
Quitman County, 8, 30, 123

Race riots, 61–62
Railroad Segregation Act, 53
Railroads, 135, 164–67; regulation of, 97–101. *See also* Segregation, on railroads and streetcars
Rankin County, 45, 113, 185
Ratliff, W. P., 127
Raymond, 35
Reapportionment, 95, 110–11, 120–22
Reconstruction, 3–6
Redeemers, 89–92
Redmond, S. D., 233
Reed, Walter, 183
Republican Party, 4–7, 99, 125–28
Richardson, Edmund, 144
Rienzi, 20
Ripley, 167
Roads, 168–74
Rose, Sumner W., 174, 211
Rosenwald, Julius, 77, 248n16
Rothenberg Brothers, 175
Rural free delivery, 125, 128, 168

Safety, 150–51, 167
Sawmills. *See* Lumber industry
Schlitz Brewing Company, 132
Schuyler, George S., 79
Scott, Charles, 114, 197
Secret caucus, 202–5
Segregation, 53–58, 197; on railroads and streetcars, 53–56, 86
Sharecropping. *See* Tenant farmers
Sharkey County, 127
Ship Island, 166
Ship Island, Ripley, and Kentucky Railroad, 167
Shipbuilding, 163
Shrimp fishermen's strike of 1915, 161
Sillers, Walter, 114
Simmons, John M., 100

Simpson, J. A., 141
Simrall, Horatio F., 114, 116
Sirley, W. V., 35
Slovenian workers, 132
Smith County, 139
Socialist Party, 79, 153, 174, 211, 223
Somerville, Nellie Nugent, 213–17
Spanish-American War, 125, 194
Steam loader, 136
Steam skidder, 136
Steamboats, 167–68
Stennis, John C., 241
Stokes, Allie, 58
Stokes, Lillie, 104
Stone, Alfred H., 42
Stone, John M., 7, 93, 109, 113; and racial disturbances, 59–60, 63, 153
Stoneville, 31–32
Street, Hugh M., 113, 203
Streety, Eva, 152
Stubblefield, Louis, 72
Sturgis, 209
Subtreasury, 27–28, 97, 125, 211
Sullens, Fred, 170, 207, 209
Sullivan, William V., 64
Summit, 59, 126
Sumner, Charles, 91
Sunflower County, 8, 30, 78

Tallahatchie County, 137
Tariffs, 96, 206
Taylor, 182
Taylor, Laura, 164
Taylor, R. H., 116
Telephones, 174
Ten Mile, 139, 150
Tenant farmers, 13, 17, 38–44, 71, 99, 231–32; mobility of, 48–49
Tennessee Valley Authority, 241
Terry, 22
Textbook selection issue, 98
Textile industry, 142
Thaten, Henry W., 34

281

Thigpen, Samuel G., 168
Timbering, 131–42
Tomato Clubs, 230
Townes, Duncan, 41
Treadway, L. N., 15
Treadway, Lucy, 213
Truck farming, 35
Truly, R. H., 126
Tunica County, 37, 70–71
Turpentine. *See* Naval stores industry
Tylertown, 140

Unions, 156–62, 236
United Daughters of the Confederacy, 154
Universal Negro Improvement Association, 239
Usury, 198
Utica Institute, 70, 78–79

Vagrancy Act, 48
Van Cleave, 152
Vardaman, James K., 127, 159, 183, 221, 233; in 1903 election, 195–97; in 1907 Senate election, 200–1; in 1910 secret caucus, 202–5; in 1911 Senate election, 205–9; in 1918 election, 223–24; early political career of, 193–95; and Frank Burkitt, 94; as governor, 197–200; and imperialism, 125, 203; and lynching, 64–65, 196, 200, 225, 227; and Progressivism, 225–26; and prohibition, 219; and railroad strike, 170; as Senator, 211–12; and whitecapping, 60; and woman suffrage, 215; and World War I issues, 222–23
Vaughan, A. J., 20
Vicksburg, 3, 34, 108, 126, 166; prohibition in, 220; and streetcar protests, 56; unions in, 156–57; and yellow fever, 180
Violence. *See* African Americans, as victims of violence; Political violence

Wagon-making, 163–64
Wahalak, 61–62

Waldauer, Joseph, 56
Walker, Joel P., 24
Walthall, Edward Cary, 27–28, 92, 190
Ward, B. F., 225
Warren County, 106, 115, 220
Washington, Booker T., 69–70, 77, 198
Washington County, 51, 69, 172
Water Valley, 158–60, 163, 180
Waterpower, 149, 236
Watkins, A. K., 222
Wayne County, 170
Webster County, 115
Wells, Ida B., 80–83
Wesson, 34, 142–45, 153
Wesson, J. M., 143
West, Absalom M., 164
West Point, 152
Weston, Moses, 69
Whitecapping, 58–61, 96, 152, 199
Whitten, Jamie, 241
Wiggins, 62
Wilkinson County, 187
Willard, Frances, 103
Williams, John Sharp, 97, 103, 168, 170; and 1907 Senate election, 200–1; supports woman suffrage, 215; and Vardaman, 197, 209, 211–12; and World War I issues, 222–23
Williams, Sandy, 134
Williams, W. L., 20–21
Williams v. Mississippi, 124
Wilson, Flowers, 59
Wilson, Woodrow, 211, 223–24
Windom, William, 74
Winona, 25, 106, 180, 193
Wisner, 139–40
Woman suffrage, 116–17, 213–17
Women's Christian Temperance Union, 103, 154, 217–18
Wool Hat pamphlet, 93
World War I, 237–39; coming of, 222–23, 236–37
Wright, Charles E., 194
Wroten, V. J., 132

Yalobusha County, 113, 114, 160
Yazoo and Mississippi Valley Railroad, 165–66
Yazoo City Yarn Mills, 155
Yazoo County, 86, 127
Yellow fever, 176–83
Yellow pine, 132–33
Yerger, William G., 121
Yewell, T. O., 205
Young Men's Christian Association (YMCA), 139, 141

www.ingramcontent.com/pod-product-compliance
Lightning Source LLC
Chambersburg PA
CBHW030337240426
43661CB00052B/1660